Francis Green is Principal Lecturer in Economics at Kingston Polytechnic, where he has taught since 1972. He graduated in Physics at Balliol College, Oxford. He then studied economics at the London School of Economics and at Birkbeck College, London University, where he received his Ph.D. From 1985 to 1986 he was Visiting Lecturer at the University of Massachusetts (Boston). He is the author of numerous articles and co-editor and co-author of three previous books: *Economics: An Anti-text* (1977), *Issues in Political Economy* (1979) and *Unequal Fringes* (1984).

Bob Sutcliffe is a writer and lecturer on economic questions. He has taught at the University of Massachusetts (Amherst) and at Kingston Polytechnic and worked as an economist in Africa and Latin America. He is the author of *Hard Times: The World Economy in Turmoil, Industry and Under-development*, co-author (with Andrew Glyn) of a Penguin Special, *British Capitalism, Workers and the Profits Squeeze*, and co-editor (with E. R. J. Owen) of *Studies in the Theory of Imperialism*.

The Profit System

Francis Green and Bob Sutcliffe

PENGUIN BOOKS

Penguin Books Ltd, Harmondsworth, Middlesex, England
Viking Penguin Inc., 40 West 23rd Street, New York, New York 10010, U.S.A.
Penguin Books Australia Ltd, Ringwood, Victoria, Australia
Penguin Books Canada Limited, 2801 John Street, Markham, Ontario, Canada L3R 1B4
Penguin Books (N.Z.) Ltd, 182–190 Wairau Road, Auckland 10, New Zealand

First published 1987

Made and printed in Great Britain by
Richard Clay Ltd, Bungay, Suffolk

Typeset in 9 on 10 pt. Times

Contents

List of Tables

List of Diagrams

Acknowledgements

We would like to thank the following friends and colleagues for their help when we were writing this book: Sally Benbassett, Mairin Byrne, Wendy Carlin, Court Cline, Howard Cox, Alison Culverwell, Sami Daniel, Andrew Glyn, George Hadjimatheou, Colin Hatcher, Beatrix Hoffman, Arthur MacEwan, Steve Miller, Petter Nore, Jenny Overton, Bernadette Reed, Jacek Rostowski, Steve Scotland, Peter Skott, Ron Smith and Ian Walker. We are very grateful to them all.

We are especially indebted to our friend Paul Auerbach. He commented on all our drafts. And he gave us indispensable encouragement through the whole process of writing the book. His input to it has been tremendous and we count ourselves very lucky to know such a generous scholar and person.

PART ONE

CAPITALISM AS A SYSTEM

CHAPTER 1

Production, Profit and Human Need

I. HUMAN SOCIETIES

(i) *Human life and labour*

Whether you are black or white, progressive or conservative, atheist or devout, poor or rich, gay or straight, old or young, female or male, you are likely to agree on at least one idea: that in the world of nature, the human race and its history have a very special place. Even if you do not believe that human beings are the summit of evolution, you are almost certain to believe that they are qualitatively different from any other kind of living creature. There are many contrasting views and theories about what the difference consists of. But nearly all of them are based partly on the idea that human beings react consciously rather than merely instinctively to the world they inhabit.

In many activities there are close parallels between what humans and other animals do: they eat, exercise and have sex. The difference is that humans have the capacity to do even these things consciously and to change the way they do them as a result of their ideas. So nightingales, despite the beauty and complexity of their song, can hardly be said to write music. And although some termites actively distribute the spores which produce their food they could not be said to be practising agriculture, any more than beavers which build dams could be called engineers.

Early in the evolutionary pre-history of the human species the greater part of its behaviour would have been instinctual. But as the human being developed, an increasing number of its activities became non-instinctual. They had to be learned. This is most obviously true in relation to what we now call art. But it is also true of the activities necessary to survive physically. While human beings began by hunting and gathering whatever food was available naturally in their environment, they later came to do more and more to enhance their ability to survive in that environment. They attempted to improve on nature; in other words they came to perform *labour* or *production* (two terms we shall often use interchangeably).

About 100,000 years ago, according to the latest archaeological research, they started making tools such as spears and arrows with which to catch food more effectively. About 8 or 9,000 years ago they began to practise settled agriculture; and roughly 2,000 years after that to smelt and fashion metals. With these changes human beings began to live much more varied lives. Whereas in the early history of our species everybody would do the same kinds of work (hunting, gathering, building shelter, preparing food), since then tasks have increasingly been divided up.

(ii) *The division of labour and the surplus*

The first division of labour was a biologically determined one between women and men. Women bore and suckled children. That division almost certainly led early in the history of the species to other socially determined divisions of tasks between the sexes, and probably between people of different ages, within each living group (tribe, clan, family). However, in the early stages each unit as a whole was self-sufficient and economically independent of the rest of humanity. Farming, cooking, house-building, cloth-making and child-rearing were done by every group, so that there was as yet no division of labour between communities.

Over the millennia, in some parts of the globe, the amount which each human being could on average produce (the *productivity of labour*) increased so that some people regularly produced more than they needed: they produced a *surplus*. This created the material conditions for three developments which occurred at various speeds and in various combinations. First, the surplus food produced by one group or community was exchanged for the surplus of another. Second, and more complex, some labourers stopped producing such necessities as food and specialized in non-food goods, eating the surplus food produced by others. Here was an end to self-sufficiency. The non-food producers began to live in separate communities and in this way urbanization developed. Third, communities emerged in which some privileged members did not produce anything at all but lived entirely off the surplus goods produced by others.

The first record of exchange of surplus goods between communities is from 10.000 years ago but it certainly took place long before that. The first development of urban communities was in the 'Middle East' in the Bronze Age (about 5 to 6,000 years ago). And the first record of groups of non-producing members of society is from about that same date.

(iii) *Money*

Some time in this long history another parallel development took place, the emergence of money; that is, of a substance employed not for its intrinsic usefulness but for its acceptability in exchange for other goods. Money greatly facilitated the extension of the division of labour because the transmission of the surplus product no longer depended on the presence of an acceptable exchange or on the use or threat of force.

Any human individual able to acquire money could use it to buy the increasing number of goods available in the market. People also bought goods not for their own consumption but to sell again for more money. They lent money to those who needed it urgently to survive, and charged interest on the loans. And they came to use money to buy human labour services: men bought wives, masters bought slaves, employers purchased the labour or products of particular labourers for a specified amount of time. And some people began to buy productive tools and equipment for their own use, and then for use by workers whom they employed.

(iv) *The social relations of production*

The forms and institutions mentioned so far already existed 5,000 years ago. The last five millennia have seen few entirely new ways of organizing human production and labour, or distributing what is produced. But the various forms and institutions have been combined in a vast number of ways. Each society has had its own way of producing and distributing wealth and its own distinctive set of relations between human beings. The sum total of these relations we shall refer to as the *social relations of production*, a blanket term for the way in which groups of human beings relate to each other as part of an overall process of production and distribution.

In defining each particular collection of social relations of production for a given society, we need to look at a number of questions:

(a) Does everyone share the labour necessary to the society's physical survival, or is it done by a limited number of people? Why is it *they* who do it and not some other group? Were they born into a certain caste, are they slaves, or do they sell their labour for wages?

(b) *Why* do people work? Is it to produce the goods they need in order to survive? Are they obliged on pain of death or punishment to produce tribute for someone else? Are they ordered by their masters to work? Do they work because they need money to satisfy their survival needs? Or do they work because they like to?

(c) How is their work organized? Do they themselves decide, individually or in groups, their speed and methods of work? Is this imposed on them by a master or manager?

(d) Who owns and controls the *means of production* (the land, tools, equipment, machines and buildings) with the aid of which work is carried out? The workers or someone else?

(e) What is the determining force – the purpose – underlying production? Do the individual workers decide to produce in order to survive? Does society have institutions which direct the production processes necessary for collective survival? Or do some people establish a production process with the objective of enriching themselves?

(f) If some people in the society do not work, who are they and how do they receive enough food and other goods to survive? This incorporates many other questions: are there particular castes into which people are born which do not require them to work? is there a sexual division of labour which requires one sex to do less work than the other? is there a class of people who manage to receive an income without working?

(g) What is the variation between different groups' and individuals' standards of living and levels of income? And what is it which decides these differences?

(h) What is the distribution mechanism by which society's product is transferred by those who produce it to those who are entitled to receive it?

These questions give us a way of categorizing any particular society's method of producing and distributing goods and services – its particular conglomeration of the social relations of production, as unique as a fingerprint.

If we can put together a set of answers from the present era we shall arrive at a way of understanding the nature of modern societies.

2. CAPITALIST SOCIETY

(i) *Capitalist relations of production*

Capitalism, the subject of this book, is the name we give to the system, now prevailing in large portions of the world, which is identified by the following fingerprint:

(a) the majority of the population, who may broadly be termed the 'working class', either work in the home or else work for pay by selling their *labour-power* (their potential and their assent to work) to others. The majority of wage workers are men; the great majority of at-home workers are women.

(b) Wage labourers work because they need to earn money to survive, since they own no land to grow food on, and no other means of production. If they cannot sell their labour-power they may become destitute. Those who work at home produce the services necessary for each working-class family or living-unit to survive.

(c) Wage work is usually carried out under the close supervision of managers and foremen. Workers have little say over their own production processes although they may conflict with the management over establishing work methods.

(d) The means of production with which they work are owned by other people, the capitalists.

(e) The purpose underlying production activities is the capitalists' aim of making profits; if they cannot do so they will not be willing to employ labourers. This is why we also refer to capitalism as 'the profit system'.

(f) The owners of the means of production may themselves choose to do some necessary organizational work but, even if they do nothing towards production and hire others to do the management and organization for them, they will still receive an income, through profit.

(g) There tends to be a very wide range of incomes and standards of living; through unequal wealth ownership capitalists generally live better than workers although there may be exceptions.

(h) Almost all services and goods (except those produced in the home) are distributed through exchange, via the medium of money. Thus the surplus product is transferred from those who produce it to those entitled to receive it through monetary exchange (not, in general, through violence or legal compulsion).

No other method of producing goods and services in past history has exactly these same characteristics. But the profit system does have some features in common with other systems of production. The most important of these is the fact that a proportion of the population can live in a relatively privileged manner without doing any productive labour. Under the feudal system, for instance, the aristocracy and the clergy were able to live without doing productive labour because the rest of the population were obliged by right, duty, custom and, if necessary, force, to hand over a proportion of what they produced. Under the slave system the whole product is the property of the masters and they concede a portion of it so that their slaves survive.

This characteristic of production systems can be called exploitation in the sense that some people are able to live as a result of the work of others. Capitalism, along with feudalism, slavery and a number of other systems, is an exploitative system in this sense. The nature of this exploitation, however, is much more complex and hard to perceive in capitalism than in other exploitative systems, because it takes place through the circulation and exchange of commodities.

(ii) *The coming of capitalism*

Societies where capitalist relations of production predominate have existed for only a few centuries, but the history of capitalist enterprises goes back thousands of years. In any single capitalist production unit – nowadays known variously as a firm, business or corporation – there is an owner or group of owners whose ultimate objective is to make profits. Labour is carried out by hired workers, under the supervision of the owners or of a manager who is their agent. They produce *commodities* (useful products of human labour, made to be sold to other people). As time passes, the wealth which the owner advances as *capital* continually shifts between money, materials, machines, labour-power and finished products, and as it does so it can be expanded.

Forms of business basically of this kind existed in ancient Sumeria and Egypt and later in Greece and Rome at the height of their civilizations. But they were not numerous enough for those societies to be called capitalist societies.

For a long time after the deline of the Roman Empire there were very few capitalist businesses in the world. Then, starting around 1550, a growing crisis of the old feudal system allowed the capitalist organization of trade and then production to spread like a fire through western Europe.

More and more of the decisions made in society about how human beings spent their lives came to be associated with monetary calculation and the balance of profit and loss. Increasingly workers came to produce not the things which they themselves would consume but things for consumption by others. Their relationship to their labour took a monetary form. They sold their working ability for a money wage which they could then spend on the goods and services they needed. The relationship between work and survival was as essential as ever but it was more indirect. Workers could only survive if an employer would pay them enough money to live on.

The employers' decisions were also based on monetary calculations. They would employ labourers only if they believed that their enterprise would yield a profit in terms of money. So the most important decisions about what was produced, and how, came to be based on the profit motive.

In this way the advent of capitalism changed the nature of human life and human relationships. A person's position in the social hierarchy became less rigidly fixed by birth and inheritance than before. Of course the majority of people were born poor and remained so all their lives. But there were more exceptions who, like the rising capitalists, initiated new transformations of society. It was near the top rather than the bottom of the social hierarchy that most changes took place.

The things which had bound society together in the pre-capitalist era remained but became less important: right, duty, obligation and physical violence. Money came to *mediate* all these human relationships and to hide them, so that, though they still existed, they were misted over by the relations of money or the relations of commodities.

(iii) *The pursuit of profits*

The successful pursuit of profit proved to be a complex and difficult endeavour. Employers had to ensure regular and cheap supplies, manage the production process efficiently, keep accounts, organize the finance of production and sales, ensure their markets and protect their property from theft, sabotage or deterioration. All this had often to be done in conflict with their workers, and virtually always in competition with each other and in conditions of ceaseless change and much uncertainty.

The squeeze of competition forced them to search ever more widely for profitable markets for their products. It led, therefore, to a massive increase in the means of transportation, in travel and in commercial interchange between communities.

And in the race for profits and the struggle against bankruptcy, costs of production had to be kept down as much as possible. One of the ways of doing that was to squeeze the maximum amount of effective labour from workers. The early years of capitalism thus witnessed extraordinary levels of cruelty towards workers based on heavy discipline and long hours of work, often in conditions worse than those of slaves. The extent to which workers could be driven depended on their power to resist and on the general political climate.

However weak their resistance, there is a physical limit to the amount of work that can be forced out of one man or woman or child. In the race for profits capitalists have always wanted to transcend that limit. They have, therefore, continually been on the look-out for new mechanical or other techniques which could expand the productivity of labour and for new methods of organizing work. In the profit system the surplus has more often been invested in new means of production than, as was commoner in previous systems, in temples, pyramids, cathedrals or orgies.

(iv) *Capitalism and progress*

The use of the surplus to employ workers on new means of production is a process known as the *accumulation of capital*. Accumulation in the capitalist system has led to the fastest growth in the productivity of human labour ever seen in the history of the human race. It took humanity about half a million years to invent the sailing ship; another five thousand to invent the steamship; but only another hundred to invent the spaceship. Such extraordinary acceleration is paralleled in virtually all fields of production.

For most people this has completely changed their relationship to production. Once, in order to survive, a human being needed to know something about the whole production process of, say, potatoes or corn and to carry out all stages of the process himself or herself. Nowadays most workers need to know little or nothing of the total production process in which they work. What they produce is largely irrelevant to them since they work to earn wages and instead of producing a complete commodity they repeat a small number of tasks which contribute to the production of a commodity.

(v) *Capitalist prosperity and depression*

If the accumulation of capital and technical progress under the capitalist system had continued uninterrupted at the pace sometimes achieved, by now little human labour would be necessary to produce a very generous standard of living for the whole population. In fact, however, the process has been extremely uneven and erratic.

Capitalist production has been interrupted, as in previous economic systems, by natural disasters and by wars. But it has also been interrupted frequently and sometimes disastrously by causes which are altogether more mysterious, in ways quite unknown in any previous system. On numerous occasions, without any outside stimulus or any real shortages of material resources, the process of capital accumulation has simply broken down, producing crashes, financial panics and slumps. In these recurrent periods large parts of its means of production have been unused, and large parts of its potential workforce involuntarily unemployed. The mystery of the origins of this alternation of prosperity and depression has led to major controversies in economic thought.

It is obvious to everyone, no matter what their ideological persuasion, that there must be something wrong with the functioning of a system which has periodically condemned many millions of people to unemployment and sometimes even starvation. The controversy therefore is less about the dire consequences of failure, more about whether such things are really necessary or inevitable in the capitalist system. Many defenders of capitalism as a system would argue that slumps, unemployment and poverty are not unavoidable aspects of the profit system but rather the results of the system working imperfectly.

Some argue that economic disasters are the result of inappropriate policies or rules regarding the money or the banking system. Others say that the capitalist system functions badly at times because there are too many restrictions on competition and the free functioning of the market mechanism. Conversely, yet others argue that capitalism sometimes produces slumps and depressions because there is too little or inappropriate intervention by the state authorities to control and plan the economy.

Despite the large gaps which exist between those who hold these various points of view, they all accept that in principle the profit system could operate without extremes of boom and slump. In essence, they say, it is a system which is capable of equilibrium and stability.

There is a chasm between all who hold those views – the various schools of orthodox economics – and those who, following in the tradition of Marx or other socialists, argue that capitalism is essentially an unstable system in which periodic crisis is virtually inevitable. Those who take this view are no more in agreement among themselves than the supporters of capitalism.

Socialist economists however do agree on their wider criticisms of the profit system. The problem of slumps and depressions is one aspect of a more general question of whether capitalism as a productive system effectively meets social needs. Its critics generally argue that even in conditions of economic boom capitalism fails to meet many human needs; in slumps and depressions the failure is more obvious and extreme.

In contrast its defenders argue that despite its periodic lapses capitalism is in general the best way of supplying the needs of society, and that the capitalist system of production and distribution responds flexibly to those needs through the price or market system. We shall return to this debate repeatedly.

(vi) *The economists' dispute about profits*

The debate about capitalism and social needs is closely related to another debate about the lifeblood of capitalism – profit.

Although a bit of an over-simplification, it is not an absurd caricature of pro-capitalist economists to say that they see the capitalist system as essentially a system of interlocking markets. As a result of this, their central concepts used in analysing the system are the counterposed forces of demand and supply, and equilibrium, both of price and quantity sold. This is true not only at the level of a single commodity or business (microeconomics) but also at the level of the economy as a whole (macroeconomics).

Their view tends to emphasize the qualitative equality between different human beings. In economic relations people are seen as owners, buyers and sellers of goods and services. And, according to this approach, it is possible, at least in theory, that they should all receive the just price (the true value) of the goods and services they have to sell. Out of this conception comes a particular view of the nature of profits and wages. They are seen as forms of income which are in many senses equivalent to each other. Both are rewards to different factors of production for their *services* to the production process. Both are equally just and fair and so neither exploitation nor cheating can be part of the normal functioning of capital.

Markets and exchange – the buying and selling of commodities – is certainly one crucial part of the functioning of the profit system. But it is not all there is to it. Equally important is what happens in the physical process of producing goods and services in the factories, the offices, the salons and the fields. Here the participants in capitalist production do not relate to each other as qualitative equals – all buyers and sellers. They relate as employers and employed – those who own the means of production and can hire and fire labour, and those who do not and cannot.

Within production the relationship between employer and employed is an unequal power relation in which the capitalist has property rights and the worker has none, even though workers may acquire some countervailing power against their employer by union organization, threats of withdrawal of labour or other actions.

Thus capitalism contains two main spheres of relationships: production and exchange. This leads to an altogether different explanation of the origin of profits. In the conventional view, described above, profits originate in market or exchange relations. In the alternative view, which derives mainly from the theoretical writing of Karl Marx, profits depend on the successful functioning of both spheres in unity with each other. In the labour process workers must produce commodities which are worth more than the labour-power and material inputs which went into producing them; in other words the productivity of labour must be sufficiently high. Then the commodities must be sold on the market at a price equivalent to their worth. The profit must be realized.

In the first part of this process profit is only potential; it is only when the second part is fulfilled that profit becomes real, that is, converted into money. Both parts are absolutely essential. Profit cannot be realized in the market out of thin air; it must first of all have been produced potentially in the production or labour process. Yet equally, if the potential profit fails to be realized because of the failure of the market, then it evaporates. And capitalists will not go on producing commodities on which they cannot realize profits.

(vii) *Capitalism today*

So far we have discussed the profit system by means of an abstract model designed to capture its essence. The real world of capitalism can never correspond exactly to such a model. But an understanding of these essential rules of the system is indispensable for making sense of some of the complexities and apparent contradictions of the real world. To understand a chess game the onlooker must know the rules; only then will the moves cease to seem arbitrary and unconnected.

So it is with capitalism, which continues to dominate the economy of most of our planet. No exact estimate has been made, but almost certainly no less than four-fifths of the monetary value of production of goods and services in America, Africa, western Europe and non-Communist Asia comes from privately owned businesses operating in search of profit. The rest is largely produced by state- and municipality-owned enterprises, some by small-scale independent producers who employ no labour (especially in agriculture) and a very tiny proportion by co-operative enterprises. (In

Chapter 2 we shall examine in some detail the characteristics of these different types of businesses.)

The figure of four-fifths in a sense underestimates the extent of the capitalist nature of production. Very many state- and municipality-owned enterprises, though not privately owned, operate on virtually identical principles to capitalist businesses. They are usually expected to make profits on their operations and may often need to do so in competition with capitalist-owned firms. And production in such enterprises is usually identical to that in capitalist firms. The workers sell their labour-power for wages and have their work decided and managed by unelected managers.

The great majority of the means of production continues to be owned and controlled by a small capitalist class. A few years ago it was commonly claimed that as the directors and managers of firms were not the owners, the management was free to pursue goals other than profits. Some even talked of the 'soulful' corporation which eschewed exploitation of its workforce and cared for the 'public interest'. These views are less fashionable now. Managers, it is realized, overlap substantially with owners of capital and almost always share their objectives. There may be quite a large number of people who own a few shares, giving rise to the illusion of the 'property-owning democracy'. But in reality only a small proportion of them is substantially wealthy and able to wield any control.

At the same time the real wages of most workers in the advanced countries have risen very substantially (if very erratically) during the history of capitalism. It used to be held, in the time of the boom, that this also contributed to greater security for people. The renewed crises and mass unemployment of the 1970s have shattered this illusion. Yet it is fair to point out that there are sizeable groups of people earning relatively high incomes who are neither obviously part of the working class, nor capitalists. This has led some to argue that class is no longer important in society, that a tendency towards classlessness has accompanied a trend towards equality.

The two-class model of capitalists and workers is, and always was, an over-simplification of the real world. None the less we hold that it remains a fundamental division within modern societies. It is true that in the advanced countries the relative and even absolute numbers of industrial manual (blue-collar) workers have been falling. But although many people define the working class to exclude non-manual (white-collar) workers, the great majority of them have the same social and economic relations to their employers as the manual workers do.

Some of the self-employed, professionals, senior state bureaucrats and middle and upper managers are not part of a simple worker/capitalist dichotomy. The class structure is in fact quite complicated. But the expansion of varieties of the middle class does not eclipse the division between

owners of the means of production and wage workers as the most characteristic and basic of the class divisions of capitalism.

In Chapter 2 we shall examine in more detail the characteristics and
motives of the capitalist class, and the forms of businesses which it owns.

If the significance of some of the above transformations of modern capitalism has been overstated, there are others of greater significance. One is the
astounding increase in the economic role of the state (the theme of Chapter
11). In the advanced countries the state is now responsible for at least one-
third, and in one case (Sweden) nearly two-thirds, of total national expenditure. Much of the increase since the nineteenth century reflects the rise
of the 'welfare state' whereby governments have assumed responsibility for
providing education, paying for health services and supporting the aged,
the unemployed and so on. Some also comes from increased military and
police spending. The activities of the state may have somewhat modified the
gross extremes of inequality characteristic of the nineteenth century, but, as
we shall see in Chapters 8 and 12, there remains a staggering inequality in
access to economic resources. The growth in the state's role has been much
more on the side of consumption (deciding what is spent) than on production. Thus in so far as the state has changed what is purchased it has
controlled what it is profitable to produce; but it has not changed the basic
fact that profits are the necessary stimulant of most production.

It is not only the defenders of modern capitalism who emphasize the
changes which the system has undergone. They and others have attached
importance to what is seen as a growing internationalization of the capitalist
system. They point to the very rapid recent development of world trade, far
in excess of the growth of world production, thus indicating a new wider
international division of labour. They point to the growth of international
economic institutions like the International Monetary Fund (IMF), the
World Bank, the Bank for International Settlements (BIS) and the European Economic Community (EEC). And perhaps most important of all,
they stress the post-war emergence of the multinational company as the
typical productive unit of capitalism.

In Part Four we assess the significance of a number of transformations of
capitalism in detail. Some of them, we conclude, have had profound effects
on the working of capitalism. But they have not changed its essence, or
given it a new fingerprint. Its driving force continues to be the profit
motive.

3. THE PROFIT SYSTEM AND HUMAN NEEDS

An important issue underlying much of our discussion will be the extent to
which the profit motive is compatible with the satisfaction of social needs,

the sum total of the needs of all the individuals in society. The tremendous advances in productivity suggest also that capitalism must have had a major impact on some material satisfactions.

Yet material needs, as everyone knows, are not all. There are also spiritual and psychological needs for such things as security, adventure, love, friendship, sex, culture, creativity and freedom. To many, the satisfaction of material wants may seem a secondary question, albeit a very important one.

We should distinguish also between those general needs which humans would have no matter what kind of society they live in (food, means of communication and so on) and those which are socially determined and which may vary according to the type of society. Given that, the question may be put: how far does capitalism lead to the satisfaction of human needs compared to other possible societies? Or, a closely related question, how far are those needs met relative to capitalism's own technical potential?

It would be absurd to deny that the profit system does meet some human needs. It produces shoes, ships, sealing wax and a million other things which are needed and purchased by people. It provides education, culture and health services. Many economists, while not denying that deficiencies remain, would argue that capitalism is in fact the best possible way of meeting needs for the majority of people. We do not agree.

(i) *Profit and material needs*

In all the advanced capitalist countries, paid workers now receive substantially higher real wages than a century ago. They can more easily meet their general material needs, for example by feeding themselves better, and also more often meet many socially created needs, such as the desire to watch television.

Yet even after the longest and most successful boom in its history (from 1950 to 1970), the system has been unable to provide for everyone a life free from material want. The number of people suffering from starvation and malnutrition around the world, and even in the richest country of all, the USA, certainly grew in absolute numbers and perhaps also relative to the size of the population of the world as well. Even in the advanced countries, with very few exceptions (such as perhaps Sweden and Switzerland), there is evidence to suggest that relative full employment and rapid economic growth did not eliminate widespread poverty.

Part of the reason for this deficiency is the chronically unequal distribution of income, of the power to consume, both within each country and between different countries. Another factor has been the kind of products which the available resources have been used to produce. The most obvious example is the production of armaments and other forms of military expenditure. Not far off one-twentieth of the productive resources of the world in the last thirty years has been used to produce means not of sustaining human life but of producing human death. Many more resources are spent in polluting the natural environment, dirtying the air we breathe, the water we drink and so on, not deliberately but as a by-product of the search for profits.

Much economic effort is also devoted to satisfying socially determined needs intrinsic to capitalism, such as producing drugs to combat stress, or goods and services to counteract the effects of pollution.

There is no way of estimating what proportion of resources are used in these various 'unnecessary' ways, but it must be very substantial. On top of all the unnecessary production is the waste of leaving resources unutilized: the machines, land and other productive equipment which lie idle during periodic depressions, and the masses of unemployed and short-time workers.

The consequences of economic slumps under capitalism are very far-reaching. Their instant result is physical want for a sizeable section of the population, mainly those who already occupy an underprivileged position. Physical want and insecurity result both in material deprivation (even starvation, disease and death) and psychological damage (slumps and recessions produce more stress, fear, mental illness and suicides).

(ii) *Capitalism and politics and culture*

The economic workings of a system of production cannot be separated from its associated culture, ideology and politics. Capitalism, via the political and ideological systems it fosters, affects also the ways people love, create, enjoy culture and indeed experience almost all aspects of their lives.

At its early entrances on to the political stage the capitalist class preached the ideology of freedom and equality. The slogan of the French Revolution was 'freedom, equality and brotherhood'; and the US constitution declares that 'all men are created equal'. Yet the implementation of this ideology has, even at the best of times, been incomplete. Even formal democratic rights, such as the right to elect parliamentary representatives, have failed to result in real equality of political power. Formal equality has not been able to overcome the relations of dominance inherent in a productive process where one relatively limited class of people owns most of productive wealth; and where the livelihood of the majority is dependent on their ability to work in such a way that the minority gain a profit.

A similarly ambiguous verdict must be given on capitalism's record in meeting the need for creativity. In the advanced countries the number of working hours has been reduced and people have more spare time than they did in the earlier days of capitalism. Yet most people still have to spend the great bulk of their lives working for others in order to survive rather than expressing their free creativity. Much of their leisure is needed simply to recover from fatigue. And for the majority, the content of paid jobs has tended to become more routine and less skilled. Only for a minority can work be the positive expression of their individuality rather than the negative cost of physical survival.

As for culture generally, it has often been observed that the development of capitalism destroys old and sometimes valuable traditions, such as ancient crafts and vernacular art. What does it put in their place? There are valuable new forms of popular culture – novels, popular music and, more recently, movies and television – which have grown up largely with capitalism. In the advanced countries, at least, access to the consumption of these forms of culture has become very widespread. Undoubtedly much of this cultural output is of very high quality. On the other hand the commercialization of culture under capitalism often results in the pursuit of the safe and the mediocre rather than the experimental or the excellent. Access to cultural and sporting activities is normally determined by considerations of profit and finance. And a growing proportion of people are consumers of culture rather than producers of their own cultural expressions.

Thus, even under the best of circumstances, there are many ways in which capitalism has limited the satisfaction of non-material human needs. It has made room for only a limited degree of formal democracy, it has produced jobs which stifle the creativity inherent in people and it has widely reduced cultural values to the common denominator of profit and loss.

And circumstances are by no means always so good. There have been periods, even in modern times and in the advanced capitalist countries, when the most basic political, individual and cultural freedoms have been suppressed, especially in times of economic crisis; political responses to the potential breakdown in the existing order created by mass unemployment and the failure of the system to meet many elementary needs. Thus capitalist economic relations are no guarantee against totalitarian dictatorship.

It is arguable that economic pluralism may in the long term be conducive to some form of political pluralism. This proposition however is often reduced to an openly 'apologetic' view, that only private ownership of the means of production can ensure democracy – a notion which we repudiate thoroughly in Chapter 20. In fact multiparty parliamentary systems are extremely rare in the less developed parts of the capitalist world. There one finds military or civilian dictatorships almost everywhere, and many forms of political repression. These tend to be associated with the glorification of a particular leader, a race or a nation, or with the demands of a funda-mentalist religion.

These are typically only the extreme form of reactionary ideologies commonly found also in more prosperous places. Wherever you look you find multiple forms of discrimination and inequality against people of races or colour or nations other than the dominant one, against women, against lesbians and gay men, against the physically or mentally handicapped, against the aged, against children and so on. The ideologies and institutions which are associated with these forms of inequality – class prejudice, im-perialism, sexism, racism, the family and so on – are not themselves peculiar to capitalism. But they are sometimes adapted and used by the capitalist class for its own benefit. Sometimes they have called on pre-capitalist values, especially religious ones, in their support.

All these issues, and more, are elaborated in Part Three, which examines the profit system from the point of view of working people who live under it.

With all the various political and ideological phenomena we have men-tioned, capitalist nations at different times adopt widely diverging practices. This has led some people to draw the conclusion that there is no connection between the nature of the economy and the cultural, moral and political conditions of the society, which can therefore be ignored when writing about an economic system.

We do not agree with that; but nor do we think there is a rigid, mechanical connection between the economy and these other non-economic features of society. That view, often characterized as 'economic determinism', has been a common one among those influenced by a crude version of Marxism. But we are influenced by the conviction that there are many important links in both directions between capitalism as a way of organizing economic life and the politics, ideas and culture of capitalistically organized economies.

CHAPTER 2

Business

The world's most renowned capitalist today is the product of capitalist imagination – J. R. Ewing. The legendary J. R., however, is head of a rather untypical big corporation. It is largely national in its operations; it produces a single product, petroleum; its ownership and control is confined to a single family. There no doubt remain some real-world corporations which resemble the fictional Ewing Oil Company. But as a visual aid to a course in the changing nature of the modern capitalist corporation *Dallas* is a non-starter.

If we look for a wide overview of the real world of modern business we shall find instead a picture in which corporations have been growing larger, increasingly spreading across national boundaries, diversifying into the manufacture of many products and owned by a much more diffuse oligarchy than their original founding families.

I. VARIETIES OF BUSINESS

If Karl Marx (1818–83) or Adam Smith (1723–90) could time-travel to the late twentieth century they would see that the number of capitalist businesses has expanded immensely; that the size of the larger ones has increased beyond recognition; that the largest businesses are very much less commonly owned and controlled by individuals and families. And they would probably be amazed by the sophistication with which businesses can nowadays be managed and controlled, which surpasses by far the methods of earlier times.

Such changes have resulted from many causes and pressures: partly from the gradual evolution of business structure and organization over time in all capitalist countries; partly from sudden upheavals in structure which have happened, for instance, in the aftermath of the world wars, or in the Great Depression, or in merger booms at other times; partly from the changing significance of different capitalist countries with different traditions of business structure; and partly from changes in the relative importance of different industries.

The result of all this is an extremely heterogeneous modern set of capitalist institutions. At one extreme, for example, stands Exxon, the world's largest manufacturing company, whose sales in 1984 amounted to $91 billion (about equal to the national income of the continent of Africa); or Citicorp, the world's largest bank whose assets in 1984 were over $150 billion. At the other extreme are literally millions of small capitalists employing only a few workers, or self-employed small businesspeople who are capitalists in the limited sense that they are seeking profit through the provision of goods or services, though they do not employ labour.

Besides variations in size, there are also different types of legal forms of capital: joint stock companies whose shares may or may not be publicly quoted (that is, for sale to outsiders), partnerships, public corporations and so on.

So there is no single typical capitalist firm and probably there never has been. There are, however, a number of *types* of firm which have many characteristics in common.

The most usual way of classifying firms is according to their size, measured either by sales, output, capital assets or employees. The difference between big and small business is not an arbitrary and quantitative one. It reflects more qualitative differences in such matters as financial standing and relations with the workforce. The large corporation usually stands in a qualitatively more favourable relation towards its banks and its supply of finance than the small firm with less security to offer. Also large companies have generally much more stable and secure workforces than small ones.

(i) Big business

Only a tiny proportion of the world's businesses come into this category. Yet the majority of the production of goods and services takes place in very large corporations, each with vast numbers of workers on the payroll.

The biggest private employer in the world, General Motors, had by 1983 nearly three-quarters of a million workers (more industrial workers than in many whole countries). Less exceptional are companies such as Union Carbide, the giant chemicals concern, with nearly 100, 000 workers; while a famous company like Coca Cola employed only a modest 40,000. In western Europe 32 corporations had more than 100,000 employees, in the USA 17, in Japan 4 and in South Korea 2.

Table 2.1 shows the world's ten largest industrial corporations ranked by sales. All of them are privately owned. The table shows how the big business sector is dominated still, as it has been, by the petroleum and motor vehicles industries, with electronics gradually moving up the list. This underlines the remarkable power of the US oil and motor industry and its infamous

Table 2.1 The World's Ten Biggest Corporations, by Sales, 1984

Corporation	Industry	Sales ($ billion)
1. Exxon (USA)	Petroleum	90.8
2. Royal Dutch/Shell Group (UK/Netherlands)	Petroleum	84.9
3. General Motors (USA)	Motor vehicles	83.9
4. Mobil (USA)	Petroleum	56.0
5. Ford (USA)	Motor vehicles	52.4
6. British Petroleum (UK)	Petroleum	50.6
7. Texaco (USA)	Petroleum	47.3
8. International Business Machines (USA)	Electronics, computers	45.9
9. Du Pont (USA)	Chemicals	35.9
10. American Telephone and Telegraph (USA)	Electronics, appliances	33.2

Source: Fortune, 19 August 1985

tycoons (the Rockefellers, Gettys, Fords, Morgans and Sloans) in the last century of capitalist history. If not in other respects, then Ewing Oil and its close TV rival Carrington Oil are representative of their industry.

Table 2.2 shows the world's ten largest banks ranked by their assets (which are a rough guide to the extent of their influence in the economy generally). The predominance of the Japanese banks is testimony not only to the concentration of the banking structure there, but also to the successful expansions of Japanese industrial businesses.

Table 2.2 The World's Ten Biggest Commercial Banks, by Assets, 1984

Bank	Value of assets ($ billion)
1. Citicorp (USA)	151
2. Dai-Ichi Kangyo Bank (Japan)	125
3. BankAmerica (USA)	118
4. Fuji Bank (Japan)	116
5. Sumitomo Bank (Japan)	115
6. Mitsubishi Bank (Japan)	111
7. Sanwa Bank (Japan)	102
8. Banque National de Paris (France)	98
9. Caisse Nationale de Crédit Agricole (France)	92
10. Crédit Lyonnais (France)	90

Source: Fortune, 10 June and 19 August 1985

Capitalism as a System

The relative importance of large industrial corporations can be judged more precisely by examining a measure of *aggregate concentration*, the proportion of total output that is produced by the 100 largest firms. Table 2.3 shows how in two countries, the USA and the UK, this proportion increased steadily, at least until the 1960s and 1970s. In one sense these shares even underestimate the impact of big corporations since many of the smaller firms are merely satellites of the larger ones, because they are partial subsidiaries or suppliers.

Table 2.3 Share of the Largest Hundred Firms in Manufacturing Net Output

UK	1909	1924	1935	1949	1953	1958	1963	1968	1970	1980
% Share	16	22	24	22	27	32	37	41	41	41

USA	1909	1924	1935	1947	1954	1958	1963	1967	1977	
% Share	22	25	26	23	30	30	33	33	33	

Sources: S. Prais, *The Evolution of Giant Firms in Britain*, Cambridge, Cambridge University Press, 1981; Y. Brozen, *Mergers in Perspective*, Washington DC, American Enterprise Institute for Public Policy Research, 1982

Not only have big firms in the last century been turning into giants, they have also been geographically extending and diversifying their activities. The international corporation is not a new phenomenon. Several have existed for many decades, for example Unilever (incorporating the United Africa Company), the United Fruit Company, the British South Africa Company and so on. But since the end of the Second World War many other corporations, which were formerly regional or national in scope, have become international by investing much further afield. The large corporation without foreign activities is now a rarity. In a few cases there are companies to which it is hard any longer to ascribe a nationality.

We are rapidly approaching the time when the typical big firm will also be a conglomerate without any single preponderant activity – producing not one product, nor a number of related products, but many unrelated products. This process has long been going on either through the establishment of new investments in previously unfamiliar fields, or through old firms developing new products. But in recent years the characteristic way in which it has occurred is through corporate mergers and take-overs.

Diversification is far from a new phenomenon, but corporations in the post-war epoch became more than ever pure profit-seeking machines, neither rooted in a particular place nor tied to producing a particular product. Today it would not be a surprise to find that a company which produced and marketed T V soap operas also made T Vs, sponsored operas and manufactured soap.

That example is imaginary, but in reality a Londoner in the 1980s could buy a Sunday newspaper produced by a subsidiary of a US-based multi-national oil corporation or hold an insurance policy issued by a subsidiary of the Greyhound Bus Company. The US Steel corporation, to the dismay of steelworkers, has been redirecting its investment into the oil business; and British Petroleum has opened a bank. Here is money capital chasing profits with more freedom than ever before.

(ii) *Small firms*

Despite the dominance of big business it would be very premature to toll the funeral bell for the small capitalist. Every year many thousands of people across the capitalist world with a little capital or the chance to borrow set up their own business. Many fail even in good times; but many others succeed, at least for a while. Accurate figures are hard to obtain. In the U K in the declining 1980s there remained somewhere between 1 and 2 million small firms (with up to 200 workers each, though on average many fewer). In a more vigorous economy such as Japan's, small businesses thrive particularly well; a growing industry makes spaces for new entrepreneurs and has plenty of finance to lend to them when necessary. And they have always played an important role as subcontractors to the main conglomerate corporations (called *Zaibatsu*).

Praise for the values represented by small business is frequently heard – and from different parts of the ideological spectrum. Some have extolled their embodiment of the entrepreneurial spirit; others argue that the closer, less impersonal, relations possible between boss and worker can lead to more fulfilling and less alienating work. It is true that on average workers in small enterprises are less likely to be in a trade union and less likely to strike than those of larger corporations. The evidence suggests also that they are generally paid less and are less secure in their job than their equally qualified counterparts in big business. Only where the smallness of the production unit is coupled with full participation of the workforce in its decisions, as in some co-operatives, are more democratic ideals achieved. Often small business is characterized by exceptionally bad working conditions and exceptionally oppressive management regimes.

2. THE WORLD OF THE CAPITALIST CLASS

These basic facts about the structure of business provide the background to three questions about the nature of the capitalist system. Who are the members of the capitalist class in the modern world? Have the willingness and ability of capitalists to go after maximum profits changed with the arrival of large corporations? And has the degree of competition fallen or risen?

(i) *Today's capitalists*

Most small companies are individually owned by families, small groups or individuals. The ownership of big business is much more widely spread. In the USA only two or three big businesses continue to be privately owned by individuals or families. The great majority are owned by shareholders and normally there are many such shareholders for each company.

Even so, in the advanced countries, those who own shares in any quantity tend to be a very small minority of the population. In both the UK and the USA over nine-tenths of the value of all privately owned company shares are held by one-tenth of the adult population; in Canada, 93 per cent of business shares belong to the richest 20 per cent; in Sweden, often regarded as a hotbed of egalitarianism, the concentration is even greater – the richest 5 per per cent own over 95 per cent of privately held shares. And most of the shares are owned by a small minority of the minority. Though, as in any categorization, there will be borderline cases, it is possible to identify a very small group of people (much less than 1 per cent of the adult population) who gain the bulk of their income from the ownership of business. In one respect, however, such figures exaggerate the concentration of ownership. In a number of countries a rising proportion of company shares are owned by institutions like pension funds and insurance companies. In the UK where this trend has gone furthest, over two-thirds of shares are institutionally owned in this way. The nominal owners of pension funds and the holders of insurance policies include millions of workers.

This development does not, however, represent a very significant move towards an egalitarian capitalism. Pension rights and insurance policies are themselves very unequally distributed and heavily weighted in favour of the relatively rich. And they give employees no power in the running of capitalist firms. You would not be able to tell from managers' actions on the shopfloor whether some of a firm's shares are held by pension funds. In any case the funds and insurance companies are for the most part administered by executives of financial capitalist companies.

The ownership of the means of production is not the only question at issue. Most studies of modern capitalism have reached the conclusion that there has been a powerful tendency towards the separation of ownership and control, especially in big businesses. Increasingly these are managed not by their owners but by a professional management. A manager-controlled firm has been defined as one where no family or coherent group could be identified as owning more than 5 per cent of the share capital. In the USA it has been calculated that of the largest 200 non-financial companies over 160 are now in this sense manager- rather than owner-controlled. Though similar studies in the UK have concluded that the figure there is much less (probably still under 50 per cent), the trend appears incontrovertible.

Despite the spread of managerial control, the day of the distinctive individual capitalist personality has not yet passed altogether. For there are still many important large businesses and very many small ones in which control is still significantly exercised by their owners. A number of the most famous families in the history of US capitalism continue to keep large shareholdings in the firms with which they have been historically associated: the Dow family (Dow Chemicals), the Du Pont family (chemicals), the Rockefellers (Exxon), Ford, the Gettys, the Mellons (Gulf Oil), the Hewletts and Packards (computers). It is also true that there seems to be a continuous, if limited, supply of old-fashioned industrial barons – such men as Rupert Murdoch and Tiny Rowland – in the ruthless pursuit of great capitalist empires. Their importance is easy to exaggerate because of the lurid and colourful nature of their activities.

Not all the means of production are in private hands. Apart from the goods and services produced and distributed non-commercially by the state, a small proportion of commodities are produced in public corporations. These typically include some of the infrastructural activities, fuel and power, transport and telecommunications. In addition the national or local state may own parts of capitalist corporations through public shareholdings. This is clearly more significant than it was a hundred or even fifty years ago, though in very few countries would more than one-tenth of production come into this category.

Four main motives have produced the growth of public ownership: the spread of state-provided public services like health, education and welfare, as well as the rise of the military; the take-over by the state of loss-making capitalist industries which provided indispensable inputs to the rest of productive industry; the take-over of assets as a punishment for owners who were fascist collaborators during the Second World War; and finally (and least significantly) the take-over of private firms by governments with an ideological commitment to public ownership and socialism. The last motive, as well as being the least significant, is also the most fluctuating since strongly pro-capitalist governments have also from time to time re-privatized publicly owned industries.

The extent of public ownership and the growth of other economic functions of the state (which we shall discuss in Chapter 11) have led many people to argue that what we are calling the capitalist countries are capitalist no longer. They have become *mixed economies* with a private and a public sector. There is a mixture of public and private ownership in all capitalist economies.

We recognize that this makes a difference when these economies are compared with their nineteenth-century predecessors, but we are quite unconvinced that this has abolished their capitalist character. The nationalized sector for the most part complements rather than rivals the private sector. Public corporations have often been operated in a way which constitutes a subsidy to private capital. They frequently sell their products at relatively low prices so that costs to private business are reduced and private profitability raised at the expense of public sector profitability.

Nationalizations have often amounted to rescue operations for capitalist owners. Instead of being stuck with unsaleable, unprofitable means of production, they have been compensated (often very generously) in assets which they can use to make profits in new activities. Such nationalizations can be said to have been carried out for the health and efficiency of capitalism in general. In addition state corporations are almost invariably run on very similar lines to private enterprises. Though they may sometimes be under less compulsion to make profits (because they are being used to subsidize private profitability), their forms of management and their relationships with the consumers of their products are similar to those of private capitalists. In fact there is frequently interchange of higher management between state and private corporations. All in all they have not become elements of a new form of non-capitalist economy but remain adaptations of a capitalist economy – a form of state capitalism which is symbiotic with private capitalism.

We can now answer the question of the nature of today's capitalist class. It consists of that very small proportion of the population who own and control the means of production. Given that these two functions have become increasingly separated, it is necessary today to see the capitalist class as being composed of those who perform both roles. Along with the tiny minority of major shareholders, the leading managers and executives of capitalist business must also be included. But what level of management is the dividing line? If we include the executives of the major private corporations, why not the executives of nationalized industries? And given that there is a constant interchange of personnel between senior management and the higher echelons of the civil service should not the individuals who occupy senior government posts also be included?

There is no definitive answer to these questions. But the difficulty in answering them does not invalidate the concept of a capitalist class. Since classes are defined in terms of social functions the complexity of social life will always mean some ambiguity. But there is overwhelming evidence that a relatively very small number of people in capitalist countries either live on income obtained not from work but by virtue of owning property, or govern the lives of the majority through their ability to control the use of society's means of production. These are real flesh-and-blood human beings and not just a figment of sociological imagination.

(ii) *Capitalist motives and techniques*

Managerialism is said by many mainstream economists and sociologists to result in a conflict of interest between owners and managers. Whereas owners only want to maximize their profits over the long term, managers' motives are to increase their own emoluments, their social prestige and their security, to enjoy thick-carpeted offices, rich expense-account lunches and so on. Hence it is argued that the trend towards managerial control implies the modern corporation is less concerned with profit than its nineteenth-century counterpart.

This is the precise opposite of the truth. Modern businesses can and do pursue profits with an aggressiveness and ability unmatched by their Victorian predecessors.

A first hint that the top managers, at least, are deeply concerned with profits can be obtained from a glance at their rewards. The average yearly compensation of a Chief Executive Officer in one of the 250 largest US corporations is over \$1 million. In 1984 T. Boone Pickens of Mesa Petroleum, the highest paid of them all, received nearly \$23 million. But much of these grotesquely large salaries is paid in 'stock options' and other devices which relate managers' rewards to profits.

We can safely assume that modern owners of capital have as their motive the making of profit. This was probably true too of many of the owner-entrepreneurs of yesteryear. Even so, the history of capitalism abounds with stories of owner-entrepreneurs sacrificing maximum profits to personal obsessions, eccentricities and madnesses in a way which could not happen in the much more structured atmosphere of the modern corporate bureaucracy. Moreover, it is well known that even the owner-rentiers of the past tended to be overly concerned with annual dividends rather than capital gains and long-run profits. Many managers used to retain secret funds in years of high profit, rather than declare full profits and push up the price of the shares, so as to be able to pay out dividends in leaner years.

It is, of course, true that the modern corporation does many things which do not appear to be directly related to making profits. But you do not have to be pathologically cynical to doubt whether the reason that oil companies sponsor operas or tobacco companies finance sporting events is their devotion to culture and health. Activities like these, and the more obvious expenditures like political lobbying, illustrate that the modern business corporation has acquired a much wider view of its own sphere of activities than its predecessors. It must not only do its own business but also help to perpetuate the environment in which its business can profit.

Aside from the question of managers' motives, the twentieth century has brought great advances in their abilities. In the nineteenth century, technically competent managers were a rarity, and the information about production, costs and markets was typically primitive guesswork. Nowadays, many managers have been through business schools and universities, and they have access to much wider information and more sophisticated ways of using it. What used to be shots in the dark have now become carefully prepared, rational and calculated decisions.

Equally important, there have been great advances in the abilities of owners to monitor their representatives. Increasingly the ruling class has counteracted the scandals of wayward managers expropriating rentier capitalists by supporting increased regulation of stock markets and corporations and increased accountability to their shareholders. These were effected in the USA through the various Securities and Exchange Commission Acts in the 1930s, in the UK by the Companies Act in 1948, and elsewhere by similar legislative measures. At the same time, a steadily improving accountancy profession and an emerging cadre of financial journalists and investment advisers have served to protect the interests of owners better than ever before.

The net consequence of modern managerial capitalism would appear to be that the profit motive of the capitalist class is undiminished; and its ability to pursue that motive single-mindedly, rationally and in an all-embracing way has been enhanced.

(iii) *The extent of competition*

It seems obvious from the figures quoted in Table 2.3 that business has, over several decades, become more concentrated. Some imaginative observers have extrapolated some date in the not-too-distant future by which all capitalist production will be concentrated in one firm. A monopoly indeed! Yet this fantasy is quite unreal, not least because it ignores the vigour of smaller businesses. Even though small firms may account for a lower proportion of output they are in an absolute sense more numerous than ever before.

But what is the significance of the rise in aggregate concentration? By far the commonest answer is that higher concentration has led to less competition and that competition has assumed new forms. Some even argue that the modern era is so dominated by monopolies that there has been a qualitative change in the way capitalism operates.

We disagree. The evidence suggests that the 'chemically pure' model of rival capitalists pursuing profits and accumulating capital under the coercive forces of competition is becoming more closely approximated in reality.

Before proceeding to see why, it is necessary to clarify what is meant by the 'degree of competition'. In the 'pure' model, capitalists are assumed to be concerned with making as much profit as possible. It is irrelevant which particular goods or services are produced, provided they yield maximum profits. Each capitalist, therefore, would invest money-capital in whatever industry he or she chooses, based on the best information available. So where there is an industry with above-average profits, capital would tend to flow into it, and away from less profitable industries. If many businesses turn to the high-profit activities then the profits available to each would tend to fall; and the profit available to those which remain in less profitable fields would tend to rise. So there would be a tendency for the profit rate (profits as proportion of capital advanced) to become equal in all industries.

In the real world, however, some areas of high profit may be defended from invasion. The existing firms may erect barriers to the entry of others; and capitalists may be reluctant to move into new industries with which they are not familiar. Hence any tendency for profits to be equalized has been restricted. The definition of the degree of competition relates to the strength of this tendency: *the more competitive the business environment is, the more the profit rate in different industries tends towards equality.*

It is also necessary to clarify the notion of an 'industry'. Most studies of the capitalist economy have shown a marked tendency for increasing concentration. In the case of individual industries, however, it is difficult to attach an unambiguous meaning to the statistics. An industry as usually defined for statistical purposes – for example, 'chemicals', or 'wood products' – is not a meaningful concept from the point of view of industrial concentration because it encompasses the production of so many different, non-competing products. An apparently very low degree of concentration in an industry could, for example, be consistent with there being a 100 per cent monopoly in the production of all its different products (in other words each different wood product being produced by a single, different firm).

Mention of this problem is not intended, however, to negate the impression given by Table 2.3. Statistical studies of concentration in *well-defined* single products as well as more anecdotal descriptions of industries make it abundantly clear that big business is dominant in many economic activities.

It is well known that the international petroleum industry used to be almost entirely dominated by a handful of giant firms, the seven sisters (five American, two European). The diamond industry is a virtual monopoly of the South African De Beers corporation. The I B M company had in 1980 about half the world market in computers and peripherals. Between them the Boeing, Douglas and Lockheed companies produce virtually all of the world's long-distance aircraft. Many other examples of this degree of large-firm dominance could be found in other products on a world scale. And in each national market there are many other equivalent examples of large firms monopolizing a very large share of the sales of particular products.

Economists, both supporters and critics of capitalism, have related the degree of competition to a one-dimensional spectrum of 'market' situations. This ranges from 'perfect competition' (so many producers that each one is too small to affect the market price) to monopoly (a single producer). Under perfect competition firms are free to enter and leave each industry at will; so in the search for maximum profits the profit rates in different industries will be equalized. Under monopoly, the firm prevents new entrants to the industry, and thereby can control price and in principle achieve an above-average profit rate which can be sustained.

Those observers who stress the economic significance of the higher aggregate concentration figures of Table 2.3 see them as reflecting higher concentration in each industry and hence a move along the spectrum from perfect competition towards monopoly. That is why it is thought that there is less competition in today's world than fifty or a hundred years ago.

That this conclusion is misleading we can see by bringing together the trends we have looked at earlier in this chapter.

The idea of a simple spectrum of market situations, ranging from high to low competition, is at best a highly over-simplified one. Even a monopolist encounters competition – either from substitute products or from the *threat* of entry of new producers into a market. The extent of such a threat depends partly on technical factors such as the minimum feasible size of a single productive unit (one of the barriers to entry), and partly on institutional factors such as whether the existing monopolist is controlled or protected by the state. In the case of oligopolies (a small number of firms in an industry) there is in addition the direct competition between them.

Concentration does not eliminate sources of competition. And in principle there is no reason why the intensity of competition within a market should vary just with the *number* of competitors. It will depend on the attitudes and behaviour of the businesses concerned. Economic history offers examples both of two or three competitors trying to cut each others' throats and of multiple producers refusing to compete with each other by price fixing, as well as examples of the opposite.

We have seen that it is difficult to define 'industry' or 'the market' in which sets of producers compete. Statistics which purport to show greater concentration in individual industries typically hide the fact that the realm of operation of industries has been widening both geographically and in terms of numbers of products. There may be increasing competition from capitalists in other countries so we cannot conclude much from national-based industry trends in isolation. There are also many more possible substitute products available in the modern era, thereby further clouding the dividing line between industries.

So whereas aggregate concentration statistics like those in Table 2.3 are a useful indicator of the aggregate dominance of big business, individual industry concentration figures are often virtually meaningless.

Finally, whatever the statistics say about concentration, the changing behaviour of modern corporations – the single-minded, rational and all-embracing way in which they can now pursue profits – should alert us to the increasingly *competitive* nature of the modern capitalist world.

The modern corporation is less than ever hidebound by the particular industry in which it began life. It is no longer held back by lack of finance from pursuing what it perceives to be the best profit opportunities. It has no fear of crossing frontiers. So, increasingly, the firm which thinks it has cornered a little niche of very high profits is unable to shelter there for long.

The editors of *Fortune* magazine summed up this new competitive behaviour in 1970, in a passage quoted by Paul Auerbach in *A Critique of Industrial Analysis*:

Formerly, men in, say, the cement business knew exactly what to do with their profits: pay out part of them to stockholders and reinvest most of the balance in cement plants. But anyone who sets out to clarify his ultimate objective comes, fairly rapidly, to the proposition that his main objective is maximizing the return on his capital and, thereby, raising the value of his stock. And when he gets to that, he proceeds inexorably to the thought that alternative investments may yield higher pay-offs than cement. When he gets used to the idea that alternative investments are not only legal and moral, but profitable, he is pretty far along the road to becoming a conglomerator.

3. THE CAPITALIST PROCESS

In this chapter we have established the dominance of private business and looked at the various types of business in which profits are made. All of these are real-life embodiments of capital, the basic unit of capitalism, and (with the exception of banks, which we shall turn to in Chapter 7), each must in principle be part of both the spheres of capitalism referred to in

Chapter 1's abstract discussion: they are involved both in production and in exchange.

Just as a growing tree passes through changing seasons, so *capital* passes through the seasons of its spiral progression as illustrated in Diagram 2.1. These occupy the next part of this book.

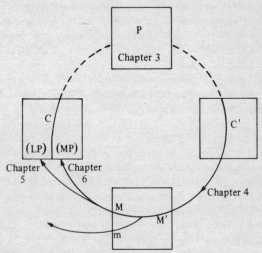

KEY
P: Capital in the production stage
C':   Produced commodities with incorporated potential profits
M':   Money-capital with incorporated realized profits
M: Money-capital
m: Realized profits
LP: Labour-power
MP: Means of production
C: Commodities

Diagram 2.1   The Stages of the Capitalist Process

In Chapter 3 we begin with the production sphere, where the potential for profit is found, and where capitalist confronts workers in an unequal power relationship. Then in Chapter 4 we enter the sphere of exchange by looking at the process whereby commodities are sold and hence profits realized, concentrating on the particular problems of selling to consumers. In the diagram, C' indicates the produced commodities, and M' the money for which they are sold, including the profits (plus interest, rent and dividends) that have been realized. These profits, represented by m, may or may not be invested in an attempt to expand the business. Either way, the rest of the money, M, is reused to continue the capitalist process. Still in the sphere of exchange, business must enter the market to buy more commodities, represented in the diagram by C: both labour-power (Chapter 5) and the means of production (Chapter 6). This puts the firms back in the position to start the production process, taking us again to the beginning of the circuit.

In Chapter 7 we conclude Part Two with a discussion of markets and money: the general economic soil and financial fertilizer which promotes the life-cycle of capital.

PART TWO

THE CAPITALIST PROCESS

CHAPTER 3

The Production Process

I. CAPITALISM AND PRODUCTIVITY

Humanity's oldest profession, in fact as opposed to fable, is that of the farmer. Throughout human economic history most people have practised agriculture or animal husbandry. The long life of this activity, therefore, provides the most vivid illustration of the scale of the explosion in productive potential released by modern capitalism. In the nine millennia or so since the revolutionary dawn of settled agriculture the provision of food for human communities occupied most of their labour force, as in the poorer parts of the world it still does.

Some important improvements in technique took place – in the design of the plough, the use of draught animals and irrigation. But century after century saw little change in the basic nature of the farming process: much manual labour combined with traditional farming methods, basic tools and at times some help from animals.

Then quite suddenly in a few countries in the seventeenth and eighteenth centuries the velocity of technical change accelerated to allow agriculture to escape from the gravity-like pull of tradition.

By the middle of the twentieth century, Sigfried Giedion in his classic study *Mechanization Takes Command* (1969), could describe a modern 'factory farm' in the following terms:

Yonder, in the vast gambrel-roofed barn, stands the machinery of the American farm. And nearby, 160 acres of grass, wheat, or corn land are ready to be reaped. Three people suffice to carry on the work. Twenty cows in the stalls are milked by machines, which automatically stop as soon as the udder runs dry. The farmer does not have to be in the fields at five in the morning. He sometimes leaves the house between nine and ten, to sow or to harvest. For the first time since it has been tilled by men, the soil no longer exacts sweat and unceasing tenacity. (pp. 164–5)

Thus a fundamental change had occurred in the way agricultural production was organized: it had become mechanized and already to some extent automated.

Along with this technological advance went changes in the economic and social relations under which production was carried out. As in industry, capitalist agriculture is largely carried out by people working for wages; and the products are not destined to be consumed by the producers, but are to be sold on the market. Giedion continued his study as follows:

The commercialization of the farm is pointed out by Californian agriculturalists, 1926: 'We no longer raise wheat here, we manufacture it . . . We are not husbandmen, we are not farmers. We are producing a product to sell.' (p. 166)

It is not only the way things are produced and products distributed that has been transformed: it is the products themselves. Advanced capitalist countries nowadays overfeed themselves with no more than one in twenty of their workers still in agriculture. Many of the rest produce goods and services which were not even imagined two centuries ago. Even the more traditional activities have, like farming, undergone radical changes that have raised the productivity of labour to levels that would have been beyond belief for our ancestors of a few generations ago.

To recognize capitalism's revolutionary achievement, however, is very different from endorsing the character of modern production processes. Despite the massive productivity gains, there are countless millions of people, even in the advanced capitalist countries, who continue to feel the oppressive imperatives of hard work, numbed by the long day's drudgery or meaningless routine. And there are new ways of making sure people work hard, new techniques which capitalist managers can use to cut down the time 'wasted' during the working day. In his profound comedy *Modern Times*, Charlie Chaplin vividly ridiculed this tendency through the farcical 'eating machine', devised so that workers could eat on the production line instead of stopping work for meals. And via the image of the worker who cannot stop twisting imaginary nuts even after the production line has been switched off, he made countless people laugh at the absurd way in which modern machines seem to enslave human beings.

What Chaplin illuminated is the fact that production is not just a question of changing technology but of achieving the social relations under which it is carried out. In fact the technology itself is not some neutral outside factor which inventors happen to discover. It is increasingly designed, under capitalism, with profits in mind. So in this chapter we explore the modern capitalist production process from both points of view: the technical and the social.

2. THE POLITICAL ECONOMY OF PRODUCTION

(i) *Ideologies of technology*

Technology is constantly idealized by politicians and social theorists: advancing technology, it is claimed, will solve our human problems and should be welcomed with open arms. We are called on to worship the god of new technology, to forget its detrimental effects on people or on the natural world. Those who resist, the infidels and heretics of the religion of technology, are damned as Luddites, selfish enemies of the common progress. But not everyone has joined the church.

Many sociologists, writing within the traditional framework of 'industrialism', have seen an inevitable trade-off between progress in material standards through industrialization and a developing tyranny of machines over the human race. In this approach people may have to become more alienated at work if they want to get richer.

Orthodox economics by contrast remains neutral and agnostic. Its concern is with the allocation of given resources and it regards labour as just another input like machines: the services of 'human capital'. (Since in orthodox economics machinery is termed 'physical capital', the term is equivalent to 'human machinery'.) Unless one accepts the morality of slavery (which even capitalists normally do not), 'human capital' cannot be bought like machines; one can only buy its services for specified periods of time. Beyond this, orthodox economics recognizes no distinction in principle between humans and machines in the context of production.

Most economists do not see the management of labour as an *economic* problem; and those few that do, tend to see it in terms of an 'optimal exchange' between worker and capitalist rather than as an inherently hierarchical and conflicting relationship. Hence they use the concept of a 'production function', which mysteriously and mechanically relates the quantities of inputs into a production process with the amount of output produced.

Both these viewpoints – of 'industrialism' and orthodox economics – are limited and distorting, as a consequence of their failure to set their conception of modern production in its capitalist context. But neither approach is simply wrong. Each misses the essential truth not by stating the opposite but by only looking at the surface of things. To say that workers are oppressed by machines is to recognize a real tendency, which is that workers may directly experience and perceive their oppression in this way, without seeing through the surface to its essential basis in capital's domination over labour.

Similarly, the notion of 'human capital' expresses a real tendency under capitalism. Getting effective labour out of workers would be easier if they could be made to behave like objects; after all, machines do not go on strike, nor do they have an independent existence. In attempting to control the detailed production tasks of workers, either through technological design or through management techniques, capitalists are effectively trying to convert labourers into objects – into the equivalent of inanimate appendages of the machines. In an extreme instance, a British subsidiary of a Japanese company recently prohibited its employees from laughing at work. So 'human capital' is not such a bad term after all, as long as one remembers that it is the accumulation of capital which tends to turn humans into objects.

But if we are looking for a theory that can explain the changing ways in which production is organized and the kinds of technology which capitalist innovators aim to introduce, we must dispense with the simple idea of a production function and go deeper. We must enter the gates of the factory, open up the office door and see what goes on inside.

(ii) *The duality of the labour process*

A *production* or *labour process* is simply the action of humans upon nature in order to produce something that is useful. In general, in all eras of human history, production involves three elements.

(a) *The purposeful activity* is the conscious transformation of nature.
(b) *The object of labour* is that which is to be changed. It could be a raw product of nature, such as fish in the sea, or the output of a previous act of production, such as bricks to be used in building a house.
(c) *The instruments of labour* used by humans to assist in the transformation of nature; for example, tools and machines of all kinds.

The second and third elements together make up the means of production.

But in the capitalist era the labour process has some further specific elements which did not previously exist – whorls in the fingerprint of the profit system: these are the kind of control and the motives involved. Workers do not own the means of production and they must work under the control of capitalists. They sell their own special commodity, their labour-power. The capitalists who buy it must ensure that the potential work is turned into effective work. And their principal objective is to make as much profit as they can.

Thus *production under capitalism is a unity of two processes – the labour process in general* (*which is common to all human societies*) *and the profit-making process whereby money-capital is advanced for the purpose of expanding it*. This dual approach underlies the analysis of production which follows.

(iii) *Ways of increasing profits*

Capitalists cannot stand still for long in a competitive world. To survive they must attempt continually to modify and in some cases even to revolutionize the production process.

There are broadly five ways in which they can try to increase their profits.

(a) Get workers to work for longer each day (without paying them appropriately more).

(b) Get workers to work harder or more intensively.

(c) Buy more tools or machines and thereby use the workforce more effectively.

(d) Buy new tools and machines which embody new techniques of production.

(e) Improve the allocation of a firm's given resources by rationalizing the administrative process, for example through improved accounting techniques.

The first four strategies can have a direct bearing on the production process. They do not necessarily always bring a greater profit return on capital outlay and different approaches were therefore more prevalent at different times.

The lengthening of the working day was particularly important in the early years of capitalism in England. Early factory owners made their workers work up to twelve hours a day, and well beyond, sometimes seven days a week. Even though this may have meant paying more wages, the extra profits produced easily made the system worthwhile for capitalists. As for the workers, they were often in a particularly weak position to resist such extreme exploitation, as even if they could survive on the lower wages of a more reasonable working day the capitalist could threaten them with dismissal. Resistance to the free reign of capital arose eventually via the state: the British Parliament passed several laws, beginning in 1833, to restrict the hours during which workers were allowed to work. These 'Factory Acts', which applied initially only to certain industries (textiles) and types of workers (children and women), were gradually generalized; they became the focus of a considerable class struggle.

In later times this strategy became relatively less important than the others. It became a question of how, with a fixed or even declining length of the working day, the capitalist could increase the amount of profits obtained.

The second strategy involves reorganizing work to increase its intensity, as when the capitalist increases the speed of an assembly line, so that workers have to work faster in order to keep up. Naturally this tactic is also the focus of some struggle on the factory floor. There are, however, a host of management tactics that come into this category, including the rise of the factory itself, the expanded division of labour and yet more tactics specific to the twentieth century, which we shall describe below.

The third and the fourth strategies both involve new investment, though only in the latter case, where new techniques are involved, could the change in the production process be called 'revolutionary'.

In choosing a strategy to adopt, capitalists are in effect deciding on a set of concrete production conditions which affect the lives of everybody associated with the firm.

The most frequent decisions which capitalists must take concern 'short-term' responses to market decisions – for example, how much overtime to employ, whether to raise or lower the price or output, and so on. These must normally be taken assuming a given technology, machine stock and method of work organization.

It is in the medium term, however, that occasional *strategic* decisions have to be made about a normal mode of operation – the normal length of the working week, the best combination of labour-power and means of production, the method of work organization, etc.

In a still longer view, technology itself is changing and infrequent decisions have to be made about which technologies to research and which to adopt.

It is with these medium- and long-term strategic decisions that we are concerned in this chapter. The choices are influenced partly by technical factors, which is why we shall look first at the principal, purely technical reasons for productivity advances with different systems of production. But they are also partly determined by social factors concerning the capital/worker relationship, to which we shall soon return.

3. FIVE SYSTEMS OF PRODUCTION

It is not easy to sum up the vast and complex story of the principles and types of production method that have been seen in capitalism. The following fivefold classification hides a host of complexities, but suffices for us to build up our picture of the twofold nature of capitalist production.

(i) *Co-operation*

'Simple co-operation' occurs whenever many people work together, according to some plan, all doing the same action. Suppose for example the job is to take many buckets of water up a ladder. One individual would be forced to make several successive trips up and down, but several people co-operating could form a chain to pass the buckets. Productivity will be greater with many people working; that is, more buckets will be carried for each person helping, in a given period. Other tasks, such as the lifting of heavy materials, would be impossible without co-operation.

Inherent in this principle is the idea of 'economies of scale', which economists have been familiar with for hundreds of years. In technical terms, economies of scale exist whenever increasing all the inputs into production increases the output *more than proportionately*.

However, the advantages of simple co-operation are limited. Beyond a certain point it makes no sense to increase the number of workers because further improvement is constrained by the techniques of co-ordination. Moreover, productivity is naturally limited by the human capacities of the individuals involved.

Simple co-operation became a particularly useful means of expanding productivity, alongside the rise of capitalism, since it became possible in factories to get numbers of people working together in the same place. But there is no era when we can say this was the predominant system of production. Rather it is found to varying extents in all times and places. Moreover, the principle of co-operation – that the collective labourer can be more productive than the individual – lies behind all subsequent technical means of expanding productivity.

(ii) *Division of labour*

Adam Smith, in his classic *The Wealth of Nations* (1776), regarded the 'division of labour' as the key to prosperity. Capitalists employed such a system before and after the onset of general mechanization, both in the home, as happened in the 'putting-out' system of production, and in the factory.

The concept must not be equated with a closely related idea, that of the overall division of labour in society, in which people specialize as doctors, lawyers, craftsmen and so on and sell their specialized products to the market. Here we are considering the divisions that occur within the factory or workplace. They involve two elements: (a) the differentiation of tasks, wherein a production process is split up into separate detailed parts, and (b) specialization, wherein workers specialize in the performance of one or a few tasks. It is possible to have (a) without (b), if one worker switches from task to task or if several workers are involved but they regularly rotate the tasks between them. Such an arrangement has occasionally been demonstrated, for example in many Japanese factories. But it is fair to say that generally the two elements have been developed together in most capitalist production processes.

The system had technical advantages which enabled productivity to be increased. First, the fact that tasks were differentiated, and that people specialized in a particular task throughout their working lives, increased their expertise at that task. Moreover it increased their inventiveness, encouraging them to find improved ways of doing each task. Second, the principle of specialization allowed tasks of different kinds to be allotted to different people with matching skills. This was the most important source of gradations in the workforce: unskilled workers employed at unskilled tasks, skilled machinists concentrating on the task they are trained for. This is often referred to as the Babbage principle after Charles Babbage (perhaps better known as the inventor of the calculating machine) who explained its advantages in 1832. A third, relatively less important, advantage of the division of labour, compared to individual production, is the time saved in changing position or in taking up a different tool.

Yet there remain clear technical limits to the pure system of division of labour: it is ultimately constrained by the physical and mental powers of the workers. Further strides in technical advance required the onset of mechanization.

(iii) *Machine production*

A machine is a mechanism that can perform with its tools the operations that were formerly done by the worker. That is, the immediate control of the process passes from the hand of the worker to the machine. This is the fundamental basis for the increased productivity which mechanization brings.

Thus a machine is not just a complex tool – many machines are much simpler in construction than some non-mechanical instruments of labour. Nor is it a question of where the power comes from. Many a plough was pulled by an ox but this did not allow the ploughing process to pass from the direct control of the ploughman.

But the machine allows the possibility of much greater complexity, in that many tools can be handled at once. Further it allows for immensely greater forces to be used in production, and thereby calls forth the development of greater power sources. Early textile mills often used waterpower to run the looms but were later converted to steam power, which became the main power source in the early period of industrialization in Britain. The later developments of electrical power, internal combustion engines and even nuclear-powered engines have added immeasurably to the force available to be exerted by machines. It requires no great elaboration to appreciate the way the machine takes away the need for human dexterity with the tool and furnishes the worker with a productive capability far exceeding anything that was previously possible.

The further development of production is a matter of moving to increasing levels of mechanization and thereby higher levels of productivity. The classification of such levels is not well agreed. Writers have identified as many as seventeen levels ranging from hand production to fully automatic production systems. But for the present purposes it is helpful to identify two more systems only.

(iv) *Integrated mechanized production*

Mechanical 'assembly line' production is applicable in certain industries where production involves a continuous flow from raw material to finished product, with parts of the product being assembled at successive stages by workers or by machines controlled by operators. The specific technical advantage of such a system is that it reduces the time and energy required to move either the worker or the half-completed product to the next stage. Instead, the conveyor belt moves the product at a steady machine-powered pace from worker to worker. This sytem was introduced first in the USA in textiles, meat-packing and lamp production, but it is most commonly associated with the automobile industry. And as this latter case exemplifies, the advantages of this system only appear with a large scale of production.

(v) *Automatic machines*

The final stage is 'automation'. Production processes that come into this category range from the automatic washing machine to the modern, fully automated process plant characteristic of the chemical industry. Automation means more than elaborate mechanization and the replacement of human labour. It means the replacement of the *judgemental* part of labour.

In the case of the washing machine, for example, the judgement is simple: when a given amount of time has elapsed at one stage of the production cycle, the machine by itself moves to the next stage according to a pre-set pattern. With the advance of computers and microelectronic technology, highly automated systems now allow machines to measure and correct their performance while operating and even to anticipate required actions. This sort of control is possible in the oil and chemical industries. Similarly advanced is the system of robot production, which has the advantage of judgement combined with flexibility, thus allowing automatic production when only a small number of units are being produced. Most observers predict that an increasingly wide range of manufacturing functions will become amenable to automation in the 1990s. And at the same time the revolution in information technology is automating many clerical functions and changing the face of the office.

4. TECHNICAL EFFICIENCY, WORK INTENSITY AND PROFITS

These various systems of production may all be found in use in present-day capitalist enterprises either on their own or in combination. Our order of presentation roughly corresponds to historical trends, but the principles of the first two – division of labour or simple co-operation – persist even in this age of automation. How did they evolve? What prompts capitalists to use one method of production rather than another?

Worshippers of technology believe that the answers rest purely with the technical data: the most technically efficient methods are eventually chosen. But if we relate our answers systematically to the profit motive, we find that it is not purely a matter of technology; economic and social factors are at least as important.

(i) *The decision to use more machines*

The strategy of using more machines can best be examined if we assume for the moment that technology, the method of work organization and the normal length of the working week are unchanged; these assumptions imply a constant average intensity of work.

In general the addition of machines should increase the productivity of labour; but this does not necessarily improve profits, for the extra machines have a cost. The capitalist must decide whether they will increase profits – in other words whether their introduction will be economically efficient, a complex question which is determined by two factors: first by technical efficiency, and second by the relative prices of machines and labour.

The best way to explain technical efficiency is by showing what would count as technically inefficient. A production method is inefficient if there is an alternative method which gives

(a) more output from the same quantity of both inputs, labour and machines, *or*
(b) more or the same output from
    (i) less of both inputs, labour and machines, *or*
    (ii) less input of labour and the same of machines, *or*
    (iii) the same input of labour and less of machines.

A technically efficient method of production is one where there is no alternative with any of the characteristics in (a) and (b).

There can be several methods which are technically efficient to produce any particular level of output. It may be technically efficient to use a labour-intensive method of producing things, because although mechanization saves on labour it involves using *more* of the other input, namely machines. Setting aside technically inefficient production methods, the real question is which of the possible technically efficient methods will give most profits: the more mechanized or the more labour-intensive one? A simple example shows how this question must be answered. Street cleaners can clean the streets more quickly if they are all equipped with vacuum cleaners. But this will not necessarily be profitable. If the vacuum cleaners are very expensive, it may cost less to use a more labour-intensive method. If the machines are cheap enough, then it pays to become more mechanized.

So which method of production is *economically* efficient, in the sense that it maximizes profits, depends on the prices of the inputs, machinery and labour. It follows that there can be two reasons why an existing method of production will be replaced by another, more mechanized one.

(a) If there is some technical change which renders the existing method technically inefficient, in the sense defined above, profits are certain to improve as, after the technically inefficient method has been discarded, less needs to be paid out on inputs for a given output.
(b) If the price of the machines relative to the wages of labour decreases sufficiently, it makes it profitable to mechanize.

Technical Annexe 3.A derives these conclusions diagrammatically.

The conclusions, however, are only valid given the rather restrictive assumptions made at the start of this section. They must be amended as soon as we allow for variations in the level of work intensity. To treat labour simply as a technical input is to ignore the distinction between labour-power (which is what the capitalist pays for) and what we may call 'effective labour' (which is the actual amount of productive effort put in).

The definition of technical inefficiency above refers to effective labour inputs. It becomes a less useful concept when *the intensity of work* – which measures the relation between effective labour time used and labour time paid for – becomes a variable which can itself be influenced by the choice of production method.

With fixed work intensity any given amount of labour-power purchased by the capitalist would yield a known number of effective hours of labour. But if work intensity increases, the same amount of labour-power can be converted into a greater number of effective hours of labour. The consequence of this is that the cost per unit of effective labour with a method of production depends not just on wages but also on the intensity of work which it enforces.

It is even possible in principle therefore for a method of production which is 'technically inefficient' to be the one which gives the most profits, if it involves a method of work organization that guarantees greater work intensity.

The rise of factories was followed in the nineteenth century by widespread mechanization that rendered earlier production methods obsolete and inefficient. But it seems likely that in a large number of cases the immediate profitability of the factory method of work organization had nothing to do with technological superiority over the cottage industry which preceded it. This was evidently true of the weaving industry where the technology used in the factory was the same as had previously been used in the home. Rather, the early factories were profitable for capitalists because they enabled them to get workers to work harder and longer hours under the supervision and discipline of the factory manager. Output was increased by factories and so too were profits; but this was achieved by applying more effective labour inputs, not less, at a much cheaper rate due to the increased intensity.

(ii) *The evolution of technology*

In the long term, not only the method of work organization but also the technology can be changed. Present-day technology is the legacy of research and design decisions made in the past. While production systems must obey natural laws of physics and chemistry, they also bear the imprint of human design. This means that under a capitalist system technology is generally designed to meet the needs of capitalists.

It is a fact that Britain, the first capitalist country, supplied the vast majority of inventions to be made in the eighteenth and nineteenth centuries. Invention and capital accumulation interacted with each other to produce an upward spiral: the former stimulated the latter, while the prospect of profits increased the propensity to invent new technologies or to innovate where they were already in existence but unused. From the last decades of the nineteenth century onwards this process was intensified as scientific advance was firmly harnessed to the needs of capital. Invention ceased to be the province of the amateur scientist or engineer, and was increasingly dominated by the research and development departments of the large corporations.

In discussing the choice of production systems in the long term we must therefore remember that the technology which they use is in part within the choice of capitalists. But, as with changes in work organization, changes in technology do not just bring greater profits by increasing the technical efficiency of production, but also by increasing the intensity of labour. A machine operator has to work at the pace of the machine, often harder than he or she would in the absence of the machine's tyranny. A specific modern example is the word processor, a machine backed by a modern computer which has helped to cut drastically the costs of clerical work. By eliminating the need for retyping it reduces the time required for secretarial tasks and represents a definite technical advance, making the old typing system inefficient. But in addition word processor systems have been designed to increase greatly the control that management has over the secretary at work.

By automatically measuring and checking the work and allocating more as soon as each task has been finished, the pace is intensified and office costs are thereby reduced.

(iii) *Alternative routes to profit*

The conclusion that there is more than one way for capitalists to try to maintain or improve their profits is summed up schematically in Diagram 3.1. It summarizes the central proposition of this section, that there is more to modern production than technology alone. But the different decisions are not always simply a question of balancing up the pluses and minuses of the various technical and socio-economic factors; these factors are interrelated and, in particular, certain types of work organization may be more conducive to the advance or acceptance of technical knowledge (the inventiveness ascribed to specialization by Adam Smith would come into this category). So decisions about, and the evolution of, technology and work organization are a more complex matter than they appear in Diagram 3.1.

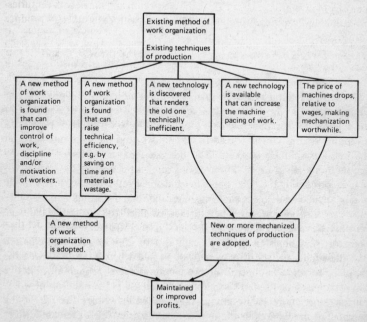

Diagram 3.1   Alternative Routes to Profit

(iv) *Another look at the systems of production*

Finally, we can look at some of the systems of production which we earlier considered purely from the technical point of view. We can now examine the economic and social advantages each could bring.

In the case of the division of labour, the advantages to the capitalist are attended by disadvantages to the workers which are soul-destroying. The minute, detailed specialization that accompanies the capitalist-controlled division of labour means that each specialized worker has to concentrate on one task indefinitely. This 'fragmentation', wherein workers lose sight of what is being accomplished in the overall production process, is present to some extent even under simple co-operation – since the plan of production is not theirs but the capitalists'. Under the division of labour it is carried to a much greater degree. The real implication of the Babbage principle – the matching of skills with the tasks requiring them – is the creation of an unskilled workforce and the systematic stunting of human capabilities. The classical economists were aware of this drawback. Even Adam Smith, the foremost advocate of the division of labour as the vehicle of progress, could say in *The Wealth of Nations*:

The understandings of the greater part of men are necessarily formed by their ordinary employments. The man whose life is spent performing a few simple operations . . . has no occasion to exert his understanding . . . He generally becomes as stupid and ignorant as it is possible for a human creature to become. (Book V, Chapter I, Part 3)

These disadvantages to the system are not necessarily a problem for capitalists – who are interested in the technical properties of a system of production not for their own sake but only in so far as they promise a profitable return. Unless forced to, capitalists need not take into account the interests of their workers. The degraded status conferred on many people by the divisions of labour is not of direct concern.

In reconsidering the third stage, machine production, we must add to the purely technical advances that machines indubitably brought, the specifically capitalist advantages. They further extended the use of the Babbage principle by replacing in many cases the skilled craftsman with an unskilled operator, sometimes enabling the capitalist to draw women and children into the supply of labour-power. And, as stated before, they allowed the capitalist to begin to control the production process through an objective force, the machine itself. This enabled an increase in the intensity of work. Finally, since by replacing labour they tended to weaken the bargaining position of the worker in the market, machines enabled the capitalist to keep wages down and to increase the length of the working day.

In the case of automatic machine production, the same general principle applies. Automatic systems are in a purely technical sense progressive because they permit substantial savings in inputs. Yet, as was illustrated in the case of word processors, they also enhance capitalist control over workers. Moreover, as with machine design, automatic systems are constructed to serve the profit-maximizing aims of the capitalist and these do not necessarily coincide with the human needs of the workers – in particular, they have not been extensively used to eliminate boring unskilled tasks.

It is with assembly line production that purely technical advantages form relatively the smallest part of the attraction for capitalists. Although there are some such benefits, deriving from the more efficient lay-out of work, the reason why the assembly line constituted a distinct stage in the evolution of capitalist production systems and why its introduction enabled capitalists to reap enormous profits, is that it permitted greater control over the worker.

This is exemplified well in the history of the Ford Motor Company, from its inception in 1903 with only a few skilled workers to 1914 when the mechanically driven conveyor-belt line for final assembly started rolling. Between 1903 and 1908 Henry Ford expanded the use of the division of labour to create unskilled tasks, and with a more efficient lay-out increased productivity to some extent. Between 1908, when the Model T was introduced, and 1914, he experimented constantly with the production system in order to meet the enormous demand for the product. When the assembly line was introduced and mechanized, the final assembly time of the chassis was reduced from over twelve hours to about one and a half hours.

Only about one-fifth of this extraordinary rise in productivity has been attributed to the purely technical advantage of the assembly line. A small part of the rest came from an improved division of labour. But by far the largest part of the time saved came from the increased pace of work which the conveyor belt enforced.

5. MANAGEMENT

Speeding up the labour process was another of the themes of Charlie Chaplin's *Modern Times*. We see the factory manager in his control room before a TV screen observing the rate of work at different places in the factory, and hotting the pace up where he chooses. This image also focuses attention on the manager.

We cannot explain the production process in capitalist society without an analysis of how workers are managed. After outlining the five production systems, we referred to the specific advantages for capitalists in each case. And the choice between different methods of production depends on social factors and hence on the effectiveness of management control.

Indeed *the problem of management of labour follows from the essentially antagonistic nature of capitalism*. In the exchange process workers sell their labour-power (not their labour) to capital. Having got rid of their time by selling it to the capitalist, workers have little reason to show an interest in the labour process, since it is not theirs; it becomes the responsibility of the capitalist.

(i) *Control*

There are three kinds of control that capitalists maintain: first, over the disposition of the means of production and the allocation of resources; second, over when, where and indeed whether workers work, if so for how long, and so on; third, over the specifics of the production process – what the worker actually does. It is the second and third levels that are of concern here.

Given the aim of maximizing profits, it might be thought that capitalists would seek as much control as possible at all three levels. But that would be to ignore the productive advantages from flexibility and workers' initiative. A comparison of nineteenth- and twentieth-century management philosophies will exemplify the balance of gains and losses from close control of work.

(ii) *Early management systems*

In the heyday of *laissez-faire* capitalism the methods of controlling the worker and work itself were for the most part indirect. Only a small fraction of production was managed in a direct and despotic way by a capitalist boss. In many firms this job would be given to a foreman who had authority over the other employees of the firm – a method that was widespread in Britain and the USA. Also common was a system of 'co-exploitation' whereby specific jobs would be subcontracted to skilled workers who would then hire unskilled workers or make use of the firm's pool of labourers.

These systems for the indirect control of work were complemented by an arms-length impersonal relation between worker and capitalist, which sociologists refer to as the 'cash nexus' of the wage system. Neither party to the exchange had any obligation to the other except to honour the terms of the deal: the worker to supply labour-power, the capitalist to pay wages. Capitalists were not expected to care for workers' welfare or to take any interest in the non-work part of their lives. The cash nexus remains the basic relationship in modern capitalism but is often supplemented by other forms of obligation – such as pensions, sick pay and so on.

These nineteenth-century methods of control were often successful because they struck a balance between the need to increase the intensity of work as much as possible and the need for flexibility to deal with detailed, changing production problems, which depended on the expertise of the skilled worker. Too much direct control of workers' actions by capitalists, even assuming they could overcome the resistance of skilled craftsmen, would have stultified production.

This balance began to shift towards the end of the nineteenth century, principally because of increasing size of corporations but also because with changing technology the traditional skills of craftsmen, and hence also their role in the direction of production, became obsolete. One response to this was the use of piece-rate systems ('payment by results') which by the end of the century were widespread in Germany, the USA and Britain. The purpose was to stimulate workers to work harder by the incentive of more pay. Simple as this system may sound, it is less than ideal because it entails endless struggle, in a changing world, over the rates for each job, the quality of the products and other issues – and this struggle itself could and did reduce the intensity of work, as workers discovered that hard work in order to make greater wages would often be met by a rate cut by the management.

In consequence, management in the twentieth century has increasingly, though not invariably, tended to equate the desire for maximum profits with a need for greater control of work.

(iii) *Modern management principles*

The change in management philosophy was reflected in a rise in the number of managers and the conscious teaching of management as an occupation.

The most striking new philosophy to emerge was dubbed 'scientific management' by its American founder, F. W. Taylor. At the turn of the century, he developed a system whose express purpose was to counteract what he called 'soldiering', the problem of workers not working hard or effectively. There were three general principles to this strategy.

(a) Managers should 'scientifically' (i.e. systematically) pursue the utmost extension of the division of labour. This required, for the first time, a careful study of the production process by managers, and its fragmentation into separate and simple tasks.

(b) A particular fundamental division of labour should be pursued, that between brain and hand. Production workers should have to think as little as possible about their work: the process of conception should be separated from that of execution.

(c) Managers, with their newly acquired monopoly of the knowledge of production techniques, should plan production tasks and direct workers to them.

It is the first principle which spawned 'time and motion' study, and on the basis of this detailed analysis of job tasks a more rational incentive scheme could be drawn up, with clearly defined rates for each task. Workers were treated as self-interested and rational (even if not intelligent), and work was therefore only to appeal to them as a means of getting wages.

The second principle elevated the contempt for workers as human beings to a new plane. If conception is what distinguishes human from animal production processes, then the objective was literally to dehumanize and to degrade labour. In concrete terms, Taylorism made tasks, as far as possible, routine, standard, less skilled.

The basic principles of Taylorism were first put into practice in the USA by about 250 firms in the period 1900–19, through new techniques of rational management. After the First World War the techniques spread within the USA. By the end of the 1930s they had begun to be widely used in Europe, with even British capitalists somewhat tardily relinquishing traditional delegated control systems to some extent. Even those new management systems which did not claim to be Taylorist were strongly influenced by its central philosophy, which was to take increased control of the production process.

One principle that built on Taylorism was 'Fordism', the idea of maintaining control through the specific design of technology, as in the assembly-line technology at the Ford Motor Company. While Taylorism is a philosophy of management and Fordism one of technological design, they dovetail with each other, are often used together and have the same object in view: increased work intensity.

(iv) *Alternative management strategies*

Dominant as these new rationalized techniques were, the pursuit of total control over production processes did not necessarily lead in all cases to maximum profits. As before, the need for flexibility in dealing with production problems as they arose was less easily met when the production workers could not take the appropriate decisions. The complex management process could therefore become unwieldy and costly, so that despite the gains in work intensity the losses elsewhere could be equally great. It is inefficient, from the technical point of view, not to use workers' capacities to the full. Moreover, in many cases the attempt to introduce rationalized management practices was met with strong and often successful resistance from skilled workers.

In 1914 Ford's workers started quitting in droves and though they were easily replaced from the large pool of unskilled labour-power in the Midwest, the high turnover was a waste and a drawback. So in 1915 he intro-duced his famous 'Five Dollar Day', a relatively high wage at the time, to be paid only to those over twenty-one, after six months' continuous em-ployment, and given satisfactory moral behaviour, the latter to be deter-mined by his infamous 'sociological department'. Direct control over work, it seemed, was not enough; it was necessary to exercise some further control over the worker.

This latter observation lies behind a variety of alternative approaches to modern management which have this in common: that their method of gaining maximum profits through a combination of high work intensity and high technical efficiency entails a modification of the pure cash nexus, so that the capitalists' control over the worker extends beyond the mere exchange of a wage packet, and if necessary involves a relaxing of direct controls over work.

Such methods are found throughout western capitalism – evidence includes the payment of pensions and other fringe benefits to certain classes of workers, which tie them to the companies they work for, and the in-corporation of and accommodation with trade unions, rather than con-frontation over production disputes. They are, however, best illustrated by Japanese capitalists' methods of control, partly because those represent the most substantial modification of the cash nexus, and partly because they have been remarkably successful in reaping profits and assisting capital accumulation.

In Japan, as elsewhere, capitalists encounter the problem of the con-version of labour-power into actual labour – specifically the directing, motivation and rewarding of workers. Early methods of control had depended partly on an indirect employment system not unlike that in nine-teenth-century Britain. Employers often relied on *oyakata*, independent labour contractors, to find workers, supervise production and so on. As in western capitalism, this method was adequate to the needs of early capital-ism but became a drawback when large-scale industrialization took off in the twentieth century. The problems of work organization and the need to raise work intensity, especially of skilled workers, were not, however, met by the Taylorist technique of job analysis and an extreme division of labour. Certainly, skills were destroyed by heavy investment in new machinery and technology. But the power of the remaining skilled workers was removed by a policy of training them from a young age and keeping them within the company.

In the modern Japanese corporation hard work is gained not by close authoritarian control but by building on the values of team work. The basic work unit is a small group, within which workers regularly do a wide range of jobs. Allegiance to the other workers in the group and loyalty to the company are the forces relied on to motivate workers, and the direction of work tasks is within limits a matter of group decision.

Relaxation of higher management's direct control over production is made possible by the lifetime employment system. Loyalty to the company, rather than to an occupation or profession, is emphasized ideologically and enforced economically by guaranteeing some employees a secure job for life. All required skills are generated within the company. At the same time workers are effectively tied to the company by economic as well as ideological chains, since they would suffer a large drop in wages if they took a job elsewhere. The reward system is such that wages and other benefits are linked automatically with age and, to a certain extent, need (family commitments). Unlike in Taylor's system of control, in Japan's system of 'bureaucratic paternalism' the immediate link between individual performance and monetary reward is a tenuous one.

This system was a result partly of managerial choice and partly of class struggle. The specific historical conditions in which Japan found itself in 1945, a defeated power under US occupation, could have resulted in other forms of development. But Japanese capitalists sought to utilize the lifetime employment system for an elite group of non-manual workers that had developed before the war. Considerable worker resistance and strike action led on the one hand to the system being expanded to include many manual workers. On the other hand the independent strength of workers in the future was lessened by the incorporation of company unions.

Thus Japanese capital's method of control involved a modification of the cash nexus, in an attempt to reduce the frequency of overt conflict in industrial relations. It cannot remove the antagonism inherent in the capitalist labour process. Its success is interesting because it demonstrates the possibility of alternative methods of control that do not rely on the exercise of *direct* authority. That Japanese managers can eat in the same canteen as their workforce gives the lie to the oft-expressed western belief that management requires separation and social distance. At the same time the Japanese have shown that it is possible to relax the link between effort and monetary reward, and base payments on need. But it must be remembered that the success of bureaucratic paternalism is intimately related to the other features of the Japanese labour market and to the general economy in which it is embedded.

Thus not all workers reap the benefits of the Japanese system. There are temporary workers, who can be sacked at short notice, plus outside contract workers, plus young women who work until they marry. These groups act as a buffer to the system, shielding it from recessionary downturns. When times are bad and demand for a product is low, the 'lifetime' workers are protected by sacking the other groups and if necessary by shifting protected workers to other plants producing different products within the same company. Second, while Japanese management has ensured regular productivity increases and hence contributed to the post-war success of Japanese capital, the modification of conflict in industrial relations depends in turn on the success of the system, on its ability to make room for progression of workers up the promotion scale and to provide the resources for improved wages and benefits. The orientation towards expansion and investment is helped by the financial structure of Japanese businesses which makes it comparatively easy to obtain long-term financing of projects from banks.

6. THE EVOLUTION OF OFFICE WORK

The themes of this chapter have been the ways that contrasting management styles relate to the profit motive, and the evolution of capitalist technology and methods of work organization. Elements of all of these are illustrated by the changes in clerical work over the last century.

It is a tale of a job that has gone through stages of rationalization and mechanization similar to most other production processes. Office work has been affected by the development of capitalism, in that as capital expanded, as firms became larger and as the amount of necessary complex planning and recording increased with expanded commodity production, not only did the demand for clerical work increase, but also its nature evolved under the influence of capital's search for greater profits.

In the mid nineteenth century, the (generally male) clerical worker normally belonged to the lower stratum of management, had good prospects of promotion into higher management positions or even to a partnership in the business, and had a secure job for life. His job was wide-ranging. His tools were pen, ink and so on. Towards the end of the century the demand for clerical work expanded. A greater proportion of clerks and secretaries became clearly separate from management. The larger corporations split up their planning, financial, sales and accounting functions into separate departments, and even within departments a considerable division of labour evolved. One particular division, between men and women, coincided with the introduction of the most basic office machine, the typewriter. From the start women were able to break into this production process, partly because it was new (no male traditions to be broken down) and partly because it was 'clean', the ideological requirement of a job for middle-class women. As the historian Margery Davies has described, it became accepted that 'woman's place is at the typewriter'.

As clerical work of all kinds continued to expand in the twentieth century, it became almost entirely a domain of female workers. In consequence a particularly important way of directing it was patriarchal control, an example of capital making use of and modifying a relationship traditional in earlier and different societies. The bosses, who were almost always men, were already ideologically conditioned to dominance over women, and the secretaries were similarly prepared to accept men's orders (albeit with some conscious or unconscious resistance).

Supplementing patriarchal control, the office worker was also conditioned by the status attached to non-manual work, which may have resulted partly from the earlier identification of clerical work with a managerial function. Moreover, within clerical grades there is a considerable value attached to status. Although the wages of clerical workers, particularly the lower grades in the typing pool and elsewhere, fell to levels similar to and below that of manual workers, their fringe benefits and relative job security continued to mark them out as different.

These methods of doing clerical work – partial division of labour, simple mechanization complemented by patriarchal and status relationships – meant that the degree of control over the detailed work was far from complete. Since management was able to rely to a certain extent on the self-motivation of the worker, and since for a long time clerical costs remained a small part of total costs, no attempt was made in many cases to increase control.

In some cases, however, the costs of office staff were becoming so high that managers found it profitable to rationalize the organization of office work. An American, William Leffingwell, demonstrated the productivity gains to be had by applying Taylor's principles to the office. By a combination of work measurement, routinization and simplification of tasks, and changing the lay-out of the office, it was possible to raise the intensity of work and thereby cut costs. Leffingwell explained: 'As a means of knowing the capacity of every clerk, and also as a means of spurring him to even better efforts, the planning department keeps daily records of the amount of work performed by each clerk and his relative efficiency' (quoted by Harry Braverman in *Labor and Monopoly Capital*, p. 308). These methods were applied in a few cases in the USA in the inter-war period and became much more widespread during the 1950s and 1960s.

The end of the post-war boom marks roughly the beginning of the next stage: further mechanization and automation. The need for greater control was brought on by the ever-increasing proportion of total costs taken up by the office; this in turn was due partly to the increasing if unconscious resistance to patriarchal control, as well as to the sheer volume of required work. This control was eventually to be supplied by the computer, which, in the 1970s and 1980s, revolutionized information processing. The word processor has greatly increased the technical possibilities, at the same time as increasing the management's control over secretarial work (as referred to above), and since it can simply edit out mistakes, there is no longer such a need for fast and accurate typists – their skill has been devalued. Wage clerks have only to punch or type some basic data and a computer processes it, calculates the wage and produces the appropriate cheques and payslips.

The mechanized, semi-automatic processing of data is having its impact throughout the world of clerical work. The modern microcomputer has relieved workers of many mundane and unrewarding tasks. Yet in many cases it causes redundancies by increasing the productivity of labour at a time when there are no other jobs to go to, and reduces the remaining jobs (except for a few elite systems analysts) to simple, routine, unskilled manual labour. In the office, or in the factory, what gives the capitalist more output and more control robs the worker of individuality and skill. So we will return to this theme from the worker's standpoint in Chapter 8.

The remaining chapters of Part Two continue to trace the stages in the circuit of profit through which capital passes after it emerges from the production process as new commodities in search of a market.

Technical Annexe 3.A The choice of production method

We have argued that, while a technically inefficient production method would not maximize profits, given fixed working intensity, the choice from the menu of technically efficient methods depended on the prices of the inputs.

This proposition can be shown more clearly and rigorously by the following hypothetical example. Consider a capitalist that employs two inputs, labour-power and machines, in order to produce a single output. Given the assumption of fixed work intensity, any quantity of labour-power bought on the market translates into a known amount of effective labour, measured in hours.

Diagram 3.A.1 shows four ways in which the inputs can be combined in order to produce a given quantity of the output. Suppose that initially the firm is using method A, which requires only a few machine-hours but the largest amount of labour-hours. The three other methods of production, B, C and D, all involve replacing an amount of labour services with more machinery, with D being the most mechanized method.

In addition to methods A, B, C and D, we could allow for the possibility of combining two production methods in the one firm. To produce the same given quantity of output, for example, a combination of methods D and C would require more labour than method D alone, but less than C alone; however, it would require less machinery than method D alone and more than C. In fact, the dotted line joining D and C shows us what would be needed from the inputs when various combinations of D and C are used. Similarly the line AC shows combinations of methods A and C. The full dotted line ACD is called an 'isoquant' (or 'equal-product line').

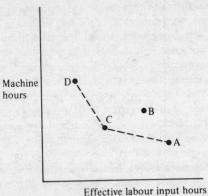

Diagram 3.A.1   Techniques of Production

Would it be advisable ever to use method B? The answer is no, because by using C the capitalists could save on both inputs, effective labour and machinery, thus reducing costs. B is therefore technically inefficient – we might perhaps think of it as representing a production method that uses an outmoded technology.

By contrast methods A, C and D (or the combinations represented by the lines AC and CD) are all technically efficient because it would not be possible to save on one of the inputs without having to use more of the other. For example, you can replace labour by switching from A to C, but you have to use more machines in order to do so.

The capitalist's problem of how to choose a production method is not yet solved because there are still three methods (and various combinations of them) to choose from that are technically efficient. The solution derives from the principle of profit maximizing. In this case, since we are talking about a given quantity of output, profit maximizing amounts to minimizing the cost of producing this output.

To examine this, we shall assume that each input has a fixed and known price. In the case of labour it is simply the hourly wage rate. In the case of machines it is the cost of using a machine for each hour. To calculate this is easy if we assume that the capitalist hired the machinery. It is more difficult if the capitalist has bought the machine outright – for then its hourly cost depends on the price of the machine and also an estimate of how long it will last before it needs to be replaced – but we shall assume that the capitalist knows this hourly cost (sometimes referred to as the 'rental cost').

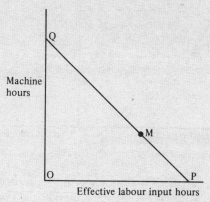

Diagram 3.A.2   The Budget Line

Diagram 3.A.2 shows a budget line, PQ. Given an amount of money to spend on inputs, the prices of the inputs determine how much can be spent on each. If all the money were spent on labour-power, then OP represents the amount of hours of labour obtained. The lower is the wage rate the greater is OP. If all is spent on machinery, then OQ represents how much machine service is obtained. The lower is the hourly cost of machines the greater is OQ. Spending the money on some combination of the two is represented by a point such as M. The line PQ shows all the possible combinations of labour and machinery that could be purchased with the given budget.

The steepness or 'slope' of the line depends on the prices of the two inputs. As we move along the line from P to Q, less is spent on labour and more on machinery. The higher the price of machinery (or the lower the wage rate) the less extra machinery for any given fall in the amount of labour. Diagram 3.A.3 compares two budget lines, WX and TU. In the case of WX the cost of machinery relative to the wage rate is greater than in the case of TU.

The *position* of the budget line depends on the total amount of money to be spent on inputs. Diagram 3.A.4 compares two budget lines, PQ and RS. With RS it is assumed that the prices of the inputs are the same as with PQ, so that its slope is the same (the lines are parallel). But with RS there is a greater amount of money spent on inputs – more can be spent on both inputs if desired.

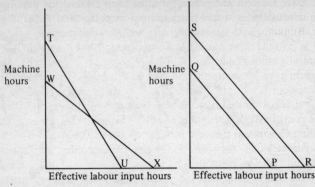

Diagram 3.A.3   Varying Relative Prices   Diagram 3.A.4   Varying Cost

Diagrams 3.A.5 and 3.A.6 put together the separate items of analysis from the earlier diagrams. They show how the capitalist can combine knowledge of the input costs with knowledge of the available technically efficient production methods, A, C and D.

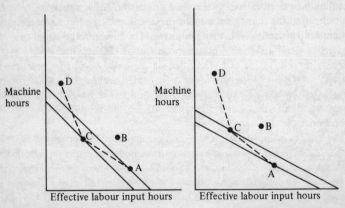

Diagram 3.A.5   Choosing a   Diagram 3.A.6   Choosing a
Mechanized Technique   Labour-Intensive Technique

In Diagram 3.A.5 we assume that to start with the firm is using production method A. Does it pay to buy more machines and move to a less labour intensive, more mechanized production method? The answer is yes, because the budget line which passes through A is at a higher level of cost than that passing through C. In order to produce the given quantity of output, method

C will lower the cost and hence raise the profit. The same argument in reverse tells us that it would not pay to move to method D (or, for that matter, B); that would increase the cost necessary for producing the given output as it would mean moving to a higher budget line. So method C is the economically efficient one.

Diagram 3.A.6 shows a situation where the machinery is relatively more expensive than 3.A.5 so that the budget lines passing through A and C are flatter – so much so, that now the line going through C is further out than the line going through A. In other words, to buy more machines and move to method C would in this case increase costs and hence decrease profits. The capitalist would therefore decide not to mechanize. A remains the economically efficient method.

Thus the analysis supports the propositions made in the chapter. But equally, as argued there, the conclusions break down immediately we drop the assumption of a given work intensity. This is because there would now be a disjuncture between the budget line represented in Diagram 3.A.2 and the isoquant in Diagram 3.A.1. Since the capitalist pays for hours of *labour-power*, that is what should be on the horizontal axis of Diagram 3.A.2, while Diagram 3.A.1, representing purely technical factors, needs to have *effective labour input hours* on its axis. With variable work intensity there is no equality or fixed ratio between the two, and so they cannot logically be combined. In this case the choice of production method is more complex and cannot be neatly shown with the standard diagrammatic analysis.

CHAPTER 4

Selling to Consumers

The production process is just one step in the circuit of profit making. No commodities will be produced unless they are expected to sell – and realize their potential profits.

Analysts of the economics of capitalism have held widely differing interpretations of the significance of this next stage. They have ranged from those who dismiss the problem of selling commodities as trivial because 'supply creates its own demand' (see Chapter 14), to 'underconsumptionists' who see a chronic and necessary insufficiency of demand for commodities as the Achilles' heel of capitalism. The material in this chapter (some of it technical) should help to support an interpretation that the maintenance of sufficient demand for commodities is a real and serious problem for the profit system – sometimes a health-threatening one. But it is one among a series of problems which the profit system encounters simultaneously.

Broadly speaking, business profits are realized by selling goods and services to other businesses, to the state and to individual consumers. We leave the first to Chapter 6, and the second to Chapter 11. Here we examine the techniques, issues and problems relating to the third: individual consumers' needs and wants; producers' efforts to create and control these wants; the laws of demand for individual products; and the determinants of consumers' demand for products in the aggregate.

The sale of produced commodities is neither automatic nor accidental. The conditions for successfully negotiating this stage of the circuit of profit are as complex and demanding as those for successfully producing the commodities. Fields and warehouses filled with unsold goods, sales of surpluses at 'give-away' prices, are common symptoms of failure at this point in the circuit.

I. WANTS AND NEEDS

Some wants for commodities arise from the natural needs of humans. They are living animals and hence they must eat. Survival requires other basic needs to be satisfied, such as shelter, hygiene and so on. To sell their labour-power, workers must be fed and reasonably fit. Beyond this there are many other human needs, both material and spiritual, and from these arise certain wants which would exist in any human society.

Other wants are specific to certain kinds of societies. For example, the demand for keys and locks, security guards and so on, does not exist in societies without a strong sense of private property. Many other kinds of wants in the present-day world, such as armaments, are unnecessary in the sense that in another kind of society they would not exist.

Most wants in modern times are generated by social interactions. Whether or not they would vanish in a different context, they bear at present the imprint of the capitalist society in which they appear. They cannot be explained by examining the nature of a mythical isolated human.

(i) *Automatic social needs*

Many wants arise automatically from social or economic circumstances. For example, workers need eating-places near their place of work; if there is no public transport, people will want cars. In such cases the social compulsion is so strong that the commodity becomes a necessity, whereas in other circumstances it could be regarded as a luxury.

(ii) *Wants from social intercourse*

Wants and needs are also formed through the many and various social interactions that are part of everyday life. People acquire a 'taste' for television or admire a neighbour's video; they may see the uses of such products, or alternatively may simply want to keep up. The desire of the better-off people to demonstrate their wealth and superiority by spending ostentatiously was described by US economist and sociologist Thorstein Veblen, in his famous book *The Theory of the Leisure Class*, as 'conspicuous consumption'.

Some wants can be formed from a combination of social interaction pressures and of automatically created needs. Addictive drugs (including cigarettes) may be taken initially for pleasure, or as part of participating in a group, but they are habit-forming and later acquire a physiological compulsion.

(iii) *Want creation for profit: advertising*

Capitalists can consciously and deliberately manipulate many wants through the expenditure of vast sums of money on advertising and the selling process.

In 1984 some $88 billion, over 2 per cent of GNP (Gross National Product), was spent on advertising in the USA; and a further unspecified sum was spent on want-creation as part of the job of sales personnel. Table 4.1 gives some comparative figures, indicating that a relatively high amount is spent in the USA (the richest country). It also shows that much less was spent in the nineteenth century when firms were much smaller. Advertising grew rapidly at the turn of the century, which was also when many large firms grew up, although the high levels of the 1920s have not since been exceeded.

Table 4.1   Advertising Expenditure (percentage of GNP)

(a) International comparison, 1979	
	%
Belgium	0.57
Brazil	0.95
West Germany	0.52
India	0.15
Italy	0.34
Japan	0.93
UK	1.3
USA	2.1

(b) The USA, 1867–1980			
	%		%
1867	0.5	1930	2.8
1880	1.1	1940	2.1
1890	1.4	1950	2.0
1900	1.4	1960	2.4
1909	2.0	1970	2.0
1920	4.0	1980	2.1
		1984	2.4

Sources: US Department of Commerce, Bureau of the Census, *Historical Statistics of the United States, Colonial Times to 1957*, Washington DC, 1960. US Department of Commerce, Bureau of the Census, *Statistical Abstract of the United States*, Washington DC, 1984. Brian Chiplin and Brian Sturgess, *The Economics of Advertising*, 2nd ed., London, Holt, Rinehart & Winston for the Advertising Association, 1981

Advertising can succeed as a want-creator because it really can influence people's ideas and values. It may do this by purveying half-truths, deceptions and vague lies. In 1928, during what was perhaps the greatest orgy of advertising in US history, the chairman of the Federal Trade Commission estimated that very roughly $500 million (about $3 billion in 1985 values) was fraudulently extracted from sick, poor and ignorant people by medical advertisements. Nowadays some governments try to control the more outrageous lies, but the agencies have developed more subtle methods of psychological manipulation. It is not lying to tell people that a certain drink is 'the real thing', or that another 'refreshes the parts other beers cannot reach'. But there is a real message behind the utterly meaningless slogan.

Advertising is not all fraud. Without lying it can act in one of two ways: either by conveying information or, more commonly, by persuasion with imagery. The informational mode is to tell consumers about the quality and price of available goods. Most classified ads in newspapers and magazines, including those for personal non-profit making sales, fall into this category. So, at least in part, do some other commercials. But most advertising is designed not to inform but to persuade.

It aims to persuade via association. The product is invested with the ability to fulfil human desires far beyond those it satisfies by its inherent nature. Thus a particular item of clothing (as worn by such and such a princess) may seem to fulfil a desire for social advancement, a particular model of motor car (draped with near-naked young women) to be a passport to sexual fulfilment for heterosexual men, a particular brand of fast-acting floor cleaner to look like the way to better motherhood, or a make of cigarette to give you that cool, masculine image (without, of course, troubling you with the associated health risks).

Such advertising – the great majority in magazines, on hoardings, TV and radio – conveys no information. Yet its apologists argue that it is pointless to distinguish informational from persuasive advertisements since both are in the cause of profits and sometimes the same ad can come into both categories. This ignores the fact that there is a genuine ideological difference between the two approaches; and just because it cannot always be precisely quantified this does not mean the distinction is pointless.

Advertisers devote a disproportionate amount of attention to children, who are regarded as particularly gullible 'consumer trainees' and may be especially prone to confusing TV ads and radio jingles with reality. And the projected images of the products may stay with them for life.

A similarly devastating and tragic case is that of consumers from underdeveloped countries, especially the millions who, unable to read, are regaled with incessant images of a glossy American dream of wonderland. Advertising does not only sell products; it is one of the ways in which global corporations maintain an ideological sway in Third World countries. They largely control the media, particularly TV and radio stations. They convert imports into a form of conspicuous consumption; thereby their materialist propaganda lulls the better-off people into importing the goods of the global corporations rather than developing their own economies.

But advertising, though very effective, is not omnipotent. It can modify people's tastes and even create new needs; but can it so control the human psyche as to create a want for anything and everything that might be produced? The evidence is not clear; indeed, the whole business is still far from an exact art. (A director of Unilever is quoted as saying that though half his company's advertising expenditure was wasted, he did not know which half.) There do seem to be limits beyond which intelligent humans are not easily persuaded, even subconsciously.

(iv) *Consumer sovereignty*

The natural and social origins of wants should be the starting point for understanding the market demand for commodities. It reveals the economic and ideological importance of advertising and it lays the groundwork for criticizing the kind of consumption that is encouraged in capitalism (a theme we pursue in Chapter 8). But you will not find a discussion of the origins of wants in standard textbooks in economics.

This is because standard economic theory holds that it makes no difference where wants come from. 'If a person demands something, and is willing to pay for it, then it must contribute to his or her welfare' is the way the argument goes. Who are we to say what is good or bad for someone else? As long as people are not legally or violently forced to buy things, then all is for the best.

The simplicity and forcefulness of this *apparently* liberal position is, however, deceptive. It is absurd, in a study of human behaviour, not to investigate the source of wants, especially if they are themselves affected by economic factors. To examine and comment upon the source of wants is quite different from advocating that 'better' wants should dictatorially be imposed from above. Yet 'consumer sovereignty' is one of the cherished doctrines of standard economics.

The doctrine states that (given the available ways of producing things) it is consumers who ultimately determine the allocation of resources in a free-market society. If, for example, they switch their tastes from apples to pears, this will raise the price of pears relative to that of apples, thus inducing fruit farmers to grow more pear trees and fewer apple trees.

Some critics of the unbridled free market – such as the American economist J. K. Galbraith – have argued that consumer sovereignty is dead. Giant corporations, they contend, now have the ability to mould consumer tastes as precisely as a violinist tunes a violin. It is difficult to agree completely with Galbraith. The undoubted fact that advertisers have *some* influence on consumers does not entail that consumers' own wants have no independent influence on production. Clearly, consumers do matter.

The more definitive defect of the doctrine of consumer sovereignty is that it fails to identify the real purpose and ultimate determining force in the capitalist process, namely the making of profits. It is this objective that shapes how resources are allocated in the capitalist world economy and how that economy develops over time. Selling to consumers is a necessary stage of the capitalist process, the part where the potential profits contained in final commodities is realized. But it is not, as the doctrine of 'consumer sovereignty' proclaims, the end in itself of economic activity.

2. EFFECTIVE DEMAND FOR COMMODITIES

If you have no money, it makes no difference how much you need food and shelter, or how much you want to buy the latest fashionable clothing. Capitalists selling such commodities are not interested *directly* in your needs and tastes; they respond only to such market demand as is backed by the ability to pay. Only in the most exceptional cases will a company make gifts and this will normally be to gain good publicity. Therefore we must distinguish between 'wants', as discussed so far, and 'effective demand', which is wants accompanied by spending power.

There are two main factors which, together with wants, determine the level of demand for any particular commodity: the consumers' resources, and the prices of commodities.

(i) *Income and wealth*

The first vital ingredient of demand is that the consumer has money to dispose of. For the vast majority of households this comes from wage or salary income; for many from grants made by the state (pensions and so on); for a small minority from their wealth (dividends from stocks and shares, or other assets). For some, income can be supplemented out of past savings.

For most commodities there is a simple relationship between income received and quantity demanded: the more you have, the more you can spend. These are called 'normal goods' and are contrasted with 'inferior goods', on which spending falls as consumers' incomes rise. For example, as consumers' incomes rise they may spend more on luxurious motor cars or fillet steaks; if so their demand for older standard cars or sausage meat may decline.

(ii) *Prices*

The question of what to buy, and how much, depends also on the prices charged. The absolute level of the price of a commodity does not tell very much on its own. What is important to a consumer is the price relative to the income available for spending, and relative also to the prices of other possible purchases.

The basic *law of demand* is that the higher the price of a commodity, the lower is the quantity demanded. This law assumes that there is no change in wants, money income or the price of other commodities. Its validity has been confirmed in much empirical research. There are two sides to its rationale. First, if the price of a commodity is high in relation to consumers' income they tend to buy less because they can no longer afford it. Second, if its price is high in relation to other prices they will buy less because the cheaper goods are now more attractive.

There are some exceptions to the rule. A high price can lead to a greater demand if consumers aim to establish themselves in other people's minds as owning top-quality objects. Dealers in diamonds and luxury limousines know that a high price tag can be part of a commodity's appeal if it satisfies the desire of the very rich for conspicuous consumption. Also in the absence of information consumers may equate higher relative price with quality. 'Cheap' is sometimes a synonym for bad.

Such exceptions are rare: for most commodities the law of demand holds. The law can be illustrated more technically by the hypothetical demand curve for apples in Diagram 4.1.a. On the vertical axis we plot different prices per lb; on the horizontal axis, the weight demanded in a given period, say a month, at each price level. The 'law' implies simply that the curve slopes downwards.

The steepness of the slope depends on how sensitive demand is to price

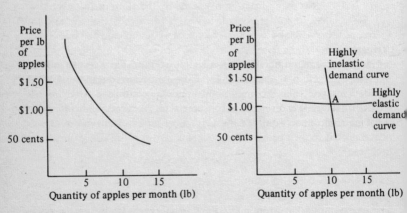

Diagram 4.1   Hypothetical Demand Curves

(a) The 'law of demand'   (b) Different elasticities of demand

changes. This may be measured by the concept of 'elasticity', defined as the ratio of the proportional change in quantity to the proportional change in price. In symbols it is written as

$$\text{Elasticity} = \frac{\Delta Q}{Q} \div \frac{\Delta P}{P}$$

where Q stands for the quantity of apples per month, ΔQ for the change in Q, P for the apple price and ΔP the change in P. (Strictly speaking it will be a negative number but the minus sign is by convention omitted.)

To give a numerical example: when the price rises from 100 to 110 the quantity demanded per month falls from 50 to 45. Quantity has fallen by 10 per cent: hence the elasticity is 10 per cent $\div$ 10 per cent, exactly 1. Suppose instead that, for the same price rise (100 to 110), the quantity were to fall from 50 to 40, that is by 20 per cent; then the elasticity would be 20 per cent $\div$ 10 per cent, exactly 2. Thus the more sensitive quantity is to price, the greater the elasticity.

In Diagram 4.1.b the nearly flat curve illustrates a special case where the demand is very elastic. Starting from the point A, a very large proportional change in quantity would result from any small change in price. In the limit, if the curve were absolutely flat, the elasticity would be infinite. The nearly vertical curve on the same diagram illustrates the opposite case where demand is insensitive to price. Even quite a large proportional change in price leads to a small proportional change in quantity demanded: it is a very 'inelastic' curve. In the limit, if the demand curve were vertical, the elasticity would be zero.

(iii) *Elasticity and revenue*

To capitalists wishing to sell commodities, the elasticity of demand for each of their particular products is an important fact: it determines the effects if they alter the prices. We can see this if we see first that there is a relationship between elasticity and the revenue they receive.

The total monthly revenue of producers, which is the same as consumers' total expenditure on a product, is its price multiplied by the quantity sold:

$$R = P \times Q$$
Revenue is   Price times Quantity

If the price goes up, the quantity goes down. What happens to total revenue depends on the elasticity of demand. If elasticity is exactly 1, a 1 per cent rise in P means a 1 per cent fall in Q, with the result that revenue stays the same. If the elasticity were 4, then a 1 per cent rise in P would mean a 4 per cent fall in Q. Hence revenue would fall (by about 3 per cent) as a result of the price rise. If the elasticity were $\frac{1}{2}$ then the 1 per cent price rise would lead to only a $\frac{1}{2}$ per cent fall in Q. So the revenue would rise. These three cases illustrate the general rules:

(a) when elasticity is above 1, price rises lead to revenue falls;
(b) when elasticity is below 1, price rises mean revenue rises;
(c) when elasticity is equal to 1, revenue is constant.

If the elasticity of demand for a firm's commodity were extremely high – in the limit, infinity – then the firm would have no freedom to vary its price. It would be a 'price-taker'. More common is case (a): it can raise its price but if it does, its revenue will fall; only if its costs fell even more would this improve profits. In the opposite case (b), a firm could gain more revenue by raising its price and in addition its costs would fall as it would be producing less; so its profits would be bound to rise. Because of this, firms which have some knowledge of the elasticity of demand for their product would not be expected to sell at a price at which the elasticity is less than 1, since if they did they would be missing an opportunity to raise their profits.

(iv) *Substitutes and complements*

The most important factor which determines the elasticity of demand for a commodity is the availability of 'substitutes' – commodities with similar properties able to perform similar though not necessarily identical functions. Taxi rides can substitute for train journeys, theatre tickets for watching TV, Coca Cola for Pepsi Cola, and so on. The apples sold in one store are (assuming identical quality) perfect substitutes for those sold in the next-door store. If a good substitute is available for a commodity then the demand for it will be very elastic, since only a small rise in price is sufficient to induce consumers to switch to the substitute. At the extreme, if a perfect substitute is available the elasticity will be infinite (the demand curve horizontal).

At the opposite extreme are vital commodities for which no substitute exists. For example, where a community has only one main source of food, say rice, its elasticity of demand will tend to be low. But the degree of elasticity depends also on how widely we define the commodity. Consider the case of oil and coal, which are substitutes because each is a provider of energy. The demand for either may be reasonably elastic because, allowing for a time lapse, consumers can switch from one to the other if their relative prices change. The demand for 'energy' as a whole, however, is much less elastic, since it is much more difficult to economize on all energy sources. Companies that wish substantially to raise the price of a commodity require a low elasticity of demand, so they are motivated to try to nullify the effects of substitutes being available. When the international oil companies took over substantial proportions of coal assets in the 1960s, this was one of their main objectives.

Advertising also has an effect on elasticity. In addition to trying to attract new consumers (thus shifting the demand curve outwards) it can keep existing ones from switching when the price rises (thus effectively making the demand curve steeper). A high proportion of advertising is devoted to persuading consumers that the advertiser's product is not substitutable by others (this is part of product differentiation).

The opposite of a substitute for a commodity is a 'complement': for example, knives go with forks, tennis balls with tennis rackets, batteries with stereo walkmen. The elasticity of demand will be lowered by the existence of important complements: the demand for batteries is less sensitive to price for people who have already bought their portable stereo players.

(v) *The meaning of demand curves*

The monthly demand for a product depends, as we have seen, on many factors. Price is only one of them. Demand can increase if price falls, but also if the other factors change – for example, if consumers' income increases. If price falls, there is a movement down the demand curve; if income rises, the whole demand curve shifts outwards. Such changes are illustrated in Diagram 4.2.

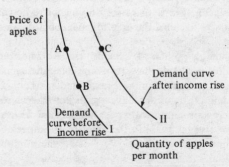

Diagram 4.2　The Effect of a Rise in Income on the Demand Curve

Starting from point A on curve I, if price falls then demand rises (say, to point B). But if income rises, consumers move on to curve II; even if price does not change, demand again rises (to point C).

For capitalists, the economic environment is always changing. This means that any one hypothetical demand curve does not plot out the actual points of quantity and price observed over time. Rather, each curve is an instantaneous snapshot of the pricing possibilities at any given moment. To show this, consider the case of Diagram 4.3.

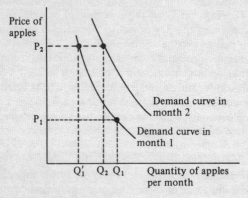

Diagram 4.3   Demand Curves over Time

Suppose that two things change: between month 1 and month 2 the price rises from P_1 to P_2, but other factors such as income and advertising also increase, so that the demand curve shifts outwards. In practice, the quantity sold would fall from Q_1 to Q_2, but we would not be observing the true elasticity of demand. If price had risen and there was no change in advertising or consumers' income, the quantity sold would have dropped much more, to Q_1'.

Although these hypothetical demand curves can never be directly observed, this does not imply they are of no use. Businesses need to calculate demand conditions in determining pricing and marketing strategies and nearly all modern corporations have significant market research departments, or employ consultants, to do this. The demand curve and the concept of elasticity can also be useful in the analysis of changes in the capitalist economy (Chapter 17).

3. AGGREGATE CONSUMER DEMAND AND SAVING

The concept of demand that has had much the greatest impact on economic ideas is not the demand for any single commodity, but the aggregate demand of all consumers (workers, businesses and the state) for all commodities. Aggregate demand is a very important concept because it affects how the many separate plans of all the different capitalist units are co-ordinated. In

Chapter 14 we shall see how it helps to determine the stability or instability of the economy.

The aggregate level of consumer demand is a major, often the largest, component of it, and we can usefully examine here the factors underlying it.

(i) *Consumption, saving and income*

Consumption is the obverse of saving. Out of a given income the amount which is not spent on consumption is in some form or other saved. This is true for both individual income and national income.

One way of investigating what determines the level of consumption is to look at what determines its counterpart, savings. A large part of the total saved in each economy is decided upon directly by business executives, particularly the top managers of the major corporations. They withhold from their shareholders some of the profits received and use the money to purchase more capital equipment or place it in the bank ready for spending later on investment. The amount saved and invested in this way depends on the prospects for future profit. Governments save part of their income when they do not spend it on consumption, but invest in durable equipment (roads and so on). Finally, individuals save when they consume less than their disposable income (the income they have left after paying their taxes).

Working people save for a variety of motives. They put money by in banks or other savings institutions for particular purposes such as an annual holiday or a new car. They save as a hedge against economic insecurity, such as possible unemployment, and they save also for their old age, either individually or through collective pension schemes (often compulsory). And in an age of inflation, an increasing amount goes in just making good the erosion of the real value of the savings which they already have.

Many working people are severely limited in the amount of saving they can do by the fact of having low incomes in relation to their needs. Almost all current resources have to be used to buy the daily means of living; in addition it is usually impossible for low-income people to borrow from banks. Hence for many people, the total level of saving is heavily constrained by their income. Only richer people can save adequately.

Some individuals who save, usually the very richest, are in fact capitalists who are living off the dividends and capital gains they receive from their ownership of capital. Much of this income is saved, as they reinsert their money into stocks, shares and other assets. For this reason and because companies do not distribute much of their profit, the proportion of profit-income saved tends to be very high; while the fraction of income saved by workers is low. This is a strong force perpetuating the existing distribution of property.

(ii) *Two propositions*

These remarks support the idea that aggregate income is a major determinant of aggregate consumption. Furthermore they give weight to two propositions put forward by John Maynard Keynes, the famous British economist who did so much to change economic ideas in the first half of this century.

(a) Keynes defined the 'average propensity to consume' (APC) of a person or household unit as the total spent on consumption divided by its income. If C is consumption and Y is income:

$$\text{Average propensity to consume (APC)} = \frac{C}{Y}$$

The first proposition is that the APC is highest for those people on low incomes. Conversely the average propensity to save (APS) (saving divided by total income) is highest for rich people – in particular, of course, for those in receipt of a large amount of profits-income.

(b) Keynes defined the 'marginal propensity to consume' (MPC) as the extra amount consumed by a person or household when income increases by one unit: or in other words the increase in consumption divided by the increase in income. Where the symbol Δ means 'change in':

$$\text{Marginal propensity to consume (MPC)} = \frac{\Delta C}{\Delta Y}$$

The second proposition is that for most people, the MPC lies between 0 and 1. In other words, for every extra \$1 or £1 of income received, the increase in spending is positive but less than \$1 or £1, a plausible view of how consumers behave when they are constrained by the level of income they receive. For example, you receive an extra \$100 income in a particular month, and you spend an extra \$90, saving \$10 extra; your MPC is 0.9.

(iii) *An aggregate consumption function*

The concept of the marginal propensity to consume plays a crucial role in the discussion of stability in Chapter 14. Both it and the average propensity to consume can also be applied to the economy as a whole as well as to individuals.

Imagine adding up everybody's income and everybody's consumption spending over a period of, say, a year. Hypothetically, the relationship between the two over a series of years might be depicted by Diagram 4.4.

This is called the 'aggregate consumption function', referring to the idea that total consumption is a function of ('depends on') total income. The second proposition, that the MPC is between 0 and 1, is reflected in the

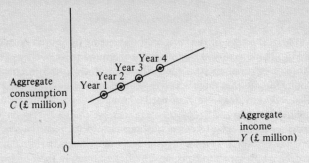

Diagram 4.4 A Hypothetical Aggregate Consumption Function

diagram. The slope of the line is at less than 45 to the horizontal: hence for every £1 million rise in aggregate income, *Y*, there is a less than £1 million rise in aggregate consumption, *C*.

Although Diagram 4.4 is only a hypothetical curve, empirical evidence has shown many times over that it is a reasonably good first approximation to understanding aggregate consumption demand in all economies. It squares with the reasonable proposition that many, if not most, people are strongly constrained in their consumption habits by their income. And, at least approximately, it fits the observed facts.

There are, however, influences on consumption other than income, so a longer term viewpoint or a more precise explanation means more research. Consumption is also affected by wealth. Since in developed countries many people own more assets nowadays than, say, fifty years ago, the consumption function has drifted upwards over time.

Also, as income increases, people spend more and develop new consumption habits; even if income decreases again they still try to keep up their accustomed higher consumption level.

In most capitalist economies aggregate consumption patterns in the 1970s have also been distorted by high levels of inflation. For all these reasons and more, simple lines like that drawn in Diagram 4.4 are not adequate for understanding total consumption very precisely.

None the less, aggregate income does remain the most important single influence on aggregate consumption. This relatively simple fact helps to show how one route to solving problems in capital accumulation may be blocked by a major obstacle. For one response of capitalists, when their profits are too low, is to lower wages. Yet wages and salaries are the main components of income, and if they start to fall so will aggregate consumer spending. The result is that businesses as a whole will find it difficult to sell their commodities, a possible contributing cause of generalized crisis in the economy (Chapter 15).

(iv) *Ideology about saving*

From at least the time of the early Puritans saving has been regarded as a virtue. Putting money by or investing it, you scored twice over, by building up a store of spiritual goodness as well as of worldly goods. Keynes, however, pointed out that high levels of saving are a mixed blessing in a capitalist economy; for businesses need consumers to spend money on their commodities.

The orthodox theory of savings is obsessed with the idea that their only source is the 'rational' savings plan of every individual. It is assumed that people decide how much to consume at different times in their lifetime and, by judicious borrowing and lending, achieve their aim. They save when their income is high relative to their consumption (in the middle years of life) and consume more than their income during retirement (and possibly early in adult life by living on credit).

This approach misses the importance of company saving which is one of the main channels for capital accumulation in western countries. Indeed it makes no distinction between workers' savings, whose purpose is usually a minor rearrangement of consumption over time, and capitalists' savings, whose purpose is the accumulation of further capital to expand profits. Moreover it grossly overstates the ability and willingness of most people to make the necessary comparison of the distant future with their present enjoyments. Much life-cycle saving, such as compulsory pension scheme saving, is forced upon people, not planned by them.

The theory becomes particularly apologetic when it comes to the question of 'wealth'. Since wealth is accumulated savings, and savings is interpreted as due to a 'rational' past choice, individuals are made to seem personally responsible for the amount of wealth they currently have. Poverty is a fault and wealth a virtue, the reward of past frugality.

In fact, there is one overriding reason why most rich people are rich: it is not because they are lucky gamblers, or because they have scrimped and saved in the past, or, except in a minority of cases, because they are self-made entrepreneurs who started out with nothing; rather it is because they inherited a large fortune and have been successful capitalists ever since. Painstaking research has shown, for example, that three out of every five rich British men who died in the 1960s with the then considerable wealth of £100,000 or more had had fathers with more than £50,000; many other rich people had married into fortunes or inherited from other relatives. These people were rich because they were members of the propertied class.

The rich, like the rest of us, are responsible for some of the demand which allows capitalists' potential profits to be realized through exchange. But consumption is not the only source of demand for commodities; some demand is that of capitalists for new means of production. For the capitalist seller, this act will be realization; for the capitalist buyer, part of the next stage of the circuit of profit – the purchase of labour-power (Chapter 5) and of new means of production (Chapter 6) so as to repeat and expand the production process.

CHAPTER 5

Buying Labour-Power

It is instructive to imagine what might be the fantasies of capitalists, en route to the labour market, as to the desirable qualities of the ideal worker.

Each would want certain amounts of different types of labour-power, equipped with various skills and able to perform specified production tasks. But it is not just a question of technical skills. They would want workers who would fit in entirely with their plans: workers who were docile and willing to take orders, who were diligent, persevering and punctual, and who were available when needed but did not mind being cast aside at other times. In fact what they would really like is to be able to treat their workforce like robots, hired when convenient from the robot rental agency. The contradiction between ideal and reality is resolved partly through the various management strategies we looked at in Chapter 3. It also affects the types of worker that are hired and modifies the way the labour market operates.

In the absence of robots, employers need workers to co-operate with each other in order to be productive; and yet co-operation can breed solidarity and collective resistance, for example through unions. They also often need workers to stay for lengthy periods in one job, so as to acquire the necessary skills; yet as workers' jobs become more permanent they develop expectations as to their rights at work which interfere with employers' demands for flexibility; such rights can be imposed either through collective action or through political institutions. And just as capitalists want to get away with paying their own workers lower wages, so they also want higher wages elsewhere to support a mass market for their products.

Such contradictions may sometimes be resolved through accommodations with trade unions, through segmenting the workforce and favouring some sections, and through balanced wage rises that are enough to provide new markets, but not enough to cancel out productivity improvements. But these are tightropes along which capitalists must always warily tread. The way the labour market develops is often well beyond the control of individual capitalists, and they are easily blown off balance by high winds.

As capitalism develops and expands, these contradictions of the labour market are periodically resolved and then exacerbated. As a result, the growth of capitalism sets up currents of change in people's lives, their institutions and their cultures.

I. FACTORS WHICH SHAPE THE LABOUR FORCE

In the nineteenth-century capitalist countries, many children of twelve were wage labourers, but in the changed social relationships of present-day advanced capitalism they are almost all at school, hence part of the non-wage-working population. This is but a small illustration of how changing social relationships can affect the numbers of working people. It is not *just* a question of population statistics. The numbers and qualities of the workers available for hire depend upon several factors.

(i) *Population*

The number of wage labourers in any country is clearly less than the total population, simply because there are those who do not do wage work. Other things being equal, a larger population provides a larger number of potential wage workers. The population itself is affected by a myriad of interrelated factors: factors such as the age at which families are formed and children reared, and the normal size of families; medical factors such as cheap contraceptive methods and cures for diseases (these affect birth and death rates, and also influence the normal size of families); and, more important, economic factors such as the level of material living standards, which can impinge on both birth and death rates.

Some of these factors, especially the economic ones, might themselves be explained as specific developments of capitalist relations, though the connection is loose. It remains true, however, that population is only an un-reached outer limit to the number of wage labourers.

(ii) *The recruitment of the 'industrial reserve army'*

Between 1955 and 1961 the Japanese economy grew at the extraordinarily high rate of nearly 10 per cent a year. How could this have been sustained by a natural rate of population growth? The fact that it could not points to the need for the supply of labour-power to be flexible – capable of expanding rapidly to meet the sometimes explosive growth of capitalist economies.

The major economic mechanism which provides new sources of labour-power is simply the expulsion of workers from existing production processes, either through their replacement by machines or through increased work intensity as a result of various changes in work organization. Capitalist expansion has an inbuilt, sometimes erratic, tendency to create what Karl

Marx called a 'reserve army': a group of people – not necessarily always the same individuals – who are available to be absorbed into capitalist employment at short notice.

As capitalism grows, the size of this 'army' varies. If the economy expands rapidly, then despite increases in productivity there is a fast-rising overall demand for labour-power and the ranks of the 'army' are thinned out. At other times the rise in productivity will outpace the growth of the economy, particularly after a crisis. Then, the demand for labour-power falls behind its supply and the reserve army is replenished.

The reserve army helps to regulate wages by reducing pressure on employers to concede rises, through the simple market relation of supply with demand. It raises the pressure on existing workers who fear unemployment and who also may consequently be forced to raise their work intensity (which can further reduce the demand for labour-power). And it can provide the leeway for possible rapid expansions of capital, both in the short term, that is over a year or so, and in the longer term over a number of years.

As the economy emerges from the recession stage of a business cycle, it can grow very fast for a short period. In this time firms employ again those that were sacked during the depression – the 'floating' part of the industrial reserve army. They may also employ some others who lost their jobs much earlier and were unable to find new ones – the 'stagnant' reserve army. But sometimes the capitalist economy can go through a prolonged successful phase of many years, during which time crises, if they occur, are weak and short-lived, and industrial capital's hunger for more labour-power may be met by the 'latent' section of the reserve army. These are people who work in backward low-productivity sectors of the economy. They are ripe for replacement by machines and provide thus a hidden source of labour-power should the need arise. The classic location of such workers is in agriculture. Both in the nineteenth century and in modern times, the major part of the latent reserve army has been found from agriculture; workers' historic ties with the land are severed and they are dragooned into an urban proletariat.

(iii) *Unions*

A third factor influencing labour supply is the resistance of workers themselves. Workers who act together can force employers, through economic sanctions such as strikes, to raise, or not to cut, wages. They can improve working conditions and sometimes safeguard their jobs for a while during a depression. And they can aim to achieve legal rights at work through political activity. Furthermore, unions and other worker organizations often impose a structure on the labour force, by restricting entry to certain types of jobs. For example, it is common for professional organizations to regulate entry – ostensibly to maintain standards but often really to restrict competition; and many male-dominated unions exclude female workers from jobs in the traditional manufacturing industries.

(iv) *The state*

Finally, governments also have a major influence. They have assumed the main responsibility for the mass of (at least) basic education. They thus provide the general technical skills, such as numeracy and literacy, that are normally necessary for people to get on and to work efficiently in the modern world. Schools can also form part of the socialization process needed to prepare young people for the later disciplines of working life. Competitive schools and exams serve to sort out those people who are going to be given the best jobs. Governments subsidize training schemes, encourage immigration or emigration, provide police (who strengthen the employer's side in industrial disputes), and so on. Moreover they themselves employ millions of workers, hence modifying the remaining market for private employers. We shall evaluate the role of state activities in Chapter 11.

2. THE POST-WAR LABOUR FORCE

Through the 1950s, 1960s and 1970s, industrial ouput in the five largest capitalist countries (France, West Germany, Japan, the USA and the UK) rose on average by about 6.3 per cent a year. Yet output per person employed rose in the same period by about 5.2 per cent a year. Thus we see two basic facts: first, that rises in labour productivity were 'setting free' millions of workers, enabling the reserve army of labour to be continually reconstituted; second, that, despite this, capitalists still needed to draw increasing numbers into the wage-labour force. The increase in numbers of wage workers in all types of business and state employment for six major countries is shown in Table 5.1. It shows especially large rises in Japan and the USA.

Some of these new workers came from natural population increase, but by no means all. For example, the US population of working age rose by about a half from 1950 to 1982, yet the numbers of wage workers more than doubled. A small part of the rise in the 1950s and 1960s might be attributed to the depletion of the officially visible reserve army, for, especially in West Germany, unemployment declined steadily in this period. But mass unemployment was later reconstituted so altogether over three decades this factor was irrelevant. To understand where the rest of the rise came from

Table 5.1   Salaried and Wage Labourers, 1950s and 1980s (millions)

	Early 1950s	1980s
France (1954, 1982)	12.5	17.8
West Germany (1950, 1982)	16.5	23.8
Italy (1951, 1975)	11.6	13.6
Japan (1955, 1982)	18.0	41.0
UK (1951, 1982)	19.8	22.5
USA (1950, 1980)	49.3	101.4

Source: International Labour Office, *Yearbook of Labour Statistics*, ILO, Geneva, various issues

we shall look first at the mass migrations that have been a prominent feature of modern capitalism.

(i) *Migration*

(a) *From countryside to town*

The industrial working class in the modern post-war world continued in most capitalist countries to be topped up from a latent reserve army of farm labourers, still the lowest paid of all workers in most countries, and easily replaced by machinery and other more advanced capitalist production methods. There were massive migrations of workers from the fields into the towns. In the USA the southern black rural workers moved north and into the cities in the 1950s and 1960s.

A further source of wage labour for the industry and service sectors were the many millions across the world who in 1950 worked unpaid for their families. These also were ripe for replacement by capitalist production techniques which rendered their own production processes inefficient, and in many countries they joined the flow of migrants into the towns along with the displaced rural wage workers and self-employed. In Japan, France, West Germany and the USA this was especially important: taken together their wage-working class rose by about 60 million in the 1950s and 1960s, some 10 million of which came from the proletarianization of rural family workers.

The result of this displacement of both farm labourers and unpaid peasant family workers was a massive rise in the size of towns throughout the capitalist world especially in Third World countries. The population of Seoul, for example, rose from under 4 million in 1955 to nearly 13.5 million by 1980, about 36 per cent of South Korea's total. The pressure on housing, transport, sanitation and other factors meant that the new industrial wage workers had generally the most appalling environmental conditions.

At the same time the countryside was everywhere losing population, either in absolute numbers or relative to the total. Although agriculture began as the most backward sector it was also advancing the most rapidly. Its labour productivity in the developed countries rose faster than productivity in industry and services. And the inevitable result of mass migrations over three decades was the dramatic change in the structure of the workforce shown in Diagram 5.1; by 1979 the agricultural workforce was a tiny minority, and this source of the latent reserve army had been virtually used up. In the advanced countries an overwhelming portion of working-class people in the 1980s live in towns, a majority of them working in the service sector.

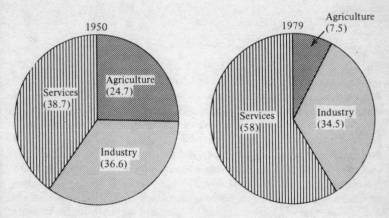

Diagram 5.1   Structure of Employment* (% shares)

Note: * Average of sixteen advanced capitalist countries, not including Japan.

Source: Angus Maddison, *Phases of Capitalist Development*, Oxford and New York, Oxford University Press, 1982

(b) *Across the border*

Vast numbers of people every year cross national borders in search of jobs. But sometimes when local supplies of labour-power are exhausted, employers, rather than move their expanding factories elsewhere to possibly unreliable areas, may turn to foreign supplies by encouraging immigration. In post-war Europe the westward and northward flow of workers ran into hundreds of thousands every year. Millions left East Germany and elsewhere to work in the Federal Republic, but these were not enough. There were special shortages of workers willing to undertake unskilled jobs and bilateral agreements between governments, aided by positive steps to recruit abroad, brought many millions of immigrants to northern Europe.

Migration from southern Italy was made especially easy by the right of open labour mobility within EEC countries, but Turkey, Yugoslavia, Greece and Spain were also major suppliers of migrants. They came simply as workers and in most cases were not given the full rights of citizenship. Regarded as temporary visitors, there to do the unpleasant jobs, *gastarbeiter* (guest workers) eventually constituted substantial proportions of the population – for example, in 1974 nearly 7 per cent in West Germany, as much as 16 per cent in Switzerland, and perhaps double these as proportions of the wage-labour force. Meanwhile the UK received immigrants from yet further afield, from its former colonies in the West Indies and the Indian subcontinent.

(ii) *Wage-working women*

The supply of labour-power available for capitalists has been further substantially augmented in some countries by a massive social upheaval which itself involved no major population movements or expansions: millions of married women, who would beforehand have worked exclusively at domestic labour tasks in the home, forsook the kitchen sink and joined the wage-labour force either full-time or part-time. In the USA the 'labour force participation rate' of married women (the proportion of all married women, including the elderly, who are employed or looking for wage work) rose from about a quarter in 1950 to over half in 1984. Table 5.2 gives the varied results of such changes over the years for a selection of countries. In the UK, the change was substantial and of special importance, for the increase

Table 5.2   Women as a Percentage of the Labour Force, 1950–83

	1950	1983
Australia	22.4	37.3
France	36.0	40.2
West Germany	35.1	38.4
Japan	38.5	39.5
UK	30.8	39.6
USA	28.8	43.0

Sources: Angus Maddison, *Phases of Capitalist Development*, Oxford and New York, Oxford University Press, 1982. OECD Economic Outlook, *Historical Statistics, 1960–1983*, OECD, Paris, 1985

in the numbers of wage-working married women itself more than accounted for the small rise in overall numbers of wage workers.

The rise was accompanied by a major cultural and social change: the new dual role of women, which generally involves working both at home and in the labour market. It has transformed the way many women experience capitalism, from one of working until they get married, to one of organizing their time to enable domestic labour, including child-rearing, to be combined with wage work. It has gone hand in hand also with the rise of women's liberation movements throughout the western world, which have questioned and sometimes begun to modify traditional patriarchal attitudes in many spheres of life, not least in regard to the sexual division of labour (see Chapter 8).

Different writers have proposed a number of causes – on both the demand and the supply side – for this increasing participation of married women, which has provided employers with more available labour-power.

(a) Substantial post-war improvements in housework technology – washing machines, fridges, wash-and-wear clothes, fast foods and so on – have reduced the time required for basic housework tasks.

(b) A fall in the average size of families in many countries means fewer years are involved in bearing and rearing children.

(c) Third, taking a longer view, it was common in nineteenth-century America and pre-industrial Europe for married women to produce goods for use in the home or commodities for sale such as butter, eggs and cloth which augmented the family's cash income. But with the rise of capitalist industry many of these production activities were undercut and rendered inefficient, thus both curtailing a source of family income and freeing women's time to some extent. Many millions of married women may have been potentially available for wage work for much of this century, even though the main rises occurred only after the Second World War. There were doubtless many social and political obstacles to their earlier participation, but an indication of the ability and willingness of women to do wage work may be gleaned from their wartime activities. In the USA and the UK their participation rate rose sharply between 1940 and 1945. The vast majority expressed the wish to stay working after the war, but they were often obliged to relinquish their jobs, partly due to ideological pressure (jobs were to be 'kept for the boys') and partly because many firms deliberately closed their day nurseries and reduced their demands for part-time workers, in order to exclude women.

(d) During the boom of the 1950s and 1960s there was a disproportionate rise of the service sector in many economies. This meant a special rise in jobs where women are normally concentrated, such as in clerical occupations, and in education, health and welfare distribution services.

All these reasons suggest that women will continue to be a major source of labour-power. The majority of families are used to, and often depend on, at least two income sources. Moreover, the experience of wage-working changes social attitudes in an irreversible way. Although we expect a continuing evolution of the sexual division of labour, we judge it unlikely that women will need or choose to return to being full-time domestic workers.

(iii) *Trade unions*

A third major fact about wage labourers across the advanced capitalist world, which confronts each buyer of labour power, is that many of them are members of trade unions, which have the power to modify and resist employers' intentions with regard to the wage contract. In very small numbers in the nineteenth century, then increasingly through the first half of the twentieth, workers joined unions in the hope that their interests would be better represented. In the post-war world the proportions either held steady or rose yet more (Table 5.3) despite the massive rise in numbers of wage workers, especially in the service sectors and amongst women, who usually had a low level of unionization. Since the crisis of 1979, comparable figures are hard to find, but it is certain that some unions have lost many members to mass unemployment: in the UK, for example, membership fell by 2 million from 1979 to 1983.

But the proportion in unions do not necessarily correspond closely with union power. That depends also on how membership is distributed among industries, the quality of leadership, and so on.

Table 5.3 Union Density, 1910–83
(actual as percentage of potential union membership)

	1910	1950	1977
Australia	24.6	56.0	54.3
Canada	15.0	32.8	34.2
West Germany	–	33.1	38.4
Sweden	8.3	67.7	92.9
UK	14.6	44.1	52.8
USA	10.1	28.0	25.3

Source: G. S. Bain and R. Price, *Profiles of Union Growth*, Oxford, Blackwell, 1980

(iv) *Segmentation of labour markets*

However much trade unions may promote solidarity among their members, the working class remains divided in many ways. It is largely segmented by national boundaries, especially since the 1970s when many countries imposed tight restrictions on immigration. In addition the wage-labour forces within each country are also split into different kinds of workers. Capitalists can often choose combinations of workers from each sector.

The segmentation occurs along the various dimensions of the wage-labour contract. Thus jobs can differ in duration and in degree of security. Casual labour, when workers turn up each day in the hope of employment, is at one extreme, being both short-term and very insecure. At the other extreme are the long-term 'tenured' jobs of many civil servants and university academics. In between, there are many jobs which are 'implicitly' long-term and secure: as long as capitalists do not lose too much profit they will continue operating and are expected to retain the workers concerned even when times are temporarily bad. This type is particularly common in companies' 'internal labour markets', the system whereby a company fills most of its job vacancies from within its own ranks, rather than opening them to competition from all qualified workers. Most companies recruit externally only when they need to, and mainly at the bottom of the firm's hierarchy.

Wage-contracts also vary in other ways. Most obviously, there are considerable differences in the levels of pay and standard of work conditions. A further dimension concerns how much responsibility capitalists take for their employees' welfare, health and pension needs and so on.

Finally, the jobs themselves vary, according to whether they require unskilled or skilled labour, whether such skills are *general* (applicable in any firm) or *specific* (only of use to the existing employer), and whether the work tasks are routine or require independent action, closely controlled or not.

Across the capitalist world we find that workers become divided along some or all of these dimensions. They are selected for and remain in certain jobs or types of job, thus creating identifiable segments, between which the degree of mobility is relatively low and competition limited.

The precise kinds of division within a nation's working class depend on its particular history. We shall here describe briefly the segmentation in the advanced capitalist world's largest national labour market, the USA, since that has been especially closely analysed by economists. There the post-war labour force developed into three broad segments of roughly equal size.

(a) A 'subordinate primary' sector consists of workers who are on the whole secure (relative to others) in their jobs, and expecting to earn increasing real wages. Their work tends to be routine, standardized and subject to Taylorist scientific management control (see Chapter 3), but they are often protected by unions which help to lay down the limits of their job tasks. Their skills where they exist tend to be specific. Typically they are employed in internal labour markets, which shut their jobs off from competition from other workers. Their unions may also impose 'seniority' criteria for promotion and improvement of benefits.

As a result there is a low turnover of jobs, with relatively few redundancies and resignations. In return for acceptance of management prerogative in production, the workers are granted some security – a partial immunity from the ravages of recession.

(b) The 'independent primary' sector contains all those salaried workers who possess high general skills – such as technicians, professionals, craft workers and managerial workers. They are relatively free from direct control, fairly mobile between jobs yet secure if they wish to remain, and highly paid.

(c) In the 'secondary' sector, workers are normally unskilled, low paid and have insecure jobs because they are especially vulnerable when the economy is in recession. Often they work under the simple and direct control of a boss, and are concentrated in smaller firms; large firms, however, also employ secondary workers. There are no internal labour markets and there are few barriers to competition. Job tenure is short on average, either because workers are made redundant or because they become bored or otherwise disenchanted and leave voluntarily. They tend not to associate much with the job or their employer. Their only motivation for working is to earn their wages.

Not all workers fit neatly into one of these sectors, for the three categories are general ones intended to capture the overall picture. Moreover, the threefold structure was developed during the post-war boom, and it is possible that the economic crises of the 1970s and 1980s may have begun to break it down. None the less the concept has proved useful particularly as an aid to understanding the persistence of poverty, of racial and sexual discrimination and other divisions within the US working class.

The growth of structured markets in the USA came at a time when more and more women were entering the labour force. Often working part-time and with interrupted careers due to their family commitments, women found fewer opportunities to learn new skills on the job. Moreover, this aided the process of segmentation for capitalists found it easier to maintain demarcations according to the sex of workers. Thus women tended to be channelled into secondary jobs, and where they found more stable employment this was normally in the subordinate primary sector. It is estimated that by the 1970s females constituted about a half of the labour force in each of these sectors, yet only between a fifth and a quarter of the independent primary sector.

Similarly a disproportionate number of black workers (about 60 per cent in 1970) found themselves channelled into low-wage secondary jobs. Expelled from the agricultural jobs of the south, they migrated north and to the cities but were often excluded from stable primary jobs by long-standing discrimination. Thus the segmentation of the labour market came to reflect also the geographical segregation of black communities in inner cities.

The traditional economic theory of the labour market was unable to account for segmentation, for it used to assume that the market was competitive and becoming more so. Orthodox economics assumed that workers would sell their labour-power to the highest bidder – that is, they could move easily to work for the employer with the highest wage offer. Barriers to mobility could only be due to mistaken intervention in the normal workings of the system. Suppose, for example, that a particular job was artificially restricted by an employer to a separate group of workers; in the long run a new firm could employ outsiders, since they would work for lower wages, make more profits, drive out the older, less profitable one, and so remove the barrier. In sum, barriers were argued to be temporary, accidental and bad for profits.

By contrast, new economic theories recognize that the wage contract is not exactly like a 'spot market' on the stock exchange where a current commodity is swopped for money; for, as we have seen, most jobs apart from the most casual ones have an implicit presumption of continuity. Second, they show how the creation of segments can be profitable for firms; hence they account for the persistence of segmentation rather than its demise. Two main reasons have been advanced as to why it has been profitable for firms to set up internal labour markets and promote the primary sector.

One approach sees it as a rational response by American employers to the aggressive union drives of the 1930s. Although the unions were weakened after the war by political attacks, they had won widespread concessions such as grievance procedures to counteract the threat of arbitrary management. Part of the rapprochement with unions was an implicit commitment to steadily rising real wages. But in addition companies attempted to weaken resistance further by a strategy of 'divide and conquer'. Thus, some workers were granted the security of primary jobs with better wages, which helped to gain company loyalty and was beneficial for maintaining industrial peace; at the same time, the weaker, less unionized workers in the secondary sector were isolated. Nowhere has this strategy been more successful than in Japan, with its divisive life-time employment system (page 56), where the aggressive post-war independent unions were eventually tamed and incorporated within each firm's internal labour market.

A second approach places less emphasis on the class struggle between capitalists and workers, but more on technology. It is advantageous for managers to keep workers with specific skills in the firm, so they do not have to train new recruits; and the workers benefit by staying (as they could command less wages from other employers).

Although we have concentrated on the US labour market, divisions can also be found in other countries. The structures differ because the economies have varying histories. One relevant difference is the size of the public sector, which is relatively greater in many European countries than in the

USA. State employment can substantially affect the structure of the market. A further important difference is in the strength of trade union movements. For example, in the UK and in Italy strong unions have resisted capitalist attempts to impose such clear-cut segments as exist in the United States, but they have maintained and imposed their own divisions within the working class, along lines of skill and of sex differentiation.

The forms that segmentation takes have also changed over time, reflecting the dynamics of capital accumulation. Following on the crisis of 1979, government policies and management strategies have aimed at 'de-regulating' markets, including the labour markets. They had tried to introduce more 'flexibility', or to remove 'rigidities'. In Europe this language has been management-speak for removing people's rights at work, such as limited protections against unfair dismissal, maternity leave and so on. A 'rigidity' for capitalists has often been a source of needed security for workers.

'Flexibility' encompasses a number of changes in labour contracts and in working practices which try to raise the competitiveness of European and American workers. It does not simply mean repealing legislated rights. It means bringing in more shift-working, making use of more agency labour and subcontracted jobs, more home-working, decentralized collective bargaining, a reduction of old-fashioned job demarcations.

It is a fair bet that the secondary sector has been relatively enlarged by this shake-up of labour markets. But employers must continue to live with the need to keep a stable and skilful component in their work-forces.

3. WHAT CAPITALISTS PAY FOR LABOUR-POWER

(i) *Disparities of pay*

Of all the dimensions along which workers are divided, pay is the most important and most striking. Taking the USA in 1981, Table 5.4 shows how pay depends substantially upon occupation. Moreover within each occupational group there are further wide disparities. A more striking indication of inequality is that whereas 9 per cent of the labour force were paid over $500 a week, 37 per cent received less than $150 a week.

Disparities of pay are also revealed in other ways. Table 5.5 (again USA) illustrates the widely known fact that men are paid on average more than women, and white people more than people of other races. And Table 5.6 shows, for a selection of countries, how pay differentiation by sex is wide-spread. In fact, sexual and racial pay inequality can be found in all capitalist countries (nor are they confined to the capitalist world only). Such disparities profoundly structure the ways in which different workers experience life under capitalism (see Chapter 8).

Employers maintain these differentials for a number of reasons. One may be custom: tradition dictates that they are adhered to, whatever their

Table 5.4 Median Weekly Earnings for Full-Time Employees in each Occupational Group, USA, 1981

	USA 1981 $	Relative to farm workers
Managers, administrators	430	2.3
Professional and technical	410	2.1
Craft and kindred workers	375	2.0
Sales workers	317	1.7
Operatives (non-transport)	252	1.3
Clerical workers	248	1.3
Labourers (non-farm)	243	1.3
Service workers	203	1.1
Farm workers	190	1.0

Source: US Department of Commerce, Bureau of the Census, *Statistical Abstract of the United States*, Washington DC, 1984

Table 5.5 Median Weekly Earnings for Full-Time Workers in each Racial and Gender Group, USA, 1982

	Whites $	Blacks $	Hispanic origin $
Females	253	231	209
Males	397	299	274

Source: US Department of Commerce, Bureau of the Census, *Statistical Abstract of the United States*, Washington DC, 1985

Table 5.6 The Male/Female Earnings Ratio,* 1982

Japan	1.89	Belgium	1.36
Singapore	1.57	France	1.24
Switzerland	1.49	Australia	1.21
UK	1.45	Denmark	1.19
West Germany	1.38	Kenya	1.19

* Ratio of average earnings in non-farm activities, 1982
Source: International Labour Office, *Yearbook of Labour Statistics*, ILO, Geneva, 1982

original cause. It is possible for customary norms to prevail for a while. But if there exists a shortage of a particular type of worker for any length of time capitalists will be tempted or forced to raise their pay in order to attract more of them. Conversely, when a group of workers is in excess supply, capitalists are in a strong position to reduce their wages relative to other workers. In the short run, differentials can usually be maintained even if there are fluctuations in demand, because capitalists can afford it and workers expect it as part of the implicit long-term contracts they enter into when they accept the terms of internal labour markets. But in the long run we can expect supply and demand forces to prevail, according to the basic rules that apply to any market.

But to explain pay differentials we must look behind the supply and demand forces to see what determines them, and to relate them to capitalist development. Fundamentally, the differentials exist because, in a stratified society, they reflect the pursuit of profit.

(ii) *Work disamenities*

Workers may receive compensating wage differentials where the required work is unpleasant or dangerous. For example, the extraction of raw materials often requires people to work in disagreeable conditions – down a mine, in an Arctic climate, or isolated on an ocean oil rig. Other things being equal, capitalists must normally pay such workers high wages. Conversely where a job is in favourable surroundings, capitalists may be able to lower the wages.

However, the 'other things being equal' clause is particularly important. Many higher paid employees also work in pleasant conditions, but there are alternative reasons why their rewards are high – see especially (v) below. By the same token, those who work in the most degrading conditions are also those with the lowest pay when they do not have the choice of better jobs elsewhere.

(iii) *Local labour markets*

Despite the mass migrations mentioned earlier, moving house to obtain employment entails high financial costs as well as the psychological and social cost involved in the disruption of communities. Thus if some regions grow faster than others the demand for labour-power can cause wages to rise relatively in those areas. Wage disparities between the same job in different regions are thus explained by the costs of migration.

(iv) *Trade union power*

Where workers are unionized to a reasonable degree they can force capitalists to concede higher wages by the power of industrial action, that is, by controlling and threatening to withhold their supply of labour-power. If they are successful they will reduce the employers' profits. They may also affect the wages of those workers not in unions: capitalists may have to raise them somewhat to avert the danger of further unionization.

This last factor makes life difficult for those who try to assess the importance of unions in raising wages. If one simply compares the wage trends of unionized and non-unionized workers one underestimates the true effectiveness of unions in gaining wage increases. On the other hand, one cannot logically deduce from observing an upward trend in wages that unions caused it, for there are many other factors involved in determining wages, underlying the supplies and demands for labour-power (it is absurd to claim that unions alone have won the wage gains of the last century).

In fact, unions are so deeply embedded within the institutional structures of modern labour markets that, while it is clear that they modify the wage-determining processes, it is virtually pointless to ask what would the situation be like without them. They are part of the market – an 'endogenous' institution – and not an external factor determining it.

(v) *Skills*

By far the most important general explanation for inequalities in pay is the existence of differential skills and abilities. It is sometimes difficult to measure skills because they involve behavioural characteristics as well as technical abilities. In many cases skill levels can become merely artificial constructions. But in all except the simplest production processes there remains a need for some specialized knowledge, for physical or mental agility.

When the employers are reasonably sure that workers will remain with the company, they will normally be willing to pay for at least some of the training required. In other cases, especially where general skills are concerned, employers are less willing to pay for training workers whom they cannot be sure of keeping. Hence workers have to bear the formal cost of paying for instruction and the informal but equally real cost of forgoing earnings during training. Skilled workers would be in short supply if they could not expect a differential to compensate them for incurring the formal and informal training costs.

Thus skilled workers are better paid because they are in relatively short supply. Traditional economics has concluded that differentials thereby reflect a choice whether or not to undergo training or to undertake unpleasant jobs (as under (ii) above), implying that the low-paid receive what they have chosen and must therefore be responsible for their own misfortunes. We also base our argument on the short supply of skilled workers, but we reject the orthodox conclusion. For in most cases the reason for skill shortage lies in the objective structure of the labour market and has little to do with personal choice.

In all capitalist countries labour markets have become structured in one way or another. Those workers caught in the secondary sectors find the way to acquisition of skills barred. Being in unskilled jobs, they do not have the opportunity to acquire skills while working, particularly if they do not remain long enough in each job.

The expansion of education has been unable to break down the pattern of divisiveness that has been created in the labour market. Low pay, insecurity and unpleasant conditions often go together rather than being substitutes for each other: the mass of secondary workers are restricted from competing for better jobs.

That female and black workers are relatively poorly paid is also easily explained within this framework. It is true that there is a certain amount of pure discrimination on sexual or racial grounds, in that white males may be paid more for exactly the same job, or irrationally preferred for promotion. But even if capitalists are prevented by law, or by union actions, from practising such discrimination, the differentials would still remain. For women and blacks are disproportionately represented in secondary jobs. Women in particular are hampered from acquiring skills through training on the job by the assumption of their continued responsibility for domestic labour, particularly child-rearing. The interruption of a career prevents them moving up the promotion ladder. Not surprisingly, the male pay advantage typically increases as workers get older.

A further reason why certain skills may be in short supply is that, independent of the market processes we have discussed, many countries' working classes are already stratified in various ways. The acquisition of skill is thus determined by factors such as family and class background.

The children of workers from poor areas generally receive a poorer education, have fewer expectations and fewer paths open to them, and are especially influenced by parental occupation; for example, the children of manual workers become manually employed when they grow up. The idea that in 'free' capitalist societies opportunities are open to all is supported by the attention given to those few who make it (as from 'barrow boy to president'), but in fact studies have shown that such social mobility is very low. Better-paid jobs require considerable training costs. If workers have to bear them, then only those whose families can afford such costs will succeed.

This helps to explain why the existing distribution of pay can be perpetuated through successive generations.

4. IS THERE A 'LAW OF WAGES'?

The theme of this chapter has been that the changes in the amount of labour-power, and in the kinds of contract drawn up for its sale, have been moulded by the advances of capitalism.

But what may be concluded about the absolute wage level, that is, the average wage taking all workers together?

The common nineteenth-century idea (often mistakenly attributed to Marx) that there was an 'iron law' of wages, which would drive them down inexorably to a bare minimum only enough for subsistence, has been discredited by fact and theory.

The more recent common contention that there is an inevitable long-term upward trend of real wages is also far from the truth.

The truth is that real wages depend upon a number of factors related to the paths of capitalist development, even over long periods, and they can move either up or down. There is neither an iron law nor a golden rule for wages.

Their movement is affected, among other things, by the rate of growth of capital, the rate of formation of the reserve army of labour, the (related) strength of the trade union movement, the profitability of capital and the stability of the state (this last because rising real wages may help to win industrial peace, hence a more stable society).

The 1950s and 1960s were the two most dynamic decades ever experienced by capitalism and not surprisingly real wages rose substantially. After the boom was over, from the 1970s onwards, the trends became more mixed. And in recent times there are many instances in Third World countries of long periods of falling real wages, even in conditions of economic growth (page 137).

CHAPTER 6

Buying the Means of Production

To compete the chapter-by-chapter survey of the circuit of profit making we need to discuss the issues connected with the capitalists' purchases of the means of production with which labour will be put to work in the production process.

I. FIXED CAPITAL

The decisions of capitalists when they buy new machines, buildings or factories are taken in relation to the profits expected. Although prospective profit alone guides these decisions, they may have major and long-lasting consequences for many other people.

If investors decide to reduce their investments or in the extreme to make no investment at all (as happened for a time in the 1930s), the result is a general slump in the economy and no prospect for any growth or improved living standards. If they decide to invest substantially, it can be at the cost of incurring present hardship for many. And what products are to be made – whether, for example, it be more private cars or more trains – and what technologies are to be used have profound effects on the kind of lives that people will lead.

New machines, and even more so new technologies, are not just temporary things, here today but tomorrow forgotten: they are expected to endure and govern production methods for a long time into the future. The term reserved for means of production which are not used up in each production process, which depreciate only gradually if at all, is 'fixed capital'. This is in contrast to 'circulating capital' such as, for example, a quantity of oil which enters the production process and is completely used up; the supply must be replenished continuously if production is to continue.

New fixed capital deeply affects the future growth and direction of an economy, and forms each year a large and volatile component of total demand; so like the horse which pulls the carriage, investment in fixed capital 'drives the capitalist system' along.

Table 6.1 illustrates the point in its barest simplicity. The first column

Table 6.1 Investment and Growth

	Annual growth rate of non-residential fixed capital stock per person employed from 1950–73	Annual productivity growth, 1950–73	Gross fixed investment as % of total demand* in 1983
Canada	2.7	3.0	19.4
France	3.7	5.1	19.6
West Germany	4.7	6.0	20.8
Italy	4.3	2.5	18.0
Japan	7.2	8.0	28.5
UK	2.9	3.1	16.5
USA	2.2	2.6	16.8

* as measured by GDP; see Chapter 14, Technical Annexe C
Sources: OECD, *Economic Outlook, Historical Statistics 1960–1983*, OECD, Paris, 1985.
Angus Maddison, *Phases of Economic Development*, Oxford and New York, Oxford University Press, 1982.

shows how fast the stock of fixed capital expanded in seven countries (during a highly successful era for capitalism), while the second shows the rate of increase of productivity. Other factors besides the level of investment help to determine how fast productivity grows; the rate and direction of technological change, the stability of demand, the organization and intensity of work are but three. None the less it is an inescapable fact that where investment has been exceptionally high, as in Japan and in West Germany, productivity has grown the fastest; and where investment was especially low, as in the USA and the UK, so also was productivity growth. The final column gives the amount of investment in each country for 1983, showing how it remains a substantial part of total demand in the economy.

It is an enduring condemnation of the profit system that decisions of such importance for the lives of everybody should be taken by a tiny minority, who are accountable to nobody but themselves and their company's other shareholders on the basis of their profit and loss accounts. In 1983 about $1,500 billion was spent altogether in the advanced capitalist countries alone on investment. This was equivalent to about $2,000 per person; but apart from the privileged few no one had any say in the matter. For the vast majority investment in productive equipment for the future remains a remote and mysterious act.

(i) *Types of investment*

By 'investment' we shall mean throughout investment in fixed capital (as opposed to the acquiring of a monetary asset like a bank deposit account, sometimes called 'investment' and sometimes 'saving'). It is useful to think of total investment as made up of three parts, even if it is not always possible to measure the proportions in each part.

The first arises from the depreciation in usefulness of fixed capital. Machines wear out, tools become blunt and factory buildings need maintaining. The cost of making good these losses to the same level of capital stock is known as capital consumption. Often the process is uneven, for a machine may last several years and not require any expenditure, but a large sum will be needed to replace it when it expires. Firms normally allow for this depreciation by setting aside sums each year, so they can avoid suddenly high expenditures in particular years. The real amount of depreciation is always somewhat uncertain, as one can only estimate the lifetime of a piece of equipment, and new technological innovations may render it obsolete almost overnight.

In any case, the amounts set aside are heavily influenced by the tax laws of each country, for firms typically use their depreciation allowances over the years to minimize their tax burdens (an art in itself). In consequence, the amounts laid by each year are no more than a very rough estimate of the true extent of depreciation. For this reason, it is often safer in economic analysis to use figures for gross investment (without deducting capital consumption).

The second part of investment is expansion through buying more of the same machines as those already in use, and the third is similar, with the addition that the extra machines are better (more productive) than the old ones, so that the result of the accumulation is not only a more machine-intensive process but also an improvement in the technology used. Sometimes a new machine may be quite unlike the old one, though designed to do the same job (for example, the substitution of a machine tool by one which is numerically controlled). At other times the new machine might be only an adaptation of the old one, such as the latest model of a car, incorporating new features.

Thus it is usually difficult to separate the second and third parts of investment, even though it is helpful to remember that these are in principle two separate channels through which the growth of fixed capital can lead to increased outputs.

(ii) *The investment decision*

What determines the amount of money that a capitalist firm wishes to invest in each period?

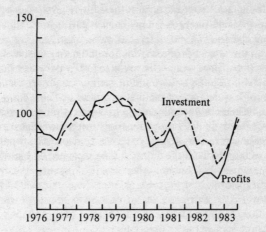

Diagram 6.1   Investment and Profits* in the USA, 1976–83 (1980 1st quarter = 100)

Note: * All data adjusted for inflation.

Source: US Department of Commerce, Bureau of Economic Analysis, *Survey of Current Business*, Washington DC, various issues.

Diagram 6.1 gives a preliminary clue. It plots indices of investment and of profits in one capitalist country, the USA, over nearly eight years. In order to display how movements in them are correlated, we have set the index for each to be 100 in the first quarter of 1980. The levels for all other (quarterly) periods are drawn relative to this benchmark. The chart shows how the ups and downs of investment and profit follow each other fairly closely and this is typical of other countries also.

The interpretation of this connection, however, is not quite as straight-forward as might be thought at first sight. It does not prove that profits cause investment, nor even that investment causes profits. They may both be moving in line with a third factor which is the proximate cause of both. But the diagram does suggest that the two are somehow connected, and indeed, as we shall shortly see, they are linked by the basic principle for capitalist investments, which is that the level and direction of investment is governed by the aim of maximizing profits. How this leads to the observed correlation can be understood fully only by looking in more detail at the various factors involved.

The most common type of investment has a typical time profile whereby money-capital is laid out in the current period to buy fixed capital, while the extra profits that this is intended to bring are gained in various future periods. A lot hinges, therefore, on how these future profits can be compared with current expenditures. A simple numerical example illustrates the principles involved.

Imagine an investment proposal which would involve spending £900 this year on a new machine, which it is envisaged will (by raising output sales) bring in an extra £250 next year, and in each of the subsequent five years. This time profile is detailed in the first two rows of Table 6.2.

One possible and not uncommon way to decide whether to go ahead with the investment is to use the 'pay-back period' method which asks how many years will pass before the original outlay is recouped. The capitalist may have a rule of thumb that if the money will be recouped within 'x' years, the investment is worthwhile, but not otherwise. If 'x' is 3, then the hypothetical investment plan would not proceed, as after three years only £750 will be received. But if 'x' is 4 or more the investment proposal would go ahead. Implicit in this rough and ready rule is the idea that capitalists prefer the returns to come sooner rather than later.

Table 6.2 A Hypothetical Investment Proposal

	Year 0 (present)	Year 1	Year 2	Year 3	Year 4	Year 5	Year 6	Sum of years 0 to 6
Outlays	£900							£900
Extra profits		£250	£250	£250	£250	£250	£250	£1500
Present value assuming $r = 15\%$		£217.4	£189.0	£164.4	£142.9	£124.3	£108.1	£946.1
Present value assuming $r = 20\%$		£208.3	£173.6	£144.7	£120.6	£100.5	£83.7	£831.4

The pay-back period approach, however, is rather arbitrary, since it depends on what is chosen as 'x', the critical period. We can see this better by examining why the returns are more valuable if they accrue at an earlier date. Suppose that the capitalist has to borrow from the bank to buy the machine: the longer the wait for the returns, the longer the time during which interest on the loan has to be paid. Even if the money did not have to be borrowed, the longer it is tied up in one particular project, the longer it is unavailable for use (maybe earning interest) elsewhere. It is clear from a simple calculation that the total return is £6 × 250 = £1,500, which is greater than the original £900; but if the interest rate were very high, the net gain of £600 over time may be more than balanced by interest payments on the original borrowed sum.

All this is part of the principle of 'discounting', whereby a future sum of money is worth less in present-day terms. For example, if the interest rate were 5 per cent, £100 this year would become £105 next year, £110.25 the year after, and so on. So if you were expecting to receive £110.25 in two years' time it would only be worth £100 in present-day terms.

Table 6.2 shows in the third row what the present value of all the expected future profits are, by discounting to the present according to how many years ahead they accrue and assuming the interest rate (r) is 15 per cent. In the fourth row the interest rate is assumed higher, at 20 per cent.

In the third row, the sum of all the discounted future expected profits is £946.1, which is greater than the present cost of £900; so, if $r = $ 15 per cent the plan is worthwhile even though interest payments have to be made. But in the fourth row, the sum comes to £831.4, because a higher interest rate means that future values are more heavily discounted in comparison to the present. Moreover, this is now less than £900, so the investment plan, if proceeded with, would result in a loss after interest payments were deducted.

This example allows us now to state two preliminary conclusions about the determinants of investment. First, it depends on the future expected profits, for the higher they are, the more likely is it that the added-up discounted present value of such profits will exceed the current outlay. Second, it depends on the rate of interest: the higher the rate of interest the less likely that a project will be found worthwhile, so that the overall level of investment spending will be lower.

Our example, however, left out a crucial feature of the decisions which capitalists face, by assuming that the future profits of £250 each year would be certain. In reality, capitalists have to guess at the most likely out-turn and take into account their own ignorance. The fact of uncertainty leads us therefore to qualify and extend the list of factors determining the level of investment.

Any factors which affect how much profit capitalists *expect* to make are highly important in explaining the level of investment. So they need forecasts of future tax rates, future rates of depreciation of machinery, future levels of demand and so on.

One way to get these is to extrapolate from present known trends into the future. For example, if demand is growing they may assume that it will continue to grow and hence they will invest more in order to meet future demand; conversely if demand is stagnant, and they assume it will remain so, they will invest little. This is known as the 'accelerator' theory of investment.

Another is that they try to be more sophisticated. Their expectations might depend on what kind of government is in power or whether the political situation is 'stable' (especially in Third World countries). And they might employ the services of a macroeconomic forecasting unit that uses all the paraphernalia of a large computer model of the economy to try to predict the future.

But a third possibility is that investors rightly recognize that the future *is* highly uncertain, they distrust or ignore whatever 'expert' predictions are made, and base their judgement on an attitude of mind: their 'animal spirits'. A major element of their expectations is therefore not really amenable to any kind of rational explanation. It has often been observed that capitalists are subject to waves of optimism or of pessimism. Clearly if everyone is optimistic there will be high levels of investment, while pessimism about profits leads to low investment. Much of the most successful prediction of future investment levels comes from surveys of the attitudes and intentions of capitalists themselves.

In the 1930s, Keynes regarded swings of what he called the 'dark forces' of investment psychology as a highly destabilizing force in the economy. It is possible that with higher current levels of government investment which is less volatile, and with a more competitive modern banking system, private investment volatility is not as crucial now as it was then. None the less Diagram 6.2 shows that investment in the USA, over the same eight-year period as in Diagram 6.1, varied much more than national income. And a similar volatility, partly to be explained by the swinging moods of capitalists, can be found in other countries too. (The implications of this for destabilization of the economy are discussed in Chapter 14.)

Another feature of capitalist investment is that though decisions are taken separately, without conforming to any overall plan, their effects are highly interdependent. Sometimes decisions can cancel each other out and lead to irrational waste, for example the development of two incompatible videotaping systems independently by competing firms. At other times one capitalist's investments reinforce those of another.

Very occasionally this interrelatedness becomes so far-reaching that the whole pattern of investment is dominated by a particular innovation for many years. Such was the case between 1880 and 1900 when over 40 per cent of all US investment was directly made by railway capitalists purchasing their requisite materials and a good proportion of the rest of investment was indirectly associated with the same innovation. Steel manufacture was in high demand, as were the construction materials necessary to build the new towns that grew up, and the whole panoply

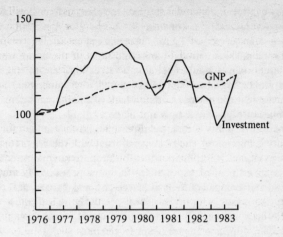

Diagram 6.2   Investment Volatility (US investment and GNP* 1976–83; 1976 1st quarter = 100)

Note: * All data adjusted for inflation.

Source: US Department of Commerce, Bureau of Economic Analysis, *Survey of Current Business*, Washington DC, various issues

of services needed by the new communities. It was truly the railway 'era'.

In the twentieth century the most profound epoch-making innovation – as far as investment levels are concerned – remains the motor car. Apart from the steel and factory machinery to which the expansion of the car industry gave rise (in the periods after both world wars), there is also the spread of suburban areas, with all their appropriate needs for highway construction and so on, the growth of the petroleum industry and a multitude of other indirect effects. That today is the age of the motor car is reflected in the fact that fourteen of the world's twenty biggest firms (by sales) are either oil or automobile companies (see Table 2.1).

Uncertainty about the future also means that the relationship between the rate of interest and investment is more complicated than in the numerical example. It is no longer possible to think of only one interest rate. A bank which lends to a capitalist who is investing in a project with good but 'risky' expected profits will correspondingly demand a risk premium and charge a higher interest rate because the future profit hopes may not be fulfilled.

Hence, when we say that the higher the interest rate the lower the level of investment that firms undertake, we should add that this applies for each given degree of risk. In reality there is a whole structure of interest rates in the money-capital markets which apply to loans and projects of different lengths and varying degrees of risk.

There is another set of factors determining investment involving the financial relationships between banks and firms. If the future were known with certainty, banks would not mind whether they lent to small or large firms. In reality the uncertainties associated with impersonal lending to small firms sometimes mean not that a high risk premium is demanded but that supplies of funds are simply not made available.

It helps if a firm has a close relationship with its bankers for then the uncertainty is minimized, the bank is involved with the firm's fortunes and funds are available. It is quite possible for banks to have some control over capitalists' investment plans, even for the same people to be managers in both bank and company. In West Germany and Japan such banks are common, one 'reason why investment is relatively high in those countries (see Table 6.1). In many other countries access to financial flows from banks is often a specific advantage of large size.

But apart from this division between large and small firms, a further important consequence of uncertainty is that firms find it much less problematical to finance most of their investments out of their own cash income. In other words, in addition to future expected profits, and interest rate factors, we see that investment may also be heavily affected by current and recent profits which are the capitalists' source of available cash. Investment may thus be constrained by profits income, just as consumers' spending levels are constrained by their incomes if the bank denies them loan facilities. In 1979, for example, 86 per cent of investment in the USA was financed internally, while in France, Germany and the UK the figure was on average 80 per cent.

In the light of these factors, we can now adduce two reasons why, as shown in Diagram 6.1, there is a correlation between the levels of investment and of profits.

First, capitalists will usually take their current profits as an indication of their future profits. Hence if current profits are high, their expectations are high (they are in an 'optimistic' mood) and so they step up their investment. Conversely, if current profits are low, they are pessimistic about the future so they invest little. Moreover, this pessimism could be yet further justified if they have excess capacity in their factories. There is no point in buying new machines if the existing ones are idle.

Second, if current profits are low then this simply constrains the level of investment that can be financed, given that borrowing from banks may be costly or difficult. So from this point of view also, investment levels are likely to move in line with profit levels.

These points, however, while valid are far from the whole story. Capitalist investors may not in practice indulge in the luxury of planning the rational allocation of their resources between consumption and investment as much as orthodox economists like to think. In the competitive struggle the very survival of their business may depend on their ability to match any investment in new technology made by their rivals. Investment can be an externally imposed survival imperative rather than a rational allocation of economic resources.

2. CIRCULATING CAPITAL

Buying circulating capital (raw materials, energy and semifinished goods) does not pose the same kind of problem for individual capitalists; they do not have to evaluate the effect on future output and profit since (by definition) these commodities are used up completely in the production process.

But producers do need to be sure of regular supplies. If their supply lines are interrupted, for example by a strike or some other failure with their suppliers, it can provoke a crisis for the firms immediately affected, which can easily spread due to the interrelatedness of various capitalist activities.

One response may be for a firm to take over its supplier, a process called 'vertical integration', but this often will not provide the answer to uncertainty as it can lead to increased organizational control problems and to being stuck with more idle fixed capital in downturns. Ultimately capitalists have to rely on the markets for a stable supply of circulating capital.

In this section we shall review two important related issues, both concerned with the regularity and consistency of supply: first, the political issues that arise in the case of raw materials which are supplied from countries in the Third World and possibly on the periphery of the capitalist system, and second, the ecological problems posed by the depletion of natural resources.

(i) *Imperialism and raw materials supply*

Much circulating capital consists of raw materials: oil, coal and other energy sources, iron ore and so on. 'Raw' suggests that these are supplied purely by nature, like windfall apples which you have but to pick up and eat. Yet coal and iron have to be mined, oil wells drilled, cotton sown and picked. Their production raises a special problem which is not merely natural, but political and social: namely that the work has to be done where the mines and ore deposits exist. If these places are on the periphery of capitalism, to bring the work under capitalist control – or indeed to control and maintain a regular supply for the capitalists in developed countries – becomes particularly problematic.

The political response has been for the advanced capitalist nations to seek imperialist control over the countries where raw materials come from. There are many other aspects to nineteenth-century colonialism and modern-day imperialism, but an important one is this assurance of raw material supply. The history of British and US intervention in Iran in the century before the 1979 revolution is an instructive instance of the use of foreign policy to secure oil supplies.

Modern-day imperialism differs in form from that of colonial days when an advanced country simply annexed areas of the world. But there are many other ways in which an imperialist power, such as the USA, can influence what happens in another country, though it would be wrong to suggest that the sole reason for such intervention is to secure supplies of raw materials. In the case of hostile regimes it can refuse aid or impose a trade boycott; it can secretly subvert them through organizations such as the Central Intelligence Agency, or it can intervene directly as happened in Vietnam. Correspondingly, 'friendly' regimes are supported by military and civilian aid, and through making loans and credits available as in Chile after the bloody coup of 1973.

(ii) *The depletion of natural resources*

The oft-repeated proposition that there is a natural limit to raw material supplies in the world, and that sooner or later the growth of capitalist (and other) economies will be brought to a halt as these supplies run short, is closely related to the first issue, since if this is true the changing structure of imperialist relations will affect how such shortages have their impact.

The raw materials said to be in limited supply are the most fundamental ones: food, since land is limited, populations are expanding, and ocean fish stocks are being depleted; fresh water, since there is not enough precipitation to meet rising demands; minerals such as zinc, lead and so on; and, most important of all, energy sources. The latter include solar and wind energy, hydroelectric power and other similar sources which, while only so much could be obtained in any one year, are 'renewable', as well as coal, oil and natural gas reserves, or uranium for nuclear power plants, which are for practical purposes 'non-renewable'.

In the case of such resources, a commonly made calculation is to state the estimated existing stock, give the rate of current and projected use and hence derive the number of years before the world runs out of each resource. Thus for example, the *Global 2000 Report to the President of the US* (commissioned by President Carter) estimated at the end of the 1970s that zinc reserves would last only 25 years, or 37 years if demand was held static at the 1976 level; that there was about 45 years' worth of natural gas, or up to 170 years if other sources became recoverable; and that coal, by contrast, was in plentiful supply.

The separate problems with each resource may well be related, in ways which compound the overall dilemma. For example, fresh water can always be extracted by desalinating sea water, but this is at present a very energy-intensive (hence costly) process.

It is not envisaged that supplies of any raw material, renewable or not, will suddenly run out in any one year. Rather the expected scenario is for rising extraction costs and decreased production relative to demand to lead to the price of raw materials rising. The capitalists who use them would make lower profits, real wages would decrease and material living standards would start to fall. Pushing the argument still further, this fall if generalized would come through a massive deindustrialization. Cars, aeroplanes and all the trappings of the modern age would become far too expensive given the price of raw materials, and there would be a return to general poverty for all people, including the majority of those in what are now the advanced capitalist countries.

On the plausibility of this scenario for the future of capitalism, there are broadly two opposing viewpoints. First, some ecologists, combining the fears of resource depletion and environmental pollution, assert on the basis of projections of current trends that ecological and hence economic catastrophe will come before too long (i.e. early in the twenty-first century) unless current policies and attitudes are changed. Often they see the only hope to be a moral regeneration, with the rich consumers of the west deciding to reduce their consumption demands and to switch them to products whose technologies require much less pollution. Such hopes are often couched in politically naive terms, which ignore the class structure underlying capitalist societies.

Second, conventional economics asserts that resources may be allocated rationally through a market mechanism, and that the existing market can prevent economic collapse even if some resources are being depleted. The argument, which is a defence of a *laissez-faire* attitude to natural resource management, starts from the plausible prediction that as a resource becomes relatively scarce its price will rise. Consumers and producers will respond in three ways: (a) they may switch their demands to substitute commodities (e.g. as the price of oil rose in the 1970s some were able to use gas or coal); (b) they may use less resources by careful conservation strategies (e.g. insulation to prevent heat losses); or (c) they may be able to avoid the problem through technical progress, and indeed there is an economic incentive for capitalists to find new methods of production that do not require increasingly costly resource inputs.

There is a good deal of truth in this repsonse. The conventional economist can point to many resource 'scares' which have been resolved and forgotten within a few years. The case, however, is not really proven, for the natural world has never before had to cope with the scale of growth in demand that came with the post-war boom and the huge rise of population. Moreover, the future situation is so uncertain that there is no way that the market mechanism can work to re-allocate resources now in order to prevent disasters twenty years hence. It is conceivable that an ecological disaster could strike before the capitalist world has time to adjust, as economists optimistically believe it would.

There is no simple answer to the global problem of resource depletion, nor is it possible to adopt uncritically either the ecologists' or the economists' attitudes. Although one can predict with reasonable accuracy the world's population twenty years hence (assuming no nuclear holocaust), predicting the capitalist economy is much more hazardous: it could come up against other crises and constraints well before then, which would render any world raw materials resource limitations irrelevant for a while. Yet the problem is a genuine one, and is capable of raising obstacles to the successful completion of the capitalist circuit of profit.

Our description of this circuit – from the production of commoditites, to the sale of commodities back to the purchase of labour, and fixed and circulating capital – is now complete. In Chapter 7 we look at the broader economic environment in which capitalists succeed or fail to complete this circuit.

CHAPTER 7

Markets, Money and Financial Capital

At every level, capitalist production is a form of social interaction. At the level of the workplace people act together, using machines and materials made previously by others, under the ultimate plan and direction of capitalist owners. And at the level of the economy as a whole there is a *social division of labour*, in which producers in one firm, though working as an independent unit, use the fruits of the labours of other workers in other firms. Even in this indirect yet real way, all workers are united in a *social act of production*.

The way that workers are united in the social division of labour, however, is a rather peculiar one. Within a single workplace or firm, different workers encounter each other directly as fellow wage earners and producers. They can, therefore, connect, co-operate and conflict in normal human ways. But the bonds between the workers of that firm and all other workers are expressed, by contrast, in the fact that the commodity they produce exchanges at certain ratios in the market with all other commodities. So the social co-operation that underlies the aggregate productive process appears not as a relationship between people (that is, between all workers) but as a relationship between the things they produce (a phenomenon which Marx characterized as the 'fetishism of commodities').

Almost all of these exchanges are mediated by money; and hence it is in terms of money that the value of things and relationships tends to be expressed. In 1985 Mantegna's painting 'The Adoration of the Magi' became famous not due to general appreciation of its sublime artistic qualities but because it changed hands for a record £8 million, defining it as 'worth' 2,000 small saloon cars; 300 'Adorations of the Magi' equal the 'value' of one Trident nuclear submarine.

The monetary calculus is not restricted to objects; it extends to people themselves. Their productiveness and worth are typically expressed in terms of the value (in money) of the things they help to produce. Courts often decide on levels of damages or compensation for incapacitating or fatal accidents on this basis; and medical committees sometimes similarly assess the 'value to society' of rival candidates for limited numbers of available kidney machines. People are said to be 'worth nothing' – a reference to their lack of personal wealth. Physical bodies are given monetary values when people insure their lives or pianists their fingers. Intimate human relations also have a price: even if an old Beatles song is right that 'money can't buy you love', it can and often does buy sex.

Since the market is an external and inconstant thing, human beings who are bound to it inevitably feel the pangs of insecurity. It can seem almost as if money acquires a character of its own. As the singer Bob Dylan declared, 'Money doesn't talk it swears obscenity'; and even the most prudish are obliged to listen. When the economy enters into a crisis this impinges upon people through the medium of money. Some capitalists are deprived of it and forced out of business, while workers with less money take a reduced standard of living. It often appears that those who deal in money – the bankers and financiers – are the ones responsible for our fortunes. Most crises are blamed at some point on money speculators.

Yet for all its power, the value which is contained in money is quite impersonal. In its appearance, money is money, no matter how it is come by or what it is going to be spent on, a fact useful to criminals. The American illegal drug trade annually netted roughly $80 billion cash in the mid 1980s, but all that 'dirty' money was easily laundered clean by a series of discreet banking transactions. No sign remains in the rich dealers' bank account to link their money with their trade.

The fact that social human relations are 'reified' into relations between things and that these get expressed in terms of money, lends a certain mystery to money itself. Karl Marx once wrote that 'money has the power to confuse and invert all human and natural qualities . . . What I as a man am unable to do, what therefore all my individual faculties are unable to do, is made possible for me by means of money.'

The previous four chapters on the stages in the capitalist profit-making process raised the question of money because they were concerned with acts of monetary exchange. In this chapter we will begin by looking more systematically at how the process of exchange is regulated through money and how it helps to co-ordinate the aggregate social production process. But we will also go on to deal with issues which concern money, as such: what it is, and what functions it serves; the role of the banks which make profits not out of commodity production but out of money itself; and the way that purely monetary issues are connected to the whole capitalist economy.

1. EXCHANGE AND THE MARKET

(i) *When the market works*

It is common to associate the idea of a market with a particular place and time. For example, at the quayside in a fishing port early in the morning, you find a market for fish. But there is no necessity for a market to be geographically confined. All that is needed is for buyers and sellers to contact each other. The foreign exchange market operates through the telephone wires linking up dealers all over the world. The labour market covers whole areas within which workers come to sell their labour-power to capitalists. When economists talk about 'the market', they refer to the abstract arenas within which buyers and sellers come into contact.

Capitalism consists of many independent producing units, each with its own plans, competing with the others to sell its commodities. Their independence seems to imply that they will produce chaos.

Although the system is anarchic, in the sense that there is no co-ordinating plan to social production, it possesses, as well, some modicum of order. Often, though not always, capitalists' individual plans are fulfilled, in that what they induce their own workers to produce can be sold at a price which yields them profits. Thus sales can equal planned production, while their own demand for inputs may also be satisfied. Considered in logical isolation it might seem unlikely that many hundreds of independently conceived plans should thus match up in the social whole. To understand what happens we must desert such static logic and look at the way capitalists' apparently independent plans can change *over the course of time*.

To some extent co-ordination of anarchic (independent) plans is brought about through continuity with the past. Capitalists learn from experience what quantities they can sell on the market and what margins between costs and prices are viable.

But this begs the vital question of how co-ordination was approximated in the first place, and as to how they can adjust to changes. The short answer is: through the price mechanism. When their plans fail, in that their planned production is substantially more or less than they can sell, firms will adjust their output plans for the future. Changes in the prices or in the warehouse stocks of commodities may help to induce such adjustments. In this sense, the price mechanism may automatically bring about social co-ordination, without any overall guiding human control. Adam Smith, the founder of classical political economy, called this the 'invisible hand' of the market.

Diagram 7.1 shows schematically how co-ordination might be achieved automatically in the market for one particular commodity over a hypothetical five-month period, starting from an initial position in which what producers

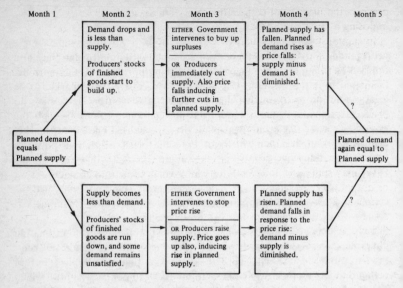

Diagram 7.1   Co-ordination through the Price Mechanism

planned to supply and actually supplied matched the market demand.

Suppose that there is a drop in demand in month 2, thereby disrupting the social co-ordination of this market. The upper half of the diagram sketches a possible course of events through which a balance is again achieved. To begin with, stocks build up as producers cannot sell all their output. In a few markets – such as in the agricultural sector of the EEC – the government may intervene to buy up such surpluses, but in the absence of such intervention producers soon (say in month 3) cut their production schedules to avoid creating too much unwanted stock. In addition, there is a tendency for the price to fall as capitalists attempt to unload the excess stock which has accumulated. This further stimulates a cut in supply plans, since they are making less profits at the lower price even if the goods can all be sold; and some less efficient producers may be forced to go out of business. Thus in month 4 we have lower supply plans; and, at the same time, the quantity demanded has increased due to the inducement of a lower price (see Chapter 4). The supply-demand imbalance has been reduced. If this balancing act continues, by month 5 an equilibrium may be restored.

The opposite train of events, when supply becomes less than demand, is traced in the bottom half of the diagram. Again, it shows how the independent plans of capitalists can be made to adjust automatically through the price mechanism. Their plans will not adjust, however, if the government prevents the price from rising either by selling from its own stocks or by imposing a maximum price.

In capitalist economies markets exist for the buying and selling of most goods and services, and interactions such as we have described can thus co-ordinate the plans of all independent producers. These markets are generally facilitated by governments, which defend private property and give basic legal protection to contracts. They are further bolstered by a number of private capitalist institutions which make profits directly from the exchange process. These are the arbitrageurs who buy as cheap as they can and sell as dear as they can, and thereby help to minimize the variation in price for a commodity at any one time. They help to keep the markets in operation.

We may sum up as follows. Whenever there are disruptions in the plans or outputs of independent capitalists there arises a disequilibrium between supply and demand, just as changing the weight at one end of a see-saw can cause it to overbalance. Yet it is possible that the price mechanism, if it is allowed to operate in the absence of government intervention other than to guarantee contracts, can bring about co-ordination. It provides incentives for suppliers and demanders, whether they be capitalists or workers, to respond to imbalances by altering their individual plans. It acts as if it were providing information to the participants. When the price of a commodity goes up it is as if the market is saying to a consumer, 'Don't buy this, it has become rather scarce: choose something else.' Of course to put it this way is an abstraction, for the real reason that people respond to price changes is economic necessity and incentive.

(ii) *When the market fails*

In the foregoing section we have been careful to use 'can' or 'may', rather than 'will' or 'do', when describing how the price mechanism might bring about equilibrium. The automatic and impersonal nature of the market has led many people, economists included, to attach mysterious, almost omnipotent, powers to it, assuming that, like a Pope, the market is infallible and will *always* work to bring about harmony and balance, even if the capitalist competition underlying it is anarchic. Their belief in the market is closer to a religious faith than to a systematic scientific analysis. Their ideology buttresses capitalists' supremacy in the realm of ideas. It extols the positive social values of self-interest and thus defends the ownership of private property in the means of production.

The facts, however, do not vindicate their faith. There is nothing automatically harmonious about the way the capitalist system works. Rather, there seems to be an inherent tendency for the market to break down in disorder every so often. The course of events shown in Diagram 7.1, which faithfully follows the argument of all the market believers, is by no means preordained. The path towards balance is not guaranteed. Capitalists do not always recoup their investments, nor can they invariably sell at a price to cover cost. The faithful typically attribute any market failures to government intervention. Even the most advanced and sophisticated economic theories of the modern day, however, have been unable to prove that, under plausible assumptions, an equilibrium that is stable in all markets simultaneously can be achieved.

There are four general ways in which the path of Diagram 7.1 may be blocked.

(a) First, the adjustment of plans to prices could be strong yet delayed, and this can cause it to 'overshoot'. Thus if demand starts by being less than supply the price mechanism could cause changes so large that after a while demand exceeds supply by a greater margin than that by which it was previously deficient. Then it might later swing back yet more violently than before. Such volatile swings and disruptions occur sometimes in the foreign exchanges and also in other specialized types of markets, usually where there is opportunity for speculation or where a long time elapses between production plans and the output of a finished product (e.g. pigs, cocoa, supersonic airliners).

(b) Second, and more fundamentally, all the different markets are related, so imbalances in one can lead to imbalances in others and possibly to a general breakdown in all markets at the same time.

(c) Third, the diagram assumed that, following any disruption, the market would have time to adjust itself. Yet in reality capitalist economies are continually open to disruptions. These can become so frequent and widespread that the market adjustment process is unable to cope. Apart from random shocks to a market (e.g. a bad harvest due to poor weather), there are intrinsic reasons why supply or demand plans are subject to change. For example, capitalists continually aim to expand through competition with each other, introducing new machinery and work methods. In so doing they reduce their costs and alter their supply plans.

(d) Finally, the demand plans in all markets contain an inherent element of fragility, owing to the fact that almost all exchanges are carried out through the medium of money. Money is not wanted for its own sake, but for what it can buy. There are, however, many reasons why demanders might want to hold on to their money for a time rather than spend it – that is, to 'hoard it'. If they do so on a wide scale, markets could experience a massive disruption to which they may not be able to adjust.

In Chapter 14 we shall discuss how this possibility of imbalance can be turned into actuality, through a cumulative process of disequilibrium, just as one piece of bad luck often leads to further misfortunes. There also we examine further the phenomenon of economic crisis, which could implicitly involve market failure in any of the above four ways.

2. MONEY

We must now look in closer detail at the functions of this mysterious factor, money.

There are in priniciple four types of market exchanges in a capitalist economy: between capitalists, as when a manufacturer buys fuel from an oil company; between capitalists and workers, when capitalists buy their supplies of labour-power; between workers; and between consumers (workers and capitalists) and capitalists. None of these exchanges could be carried out without money: uncertainty about the future and the high costs of transacting prohibit generalized barter. Moreover money, from the point of view of the capitalists, has a special purpose: it is the form in which they achieve their objective of making profits.

The uncertainty and unpredictability of the future means that there is an advantage to be gained in 'keeping one's options open', that is, by retaining some wealth in the 'liquid' form of money. If capitalists are unsure about the future prospects of selling commodities they may prefer to hold on to their money – their liquid wealth – rather than invest it immediately, hoping to profit from their freedom to choose in the future. Even workers may prefer to keep their wages in spendable form, ready to deal with contingencies, rather than commit themselves to a definite bundle of goods and services every time they sell their labour-power, though their level of income generally gives them little flexibility.

For people to be paid all their wages in commodities would be prohibitively expensive. Selling agents would have to find others who not only wanted what they had for sale but also could meet directly the seller's own wants. Trade is much more efficient via the intermediation of money.

Many conventional economists have been mesmerized by this obvious function of money. They like to compare a monetary economy with a 'barter economy', where, supposedly, exchange is widespread but takes place without money. They argue that it would be a much less efficient world. Their logic, however, is static and adds no historical insight whatsoever. A capitalist economy is a monetary one, since most production outside the home is for exchange through money, and labour-power is sold for wages in money. So the existence of something that will serve as money is clearly a prerequisite for the rise of capitalism. It is not the cause of that rise, for monetary relations had been general for many thousands of years before capitalism became dominant. Pre-capitalist economies, however, were neither monetary nor barter economies, because most production that took place was not for exchange. When exchange reached any significant level in the pre-capitalist world it was mediated by money. The economists' concept of the barter economy is an abstraction with no real foundation: it is a myth, though that is not to deny that some barter has existed in many economic systems and continues even within advanced capitalism.

The dominant role of money arose from its multiplicity of functions. Four of these are basic and interrelated (though historically they have not always held).

(a) It can act as a *medium of exchange*. It is that thing which is widely accepted by sellers in return for their commodities.

(b) It may also be a *store of value*, retained and used for the purchase of commodities in the future, at no specific date. It maintains its value relative to other commodities (when it does not – as during rapid inflation – it fails also to fulfil function (a)).

(c) It is the *unit of account* in which transactions are measured and through which the economic affairs of all institutions are gauged.

(d) It performs the *function of money-capital*. It is the form in which profits are measured and obtained, in which capital is accumulated.

Closely related to money is the concept of credit, which is the promise to pay money at some time in the future. Commodities can be exchanged for credit instead of for money; the seller obtains the consumer's IOU rather than money but normally can exchange this for money from a credit company, which is left with the job of collecting the debt owed by the consumer. Historically many forms of credit have become transformed into money, in that it has been possible to use IOUs as means of payment. The paper moneys issued by governments around the world for the last few centuries were in their origin IOUs. Formally this is still true since they are part of the state's debts to private citizens. Though they are never settled, they normally retain their value through their use in exchange.

Just as there are different types of monetary exchange, so there are different forms of credit relationship: between capitalists, between workers, and between capitalists and workers. But it is the function of money and credit as capital – that is, their use in pursuance of profit – that are central to the analysis of the capitalist economy.

3. BANK CAPITAL

Part of the mystery attached to money in popular imagination arises from the fact that it seems to be possible to obtain profits purely out of financial transactions – money out of money, without any intermediary process of production. Money seems to have an almost magical power to expand itself. It does this by being lent, and the kinds of institution which thereby obtain profits are generically known as 'financial capital', of which banks are the most important type. The banking process is therefore fundamentally different from the process of industrial capital depicted in Diagram 2.1 of Chapter 2, since it does not involve a process of production.

The powers of banks are not as magical as they appear at first sight; nor can their fortunes be divorced from those of industrial and agricultural capitalists to whom they are intimately bound. Banks are institutions which take deposits from other economic agents of all kinds. Such deposits are regarded as money by those who own them, but banks do not expect to have to pay them all back at any one time, and so can lend most of them to borrowers or use them to purchase financial assets, which yield interest or dividends. As long as these returns are greater than the interest they pay to their depositors, then the banks make profits.

In any one country the organizational structure of banks is immensely complex. Often there are a dozen or more different kinds of bank in operation. And each country has different laws or traditions. To generalize is, therefore, difficult; but it is possible to identify four broad functions which in many countries are carried out by different types of financial institution:

(a) Commercial or retail banks which maintain a direct relationship with consumers and small businesses, taking deposits from them, advancing loans and overdraft facilities to them and providing numerous other financial services, from paying bills to executing wills;

(b) investment banks, which deal more with the stocks and debts of large corporations and governments and may organize and finance mergers of firms and sometimes become directly involved in the ownership and management of industrial and commercial capital;

(c) institutions involved in longer-term assets, such as savings banks and mortgage companies (in the UK, building societies) and so on; some are non-profit institutions though they need to make a surplus on their transactions in order to finance their administrative costs;

(d) other financial bodies, which make their profits by dealing in very long-term credit, such as pension funds and life insurance companies; unlike banks, their deposits are not regarded as money since they are not immediately redeemable and liabilities to pay may not arise until decades after deposits are made.

There are thus a great variety of ways in which financial capitalist institutions make their profits, including managing the wealth of clients for a fee, buying and selling stocks and shares, and a hundred others. But what is common to all banks, the essence of financial capital, is that profit is made through the lending and borrowing of money. They are 'financial intermediaries' between lenders and borrowers. The number of institutions is so great and the organization of the sector so complex that the chains of credit are literally endless, one bank lending to another in a gigantic and constantly shifting web of credit and debt obligations. Where financial capitalists detect an opportunity, they may try to enter the web by devising some new kind of borrowing and lending in order to take a share of the available profit.

Parallel with the modern trend for production to be extended on an international basis through multinational corporations, there has been a dramatic expansion also of the international scale on which financial capital, especially the banks, operate. Virtually all the large banks in the world must now be regarded as international blocks of capital, even if they have a national base. The importance of this internationalization is taken up in Chapter 10.

4. THE ECONOMIC ROLE OF FINANCIAL CAPITAL

In order to discover the full role of financial institutions in the profit system we need to look at five things: the sheer size of the banks' operations; their role in the creation of money and credit; the monetary role of the state; the effects of money on the capitalist economy as a whole; and the condition of banks' stability.

(i) *The size of the banks*

The contribution of banks to national income is measured by the incomes they receive from providing financial services from the broad range of their lending and borrowing activities. Measured in this way, they account for only a small proportion of the total incomes generated in each country – less than 5 per cent in the USA. Even in the UK where the 'City' is relatively large, its contribution to national income is no more than 10 per cent. On this score it does not look as if financial capital is of great importance.

But the quantitative importance of banks comes not only from their income but also from their wealth which, by comparison, is enormous. New York-based Citicorp, the largest bank in the world, had assets ($151 billion in 1984) which would have allowed it, in principle, to buy Exxon, General Motors and most of Mobil Oil, the three largest US industrial corporations. And as Table 2.2 (page 21) showed, six other banks had assets of over $100 billion in the same year. These sums do not represent all the banks' net claim to assets, since they also have gigantic liabilities, the deposits of their customers. Yet they do show the huge scope of their embrace of the world's capitalist economies: their reach goes far beyond the relatively small magnitude of their total profits. Their power arises from the colossal concentration of capital into a few centrally controlled institutions.

(ii) *The creation of money*

Part of the special role of banks lies in their ability to 'create money' by lending to customers. In the act of providing credit they are expanding the amount of money in circulation. It may seem like a conjuring trick for a bank to create money apparently out of nothing. The apparent illusion is explained if 'money' is distinguished from 'wealth'. For each time a loan is made, thus giving money to the borrower, a corresponding debt is chalked up: so the borrower's net wealth is unchanged. Money is being created, but not wealth.

Banks are only able to make long-term loans because they are confident that their depositors will not all at the same time reclaim their money. Suppose £1,000 is deposited with a bank. Only a small proportion needs to be held as reserves, so that, for each such £1,000, perhaps £800 could be loaned out. The recipient of that loan has thereby obtained new money, created by the bank. When it is spent this 'new money' may then find its way back to the same or another bank and someone else's deposit, enabling a further loan to be made and more new money to be created. Diagram 7.2 follows through and explains the implications of such a hypothetical case.

The same process that 'creates money' – making loans – also yields to the banks their profits since the borrowers must pay interest. It may seem odd, therefore, that they do not lend out all their deposits rather than most of them. The reason is that they must keep some cash in reserve, since from time to time there may be an upsurge in withdrawals by depositors. If ever a suggestion arises that a bank does not have the resources to meet the potential demand for withdrawals, that bank is in trouble. The rumour can become self-fulfilling: people stampede to withdraw their funds in order to safeguard them against the bank's becoming insolvent. Such rumours often begin when it becomes known that a bank has made losses on some of its loans.

For this reason, banking is an inherently fragile business, built on a combination of confidence, respectability and secrecy. Financial institutions must always give the appearance of great wealth, hence their conspicuous occupation of the most prestigious and grandiose buildings in many towns. Bankers themselves have to cultivate an image of sobriety so as not to suggest that they may make rash decisions or bad loans. And they must go to great lengths to conceal from their depositors any problems they may have with their loans.

(iii) *The state and money*

In addition to the private banks' own prudence in maintaining their reserves, it is common for nation states to enforce such prudence through banking

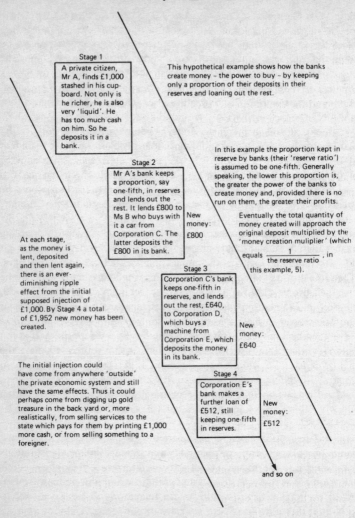

Stage 1

A private citizen, Mr A, finds £1,000 stashed in his cupboard. Not only is he richer, he is also very 'liquid'. He has too much cash on him. So he deposits it in a bank.

This hypothetical example shows how the banks create money – the power to buy – by keeping only a proportion of their deposits in their reserves and loaning out the rest.

In this example the proportion kept in reserve by banks (their 'reserve ratio') is assumed to be one-fifth. Generally speaking, the lower this proportion is, the greater the power of the banks to create money and, provided there is no run on them, the greater their profits.

Stage 2

Mr A's bank keeps a proportion, say one-fifth, in reserves and lends out the rest. It lends £800 to Ms B who buys with it a car from Corporation C. The latter deposits the £800 in its bank.

New money: £800

Eventually the total quantity of money created will approach the original deposit multiplied by the 'money creation muliplier' (which equals $\frac{1}{\text{the reserve ratio}}$, in this example, 5).

At each stage, as the money is lent, deposited and then lent again, there is an ever-diminishing ripple effect from the initial supposed injection of £1,000. By Stage 4 a total of £1,952 new money has been created.

Stage 3

Corporation C's bank keeps one-fifth in reserves, and lends out the rest, £640, to Corporation D, which buys a machine from Corporation E, which deposits the money in its bank.

New money: £640

The initial injection could have come from anywhere 'outside' the private economic system and still have the same effects. Thus it could perhaps come from digging up gold treasure in the back yard or, more realistically, from selling services to the state which pays for them by printing £1,000 more cash, or from selling something to a foreigner.

Stage 4

Corporation E's bank makes a further loan of £512, still keeping one-fifth in reserves.

New money: £512

and so on

Diagram 7.2   The Creation of 'New Money'

regulations. On the one hand governments typically lay down minimum levels of reserves which banks must hold, and on the other they can restrict the amount of credit banks can extend. At the same time, the 'central bank' in every country (the government's banker) – for instance the Federal Reserve System in the USA, the Bank of England in the UK, the Bundesbank in West Germany – usually operates as a 'lender of last resort': when money is short, certain accredited institutions are always guaranteed immediate access to its funds, thereby providing liquidity to the system and reducing the risk of a banking collapse.

The ability of governments to control bankers and the amount of money in circulation is considerably curtailed by the international nature of modern banking and the expansion of Eurocurrency deposits outside official jurisdictions. Yet it is clear that nation states remain intimately connected to money and to financial institutions. This is a chain that has existed for thousands of years, if not from the very beginnings of the history of money.

Many different goods, in frequent use but limited supply, with the right properties of portability, durability and divisibility, have been used as a medium of exchange; they include copper, iron, silver, gold, tobacco, cigarettes, cows, wampum (shells), rice and many more. But for small transactions, especially, small quantities of metal have always been advantageous. The minting of coins can be traced back as far as 800 BC, in the kingdom of Lydia, and possibly earlier. Imprinting a sovereign's image on the coin guaranteed its value and acceptability.

The participation of the state however, opened the door to using coinage to gain extra resources. Unable to raise sufficient taxes, the sovereign could order that coins be minted which did not contain the true weight of precious metal indicated on the face: the difference, 'seignorage', represented an effective tax on the people who accepted the coins in payment.

The difference between ancient and modern seignorage draws attention to the rise of paper money – sometimes called 'credit-money' – whose lineage in the western world goes back only as far as the seventeenth century. As with coinage, the nation state is intimately involved in its conception. Such money is essentially an I O U, normally issued by a government, but occasionally by private banks. Initially governments found that they could meet their expenses by issuing promises to pay in the future, which then circulated and were exchangeable for metallic money (predominantly silver). Their value was maintained to the same degree as people's confidence in the state. In fact, the chief gain for the state was simply an extension of seignorage, since the cost of printing the I O Us was negligible, yet their face value was accepted and they could be used in exchange. Generally, governments resorted to paper money in times of war when their expenditures were greatest and their ability to raise taxes through other channels limited. Despite the hyperinflations that resulted from extending the principle too far, such major historical events as the French and American revolutions and the American Civil War were facilitated by this taxing device.

In the modern era, credit-money forms the vast part of all the money in circulation. While it is true that central banks hold stocks of gold, as do some private wealth holders, almost all transactions are effected using either cash (coins or paper) or entries in banking records. The paper money remains the debt of the issuing government, and so states, the world over, remain bound up with money, influencing both its quantity and its quality. Especially this is true of the US government, which influences the quantities of dollars that flood the world's financial markets, giving it the opportunity to exercise a new international brand of seignorage.

Central banks and private companies keep reserves of foreign exchange, chiefly dollars, as a basis for their foreign trade and business operations. Since it costs the US government almost nothing to print dollar bills, while others, including non-Americans, are prepared to accept them in payment and hold them, it can acquire resources from all such dollar-holders just as if they were required to pay ordinary taxes passed by the US Senate. It can be justifiably claimed that a substantial part of the Vietnam war was financed in this way. US taxes throughout the war period were never substantially raised. Yet US citizens who held financial assets began to pay some of the war's costs when domestic inflation ate into their assets. Meanwhile foreign central banks paid through their gradual accumulation of reserves: about \$8 billion in the eight years prior to 1967, but \$58 billion from 1968 till 1974. These holdings were depreciated when the dollar was devalued in 1971 and again in 1973.

Such opportunities to suck resources from the holders of monetary assets is one of the principal reasons why states remain concerned with and intervene in the monetary system. Through inflation those assets are devalued and governments make an equivalent gain while citizens lose. (This 'inflation tax', only a variety of seignorage, is explained in more detail in Technical Annexe 14.B.) They also intervene, as they must if they are aiming to protect the capitalist economy from frequent financial crashes, to regulate the banking system. In addition they try to control the amount of money in circulation and thereby the total level of demand in the economy.

(iv) *Money, banks and the economy*

The neutrality of money
Although we showed (in the previous two subsections) that the amount and quality of money in circulation *is* affected by banks' behaviour and by the actions of nation states, a long-standing school of economic thought believes 'money is neutral', in that the monetary and the 'real' sectors of the economy are independent, and so any changes in the amount of money in circulation will affect only money variables, not the real ones. Thus, if the money supply were raised (or lowered) by 10 per cent, the neutralist school would

expect wages and prices all to rise (or fall) also by 10 per cent, leaving industrial output, employment and the 'real' wage unchanged.

If that were so, then we could safely ignore money as a kind of mirage and concentrate on analysing the real economy. Few people take such an extreme view. But it is very commonly argued that, though monetary changes or disturbances may have an effect in the short run (for example, a cut in the money supply could cause a recession), none the less its long-run effects are negligible.

This leads to many family squabbles among orthodox economists about how long exactly the 'long run' would be. Typically, the monetarists argue that it would not be very long, so that equilibrium can be restored within a few years at most, while many Keynesians believe the process will take longer, unless the government intervenes directly in the economy. Both schools, however, seem often to agree that monetary matters alone do not have lasting effects.

Keynes himself argued that such a conclusion was futile. Through his famous dictum, 'In the long run we are all dead', he ridiculed those who believed in the neutrality of money. If the capitalist economy is inherently subject to continual upheavals, it is probable that the long run, like tomorrow, will never come.

We shall look in more detail at the theory and problems of monetary policy in Chapters 14 and 15.

Money and disequilibrium

A monetary exchange economy is in a continual state of flux. If a person possesses a commodity, and intends to use it, then there is an equilibrium, a balance; the need is matched by its supply. Or if the commodity is not used but exchanged directly for another which is wanted instead, then again, after the exchange, there is equilibrium; for the purpose of the exchange has been realized and there is no reason to expect further change. But if, instead, the commodity is exchanged for money, then *while this money is being held* there is, in the very nature of the process, an element of uncertainty. There may be an expectation that the money may at some future time be spent, so as to realize the objective of the exchange. Yet until that happens there must be a 'disequilibrium' in the sense that the purpose has yet to be achieved.

Just as the physiological function of blood entails its movement around the body, so the economic function of money arises from the continuous flux of the circulation of commodities. Thus a monetary exchange economy has no overall moment of stable equilibrium, wherein economic activity comes to a stop, its purpose realized. This fact is linked closely to the idea of hoarding, introduced earlier in this chapter, as a possible source of market failure.

Banks and the industrial and commercial economy

Banks make their profits from dealing in money and are *related to industrial capitalists and to the economy generally.*

(a) Control over credit: all large companies rely on some credit, short- or long-term, to finance their activities, even if much of their investment spending comes from retained profits. Banks can enforce certain policies under threat of credit withdrawal. And they can divert their credit to areas and companies which they believe will be most profitable. But banks do not always have the upper hand. Companies may shop around for the most amenable banks, and there will be times when banks are left with available credit that is not required.

(b) Interlocking directorships: these provide a direct channel of influence, whereby the policies of industrial capitalists are decided upon at the same time as those of their bankers.

(c) 'Arrangements': these are the (often unwritten) relationships that can arise between banks and certain sections of industry, usually big business. For example, a large corporation may attain privileged access to credit from its banker in return for agreeing to continue borrowing and paying interest at times when money and credit are plentiful.

(d) Ownership of shares: investment banks buy and sell the securities of corporations from all over the world. In owning shares they play the dual role of industrial and financial capitalist. In some cases such banks are in effect conglomerate industrial holding companies – this is more common in Germany and Japan than in most other advanced capitalist countries. Some writers in the 'managerial' school hold that bank ownership does not convey much control over companies. Yet clearly if a bank holds more than a minimum of shares in any one company it can in principle exercise its power to install its own preferred managers.

(e) Interdependence: whatever short-term powers they attain, the banks are ultimately dependent for much of their profits on the success of industrial capitalists and their resulting ability to continue to pay interest out of their profits. If a bank becomes heavily exposed to the fortunes of a particular industry or corporation, its loans may become 'bad' should that corporation fail, and the bank itself would lose profits. This would add to the danger of a loss of confidence, a run on the bank and a financial panic. Conversely, if banks start to fail this would threaten to starve industry of credit and could precipitate a crisis in the 'real' economy. So the fortunes of the two sectors are intimately related.

(v) *The instability of banks*

Defaulting of an industrial borrower is far from the only thing which can precipitate a banking crash. It might be an arbitrary yet self-fulfilling lack of confidence in a bank's viability. More often, a crash is the end result of a speculative boom, whereby borrowers borrow spiralling quantities of money to chase an upward market, hoping always to repay the interest with capital gains from buying cheap and selling dear. When the speculative bubble bursts, the banks start to fail. Most recently one of the commonest reasons for fears about the financial security of banks has come from the threat of default by Third World government borrowers. But while stimuli may vary, the threat of instability is an inherent consequence of the nature of banking.

The central bank's function of lender of last resort is a tricky and hazardous one. There are occasions when emergency lending of this kind has been like throwing petrol rather than water on the flames of crisis. The intervention is sometimes seen by nervous depositors as simply a confirmation of the crisis and a run on the banks can be precipitated.

Also, too much state protection can encourage banks to be indiscriminate in their loans, with the danger of future losses. And there are some parts of the banking sector where governments exercise little sway – like a wild west town before the arrival of the federal marshal. Thus in the virtually unregulated Eurodollar market, banks respond to intense competition for business by making questionable loans, which makes the market menacingly fragile.

Ultimately the state cannot totally neutralize the inherent vulnerability of banks or completely protect banks from unfavourable winds which blow from the rest of the economy. Testimony to this fact is the continuous recurrence of bank failures which we discuss in Chapter 17 in the context of the 1980s era of crisis.

5. THE POWER OF BANKS

As long ago as 1912 the Pujo Committee in New York produced a report calling for restrictions on bankers' powers. In 1918 the Colwyn Committee in London reached similar conclusions. The most recurrent objections to the banking sector are that an oligopolistic handful of banks shares out the market and comes to predominate over industry. Thus, in their most extreme form, these objections imply that a few bankers decide the general direction of capitalist economies, where to expand resources, where to cut them, and so on.

These ideas closely parallel a theory propounded in 1910 by an Austrian Marxist economist, Rudolf Hilferding. He defined the concept 'finance capital' to depict a tendency for banks and industrial capital to become integrated, with the former exercising most of the power, through a combination of factors such as direct ownership and control, credit manipulation and interlocking directorships. Subsequent versions of the theory have supplemented this with the assertion that bankers have privileged access to governments, who have to rely on them for stable finances, and so they acquire undue influence on national policies. Orthodox economists also object to the restrictions on free competition characteristic of banking. And some leading representatives of the capitalist class on the Colwyn Committee argued that a socialist take-over would be much easier if all that was necessary to control the whole economy was to seize a few banks.

Most of these opinions are misleading. In reality, in capitalist economies, power is seldom monopolized by a small coterie of bankers; it is usually spread over a much wider section of the ruling class, including the owners and controllers of the large multinational corporations, and the capitalist national states. Periods when bankers have obtained disproportionate power among capitalists are conjunctural accidents of history rather than the reflection of any fundamental tendency in capitalism. Moreover, the expansion of the uncontrolled Eurocurrency banking networks, the introduction of new technology and of improved management techniques, and pressure from other non-bank financial institutions such as pension funds, suggest that, if anything, modern banking is becoming more, not less, competitive. Finally, in a remarkable new development, multinational industrial corporations are themselves entering the field: flushed with everyday monetary balances of billions of dollars, they have become dealers in the foreign exchange markets, lenders as well as borrowers. They have started to construct their own financial expertise. Although such dealings are still small compared to those of banks, it is by no means only the bankers that really call the tune.

Banks respond to the needs of capitalists by providing finance. They also help to meet certain genuine, if socially created, requirements of some workers, by providing normally secure depositories for their money, opportunities to save for the future, and so on. Bankers themselves claim that in doing this they are meeting human needs.

The claim does not stand up well under scrutiny. From the point of view of socialists who hold high the values of democracy, the objection to 'money trusts' is that it is preposterous for a small number of unelected and unaccountable people, almost always men, to decide the fate of millions through their strategies to make as much profit as possible.

Even if 'finance capital' and allied ideas are less relevant in the present era, both the internationally oriented banks and the multinational companies deal with astronomically vast sums of money, reflecting and measuring the enormous value of commodities being produced and traded in all sectors of the economy. Yet the activities they promote are frequently quite contrary to the wishes and needs of the majority of populations.

So in the banking world there can be a vast chasm between the imperatives of profit maximization which lead bankers to put their money into 'safe' and profitable areas, and the objective of meeting human needs. Power without accountability is exercised on a gigantic scale.

But it is misleading to see bankers as disproportionately guilty of this. They operate according to the rules of a profit system which is much wider than the banks. It is that system as a whole, rather than just a few monsters of finance, which is responsible for the widespread failure to meet human needs.

PART THREE

WORKERS UNDER CAPITALISM

CHAPTER 8

Workers and the Standard of Living

Human society, like any organism, survives by being able continuously to reproduce itself: this demands mechanisms to ensure survival both from day to day and from generation to generation. But when human society is structured into different classes, as it is in capitalism, then human beings reproduce themselves both as members of the species and also as members of a class. So what is continually re-created is not only physical – the human body – but also social – the class relations which those bodies bear to each other.

In Part Two we saw how, through the circuit of production and exchange of commodities, capitalists reproduced themselves not only as human beings but also as capitalists. That process entails the obverse one: that those who are employed by the capitalists to produce profits reproduce themselves also both as human beings and as workers. Now in Part Three, therefore, we re-examine the process largely from the standpoint of its effects on the lives of workers: in this chapter their households and families, wages, consumption and experience of life and work; and in the next, what it is that conditions the prevailing ideas about the capitalist system.

I. THE REPRODUCTION OF LABOUR-POWER

(i) *The family and the sexual division of labour*

The labour-power of workers is not on the whole produced through a capitalist process. Hence we cannot make the same economic assumptions and use the same analysis as when looking at the production of other commodities.

Most human beings are produced within a family. This institution existed long before the age of capitalism, but although its form and functions have undergone changes in most countries, it survives. Divorce, single-parent households and more communal forms of household have all been increasing. But marriage and remarriage remain widespread, and the family in which a male/female couple lives and raises children in a single unit is still the predominant social unit. For example, in 1980 in the UK, married couples with or without children made up 67 per cent of all households, and many of those in the remainder will have spent portions of their lives in a traditional family.

Within the family, and between unpaid and paid work, there is a clear sexual division of labour between men and women. It is neither an arbitrary nor an equal division but reflects the systematic existence of patriarchy, which may be seen clearly in the dominance of men in both public and private life. Politicians, managers of firms large and small, people in high-status and power-giving jobs everywhere, are almost always male.

The present sexual division of labour differs from many pre-capitalist societies. In European peasant or artisan households before the Industrial Revolution there was much less distinction between housework and the other family tasks.

The spread of industrial capitalism and the factory system throughout Europe ultimately transformed the sexual division of labour. In early factories women as well as men were employed in large numbers though women's wages were usually less than men's and their working conditions often much worse – a situation repeated in many Third World countries today. It was thought by some (for example, by Marx's collaborator Friedrich Engels) that eventually capitalists, in seeking to reduce their wage costs, would draw all women into the wage-labour force, thus breaking down the sexual division of labour altogether and ending the domestic subjugation of women and the bourgeois family.

This did not happen. For a start, the family was the essential means whereby capitalists could preserve and transmit their wealth across generations without its being dispersed on death. But neither did the property-less working-class family disappear. Hideous working conditions provoked the introduction of Britain's Factory Acts (p. 41), limiting the number of hours which women and children were permitted to work and banning them from certain occupations. Their employment became less profitable.

On top of this, there gradually developed the institution of the 'family wage' which has informed the wage bargaining of men and labour-force participation of women ever since. The principle behind it is that men need to be paid a wage large enough to support them and their families. The effect of this on the course of total wages over time is debatable. But it is certain that the family wage principle was economically debilitating for single women, who were thereby destined for poverty or compelled to seek marriage for economic reasons given the low wages and limited opportunities for women workers.

(ii) *Domestic labour*

The 'family wage' is the cornerstone supporting the current sexual division of labour, whereby men do wage work while women perform domestic labour. In fact there is a substantial proportion of families where the man's wage is not enough on its own and needs to be supplemented by the woman's, and a substantial proportion of women who do not have a man's wage to support them. Yet the idea has persisted: men ought to be paid a wage high enough to support a family, and women ought therefore to do the domestic labour. As a result most wage-working women at present finish up doing a double-day's work – paid employment and housework.

From the point of view of official statistics domestic labour does not figure as a part of the economy, unless it is performed for money, as in the case of a hired home-help. Thus, when figures are quoted for national output – such as Gross National Product (Technical Annexe 14.C) – this measure makes a large part of women's productive activity invisible. But it cannot be omitted from an analysis of the profit system – both because domestic labour bears a relation to the capitalist processes we are considering in this book, and because it has a direct bearing on the welfare of working people.

From the most general point of view there is no difference between domestic labour, wage labour and labour in pre-capitalist societies: all consist of humans transforming something to produce useful objects or services. These types of labour, however, do differ as soon as we specify the social relationships under which they are carried out.

(a) Domestic labour is unpaid, unlike wage labour. Its purpose is to produce useful things (e.g. a cleaner house, cooked food, child care) as part of a loosely defined emotional and social relationship; whereas with wage labour the aim is above all to gain the wage through an exchange relationship with a capitalist.

(b) Domestic labour time is not sharply delineated by the clock as is wage labour. The distinction between working and non-working time is blurred, the worker can switch activities several times in an hour, and it is impossible to say whether some activities are leisure or work, pleasure or duty (e.g. preparing a meal for guests).

(c) Relatedly, the distinction between production and consumption is also blurred. For wage workers, time at work is mainly production time, and consumption takes place when the wages are spent. For domestic workers the same activity can often be both production and consumption (e.g. tending flowers in the garden).

(d) Compared with wage work, domestic labour usually is subject to a more diffuse form of control. People who sell commodities are subject to the impersonal coercive discipline of the market – if they work less they can expect to receive less income. Those who work for wages are subject to capitalist workplace disciplines and controls. The pressures and controls on unpaid domestic labourers are more personal, though for many that does not mean less oppressive. Many houseworkers, however, can control their own pace of work, on the basis of their self-motivation. This in turn derives from the feeling of duty to themselves and other members of the household, supplemented to a greater or lesser extent by created images of what constitutes good housework.

(e) Associated with this lack of outside direct control, there has been no tendency to pursue a detailed division of labour, as is found in many areas of wage work. Domestic labour processes continue to involve a variety of activities, even if many are unskilled and tedious.

(f) Finally, domestic labour is, above all, a private activity – simply because it takes place in a private area, the home. Thus although there are millions of such workers doing the same job, they do not work alongside each other and they come into social contact at only a few stages of the activity – in the shops or at the launderette.

All these characteristics show that domestic labour is not in itself a capitalist process; it has a different identifying fingerprint. But, from the point of view of capitalism, domestic labour in the family performs an essential function; it reproduces the key commodity, labour-power. In the sexual reproduction of the species, in the feeding, clothing, rearing and socialization of children, and in housework and the preparation of meals, the activities of the home all serve to make available replenished and expanded supplies of potential workers, who are willing and economically compelled to sell their labour-power. Hence it is appropriate to regard domestic labour within the family as an enclave of non-capitalist relationships within a predominantly capitalist system.

The modern household technologies such as washing machines, wash-and-wear clothing, vacuum cleaners and so on, together with the availability of fast foods, have enabled capitalists to appropriate on a vast scale activities traditionally done by housewives and make a profit out of them. In addition, some tasks have been socialized in another way: they have been taken over by the state. Across the advanced capitalist world, the state had taken over the basic educating of children by the end of the last century, and has considerably extended its educational activities since then. Similarly, the care of the old or ill, traditionally domestic labour, is often now undertaken by private profit-making or welfare state institutions.

Many functions involved in the reproduction of labour-power however, remain at present 'unsocialized', in the realm of the non-capitalist family. It seems inconceivable that all of them could be taken over and done for profit because there are obstacles in the very nature of the work. It combines the roles of cook, nurse, psychiatrist, servant, friend, parent, lover. It is scarcely possible to subject this process to a capitalist rationalization involving a division of labour. It contains, for good or ill, some obstinate kernel of humanity which refuses to be turned into a mere impersonal exchange relation.

(iii) *Women's oppression*

A sexual division of labour which means that female wage workers are paid substantially less than males, while in addition they bear the prime responsibility for domestic labour, leaves most working-class women no alternative but relative poverty or dependency. This is the economic side of their oppression. Would it be possible for capitalism to dispense with patriarchy? Is capitalism the ultimate source of the oppression of women?

It is clear that patriarchy existed in previous models of production and there is no necessary reason why it would vanish if the capitalist system ended. Nor can one deduce from the abstract characteristics of capitalism, which we set out in previous chapters, that patriarchy must exist as long as capitalist class oppression remains.

On the other hand, there are mechanisms within capitalism which operate to perpetuate sexual inequality. Employers make use of patriarchal relations and give specific characteristics to women's oppression today. Sexual inequality helps to generate divisions and reduce solidarity within the working class. This is of obvious benefit to capitalists in the class struggle.

In addition, sexual divisions of labour in wage work and in the home mutually reinforce each other. Women tend to be directed towards a relatively small range of occupations – partly by an ideology of what constitutes women's work, partly by protective male prejudices which keep them from doing traditional men's jobs. The assumption that women should take primary responsibility for rearing children means that the careers of women wage workers are interrupted often for several years, sometimes indefinitely. That, as we saw in Chapter 5, in turn means a lack of access to the security of internal labour markets, and opportunities for gaining skills. Their consequent relatively low wages serve to perpetuate their subordinate position in the home. The inequality is overlaid and yet more reinforced by home-based patriarchy, limiting the amount of housework done by men even when their wives are wage workers too, thus producing the phenomenon of the double-day's work.

Patriarchy and capitalism have become so intertwined that it is hard to imagine a social change which is profound enough to eliminate sexual oppression leaving capitalist exploitation intact. Patriarchy may not be the original offspring of capitalism; but it has become its foster child.

2. STANDARDS OF LIVING

The most important single determinant of workers' material prosperity or poverty is the wage at which they are able to sell their labour-power. But although the wage level measures how many commodities workers can buy, the 'standard of living' must be interpreted in a wider sense if workers' experiences in modern capitalism are to be properly evaluated. Changing real wage rates are only one aspect of a whole picture, which includes the quality of both the material, cultural and spiritual life which can be pursued during 'free' time, as well as the satisfactions and dissatisfactions of working life.

Economic historians have long debated whether the world's first industrial revolution, beginning at the end of the eighteenth century in England, brought with it decreasing or increasing real wages. But as one of the participants in that debate, the historian E. P. Thompson, has remarked, whether wages rose or fell slightly is not the key issue. For most working people the changes wrought in traditional life patterns were 'necessarily painful'. Even though there may have been a small rise in real wages between 1780 and 1840,

any evaluation of the quality of life must entail an assessment of the total life-experience, the manifold satisfactions or deprivations, cultural as well as material, of the people concerned. From such a standpoint, the older 'cataclysmic' view of the Industrial Revolution must still be accepted. During the years between 1780 and 1840 the people of Britain suffered an experience of immiseration ... [This] came upon them in a hundred different forms; for the field labourer, the loss of his common rights and the vestiges of village democracy; for the artisan, the loss of his craftsman's status; for the weaver, the loss of livelihood and of independence; for the child, the loss of work and play in the home; for many groups of workers whose real earnings improved, the loss of security, leisure and the deterioration of the urban environment. (*The Making of the English Working Class*, pp. 444–5)

In this section we will apply E. P. Thompson's approach to various different economic aspects of life in modern capitalist economies as they affect the 'total life-experience' of workers.

(i) *Real wages and material consumption*

The 'real wage' constitutes the most conventional measure of a worker's standard of living. It is defined as the nominal wage rate divided by the consumer price index, so that a rise in real wages means that the quantity of commodities bought with the wage can be increased. Table 8.1 illustrates, for a selection of advanced capitalist countries, how real wages have indeed risen over a long period through the twentieth century.

In interpreting the table, it is important to remember the dangers of misusing statistics. In this case, the data for earlier years may be less reliable, and in addition it is virtually impossible to make a sound comparison between countries as each derives its basic information in its own way, so that the average wage may refer to a different group of workers in each country. None the less the overriding rising trend is clear, and indeed shows

Table 8.1   Trends in Real Wages, 1929–67

	1929	1948	1967
Belgium	100	103	187
Canada	100	156	256
Italy	100	135	238
UK	100	114	174
USA	100	154	242

Source: International Labour Office, *Yearbook of Labour Statistics*, ILO, Geneva, various issues

up in all advanced capitalist economies where the data are available. As a result, most workers, as well as those in other social classes, can enjoy considerably higher material consumption levels than their forebears. This means not only higher consumption of products which workers have always bought but also (not shown in the bare statistics of Table 8.1) of many new products which were previously unavailable – televisions, digital clocks, washing machines, package holidays and so on.

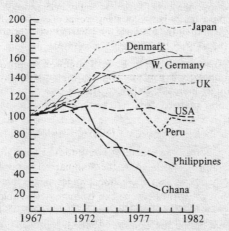

Diagram 8.1   Indices of Real Wages, 1967–82

Source: International Labour Office, *Yearbook of Labour Statistics*, ILO Geneva, various issues

So in real terms workers in developed capitalist societies can be argued to have derived some benefit from modern technology; they are better off in the twentieth century than in the nineteenth and the improvement has persisted. None the less this improvement is by no means guaranteed as an invariable feature of life under capitalism. In Diagram 8.1 we show the path of real wages for eight countries over a recent fifteen-year period. The years 1967 to 1982 cover a time when capitalism has been faltering, compared to the success story of the post-war boom. The chart shows that in some countries real wages stopped increasing and began to decrease, particularly in the USA. In other cases real wages continued to rise, though more slowly (for those who retained their jobs). The falling real wages in Ghana, the Philippines, and for much of the time in Peru, show how some workers in the Third World fared in this period. In fact, there was a variety of outcomes in the Third World, with real wages rising in some countries and falling very sharply in others.

Information on real wages is incomplete unless account is taken of the time which it takes to earn the wage. For almost all men and for the majority of women of working age, life is divided into two spheres of activity: a work life where the wage is earned, and a private life. For most people, working for a capitalist employer is not in itself rewarding (apart from the wage) so their lives are affected by how their total time is divided between the two spheres. An additional sign of increasing material prosperity in advanced capitalist countries is that for full-time wage workers 'private' time has gradually increased.

The average length of the working week has been considerably reduced in the course of this century. In France, for example, manufacturing workers worked on average 48 hours a week in 1929, but only 39.5 hours a week in 1982. In addition, people tend to start work later and retire earlier in life and to have longer holidays. Balanced against this is the modern tendency for more and more married women to go to wage work, whereas previously they stayed at home. But for men the wage is earned in less time than before, though increased travelling time and rush-hour stress may offset this.

(ii) *Collective consumption and cash benefits*

Collective goods and services which are provided free or subsidized by the state constitute a second important source of material welfare for workers. These include education, health, various municipal services and so on. In addition, old people and other groups can expect a cash income from the state, which is quite separate from earned wages.

There is no doubt that the standards of provision of these benefits for workers in all the developed capitalist economies (but not in most Third World countries) have improved over the long term. There have been both 'intensive' gains, where the level of provision rises for each person (for example, a rise in pensions), and 'extensive' gains, where services or goods are made available to a wider range or where new services are provided. Thus education has been vastly expanded since the end of the nineteenth century, so that only a small proportion of children fails to become literate, greater numbers have the opportunity of higher education, and so on. Meanwhile with the improvement of collectively provided health services and advancing medical knowledge many diseases like smallpox and tuberculosis have been controlled; and though other scourges, such as cancer and heart disease, have increased, the life expectancy of working people is greater now than at the turn of the century. Even in the short space of eighteen years between 1965 and 1983, men's life expectancy in the industrialized countries rose from 68 to 72 and women's from 74 to 79.

It is difficult, however, if not impossible, to assess exactly how much state welfare spending as a whole has contributed to an improved standard of living over the long term, and whether the improvement has continued during the last few decades. One approach might be to look at the level of these expenditures in relation to national income; this ratio, as we shall see in detail in Chapter 11, has been rising. But the increase does not necessarily mean that people's needs for collective goods and services or cash benefits are being better satisfied: changing total expenditure may not indicate changing output of needed goods and services.

Differences between the two may arise for three main reasons: (a) the size and the structure of the population may change – for example, if there are more old people, separated from their families, there is a greater need for some health and social services; (b) costs per unit of service tend to rise in public service industries because they tend to be particularly labour intensive; (c) rising expenditure may not deal with basic needs newly created by the recent development of capitalism – for example, as the roads become more congested, there arises the need for more traffic control and safety measures.

(iii) *Economic security and unemployment*

Associated with the long-term expansion of collective consumption is the rise in the principle of collective security. In the advanced capitalist countries insurance against individual disasters such as sickness, disability and unemployment has tended to improve along with wages. Thus the modern unemployed worker is not faced by starvation but can normally rely on a minimum subsistence income from the state. In the 1950s and 1960s many also thought that the risk of unemployment had been all but eradicated by the success of the post-war capitalist boom; the 1970s dispelled that myth and the chances of being unemployed rose again to approach the levels of the 1930s. Indeed, unemployment is the most tangible way in which some workers experience the crises and stagnations that periodically beset capitalist economies. The national rate rose to 10 per cent or more in most countries and for certain groups within each country the risk was far greater. In Los Angeles, for example, in 1984, over half the black population was out of a job. Although some privileged workers are never likely to know unemployment, others experience long periods of it, with detrimental effects on physical and mental health, and many who still have wage work to go to, are haunted by its threat.

(iv) *Poverty amidst plenty*

To be in 'poverty' means having insufficient resources to meet even basic needs. In the underdeveloped countries of the world, a huge proportion of the population is in this sense poor. Life is a continual struggle for survival and available resources are severely limited. In the advanced countries it might be imagined that the long-term substantial rise in real wages and state welfare provision would have eliminated poverty. Yet a trip through many western capital cities would be enough to show how staggering riches can coexist with the most glaring poverty.

In 1959 an official investigation shocked many people, revealing that in the USA, the richest and most powerful country in the world, there were 39.5 million people in poverty, some 22 per cent of the population. President Kennedy, and subsequently President Johnson, pledged a drive to remove all poverty by 1976. Diagram 8.2, which is also derived from official estimates, shows that this drive failed. Having fallen somewhat, the numbers of the poor began to rise again after 1979 (when economic depression set in), and by 1983 they had reached 35.3 million, about 15 per cent of the population.

These figures show that even according to the official estimates there remains a major poverty 'problem'. But the reality of poverty is much more complex than Diagram 8.2 suggests. To grasp it we have first to define what is meant by 'basic needs'. The official US estimates employ the absolute subsistence approach. A team of experts calculated in 1959 the cost of those basic food requirements necessary to keep a household alive and reasonably healthy, and multiplied up by a number to cover non-food physical requirements (housing and so on).

This absolute subsistence approach, however, makes the strange assumption that only physiological needs can be counted as 'basic'. But the non-physical needs to relate to other people in society can be just as pressing and basic as the need to have food. For example, most people

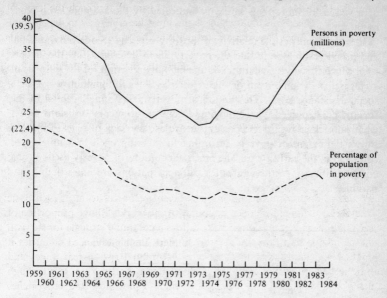

Diagram 8.2   US Poverty

Source: US Department of Commerce, Bureau of the Census, *Statistical Abstract of the United States*, 1984, 1986, Washington DC

would consider it a sign of poverty if someone could not afford the bus fare to visit nearby friends and relatives occasionally, even if not starving or homeless.

An alternative, more objective definition and understanding of poverty must start from the premise that there is a basic need for all individuals to be able to participate, at least in some minimal way, in society, and hence that some socially created needs ought to be included in the poverty criterion. One such definition has been proposed by the British social scientist Peter Townsend, through the use of the concept 'relative deprivation'. This involves looking at a large number of activities which people in society normally participate in, and examining how far those on low incomes are able to participate. When a sufficient number of such activities is impossible for a family, because it cannot afford them, it may objectively be regarded as poor, that is, suffering from relative deprivation – even if it has enough resources to prevent starvation and physical ill-health. The results of Townsend's own study and survey of the UK showed that 22 per cent of the population in 1969 were poor in the sense of relatively deprived, a lot more than would be indicated by the absolute subsistence method.

In some countries the relativity of poverty is partly recognized in official and private estimates, in that the poverty line is determined by the income level which the government uses as an eligibility criterion for the purpose of giving relief in some form or other (such as a legal minimum wage, or a social assistance level). This notion of poverty takes some account of the socially created needs, since to some extent governments' decisions reflect what politicians regard as poor and hence as deserving of relief. Table 8.2 shows the extent of poverty according to this approach in a number of countries in the early 1970s. The precise definitions of poverty used in each country differed, so the figures for different nations are not strictly comparable.

Table 8.2   Relative Poverty in the early 1970s

		Percentage of population below poverty line
Official estimates	Australia	8.2
	Canada	15.1
	UK	13.2
	USA	11.9
Private estimates	Belgium	14.4
	Eire	24.0
	France	15.0 to 20.0

Source: OECD, 'Public Expenditure on Income-Maintenance Programmes', *Studies in Resource Allocation*, no. 3, OECD, Paris, July 1976

Such evidence makes it clear that, even in the advanced capitalist countries at the end of the post-war boom, perhaps the most successful period that capitalism has ever gone through, there are substantial numbers of people whose basic needs remain unsatisfied.

Major inequality, therefore, seems to be inseparable from capitalism. Its primary source is the inequality inherent in the minority ownership and control of the means of production: a proportion of the total income every year (some 20 per cent in many countries in the 1970s, though more in earlier periods) accrues as profits to a very small proportion of the total population. In addition there is chronic unevenness in the rewards of workers. We saw in Chapter 5 how capitalist labour markets have been segmented, relegating certain sectors of the workforce to the secondary markets where incomes are already low.

Poverty, therefore, is worse for those who are imprisoned in these secondary labour markets. In the USA many writers have observed a 'feminization of poverty'. And of the millions of officially poor inhabitants of that fabulously wealthy country a disproportionately large number are of racial or national minorities. These features of US poverty are illustrated in Table 8.3.

Table 8.3 Percentage of US Population below Official Poverty Level by Sex, Race and National Origin, 1983

	White	Black	Spanish origin
Both sexes	12.1	35.7	28.4
Male	10.7	32.4	26.5
Female	13.5	38.6	30.2

Source: US Department of Commerce, Bureau of the Census, *Characteristics of the Population below the Poverty Level, 1983*, series P-60, no. 147, Washington DC, 1983

The various sources of inequality in advanced capitalist economies, which allow such vast numbers of people to remain in poverty, are so resistant to change because they are not accidental: they all reflect factors which are either in principle essential to or in practice important to the functioning of the profit system. This is why poverty has not been washed away by the tide of plenty.

(v) *Pollution*

More production has brought more pollution in its wake – and this also affects the standard of living. Factories propel their waste products into the rivers and seas and discharge dirty smoke into the air; automobiles expel exhaust gases, including unspent hydrocarbons, into the atmosphere at an increasing rate and disturb the local environment with their noise; jet aeroplanes roar overhead and pollute the stratosphere; farmers manipulate their land with fertilizers, pesticides and irrigation projects, often with unforeseen consequences on life elsewhere; nuclear power plants deposit radioactive waste in the sea; and so on.

The liberal dispersal of waste has, first of all, immediate unpleasant effects on surrounding environments and the people who live in them. Perhaps more alarming, however, are the long-term effects of pollution. Modern technology, which demands increasing energy from fossil and nuclear fuels and which increasingly manipulates nature, has a cumulative disturbing effect on the environmental balance that is as yet only partly understood. For example, the level of carbon dioxide (CO_2) in the atmosphere has risen from about 290 ppm (parts per million) in 1870 to 335 ppm in 1978. It is feared that as this goes further it will lead, through a 'greenhouse' effect, to the earth's atmosphere warming up with possibly catastrophic climatic consequences. Meanwhile, the increased burning of coal, gas and oil generates sulphur oxides and oxides of nitrogen which react in the atmosphere to form sulphuric and nitric acids. The supposedly refreshing rain and snow then bring acid death to the fish of freshwater lakes, as has been substantiated in Sweden, Norway and the USA. A third example is pollution from the heavy application of long-lived pesticides such as DDT. Not only are these effects long-lasting – in some cases they are irreversible.

There are two crucial economic aspects to the pollution problems which affect the issues we are tackling in this chapter. The first is the ignorance of humans about their transactions with nature. Despite increasing knowledge of the dangers of waste disposal it is still difficult to quantify them or to prove them beyond doubt. Ecological systems are wondrous in their complexity but alarming in their vulnerability to interventions.

The second aspect is the fact that pollution does not directly affect the agent that is actually causing it. The disposal of waste products is costly, and if a capitalist firm is obliged to bear this cost, it will have to take it into account in attempting to maximize its profits. There is therefore an incentive to keep pollution down to a minimum (for example, by recycling waste or introducing technical improvement) just as there is to minimize all other costs. The problem arises when the cost of the waste disposal is not borne by the firm – when the 'social cost' is greater than the 'private cost'. For example, if waste is discharged into a river the 'private cost' is no more than the expenditure required to convey it there whereas the 'social cost' includes the losses in production and general amenities for the people and companies that use the river downstream. There is no incentive to cut back wastes in order to reduce somebody else's costs. When the full social costs of pollution are unknown, perhaps because its impact takes effect only in the long term, the potential for expanding pollution is even greater.

We can extend this argument to classes, since just as the 'good' things of the capitalist world are very unequally distributed, so also are the 'bad'. Working-class and poor people tend to suffer the most. The rich capitalist can buy a house in a quiet and clean neighbourhood, which working people on ordinary wages cannot afford.

Even with the most imaginative approach and the best will, it would not be possible to recycle or eliminate all waste by-products of modern production processes. To solve the problem would be to ensure that decisions about recycling and waste disposal were taken rationally with a full consideration of the consequences and benefits for the whole of society.

Broadly speaking there are two proposed approaches to finding a solution. According to sections of the ecology movement, the underlying problem is that people are unaware of the dangers of pollution and expand their demands for commodities blind to the environmental consequences of producing them. The answer is to educate the public, to persuade people to accept lower growth rates and to seek political power in order to impose pollution controls where necessary. This approach unfortunately tends to ignore the fact that as long as capitalist companies are making profit from pollution, no amount of education and persuasion are liable to have much influence.

According instead to orthodox economics, the solution lies in the elimination of common property resources. Rivers, they say, get polluted because they are not owned by anyone who can charge the polluter; oceans and lakes are depleted of fish because there is no private owner to rationalize and preserve fish stocks. The solution, therefore, is to 'privatize' all resources and allow the market to ensure that waste decisions are taken rationally (since private costs will now be the same as social costs).

This would be to 'solve' a part of the problem by robbing the non-polluters of their existing rights of access to natural resources. If beaches, for example, were to be privatized in the supposed interests of pollution control, the real effect would be to restrict access to those who could afford to pay. As to the oceans themselves, let alone the upper atmosphere, the delineation of property rights seems to go beyond the ingenuity even of capitalism.

A third proposed solution is state intervention to regulate waste disposal, and prevent excessive pollution where it can be identified. To a limited extent this has occurred. But it is obstructed by the fact that those responsible for much of the pollution dominate political institutions in capitalist countries. Strong laws are difficult to pass and even harder to enforce. The film *Silkwood* provides an instructive if chilling account of the fate of workers who attempted to expose the radioactive contamination produced by a US nuclear-waste processing firm.

The legislative approach is complicated by the increasing interrelatedness of production and its international nature. State control will be futile as long as there is no international state to impose constraints on international capitalism, and incomplete knowledge to identify the culprits. It would therefore seem very unlikely that pollution can be definitely controlled under a predominantly capitalist system.

Hence in assessing the effects of capitalist relations on the living standards of working people, we note that even if most workers have more commodities than in earlier times, they must live in increasingly contaminated conditions, with no real prospect of a reversal of this trend. Moreover, some of the increase in real wages is specifically spent on countering the effects of pollution (for instance, soundproofing of houses near airports or noisy roads). In the longer run pollution may reduce real wages by raising the prices of commodities such as clean water and uncontaminated food.

There is reason to believe that in many Third World countries some forms of industrial pollution are already worse than in developed ones. This is because countries short of employment opportunities and foreign exchange have competed to attract foreign capital investment partly through offering to capitalists a minimum of state regulation of pollution or work safety standards.

(vi) *Consumption and needs*

It is implicit in most discussions of workers' standards of living under capitalism that rising levels of real income and consumption naturally mean rising levels of satisfaction. Greater quantity of consumption is taken to indicate better 'quality' of consumption.

To evaluate this assumption is very difficult because of the subjective nature of satisfaction. But it is a matter of common observation, sometimes even backed up by a bit of pseudo-social science, that higher consumption standards in the advanced countries have brought neither greater general happiness nor material satiety.

If this is true, it would seem to go against an old theory propounded by economists to explain how much consumers demanded of which commodities – the 'law of diminishing marginal utility'. This law asserts that the more you consume of a particular thing, the more 'satiated' you become and hence the less satisfaction you would get from an extra unit of it: one ice cream is 'delicious', a second may be 'welcome', a third you can take or leave but a fourth makes you sick. The law implies that as people get more and more commodities they must gradually approach satiation. Indeed this is a problem which periodically alarms capitalists who manufacture widely consumed commodities like motor cars. None the less there is in fact little sign of any letting up in people's demands for more commodities, even among the especially well-off. Despite rising consumption many people, it seems, 'can't get no satisfaction'.

The sociologist and psychoanalyst Erich Fromm (1900–80) argued that there are two opposite ways of consuming things, just as there are two ways of participating in most of life's processes: an active and a passive way. To consume actively one must relate in a positive and rational way to the thing that is being consumed, aware of its real properties and how they relate to one's own needs. By contrast, to consume passively is to be a receptacle of pressures emanating from some external source. Consuming food in an active way, for example, involves an awareness of its taste and nutritional content; eating in a passive, 'alienated' way means caring neither for taste nor nutrition but rather for image or the mere reduction of hunger. Fromm argues that passive consumption processes, which tend to be the norm in modern capitalism, do not satisfy the real needs of human individuals.

That an image can be more important than intrinsic usefulness is partly the outcome of bombardment by advertising for commodities like cigarettes, cars and drinks. In addition it may be reinforced by the prevalence of private ownership of possessions and property, and with the universality of monetary exchange society comes to be dominated by its values, both in practice and in people's perceptions. A thing's worth is thus primarily what it cost or what it will fetch on the market, and only secondarily what its usefulness to humans is. The worth of human beings is assessed more in terms of what they have than what they are or what they do.

This is the psychological basis for Veblen's concept of 'conspicuous consumption' (p. 65). Consumption expenditure is influenced by the desire to demonstrate an image of success to others. A wealthy bank builds the tallest tower block in town, a firm sends its managers around in Rolls Royces and other flashy cars, to convince their customers of their success, and individuals consume conspicuously to raise their status in the eyes of the community. This behaviour is made possible and effective by the inequality in the levels of workers' incomes. Some can demonstrate their 'success' in capitalist life by displaying expressions of their relatively high income. The obverse side is a degree of envy on the part of those not able to afford so many possessions. Some advertisements openly exploit this envy.

Moreover, most consumption is totally separated from the production processes involved in making the commodities consumed. Wage workers may have some knowledge of the processes involved in their own particular jobs, but when they spend their wages they do not need to know how the commodities are made and may, therefore, be more willing passively to accept goods which do not really meet their needs.

The failure of passive consumption to satisfy real needs may provoke people to want more. For instance, an advertising campaign promotes ownership of a particular car as an image of sexual fulfilment; a purchaser who fails to satisfy subconscious sexual needs then discards it in favour of another bigger, sleeker, faster one.

Thus the 'law of diminishing marginal utility' does not hold over the long term and there is no approach to satiation; and it is hardly surprising that many people do not perceive themselves to be happier with more commodities than before. Fromm's speculations strike at the heart of the conventional economic assumption that 'more is better than less'. They imply that economists, in evaluating standards of living, should go beyond the quantities of commodities purchased to look at the quality of the consumption process itself. Yet there is little research on this topic – most mainstream economists would consider it laughably 'unscientific'.

(vii) *Work and needs*

A final factor upon which the standard of life also depends is the nature, content and conditions of work. The conventional economic assumption is that work constitutes a 'disutility' so that 'less work is better than more'. Most people like not to be completely idle, but they would certainly prefer to work less than they do, providing they do not have to sacrifice wages.

Although this assumption may appear valid for the majority of working people, attitudes to work can differ extremely. Many people would be distressed and even psychologically disturbed if they were deprived of the opportunity to work. No doubt this depends not only on the kind of individual concerned, but also on the kind of work, on whether it can be satisfying. In creative work, humans operate on nature with a conscious purpose and with skill. They develop their potentialities, their powers of co-operation with each other, their intellect, their sense of beauty, their own individuality. There is, in brief, a close connection between creative work and human progress.

By contrast most work in modern capitalism is not creative but highly 'alienating'. Workers typically care in the end for nothing except their wages and their physical conditions at work, because there is usually no opportunity in the workplace to care for anything else.

This results from two tendencies which we identified in Chapter 3, describing the production process: the attempt by capitalists to treat workers as if they were machines (which is the consequence of taking complete control of the detailed production process), and the trend of technological and organizational advance to replace workers by machines.

If a job that previously required the use of some judgement or dexterity is analysed and split up into separate tasks, less skill is required. This was the inevitable result of the division of labour even before the onset of mechanization. In the twentieth century it was the conscious intention of Taylorism as well as of such technological advance.

But Taylorism is not the only philosophy of capitalist management, and so de-skilling, though widespread, is not an essential or inevitable development. It is an aspect of the capitalists' search for greater control, but they do not always try to achieve 100 per cent control over the detailed actions of workers. Moreover, new technologies create a need for new skills even as they destroy the basis for old ones.

Often, therefore, the consequence is a polarization of skills. The case of numerically controlled machine tools exemplifies this process. The skilled machinist is replaced by an unskilled operator and a computer, but there is then a need for computer-trained technicians to program the new machines. These new technicians occupy a privileged position among workers. But in the long run they are also de-skilled, as new equipment is designed with self-programming capabilities. The result is a small minority of graduate-level, highly skilled, workers in the design rooms while other people's jobs have become routine.

Thus, to be set against the vast increases in productivity that have been achieved in the last few centuries, and the consequential increases in material standards for those in the developed world, are the often degrading consequences of the capitalist control of technology and of work organization for workers' welfare at work.

Whether the intrinsic content of work is satisfying or not, the standard of living of workers is also affected by the conditions under which they have to work – the physical environment, the degree of danger, the extent of work-related illnesses and disabilities. Capitalists have periodically been sensitive to demands for improvements in health and safety at work; it is hard to justify death and injury in the pursuit of profit. Often under pressure from trade unions or social reformers, governments have introduced laws to improve health and safety at work and advanced countries have state safety and health administrations which monitor and enforce them. Since the nineteenth century there has been an enormous decline in the relative number of work-related accidents and deaths.

Partly this is because conditions have improved, partly because the most accident-ridden industries have relatively declined in importance, partly perhaps because of the increasing dominance of large firms which tend to enforce safety regulations more rigorously. Some work-related diseases are now better understood, though much less is known about others arising with new technologies (especially nuclear technology). But in many parts of the Third World safety and health standards at work remain at nineteenth-century levels. Inter-capitalist competition can, in the absence of rigorously enforced codes, lead to lower safety standards as a way of saving on costs. This is especially true of the more labour-intensive work processes which are not machine-paced.

In modern times the capitalist process has reproduced those who work within it, both in a physical and in a social sense. Such a complex process cannot be summarized in a few words. But even in the most advanced countries, the evidence of rising wage and consumption levels must be set against many less beneficial effects of capitalism on workers' lives: the persistence of sexual, racial and interpersonal inequalities and of mass poverty, the failure to create security of employment, the deterioration of the environment and the degradation of the quality of consumption and of work. In the Third World, where less systematic evidence is available, there are numerous reasons to believe that the situation is very much worse, in both its quantitative and its qualitative aspects. And since the onset of crisis conditions in the late 1960s it has been worsening in the advanced countries also (see Part Five).

Technical Annexe 8.A Measuring inequality

To gain a completely accurate picture of inequality in a society it is necessary to measure the quantity of *all* types of resources available to various individuals and households (including such things as access to health care, housing and public services). Unfortunately governments tend not to devote sufficient resources to gaining the full information. In the circumstances the best that economists and statisticians normally can do is to regard money income as the measure of command over resources. If we examine income distribution we can sum up in one analysis the inequality in access to all those commodities which are paid for out of this income, without taking each commodity separately. This method is not ideal, since apart from money income there are other types of resources. Two major ones are the capital gains obtained by those minorities that own shares in companies whose value rises, and the valuable benefits 'in kind', such as free use of a company car, which many managers and high-status workers receive. Both are very unequally distributed, so it should be borne in mind that they are not accounted for in the estimates of the distribution of income we shall shortly present. On the other hand, nor are some of the resources which are subsidized or provided free by governments such as certain collective goods and services.

Table 8.A.1 presents the distribution of income in three countries, using a common format. Imagine that all individuals in West Germany are arranged in the order of how rich they are, measured by the net-of-tax money income per capita of the household to which they belong. The table shows that the richest 10 per cent ('decile') received 26.8 per cent of all the income received by the whole population in that year, the next richest 10 per cent 14.8 per cent of income and so on. In all three countries care has been taken to use the same precise definition of income and also of the household, so that the figures are internationally comparable. A look will soon show that, while there is not very much difference in degree of inequality between West

Germany and the UK, Mexico has a much more unequal distribution of income. To take the two extremes, the richest decile (which will include all in the capitalist class) received not far off half the total money income, while the poorest decile got less than 1 per cent! In fact it is not untypical for developing countries like Mexico to be considerably more unequal than more advanced countries.

Table 8.A.1 Distribution of Per Capita Household Income in Three Capitalist Countries

Deciles	West Germany (1974)	UK (1979)	Mexico (1968)
Richest 10%	26.8	22.6	47.1
2nd	14.8	14.8	17.0
3rd	11.6	12.0	9.8
4th	9.9	10.5	7.6
5th	8.7	9.1	5.8
6th	7.4	8.0	4.3
7th	6.7	7.2	3.4
8th	5.7	6.3	2.5
9th	4.8	5.6	1.8
Poorest 10%	3.6	3.9	0.8

Source: W. Van Ginneken, 'Generating Internationally Comparable Income Distribution Data', in the *Review of Income and Wealth*, series 28, no. 4, December 1982, pp. 365–79

One way of illustrating the degree of inequality implied by Table 8.A.1 is through the 'Lorenz Curve'. Beginning with the richest 10 per cent we plot on a diagram the proportion of total income received by them (in the case of West Germany 26.8 per cent) – see point A in Diagram 8.A.1. Next we add their share to the second richest decile so that we have the richest 20 per cent (whose share is 41.6 per cent of total income in West Germany) – see point B. This process is continued, successively adding the share of the next richest decile, finishing up with point I, at which the richest 90 per cent obtained 96.4 per cent of total income, and J where of course 100 per cent of the population gain 100 per cent of the income. The line joining these points is the Lorenz Curve.

A short reflection will show what would happen in the hypothetical case where all income is exactly equally distributed. Then the curve would just be the straight diagonal joining 0 to J, for the 'richest' 10 per cent would then earn no more than 10 per cent of total income, and so on. Hence the diagonal may be called the 'line of equality'. The opposite hypothetical extreme, where there is so much inequality that the richest person receives virtually all the income and everyone else none, would be represented by a

Lorenze Curve that follows the outer lines oP and PJ. How far the actual curve lies away from the diagonal illustrates the level of inequality in the society. Thus the curve for Mexico shows more inequality than that for West Germany.

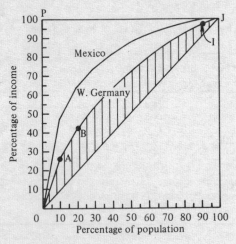

Diagram 8.A.1   The Lorenz Curve

The Lorenz Curve enables us to condense the picture of inequality which it presents into one summary statistic. The degree of inequality in West Germany, for example, may be measured by the ratio of the shaded area between the curve and the diagonal to the area of the whole triangle oPJ: this ratio is called the 'Gini Coefficient' after the Italian statistician who developed it. The higher the Gini Coefficient, the higher the level of inequality. At one hypothetical extreme, the coefficient equals 1, when the Lorenz Curve follows oP and PJ. At the other, when there is perfect equality, the coefficient is 0, since there is no area between the Lorenz Curve and the diagonal, as the curve actually follows the diagonal. In all real cases, therefore, the coefficient will lie between 0 and 1.

Table 8.A.2 makes use of this summary statistic to show the level of inequality in a selection of capitalist countries in the 1960s. The Gini Coefficients shown have been adjusted as far as possible in order to make them comparable, within a reasonable margin of error, between different countries. Thus, for example, in the case of Sweden the coefficient of 0.40 eans that the area between Sweden's Lorenz Curve and the diagonal is

Table 8.A.2 The Degree of Inequality in Some Capitalist Countries

	Gini Coefficient
Canada (1965)	0.36
Sweden (1963)	0.40
USA (1965)	0.41
West Germany (1962)	0.42
India (1962)	0.48
Brazil (1958)	0.49
France (1962)	0.52
South Africa (1959)	0.52
Mexico (1963)	0.53

Source: Jerry Cromwell, 'The Size Distribution of Income: An International Comparison', in the *Review of Income and Wealth*, series 23, no. 3, September 1977, pp. 291–308

40 per cent of the area of the triangle. The table shows in addition the particularly unequal income distributions in places like Brazil and South Africa, and further confirms the high inequality in Mexico.

CHAPTER 9

Ideas and Divisions

Capitalism is a system of production and distribution and not a system of ideas. But we have tried to show in this book that it is not a system of raw natural relations like in the animal world but the result of conscious social processes and structures of power. It was established by the action of human beings and it may be replaced by the actions of human beings.

Those facts mean that capitalism as a system is reproduced from day to day and from generation to generation not only by economic processes such as the ones we have described but also by ideas and by political domination. It is able to exist partly because of what those who participate in it think, believe and feel; and partly because its beneficiaries are able, at least temporarily, to suppress resistance to it from its victims. This, however, is not meant to imply that there is a simple common code of ideas appropriate to the profit system at all times and in all places, a kind of Bible or Koran of capitalism, nor any list of ideas which all capitalists or all workers subscribe to. The interconnection between economic life and ideas is extremely complex and very little studied in comparison with the economic and social components of capitalism. What we have to say here, therefore, is relatively exploratory and tentative.

I. CAPITALISM AND IDEAS

(i) *Religion*

In one sense capitalism is less associated with religious ideas than the systems of economic life which preceded it. Pre-capitalist systems of religion were often intimately concerned with economic life. Economic and social roles, the distribution of production and many other aspects of economic life were sometimes ordained as part of the religion. This was true, for example, of some aspects of medieval European Christianity, which held that the different estates of the people were ordained by God, and often obliged producers to render to the church a proportion of what they produced. The church thus not only justified exploitation and social stratification; it also directly participated in it as an institution.

The medieval European Christian church is only one example of a religion which was in many ways dysfunctional for capitalism. Among others are the caste system associated with Hinduism which traditionally restricted people to pre-ordained economic and social roles and which was therefore associated wth economic stagnation and the absence of structural change. Many aspects of other eastern religions with their stress on non-worldly values have also been seen as inimical to capitalist development. So, too has the Islamic ban on interest.

The growth of capitalism has often therefore been associated with anti-religious movements or at least with anti-clericalism, religious reform and change. So in Europe writers like the social historian Max Weber have linked the rise of capitalism to the rise of religious protestantism. Not only were the ideas associated with protestantism more in line with values necessary to promote capitalism (individual responsibility, hostility to ancient social codes, support for scientific progress), but also capitalism required an attack on the existing property interests of the church and its ability to appropriate a significant proportion of society's potential surplus.

Religious change has not only been associated with the rise of the capitalist class but also with the growth of the other major new class created by capitalism, the working class. The functioning of capitalism requires, as we have seen, the maintenance of discipline in the workplace and the acceptance by the working class of the economic inequalities inherent in capitalist production. Many writers, such as the historian E. P. Thompson, have seen religion as playing a key role in maintaining these in certain circumstances. In nineteenth-century Britain nonconformist Christianity spread the idea that economic suffering, if accepted without complaint, might pave the way to heaven; and the variety of Confucianism which in the late nineteenth century became the main religion of the Japanese urban working class stressed, according to the economist Michio Morishima, the values of duty, commitment and obedience (to the new capitalist employers), as opposed to the Confucianism in China where much more stress was laid on community and charity (values, it is argued, less conducive to capitalist exploitation).

If the Calvinist value of hard work is a universally valid idea for capitalism, its counterpart of material asceticism is not. Appropriate as it may have been for the growing capitalism of the nineteenth century it is singularly inappropriate for the high mass consumption capitalism of the last few decades. Coveting thy neighbour's goods has been one of the key bases of expansion of consumption in the advanced countries in the twentieth century; the seven deadly sins would appear to have become more profitable than the Ten Commandments.

A more general argument holds that religion assists capitalism because it tends to be socially conservative and hostile to revolutionary social movements. At times and places this is certainly true but it is unacceptable as a general proposition. The stress which many religions place on the values of poverty and their commitment in theory to humanitarian values is so often in contradiction to the evident effects of capitalism that it creates constant embarrassment for the authorities of the capitalist state (which is normally officially devoted to religious values).

The churches' theological authorities may also find the contradictions hard to live with. Religions tend to value co-operation above competition, charity above greed, asceticism above wealth. In every case capitalism does the opposite. The Christian capitalist has to live with the famous admonition: 'A rich man shall hardly enter into the kingdom of heaven. And again I say unto you, it is easier for a camel to go through the eye of a needle, than for a rich man to enter into the kingdom of God.'

At times, also, religions have been used to justify major reform or even revolutionary movements against capitalism. In Europe and the USA the Christian socialist tradition is a long one, while in recent times Islamic revolutionaries have frequently been in part anti-capitalist. And in contemporary Latin America liberation theology has allied itself with radical or revolutionary economic and social reform movements.

In sum, as capitalism has evolved and matured, it has developed contradictory and shifting needs for stability; and so its relationship with religions has also been complex, contradictory and shifting. When in a revolutionary phase, attempting to establish itself, capitalism has been the enemy of established religious authority. When in power and under threat, capitalism has often sought alliances with religious authorities. But complexity arises because these religions are themselves seething with internal contradictions. The so-called Christian countries, whose leaders profess a Christian faith, hold high the ideals of material wealth, of military strength and of the pursuit of profit and self-interest – hardly the values that are found in the New Testament. So although some religious values are consistent with capitalist needs, others are not. The relationship between capitalism and religions therefore is bound to be an ambiguous one.

(ii) *Individualism*

Defenders of capitalism such as the economist Milton Friedman claim that its philosophical basis is individualism – as opposed to socialism's collectivism. The essence of capitalist society is held to be the freedom of individuals to pursue their own interests and to prosper. The ideal capitalist is the simple individual who has a good proposition, invests his or her money in turning it into a capitalist enterprise and makes a profit while at the same time supplying a need. The idea is thus created that prosperity is the result of effort and achievement, and by a small step that those who are rich and privileged in capitalist societies deserve their good fortune as a reward for personal effort.

'Possessive individualism' is the basis of what are popularly known as 'Victorian values' – thrift, enterprise, competitiveness, earthly riches and heavenly rewards. Individualism is held to promote social virtues: social justice because people will be rewarded according to their own efforts; efficiency in production and distribution because the invisible hand of the market will turn the universal pursuit of personal interests into the best allocation of society's resources.

No doubt some of the propounders of possessive individualism sincerely believe that it is an effective social philosophy in the meeting of human needs. And it would be hard to deny that individuals have some control over their lives. Normally, people can choose their friends, their luxury wants, their leisure habits, and so on. But it is a far cry from that to the proposition that capitalist countries are meritocracies, where positions in society reflect individual merits. For most people's choices and behaviour are confined by the narrow perimeters of the capitalist relations they are caught up in.

One cannot escape the conclusion that possessive individualism's major use is as an apologia for the profit system: and it is usually propounded in blatant contradiction to the glaring facts of actually existing capitalism. In a world where wealth and the access to material privilege are often inherited and frequently reinforced by grotesquely unequal access to education or capital, where most of modern industry and banking are dominated by giant firms run by male members of a tiny minority ruling class, there remains relatively little space in actuality for the individual entrepreneur. This semi-fictitious being is rather a spirit raised to provide a spurious justification for capitalism.

(iii) *Freedom and democracy*

Politicians in the capitalist countries often talk of a dichotomy between the 'free world' and the 'socialist world', or the democracies and the communist countries. The word 'capitalist' is rarely used. Is there any justification at all for the association of capitalism with democracy or is it purely an attempt to delude?

There are various answers to this question. One of them, the most positive, is a historical one. In the period from the seventeenth century onwards, especially in Europe and its colonized offshoots, the new rising capitalist class was certainly to some extent associated with the political movement for democracy. The new ways of producing and making money required an attack on many aspects of the old monarchic, absolutist and theocratic order; they required the freedom to acquire and dispose of money, the freedom to move from old to new occupations, the freedom to acquire land and use it for the most profitable purposes, the freedom to pursue scientific and technical knowledge even if this conflicted with established beliefs and superstitions. All such freedoms were restricted in some degree by the power of the feudal monarchs and aristocrats, of the church and of ancient caste systems. Capitalists, therefore, became attracted to or even led revolutionary political movements. Many writers have seen the revolutions in England in the 1640s, in America in 1775, in France in 1789, in other European countries in 1848 and in Japan in 1868 as bourgeois or capitalist revolutions, and these revolutions were built around an ideology of freedom and democracy.

Capitalists might have been in many instances (and even remain today) committed to overthrowing the earlier traditional restrictions which reduce their ability to make profits. But the need for profitability, and the fact that this is based on exploitation of the working class, means that in power they must also limit the degree of freedom and democracy. Capitalist regimes, therefore, however democratic they may be, always restrict the rights of workers to some degree and seldom permit civil and democratic rights to revolutionary anti-capitalist movements.

In the inter-war period, economic and social crises in capitalist countries as advanced as Germany and Italy caused a degeneration into obscene fascist regimes. And, in the post-war world, only a minority of Third World countries retain the formal trappings of multi-party parliamentary democracy. In several of them despotic military-backed regimes which are favourable to big business have been installed, usually with the material support of the dominant 'democratic' regime itself, the USA. In some cases elected governments have been violently displaced.

A further argument against the assumed association of capitalism with democracy is that the democratic freedoms that exist are often more formal than real. In most capitalist democracies the exercise of democratic rights and civil liberties is very much constrained by economic inequalities. The law is expensive and often inaccessible to the poor; the forces of law and order are much more often used to enforce the rights of property than, for instance, the right to strike. Democracy largely consists in periodic parliamentary elections for governments which then have a term of office of several years. It is sometimes argued that these elections give no real choice; that their results are increasingly influenced by the techniques of modern advertising; that parliament is not closely answerable to electorates; that even if it were, real power resides not in parliament but in civil services which are not elected or are in the hands of the main economic interests. Such accusations may be more accurate in some places than in others.

But whatever limitations there are with regard to unequal abilities, the rights which exist are greater now than in the early years of capitalism or under fascist political systems or in eastern Europe. And whatever the shortcomings of existing parliaments, the fact remains that in the heartlands of capitalism, the advanced industrialized countries of western Europe, North America and Australasia, as well as in Japan, some form of democratic system has shone quite brightly during much of the history of capitalism.

However much democracy there actually is, it is important that the leading capitalist countries *claim* to be democratic, and seem to *be* democratic at least to the extent of possessing forms of answerability of the rulers to the ruled. It is the forms and appearance of democracy which do a great deal to give the system its legitimacy. A system which is generally regarded as democratic, even if its democracy is really mythical, may be the most ideally suited political system for capitalism.

It means that the system can politically reproduce itself without excessive expenditure of the potential surplus on the means of repressing opposition (though the mechanisms of democracy may also be very expensive to operate). But, more important, it means that it is possible for the inherent fairness and justice of the system not only to be proclaimed by the privileged capitalist class but also to a significant extent to be accepted by all classes. If the system is widely believed to be democratic then this removes the basis for revolutionary politics.

2. COERCION AND CONSENT

Some of the ideas we have so far discussed are supportive of the profit system. They appear to legitimate its existing relations, and, in so far as they are believed, are likely to lessen any resistance. But the pro-capitalist ideas are, as we have seen, full of complexities and contradictions; and the question remains. How does the system continue to exist without outright opposition from the majority exploited classes? The answer must be a combination of a number of factors.

(i) *Repression*

A first possibility is that the consciousness of the great mass of exploited people under capitalism is essentially revolutionary and anti-capitalist, but that they are forced to accept the system because of the ability of the capitalists themselves to use the repressive power of the state.

This could explain the suppression of particular revolutionary episodes in the history of capitalist states, or might even more generally explain the maintenance of the system, at least in its present form, in some places (perhaps South Africa, and certain Third World dictatorships). But it is insufficient at a more general level to explain the maintenance of the system over decades or even centuries in its main centres. Even though it is true that the state does exercise some repressive functions in these countries, the consciousness of the majority of people has not been revolutionary except perhaps for brief moments. And to see the state as simply the repressive servant of capitalism is to oversimplify drastically.

(ii) *Ideological control*

A major factor is the maintenance of non-physical, ideological control over the system by the state and other institutions of capitalist society. The state controls the education system in most advanced capitalist countries, the majority of newspapers are owned by capitalists, the radio and television are largely controlled either by capitalist corporations or by the state. These are truly formidable influences over the way people think and, while leaving to small (usually elite) groups the right to present anti-capitalist ideas, they encourage a status-quo ideology among the great mass of the population.

At its most effective this process takes place in a very subtle way. There is formal freedom to disseminate ideas; and yet in practice only a limited range of ideas is widely disseminated. The process is maintained through control exercised by owners (press barons and so on) or by boards of overseers, through selectivity in the finance of research and in publications, and only very seldom through direct censorship. This book presents the opinion that the capitalist system is exploitative and should be replaced. Yet it is being published by a capitalist publisher; we do not expect it to be serialized in the popular press, but nor do we expect it to be burned by order of the Ministry of Truth or formally banned from public educational institutions (though ironically it might sell better if it were).

(iii) *Everyday perceptions*

But the relative exclusion of those with anti-capitalist ideas from the means of ideological dissemination is not, on its own, a convincing full answer to the question of why an exploitative system is not generally regarded as such. There are also some real objective features of the everyday experiences of people which, without a scientific and systematic approach which goes beyond the 'everyday' way of seeing things, can obscure the nature of capitalist exploitation from immediate view. For people do not directly experience 'the profit system'; they experience a few capitalist enterprises. Workers may come to detest their boss but do not necessarily identify him or her with 'capitalism', which may remain a distant abstraction. Moreover, complex modern capitalist labour processes make it impossible for individual workers to identify their own 'product'; so no direct comparison can be made with wages.

But a further and more fundamental feature is the way capitalism is experienced and presented as a system of interlocking markets. In Chapter 1 we described how capitalism is a dual system containing both production and exchange relationships. But as a general rule pro-capitalist economists stress only the sphere of exchange and much of the popular ideology also reflects in a concrete way this limited and blinkered view. The twofold nature of labour (paid and unpaid), hidden behind the veil of monetary relations, is only discovered by the theoretical examination and investigation of reality. It is important that workers and capitalists both believe the worker is being paid for the work done. The payment sometimes seems insufficient and unfair, but it is undoubtedly part of the general perception of the capitalist system that there exists 'a fair day's pay' from the capitalist and an equivalent 'fair day's work' on the part of the worker.

At the same time profit seems to derive a justification from the exclusively exchange-orientated approach of much orthodox economic theorizing: if both capitalists and workers are qualitatively equal participants in production, then profits, like wages, must be the return to some 'factor of production'. The necessity of profit is often explicitly recognized. Capitalists are seen to 'deserve' some return on their money. This is often reinforced by the idea that there are just and unjust forms of profit. Unjust forms are typically seen as profits on speculation, or through capital gains and the like. The distinction which seems to be drawn is not between whether capitalists work or do not work for their profits but rather whether the profits result directly from the production of goods and services or not.

The popular justification of profit is also reflected in the very common idea that any economic activity must be 'viable': not whether it is a rational way of meeting needs given existing resources, but whether it can make a profit.

These 'natural' perceptions may partly explain why the major forms of resistance to the ills of capitalism in most places have not attacked the profit system itself. Trade unionism has largely been a philosophy of getting for workers the best deal that is possible, in terms of wages and conditions of work, without ending the wage system itself. Reformism has dominated the vast majority of political movements representing the working class: it has been at least partly responsible for state welfare improvements that might have seemed remarkable to nineteenth-century socialists. But without denying the gains attributable to reformism and trade unionism, by directing resistance away from outright rejection of the profit system they have inevitably in some ways contributed to its survival.

But we must not exaggerate the extent to which 'natural' forms of perception are guaranteed to produce pro-capitalist ideology. It is often true that workers who become hostile to capitalists do translate that into a hostility to the whole system and do look for alternative ideas and principles to rationalize their hostility. Many workers come to socialism and many do come to see the profit system as exploitative. So capitalism has no guaranteed natural mode of perpetuating itself at the ideological level even though there may be great obstacles in the way of generalizing anti-capitalist ideas.

(iv) *Divisive ideologies*

A generalized anti-capitalist ideology would require the substantial unity of all the exploited (the working class) and their recognition of common interest against the exploiters. The fact that in the history of capitalism to date such unity has never been more than partial and fleeting constitutes another major explanation of the longevity of the capitalist system. Nationalism, racism, sexism and heterosexism are all prejudices and philosophies that serve to create and maintain divisions within the exploited class.

Nationalism could be said to assist the survival of capitalism in a variety of ways. First of all nationalist consciousness may tend to inhibit class consciousness by creating something in common (nationality) between the exploiters and the exploited. From this viewpoint it is the foreigners rather than an exploiting class who seem to be responsible for economic problems. When workers are asked to forgo economic benefits or make economic sacrifices this is often done in the interests of the nation and its ability to compete with foreigners. Sometimes nationalism is reflected in economic warfare (protectionism, trade wars and so on) or in military conflict. These too can be beneficial at times for capitalism. Foreign military adventures can help sustain support for domestic policies of austerity, as, to give a 1980s example, Mrs Thatcher astutely realized in the UK war against Argentina.

In more extreme cases its functionality from the point of view of capitalism is less obvious. Economic warfare may involve an attempt at self-protection by a particular section of capital but it is undoubtedly an obstacle to the functioning of capitalism as a whole. And while there are always groups of capitalists who get rich in wars and who as a result may foment them, wars also destroy capitalists, both physically and economically, and may lead to the breakdown of the traditional order and the spread of revolutionary ideology. Both the First and Second World Wars were followed by revolutionary crises in a number of the main capitalist nations.

So nationalist ideology, like the nation state, represents a contradiction: a moderate degree may benefit capitalists in concealing class consciousness; yet its extreme form may become dysfunctional.

The 'alien' or 'enemy' in nationalist thinking is usually distant. The related ideas of xenophobia and racism are much closer to home. They are frequently directed, in many countries, at a minority section of the population. Such ideas are neither new nor peculiar to capitalism. But because ideas about the inferiority of certain races were an important part of the development of both slavery and of colonialism, racism played a major role in the birth, early development and history of capitalism.

Since then racist ideas have been endemic though they have been particularly strong in a few countries with populations of different races, usually the countries which experienced slavery or major immigrations. The profit system does not in itself produce racism but there are a number of ways in which businesses can take advantage of it, whether consciously or not. Like nationalism, a racist consciousness may be advantageous in disguising the nature of class oppression and exploitation. If white workers can be made to hate their black fellow workers and blame them for their economic problems, then exploitation may be safeguarded. Disunity in the working class may make the working class as a whole less militant and less anti-capitalist.

Racism has thus been an element in the development of segmented labour markets which we discussed in Chapter 5. People of oppressed races tend to find themselves confined to low-paid jobs in the secondary sector, with little job security. Workers can do surplus labour regardless of their colour or of the God they worship. And it is true that even in societies where racism is strong some capitalists try to avoid implementing racist employment practices. But despite the fact that in an economic sense all workers of equal skill are of equal use to companies, it is truly remarkable how seldom corporations have taken the lead in resisting racial discrimination, and indeed how often certain business leaders have been at the forefront of spreading racist ideologies. We conclude that many sections of the capitalist class have been and are aware of the less tangible and less directly economic benefits which racism gives to capitalist exploitation.

Like oppressed races, women in all capitalist societies have been and are discriminated against in terms of pay, conditions of work, access to qualifications, promotion and so on. Sex or gender discrimination and oppression could be analysed in part by making exactly parallel points to those made about race. Women also are disproportionately concentrated in the secondary labour market, with the same ambiguous relationship to the needs of capitalism as racial minorities in the same labour market. The political impact of unemployment can be blunted by imposing it disproportionately on women, who are forced back into the home, and on immigrants, who may be forced to leave the country. The ideology which says that immigrants and foreigners are inferior and have no rights is equivalent to the ideology that says women should be occupied in the 'womanly' tasks of cooking, cleaning and mothering in the home.

The question of the family and the organization of women's labour within it is therefore central. Here the parallel between the oppression of women and the oppression of racial minorities ceases. The overwhelmingly prevalent form of social organization within capitalist countries is one where women do a disproportionate amount of domestic labour (p. 133). So capitalism depends economically not only on what happens in the workplace but also on what happens in the home.

This, however, is not the sole importance of the household. Its form of organization also seems to have an important ideological relationship to capitalism. There appears to be some correlation between reactionary support for the profit system and a whole series of ideas relating to the family and personal life, such as glorification of marriage and the institution of the family, opposition to divorce, adultery, abortion, homosexuality and belief that the primary role of women is in the home as housewives and mothers.

None of these ideas is peculiar to capitalism. Restrictive morality and rigid sex roles are also characteristic of pre-capitalist societies and their source is often to be found in religion. And it could be said that modern capitalist societies have transcended Victorian sexual and other moralities more liberally than the non-capitalist societies of eastern Europe or China. In practice the archetypal 'bourgeois nuclear family' is not as predominant as it once was in the most advanced capitalist countries. The emergence of new domestic arrangements, the emergence of a gay lifestyle, these have in a sense been permitted by capitalism, both materially and also because they seem to coincide with some capitalist ideologies of free choice and individualism.

Yet the fact remains that these changes are frequently cited as examples of the degradation of ordered capitalist society, and capitalist politicians, not unlike Stalin in the USSR, periodically rediscover the family as the clue to social stability. Some of the 'permissive' and liberating personal mores discovered in previous decades may yet recede and allow the return of more tight-lipped restrictions on behaviour familiar to earlier generations.

Whether or not the family is indispensable for capitalism from a purely economic point of view, it is functional for capitalist society in other ways. It is partly a source of micro-authority which supplements the authority of other institutions in capitalist society – the factory, the school and the state apparatus. To that extent the ideologies and moralities which are connected with the institution of the family are an essential part of capitalism not so much as an economic system but more as a hierarchical social system which must ultimately constrain the freedom of its citizens in the interests of social stability, private property and profit.

The periodic popularity of traditional moralities and the glorification of the family seem to correspond to periods in which capitalism is in crisis, and reflect a belief that the questioning of authority in personal and sexual relationships will also help to undermine authority in the workplace and in society as a whole. Emphasis on the family also preserves unequal opportunities, since if the family, as opposed to more communal organs, is the main mechanism channelling the existing culture and repertoire of skills, then the patterns of inequality are reinforced from generation to generation.

Our conclusion is brief: it is that though the ideas and beliefs which permeate capitalist societies are related to capitalism's need to reproduce itself, to continue to find acceptance among people, the interconnection is complex and full of tension, and many factors are involved.

Thus, we cannot say, for example, that sexism, heterosexism or racism are the offspring solely of capitalism's need to divide the opposition, or that they would be eradicated if capitalism were to be replaced by a new system. Not yet, at least, have the Thought Police of George Orwell's *1984* taken control. Indeed, people in advanced capitalist societies are to some extent freer to think their own thoughts and pursue their own ideas, than in previous eras when heretical beliefs, or atheism, could be punishable by death.

None the less we have also seen how many ideas favourable to capitalist principles have arisen, either through impersonal economic encounters with the market or through the conscious production of capitalist propaganda. And the cultural freedoms we have, together with the cultural and psychological needs which they satisfy, are bound to be hemmed in by the constant emphasis in life on the principles of profit.

PART FOUR

TRANSFORMATIONS OF CAPITALISM

CHAPTER 10

Internationalization

Capitalism inherited a fragmented world of national states, each with its own largely self-sufficient economy. Yet in its brief history it has come closer than any previous system of trade and production to creating a single economic world. A localized economic event can transmit its effects around the globe. It is easy to stand amazed at the extraordinary extent of integration.

But at the same time it could also plausibly be argued that such amazement was misplaced: what could be regarded as amazing is just how limited is the economic integration of the world. To support this approach we could cite the persistence of the nation state and nationalist ideology long after its economic rationale seems to have vanished. Or we could observe the extent of trade controls and restrictions between countries; or the difficulties placed in the way of migration by workers and their dependants.

Which of these two outlooks is more accurate? Perhaps each reveals part of a very complex truth. We shall look in detail at the ways in which the capitalist process spreads itself across national borders: through international trade, through capitalists buying inputs (both means of production and labour-power) from other countries, through locating production processes in two or more countries and through international credit. A more detailed picture of these areas will allow us to make a truer judgement about the real extent of capitalism's internationalism, and who benefits from it.

I. TRADE

(i) *Principles of trade*

The next time you undress, look at the labels in your clothes. You would not be untypical if your shoes were made in Taiwan, your underclothes in Portugal, your jeans in the USA, your shirt in India and so on. You could easily be wearing the products, direct and indirect, of a dozen countries or more in three continents, transported over thousands of miles: an elementary concrete confirmation of the fact, well known in the abstract, that the capitalist system involves a vast amount of international trade.

In one sense international commodity trade is only a special case of a more general phenomenon, the social division of labour. Whether exchange involves international trade depends upon the partly arbitrary fact of where national borders have been drawn. The sale of Californian wine in New York is not international trade but involves much greater geographical separation of producers and consumers than the sale of Dutch cheese in Belgium. The laws which determine international trade, therefore, are partly a subcategory of the laws which determine the division of labour in a more general sense.

But international trade is different from internal trade in the sense that it is governed by an extra set of rules and regulations. Within countries there are usually not many restrictions on the free movement of goods; whereas across national borders trade can be restricted by customs tariffs and duties, quantitative restrictions and regulations relating to hygiene, standards and so on. And international trade involves the exchange of different currencies; the regulations governing this can be at least as involved as trade regulations.

The history of the study of international trade has been dominated for one and a half centuries by a famous theory – the theory of comparative advantage as outlined by the renowned English nineteenth-century economist and politician, David Ricardo. It argues that those who live in different countries can gain if in each country production is concentrated on those commodities with the greatest comparative advantage: that is, where costs are lowest compared to other commodities, so that both countries should specialize and then trade with each other. Consumers can then buy the whole range of goods and services through trade. Thus, trade restrictions should be removed to enable maximum benefits to be gained from exchange. If the model is generalized to the whole world then the productive capacity of the world's labour force would be maximized and each country would be better off than with national self-sufficiency.

The theory makes no explicit reference to capitalism. Indeed as a principle it has been applied to individuals and to many kinds of economic system. But traditionally it has been closely associated with capitalism. It carries the assumption that the division of labour which it recommends will be best achieved by the unfettered working of the market system. Businesses in each country will specialize in the commodities in which they have comparative advantage because it will be more profitable to do so.

But since profits in international trade are partly determined by exchange rates between currencies, the model makes an assumption also about the determination of exchange rates. There are two possibilities.

(a) It could assume that exchange rates are settled by means of competitive financial markets for currencies. Thus when one country has a surplus in its balance of trade there will be an excess demand for its currency. This will tend to drive up the price of its currency, thereby reducing the competitiveness of that country's products. In this way exports are brought into balance with imports; and international specialization based on comparative advantage will be automatically assured by the operating of free markets and the pursuit of profit by producers, traders and currency speculators.

(b) Alternatively, exchange rates may be fixed by governments intervening in the currency markets. If one country has a deficit in its trade, its government will continually have to support its currency by buying it up, using its stocks of gold and other international reserves. It is assumed that this would so drain away the gold in the country that prices would generally fall, and continue to do so until its commodities became more competitive and its trade deficit eliminated. So the comparative advantage theory could equally work, on these assumptions, when there are fixed exchange rates, as long as in each country prices are free to move up and down with ease.

Since Ricardo's time, the model of comparative advantage has been elaborated and modified. The Hecksher–Ohlin theory (named after its founders) argues that the basis of comparative advantage is the factor-intensity of production. A country will therefore have comparative advantage in producing those goods which use a relatively large amount of those factors of production (labour, machinery and land) which it possesses in relative abundance.

In this slightly more complicated version the theory still sounds reasonable enough, almost commonsensical. But empirical studies have shown that the world does not work, or so it seems, as the theory predicts. For instance, the exports of the USA, contrary to expectations, turn out to be more labour-intensive than its imports – the oddity is known as Leontief's paradox after its discoverer. It may be less paradoxical if the model is made even more complicated by the addition of more differentiated factors of production.

Studies which have produced these kinds of conclusion still basically maintain the comparative advantage notion. But there is another tradition which rejects it, completely or in part. Comparative advantage was used by Ricardo and his followers in the nineteenth century to justify Britain's policy of free trade. Other countries, however, saw the matter very differently. In Germany and the USA economists and politicians regarded the free trade policy not as a way of maximizing mutual benefit through international trade but as a way for British manufacturers to maintain their superiority in world trade. The most famous advocates of protectionist policies were Friedrich List in Germany and Alexander Hamilton in the USA. Ideas such as theirs have been followed by states wishing to industrialize.

Nowadays protectionism in relatively less developed economies is normally justified by a partial or complete denial of the validity of the comparative advantage principle. Orthodox economists have occasionally accepted minor doctrinal modifications of this kind. They accept that efficiency can sometimes change as a result of gaining experience, so tariff protection for 'infant' industries may be justified for short periods for specific industries. But the opponents of comparative advantage go much further than this and economists usually condemn them for heresy.

They say that comparative advantage is invalid as a principle for organizing world trade under capitalism because it tends to freeze the existing structure of world production to the disadvantage of the underdeveloped countries. The doctrine is used, it is argued, to lock the underdeveloped countries into a world division of labour in which they remain primary producers while the richer countries maintain their industrial prevalence. In this way the international trade system is seen as a mechanism which exploits the underdeveloped countries and which helps to perpetuate underdevelopment. Trade is thus held under certain circumstances to be not an instrument of enrichment, as Ricardo had claimed, but rather an instrument of immiserization.

In other words, the comparative advantage principle may be logical and valid in a hypothetical *static* unchanging world of acts of exchange, but in a real dynamic capitalist world market its prescriptions are often perverse. We shall examine the trade of underdeveloped economies in the next chapter.

(ii) *Growth of trade*

The growth of world trade has been erratic and far from universal. In some periods, its value grew substantially, as in the four decades from 1840 to 1879 when it rose by about 336 per cent, far outstripping the 165 per cent growth of industrial production. Throughout the nineteenth century, trade grew so much that by one estimate it was as much as a third of output by the eve of the First World War.

In other periods, as during the Great Depression in the 1930s, capitalist countries became inward-looking and protectionist, and world trade fell. Overall, by 1948 world industrial production was about 2.7 times its 1913 level, but trade was virtually the same as in 1913.

The post-war period has seen a renewed trend towards internationalization. The volume of trade grew on average by just under 7 per cent per annum from 1948 to 1979, which was roughly half as fast again as the growth of output. In the latter years trade was beginning to slow down, and in the world recession of the early 1980s it began to fall again. But the amounts remain enormous: $1,700 billion worth of goods and services were exchanged across national borders in 1983, just under one-fifth of the total value of commodities produced in the world.

A closer examination shows also a substantial change in the geographical patterns of trade. The post-war period has been the era for expanded trade between the advanced capitalist countries. In 1935 in the aftermath of the tariff protection, trade controls and restrictive currency areas which the major capitalist countries imposed in response to the Great Depression, trade between the advanced industrial countries was only about 26 per cent of total world trade. Partly as a result of tariff-reducing exercises like the EEC and the 'Kennedy' and 'Tokyo' rounds of tariff-reduction, the markets of the advanced industrial countries became more open to each others' products after the Second World War. So by 1970 they had cornered as much as 66 per cent of the world trade.

So from the point of view of the advanced capitalist countries the market is much more of a global arena than it was fifty or even a hundred years ago. In 1870 their trade was on average about 14 per cent of their national products, by 1938 it had dropped to 8 per cent; but in 1983 it was as much as 23 per cent. When account is taken of the fact that some commodities, such as accommodation or haircuts, have to be consumed on the spot, the overall significance of their trade appears even greater.

But many parts of the Third World, such as most of Africa, India and China, failed to participate in the trade boom and now account for a much lower share of world trade than they did before. They have a much smaller place in the international division of labour.

2. INVESTMENT AND PRODUCTION

(i) *Foreign investment and the multinational corporation*

Capital can become internationalized not only by the migration of its commodities through trade, but by the migration of all the other elements in the capitalist process which are represented schematically in Diagram 2.1 (p. 32).

What is most striking about the post-war era is the rise to prominence of the multinational corporation, as a form of international investment. But foreign investment is by no means a new arrival. The earliest phases of capitalism saw the development of international trading companies, like the East India Company, which invested their capital thousands of miles from home, both in trading activities and in plantations and mining ventures to supply raw materials to the industrializing centres. Also the industrialization of some of the major capitalist countries was accelerated by the inflow of foreign investment especially in infrastructural investment. This was particularly important in the development of the US railroad system.

The fluctuations in the history of foreign investment under capitalism follow those of international trade. The nineteenth century was on the whole a period of expansion of foreign investment. The fifty years before the First World War are often regarded as its classic period. By 1914 British capitalists, the major investors, owned about £4.2 billion of foreign assets (mainly bonds), not much less than what they owned in Britain itself, This was not surprising, since in the previous two decades a half of all their investments had gone abroad.

Many of the foreign assets were sold off or devalued during the First World War and capitalists were much more cautious about investing abroad in the years that followed. There was some recovery of foreign investment during the 1920s but a lot of this was a by-product of the penal reparations which were imposed on Germany. During the Great Depression it dried up again and it was not until after the Second World War that it started to flourish and grow.

During the post-war boom foreign investment expanded enormously taking many different forms, the principal ones being direct investment in productive activities, short-term financial flows through the banking system and long-term flows of lending, usually to governments. The multinational corporations arose with the expansion of direct foreign investment, at first chiefly by US corporations and some UK ones, subsequently followed by the Japanese and the German companies. The biggest corporations in the 1980s are still largely the USA-based companies; Table 10.1 shows how much each has become internationalized.

Modern foreign investment has thus taken a different turn from the nineteenth-century version, which was more concentrated on ownership of foreign bonds. But in relative terms it remains at present much less important than last century.

In 1983, the money flowing abroad from the USA to pay for direct investments and other long-term assets reached $9.8 billion, less than 2 per cent of the new long-term investments within the USA itself. This is still relatively much lower than for the major investing countries in 1913.

(ii) *The multinational factory*

A third way in which industrial capital can become internationalized is in regard to the direct production process, the subject of Chapter 3. Some forms of international investment involve the production of a commodity being split into separate stages, with successive ones being performed in different countries. It is as if the factory itself is straddling the world.

Table 10.1   The World's Ten Biggest Multinational Corporations, 1981 (by employees)

	'Home' country	Industry	Percentage of assets abroad	Percentage of workers abroad
1. General Motors	USA	Motor vehicles	30	29
2. Ford	USA	Motor vehicles	48	50
3. International Business Machines (IBM)	USA	Electronics, computers	47	42
4. Phillips	Netherlands	Electronics appliances	76	78
5. General Electric	USA	Electronics appliances	25	29
6. Siemens	West Germany	Electronics, computers	n.a.	32
7. International Telephone and Telegraph (ITT)	USA	Electronics, communications	37	58
8. Unilever	UK/Netherlands	Food products, soap, cosmetics	40*	55*
9. Fiat	Italy	Motor vehicles	n.a.	20†
10. Volkswagen	West Germany	Motor vehicles	n.a.	37

* outside the EEC
† 1980
Source: J. M. Stopford, J. H. Dunning and K. O. Haberich, *The World Directory of Multinational Enterprises*, London, Macmillan, 1980

In the integrated circuit business, for example, production can easily be split into three operations: wafer fabrication, assembly and testing. In the 1960s and 1970s US companies began to switch the middle phase to Hong Kong, Taiwan and other places in South-East Asia and Latin America. At the same time, computer and electronics companies can integrate backwards by taking over their suppliers of integrated circuits and other inputs. Thus Digital Equipment, the US computer manufacturer, makes its keyboards in Boston, its display monitors in Taiwan, assembles and tests its floppy disk drives in Singapore, some of its circuit modules in Puerto Rico, and so on.

Similar internationalist trends can be found too in the automobile industry. Frequently, design can be developed in one country, components in another, final car assembly in a third.

Wherever the technology lends itself to separation of the major stages of production, the potential for locating assembly and other low-skill activities in areas with low-cost labour can be exploited. There is no way of measuring exactly how much of modern production is internationalized in this way, though accounts of several industries make clear it has been increasing during the post-war period.

(iii) *Motives*

Whereas traditionally much foreign investment went in search of raw materials in the Third World (see Chapter 12), in modern times we can add three further major reasons why it has been profitable for capitalists to break loose from their national borders.

First is the search for cheaper and more docile labour. Businesses can make more profit by selling in the same market (the advanced countries) but producing elsewhere. This has been a very common reason for foreign investment in border industries, such as in northern Mexico. It is one of the motives for some of the recent investments in the Third World but it does not seem to have been the predominant one.

Second is the search for new markets. By far the majority of modern foreign investment from the advanced capitalist countries has been made in order to capture overseas markets, an inducement so powerful that most of it has been made in other rich countries. So by far the largest amount of US foreign investment has been in Canada; European capitalists have invested in the USA or in EEC countries, Japanese capitalists in Europe and North America. Internationalization of capitalism in this sense, therefore, has tended, like internationalization through trade, to confine itself to the already developed parts of the capitalist world.

Third is to avoid as far as possible the constraints of the modern state. That means setting up factories in countries with few laws and regulations controlling pollution or protecting the rights, the health and the safety of workers. It also allows companies to minimize their tax bills by the system of 'transfer pricing' on trade within each company, which in essence allows them to declare their profits in those countries which will tax them the least. It has been estimated that up to a third of international trade involves different subsidiaries of the same multinational exchanging goods with each other, so the scope for tax avoidance is huge.

3. FINANCIAL CAPITAL

The internationalization of capital has brought with it enormous movements of money across national borders. And profiting from this flow there has emerged a powerful oligarchy of international financial capitalists. Money flows across borders to finance trade, to buy factories and plantations, bonds and securities, to make loans to governments or corporations, to return the interest and the profit, to speculate on anything under the sun and moon. Virtually all these money transactions flow through the international banking system. As a consequence, all big banks of necessity operate in many different countries.

If we were looking for a single distinguishing feature of modern capitalism the global spread of these banks would be a strong candidate. It is symbolized in the shape of modern cities from New York to Bombay to Hong Kong. The central clusters of glass skyscrapers in the financial districts are mainly the property of the international banks.

Governments have frequently attempted to impose limits on the ability of capital to move across national boundaries. This is practicable enough in relation to direct foreign investment but, with the advent of computer technology and modern telecommunications, it has become all but impossible in relation to movements of money. Many governments of advanced capitalist countries in liberalizing capital movements during recent decades have been bowing to the inevitable. Like the Greek god Proteus who could change shape at will and reappear anywhere he wanted, capital can convert itself into the easily transmittable form of money, and has gained an immense power.

Thus, modern international finance represents capital in its freest possible form. It is capital relatively free from ties on production and markets, and relatively free from controls on its activities imposed by states or other institutions.

The institution which most clearly expresses this free capital is the Eurocurrency market which has developed since the late 1950s. A Eurodollar is a bank deposit or loan denominated in dollars but located outside the USA. Such money developed in Europe, mainly in London, during the

1960s as a result of various controls on the movement and use of dollars imposed by the US government. The banks received deposits in various currencies, but largely in dollars, and were able to make loans denominated in dollars (i.e. to create money) with no government control over their activities. The Eurodollar system was rapidly followed by dealings in other currencies and it came to take place not only in Europe but also in the big financial centres of Asia.

The market was boosted by the enormous increase in surplus liquidity which entered the world banking system as a result of the rise in the revenues of the main oil-producing states after 1973. In the 1980s the market continues to grow, urged on by governments which have stripped away many regulations, and by the emerging possibilities of new technology. The inventiveness of bankers in finding new instruments for their business is matched only by their inevitable steadfastness in sticking to their objective of profit maximization, rather than channelling money flows to countries which are most in need.

To what extent these revolutionary changes in the banking world increase the fragility of the system, and its proneness to financial crisis, will be reviewed in Chapter 17.

4. THE STATE

So far we have seen how all elements of the capitalist process have become internationalized, and in most cases increasingly so in the time since the Second World War.

Some opponents of capitalism in advanced countries claim that multinational corporations are necessarily their worst enemies. The basis of such views is nationalism, an objection to the foreign origins of the corporations rather than their functions as capitalist institutions. None the less the internationalization of capitalism does imply that important relationships have been modified. For example, while trade union internationalism remains in its infancy, multinational corporations increasingly have the power to switch resources between countries, thereby giving them leverage over both workers and possibly hostile nation states. And at the same time competition between capitalists has been intensified because markets, once confined and localized, have widened first to a national and then beyond to a global scale.

But perhaps the most important effect of internationalization is the undermining of national states' powers to regulate economic affairs. The main way in which any government's international problems can be manifested and assessed is through the country's 'balance of payments'. This is a national account which gives for a single country an aggregate measure of all the international transactions and transfers described in this chapter.

(i) *The balance of payments*

Table 10.2 gives an example and summary of how each item affects a country's balance of payments, and illustrates the concerns facing governments.

On the credit side are all the international transactions which involve currency entering the country from abroad; these are recorded with a plus sign. This includes: the value of exported goods and services, the import of capital from abroad (which can be regarded, like goods and services, as foreigners spending on a national asset such as the purchase of a factory), the transfer of funds from other countries in the form of loans (which can also be seen as the purchase by foreigners of a national asset, in this case an

Table 10.2 The Balance of Payments of the UK and Italy, 1982

	UK (£ billion)	Italy (thousand billion lire)
Exports	+ 139.1	+ 44.0
Imports	− 133.2	− 48.8
Visible trade Balances	+ 5.9	− 4.8
Other goods, services, and income flows*	+ 6.0	+ 3.8
Net profits, interest and rent from abroad	+ 1.1	− 2.4
'Current Account Balance'	+ 13.0	− 3.4
Net direct investment abroad	− 3.6	− 0.2
Net portfolio investment and other long-term capital	− 18.1	+ 3.3
'Basic Balance'	− 8.7	− 0.3
Net short-term capital (In, +, out, −)	+ 23.1	− 2.3
Net errors and omissions	− 8.2	0.0
Increase in liabilities constituting foreign central bank reserves	− 8.7	0.0
'Overall Balance' (sum of all the above)	− 2.5	− 2.6
Fall in gold and foreign exchange reserves	+ 2.5	+ 2.6

* includes foreign aid and migrant workers' remittances
Source: International Monetary Fund, *Balance of Payments Statistics*, IMF, Washington DC, 1984

IOU or statement of future liability), the direct transfer of funds in the form of economic aid or the repatriation of wages by migrant workers, and so on.

The debit side comprises all the same items seen from the opposite point of view, leading to currency flowing out of the country, and recorded with a minus sign: such as imports of goods and services, export of capital, economic aid and so on.

In our summary for Italy and the UK in 1982, the credit and debit sides have been lumped together for each item, to give the net inflow of currency.

Balance of payments accounting follows the principle of double-entry book-keeping, whereby each transaction is entered both as a plus and as a minus item. For example, if a UK manufacturer exports a tank, paid for in dollars, it will be entered as a plus under exports and as a minus on the bottom line, indicating that foreign exchange reserves have risen. Thus, including such changes in reserves, the overall balance of payments automatically in principle adds up to zero. Also since for each flow or transaction a plus for one nation is a minus for another, then for each part of the account the total sum of balances for all countries must also be zero.

For a single country the important question concerns the surpluses or deficits created in the various parts of the account. To begin with, economists typically examine the trade balance or, more satisfactorily, the 'Current Account Balance', which includes the trade balance along with the flows of profits, interest and rent from abroad. In 1982, as Table 10.2 shows, the UK was in surplus, Italy in deficit.

The 'Basic Balance' includes also the effects of long-term investments, and is designed to show the underlying structural position of an economy in relation to the world market. Both the UK and Italy were in deficit, according to this definition. In the former case, an important factor was clearly a large outflow of investments.

The next section of the accounts illustrates some of the difficulties faced by governments: massive flows of short-term capital. The net movements over a whole year, shown in the table, are only moderately volatile compared to what is possible in short periods of time. They turn into raging currents during periods of speculation. It is in exactly the activities included in this part of the accounts that modern capitalism has found most freedom, most international integration and most ingenuity in making money – almost, it seems, out of thin air.

Perhaps that would not matter if it were not for the destabilizing effects they have on the bottom line of the accounts, the line which 'balances' all the others: the fall or rise in a country's reserves of gold and foreign exchange. In both Italy and the UK, reserves fell by moderate amounts in 1982. If reserves get too low a government will lack the wherewithal to enter the foreign exchange market. So there may emerge a substantial devaluation of the currency which a government is powerless to prevent. Even if it succeeded in imposing exchange controls, it would cause untold disruption to trade.

There are times when a balance of payments deficit creates no basic problem. For instance, during 1983 the USA had an immense Basic Balance deficit amounting to $43 billion, which it was under no immediate pressure to eliminate because capitalists and governments elsewhere were willing to hold additional dollars. Other countries have sometimes found it relatively easy to finance deficits by borrowing in a more explicit way. But when foreigners are unwilling to hold a nation's currency and when loans are difficult to obtain or burdensome, then deficits become a problem of state policy.

The balance of payments is the outcome of millions of daily actions of consumers and capitalists pursuing their needs and their profits respectively. But the regulation of a country's balance of payments is the inevitable responsibility of the state as part of its role as ultimate monetary authority. If the net result of the private decisions is the existence of a balance of payments deficit this very often requires state action to control or reverse it.

In principle, there are a variety of possible policies, which may be summarized in four categories:

(a) 'expenditure-switching' policies such as the devaluation of currencies or the imposition of tariffs on imports or subsidies on exports; these change relative prices to consumers and change relative profitability to capitalist producers and traders;

(b) 'expenditure-reducing' policies which aim to reduce imports as a by-product of reducing total national expenditure, through austerity policies like cutting government spending, raising taxes, controlling wage rates and so on;

(c) direct controls which may either be imposed against imports or against the export of capital;

(d) a number of miscellaneous policies such as measures to encourage the import of capital (e.g. tax holidays, enterprise zones, repressing trade unions to keep wages down and discipline up, and so on).

The choice of balance of payments adjustment policies is a highly political one, for they have very different effects on the various social classes. For example, deflation leading to higher unemployment in a poor Third World country affects workers and peasants, but tariffs may hinder the actions of capitalists.

There are also structural factors which are apt to affect the evolution of balance of payments policies. The growth of international banking has tended to make it increasingly difficult for governments to control the movements of short-term money-capital, even if they should want to do so. And the changing structure of economic power in the world – with the expanding role of the I M F in the wake of the debt crisis – has meant that it is also increasingly difficult for governments to regulate their balance of payments by means of direct controls on the movement of goods or restrictions on capital investments.

In the absence, under the existing structure of international economic relations, of serious pressure on surplus countries to reduce their surpluses, the burden of international adjustment falls on the deficit countries (with the exception of those who are credit-worthy, such as the USA); it tends therefore to fall on the countries, especially of the poorer Third World, which are already most disadvantaged economically. And they can only pursue policies such as devaluation, which force them to compete with each other, or austerity programmes, which fall most heavily on their most disadvantaged citizens.

(ii) *An international state?*

One result of the various problems for national governments is the emerging need for forms of international regulation. So another sense in which the capitalist system has become internationalized is with regard to the state itself.

Even the most powerful capitalist states have found that domestic economic policy is not sufficient to control their own economies. For example, government attempts to expand total demand are limited by the risk of raising imports so much that the balance of payments becomes critically in deficit. Attempts are made to resolve such contradictions by co-ordinating policies and establishing international institutions. Some of the more important ones are founded this century:

(a) the United Nations (UN): superseding the League of Nations after the Second World War, a world-based organization aimed at reducing military conflicts (through its Security Council) and promoting co-operation (through its Economic and Social Council);

(b) the International Bank for Reconstruction and Development, commonly called the 'World Bank': an agency for channelling official aid through loans or grants to the underdeveloped world;

(c) the General Agreement on Trade and Tariffs (GATT): an organization promoting free trade by reducing import restrictions and lowering tariffs;

(d) the International Monetary Fund (IMF): set up at the Bretton Woods Conference in 1944 to encourage exchange rate stability by lending funds to countries in balance of payments difficulties (loans nowadays are often used to force governments to impose austerity policies);

(e) the Bank for International Settlements (BIS): the banker to countries' central banks, which also attempts to offset the effects of international monetary speculation;

(f) the Organization for Economic Co-operation and Development (OECD): an organization of advanced capitalist countries only, for reviewing their common economic problems;

(g) the European Economic Community (EEC), also called the Common Market: a customs union of European countries, based on a philosophy of unifying their economic policies and developing a European approach to world affairs; in practice, its main economic significance is as an agriculture price-support system (the Common Agricultural Policy).

Of these only the Common Market has come anywhere near being a supranational authority, with powers to regulate economic relations across Europe, though the principal members still retain a veto over policies and programmes adopted.

From the point of view of economics, none of these institutions has established even the rudiments of a significant international state, for one overriding reason: their budgets are far too small. Modern state intervention requires a large and increasing level of spending, yet their resources are limited by international rivalries to hopelessly small amounts. Moreover an international state would need to be able to regulate international banks as well as to fulfil an international lender-of-last-resort function. Neither the BIS nor the IMF has the necessary power to create unlimited international credit.

5. INTERNATIONALIZATION AND NEEDS

The internationalization of capital is like the transferring of a TV show on to the cinema screen. The story is usually the same but the action becomes more panoramic. Nobody can fail to notice how, over the past decades, the profit system has become more and more international, the issues and stakes seemingly more grandiose.

Yet, taking a long view, there was an earlier epoch of equal or even greater internationalization, one century ago. Today, as then, there are still many limits and constraints on how far it can go.

The biggest multinational corporation is forced to contend with the existence of many nation states, which continue to place obstacles in the way of the complete internationalization of capital. Even the financial corporations, which have apparently acquired the economic freedom of the globe, remain tied in some ways to individual nation states. In the absence of an international state with its central bank, all banks are forced to rely ultimately on national states to bail them out of bankruptcy should their assets become bad debts. So the internationalization of the system, though of great importance, is less complete than it is often thought to be. And to judge by past history there is no reason to expect that the system will make linear progress towards greater and greater internationalism.

One respect in particular in which the profit system has become less, not more, internationalized is in the supplies of labour-power. With relatively few constraints, capital has roamed the globe in search of amenable labour-power, but the extent to which workers themselves can cross it in search of wages has been rigidly controlled. The ease with which bankers and industrialists fly from one continent to another as representatives of capital contrasts sharply with the humiliating obstacles encountered by migrant workers who attempt to cross international borders.

If humans are to coexist and to progress on this finite planet, there must be an open exchange of cultures and social traditions, including the right to travel freely. Yet although the rise of mass communications technology has permitted events on one side of the earth to be portrayed on television in the intimacy of people's homes everywhere, the exchange is primarily one way, being dominated by the massive American media corporations. And though tourist travel has been extended it is confined to limited areas and to those workers in western countries with enough income to afford it.

A real international need for workers is for freedom to migrate to avoid the worst pangs of poverty. But, although workers are permitted, even encouraged, to buy commodities made in other countries, and although they may be employed by a foreign capitalist, they normally nowadays find it close to impossible to leave their own country to seek work in another. Dire as were the conditions suffered by nineteenth-century migrants to the USA and elsewhere, internationalization of the working class did provide an escape route for some of the casualties of capitalist development in Europe. Some 32 million took advantage of it in the years 1881 to 1915. Even in the 1960s period of full employment, migration was relatively and absolutely smaller than this. In the 1980s it has been cut back to almost nothing. The EEC permits freedom of movement within its area but elsewhere the restrictions are so great that only if you are in the tiny minority with some special scarce skill will the obstacles to your migration melt away.

Thus capitalism has tended to produce an internationalism which is intermittent, contradictory and extremely selective. This is not surprising in a system whose international characteristics have been created out of a need to destroy obstacles to the creation of profit. Such a system is bound to be very different to one in which international relations were a response to human needs.

CHAPTER 11

The Economic Role of the State

I. CAPITALISM'S POLITICAL INSTITUTIONS

It is universally acknowledged that one of the defining characteristics of twentieth-century as compared with nineteenth-century capitalism is the vastly expanded role played by the state. If you live in an advanced capitalist country you will almost certainly directly encounter some state institution every day of your life. You attend its schools, travel to work on its transport system, are cared for in its hospitals. And if you transgress its rules you may be arrested by its police, appear before its courts and even be put away in its prisons.

Across the capitalist world the state takes a great variety of political forms. Many countries, especially poorer ones, are ruled by the naked power of military dictatorships. A few have kings, sheikhs or religious leaders who wield real power. Many others (including nearly all the advanced countries) have parliamentary democratic regimes.

In all of these countries a number of institutions compose the state: the ministries and civil service who formulate and implement policy (the executive wing); sometimes legislative institutions (parliaments); the judicial system – the courts, judges, lawyers and (sometimes) jurors who administer justice; the coercive apparatus of the police and military; the local states (provinces, municipalities and so on) who generally administer public services on a local basis; and a host of public service institutions like hospitals, schools and broadcasting services. Although together these constitute the 'state', they are a mixed lot and do not necessarily form a coherent or united whole.

Most books on economics do not discuss the nature of the state, relegating the job to the separate domain of political science. They accept that economic policies can be discussed in a 'scientific' way, but they tend to regard the policy-making and policy-effecting institutions as given data. The state is typically assumed to be a neutral body which represents the 'public interest', a kind of neutral umpire which adjudicates between the many forces pushing and pulling in various directions.

This 'pluralist' vision of the state is not without its insights. But they must remain relatively superficial unless the state is seen in the context of a society whose driving force is the pursuit of profit and capital accumulation. This inherently antagonistic pursuit not only permeates all economic relationships; it also inevitably determines the nature and activities, indeed sometimes the very existence, of political institutions.

No single political theory can adequately explain how each of the various institutions of the state has come about. Different circumstances call for separate analysis based on the particular historical circumstances of each country. None the less, because all of them do exist within the capitalist mode of production they can be viewed as components of a system which maintains and extends the domination of capital over labour, though institutions perform such a function with varying adequacy.

The military and the police are the clearest examples of institutions dedicated to maintaining the existing structure of power – they do this through the use or threat of physical force. In a complex world they play many other roles, and some of these may be beneficial (for example, road traffic control) but their most basic role vis-à-vis the capitalist process is to enforce its rules and prevent its forceful subversion. This is often a more open function in Third World countries where violent repression of dissident groups is commonplace.

Everywhere these coercive institutions are supplemented by others which can be seen as legitimating the status quo. Thus the political parties, parliaments, established churches, welfare state ministries, mass media and so on, can all play a part in gaining an acceptance, even active support, of the business ideology favourable to the ruling class.

2. ECONOMIC ACTIVITIES OF THE STATE

From the beginnings of capitalism states have played a role in guaranteeing the general conditions under which production and exchange can flourish.

Even before capitalism developed on a wide scale, governments had come to buttress the institutions of private property. To facilitate the rise of capitalist agriculture the English state permitted the privatization of large areas of common land, through successive 'enclosure' movements. Peasant farmers were driven from the land and gradually formed the nucleus of the early working class.

States also sanctioned exchanges by guaranteeing contracts. One way of doing this was through their control of money, the medium of exchange (see Chapter 7). The flag (along with the rifle and the bayonet) and trade went hand in hand around the globe. And at home there were, even in the early days of the capitalist epoch, state institutions to deal with the casualties of capitalist development, such as the dreaded 'workhouses' that evolved as part of the English Poor Law framework.

As capitalism has grown more mature, the activities of state institutions in the capitalist process have been quantitatively and qualitatively transformed. They can be grouped under two main headings, those which assist in maintaining capitalist relations in general and those that constitute direct economic interventions in capital accumulation processes (what might be called the activities of social as opposed to private capital).

(i) *Maintaining capitalist relations*

The job of guaranteeing the general framework of capitalist production and exchange has become more complex, more consciously planned and more extensive. The mass of people dependent on capital has grown so much and the threat of class antagonism become at times so menacing that extensive state actions have been needed to preserve social harmony: this subsection looks at three under the shorthand terms 'welfarism', 'Keynesianism' and 'militarism'.

The 'poor law' principles of early capitalist states were gradually replaced, much sooner in some countries than in others, by the principles of social welfare. Early examples were the social insurance schemes introduced in Germany in the 1880s by Bismarck – a clear attempt to head off the rise of the trade union and labour movements. In early-twentieth-century Britain, the Liberal government of Lloyd George yielded to increasing demands for welfare and instituted the first elements of social insurance – an unemployment pay scheme and an old age pension for those over seventy. In the USA very little in the way of public welfare was provided, beyond the early poor law relief, until the 1930s depression called forth President Roosevelt's 'New Deal'. This was a programme largely designed to create jobs and it provided only the small beginnings of a social welfare system.

Consequently, the USA remained behind most European countries when, after the Second World War, the concept of the 'welfare state' and the ideal of social insurance were enunciated in various ways across the advanced capitalist world. This did not merely involve paying out public money to the unemployed, the old and the sick. It also meant erecting a wholly new apparatus for dealing with people's needs as they arose. Perhaps the most significant of these was the development of universal and direct state health services in the UK and Scandinavia. In other countries, medical practitioners were left as private agents, but none the less a system of subsidies permitted access to some medical services for all. Universal benefits, however, did not emerge in the USA; and it remained true even in Europe that the rich were always able to buy a better service.

A second important development of state activities has been the attempt to manage and co-ordinate the economic process through systems of 'demand management', Capitalism is a system in which each of the many units operates independently, not according to any conscious plan. According to orthodox economic theory, and indeed according to observation at some times, this did not matter since co-ordination would be provided by market forces. The British economist Keynes argued, in the 1930s, that states should adopt a more interventionist role through the conscious use of fiscal and monetary policies to regulate demand in the economy. So influential was he, that the term 'Keynesianism' has come to be almost synonymous with the philosophy of limited intervention in the capitalist economy.

Fiscal policy before Keynesianism tended to be guided by the commandment: whenever possible balance the budget. By contrast the Keynesian idea was to raise or lower taxes and to raise or lower government expenditure, so as to manipulate and regulate the overall level of demand. If this meant that the budget went into deficit, so that expenditure exceeded revenue, this was no bad thing.

Monetary policy also evolved under the Keynesian approach. Previously the job of the monetary authorities was to control the amount of money in circulation and as far as possible to maintain the value of currencies. After Keynesian ideas took hold, it was generally felt that the main aim should be to keep the interest rate low if possible in order to encourage investment, and in general to back up fiscal policy in the management of demand.

Keynes's ideas were adopted at one time or another by all governments in the advanced capitalist world. In assisting the co-ordinating function of the market when it failed, states were able to modify for a while the course of capitalist development. By seemingly avoiding crises, and by maintaining fairly full employment, they appeared to contribute towards maintaining the capitalist relationships on which the economy rests. (We shall look in further detail at how far they were or can be successful in this aim in Part Five.)

A less obviously economic way in which modern states guarantee capitalist relations is through militarism. Current levels of military expenditure are quite unprecedented for 'peacetime' – in 1982 the total for the whole world was over $600 billion and it continues to rise fast. That figure is equivalent to the income of the poorer half of the world's inhabitants: *every one* of these could have had their material living standards doubled with a hypothetical reallocation of the resources devoted to military activities. Among the advanced capitalist countries the USA has, since the Second World War, been by far the highest spender, both in absolute terms and relative to national income. (See Table 11.1.) Meanwhile Third World nations have been catching up by expanding their armed forces faster than the developed world.

Table 11.1   Military Expenditure, 1980

	US $ billion	% GDP
USA	144.0	5.6
Canada	4.7	1.9
Belgium	3.9	3.3
Denmark	1.6	2.5
France	26.5	4.0
West Germany	26.7	3.2
Italy	9.6	2.4
Netherlands	5.3	3.3
Norway	1.7	3.1
UK	26.8	5.2
Austria	8.93	1.1
Sweden	3.8	3.3
Switzerland	2.1	2.0
Japan	9.9	0.9
Australia	3.6	2.5

Source: Ruth Leger Sivard, *World Military and Social Expenditures, 1983*, Washington DC, World Priorities, 1983

These high levels of military expenditure result partly from the privileged position of the private arms corporations which together with the military personnel constitute a powerful political force – the so-called 'military-industrial complex'. Another contributing factor is the technological momentum of arms competition between the two superpowers. But the expenditures also reflect some more fundamental strategic requirements of modern capitalists which states are ultimately responding to.

One of these is the 'containment of communism' and keeping as much of the world's surface as possible open to capitalist exploitation. Some of the cold war rhetoric in the west reflects this need, though it is ideologically inflated in order to secure internal political consent for vast expenditures. A second strategic requirement is to aid domestic repression where other forms of maintaining consent to capitalist relations, such as the welfare state, have failed. Armed forces are typically used in breaking strikes, subverting anti-establishment movements, preparing for counter-revolution and so on. And a third role for military power, exercised in particular by the USA, has been to back the imperialist domination of Third World countries.

Military activities are inherently wasteful – they do not meet any human needs. Yet the destructive capabilities in the world have reached proportions that are hard to grasp in their totality. The global irrationality of such an allocation of resources, when at the same time the most basic needs of many millions of people are not met, is plain. For the dominant classes of nation states militarism has a rational function in maintaining the established order through physical and ideological means, whether the order be that of bureaucratic elites of the Soviet bloc or the capitalist classes in the western world. And from the point of view of the arms corporations and traders the system is highly rational – it presents them with the easiest of ways to make gargantuan profits. Some of the biggest arms manufacturers which benefit from this privileged position in the USA and western Europe are Lockheed (USA), Grumman (USA), Thomson, SNIAS, Dassault and DTCN (all France), British Aerospace and Rolls Royce (both UK). Experience suggests that profit levels on arms (partly because prices are directly negotiated with defence ministries) tend to be higher and more secure than profit levels in general.

(ii) *Social capital*

From the late nineteenth century onwards, the mature capitalist states began increasingly to intervene directly in the basic processes of capital accumulation. State institutions came to modify substantially the exchange and production processes in certain areas, even to participate as actual producers. It is useful to classify their interventions as of two types.

First come interventions which reduce *the private cost of the means of production:* large fixed-capital investments such as roads, railways, sewerage systems and so on – that is, the physical infrastructure of economic society. The invention of the motor car and the lorry, for instance, brought with them the need for a massive expansion of road networks. The state also participates in the provision of 'circulating capital' – that is, of some basic inputs which are used up in production, such as electricity, coal and other energy supplies, and water.

Sometimes states have simply subsidized capitalist provision of these inputs, by reducing tax liabilities. Sometimes the government pays private producers to do the work as, for example, when a construction company contracts to build a road. Alternatively, it may itself become a producer – it may directly employ workers to build the road. Many of these forms of capital have been supplied by the nationalized industries, already discussed in Chapter 2.

Second come interventions which reduce *the cost of reproduction of labour-power:* state institutions now supplement money wages in the reproduction of labour-power, most importantly through the education system, whose primary function is to produce a workforce equipped with basic skills. Mass state education has expanded in many capitalist countries in roughly three waves. It began in the late nineteenth and early twentieth centuries with the provision of primary schooling for all; secondary schooling expanded later, generally after the First World War; and after the Second World War came the rise of tertiary education, including both a wide provision of universities and an expansion of technical colleges designed to improve the skills of the elite sections of the workforce.

If states failed to provide education and training, the cost would fall either on individuals (in which case capitalists would have to pay higher wages) or on firms (paying for their own workforces). Hence state provision serves to reduce the private cost of skilled labour-power.

In addition to providing skills, schools and colleges are designed to inculcate the social habits of reliability, punctuality, responsibility and respect for authority which are required for workers in places of work.

Even more broadly, schoolteachers are often obliged to engage the interests of adolescents who have no further use for education but no prospect of getting a job were they allowed to leave school. This activity is simply part of maintaining social stability and would be more properly classified under subsection (i) along with military expenditure and the welfare state.

Education provided free by the state may be classified as 'collective consumption', a category which covers also a number of other needs often satisfied in modern capitalism through the state, such as sewerage, waste disposal, roads for private (non-work) use, health services, street lights, recreation facilities and so on. Although many of these (for example, nationalized health services) came about partly as a response to liberal and working-class demands, all can also have a functional benefit for capitalists by cutting the private costs they have to pay for their required labour-power by more than the extra taxes required to finance them. In the case of medical services the concrete benefit for capitalists is the improved health and quality of the labour force.

Some elements of social consumption may appropriately be thought of as a 'social wage', in so far as their receipt is conditional on the sale of labour-power. Thus, for example, the unemployed person receives insurance payments from the state in return for contributions made previously while working. Moreover, the elderly person also receives a state pension which is partly dependent on his or her previous work record. Benefits which are paid whether or not the person has worked, are more appropriately placed in subsection (i) above, as helping to maintain capitalist relations – in other words, as part of the welfare state.

All these direct interventions of the state, whose purpose is to reduce the private costs of means of production or of labour-power, result in expenditures which are aptly called *social capital*: 'capital', because their primary function is directly to bolster the process of capital accumulation; 'social', because they are paid for through state institutions rather than by private capitalists. Social capital is essentially a phenomenon of the twentieth century, even if elements of it may be found earlier. Its growth is a response to new needs of capital as a whole, which for various reasons may not be satisfactorily met by individual capitalists.

Some of these needs are financial. Many social capital projects require the outlay of enormous sums of money which only states are large enough to mobilize through taxation. Closely related to this is the question of risk: even if a private corporation has the financial resources necessary, it may be deterred from investing by the risk involved of committing a large sum to a single project; the government may evaluate the risk differently in the interests of all capitalists (or, at least, a section of them), and find it worth taking. Similarly it may be able to take a longer-term view than a private firm which, although it aims to survive indefinitely, may have to concern itself with being profitable always in the short run and so avoid large investments with a long gestation period (like dams, bridges, roads and airports).

Social capital is also a response to the danger that some projects, if privately undertaken, might lead to monopoly exploitation of other capitalists as well as of individual consumers. If there is only one electricity supply company (because two or more would be much less efficient, with higher average costs), that company could charge higher prices by restricting supply. In these circumstances states often intervene in one of two ways: either production is nationalized as, for example, was done with electricity or gas production in the U K, or the private companies are regulated, as in the USA, by a bureaucracy whose function is essentially to control the price at which the commodity is sold.

A third source of the growth of social capital is goods and services that have 'positive externalities'. In Chapter 8 we already encountered 'negative externalities' such as pollution where one capitalist's activities impose costs on everyone else. The capitalist producing a 'positive externality' is assumed unable to charge for the benefits which others receive. A few examples will show the advantages of state intervention to produce something that has a positive externality.

Roads to meet the needs of modern transport, for instance, are not paid for by a road-producing corporation; it could never hope to receive any profits because trying to charge users would be far too expensive. Education and training also have substantial 'external' benefits for capitalists. The skills produced by a general technical training, for example, cannot be marketed by the college that imparted them. If an individual worker cannot afford to pay for training, the skills will not be acquired, and capitalists' needs will not be fulfilled. This is why governments often intervene to pay for the training. More generally, the education system for children can be made to benefit capitalists in general in several ways, but since these benefits cannot be charged for it is in capitalists' interests for the state to finance the system.

(iii) *Against 'functionalism'*

Our preceding two sections have classified the economic activities of states according to how they help the functioning of capitalism. But this may give the misleading impression that *all* the economic activities of political institutions should be simply interpreted in this light, a 'functionalist' notion we must now dispel. To begin with, although a rise of state economic activity can be observed in all capitalist countries, there remains a large variation in the scope of state activities. This variety does not simply reflect different capitalist needs in different places. In fact there is no method by which general capitalist needs are magically translated into state actions. Capitalists' general interests can be represented only if a political institution evolves which is sufficiently centralized and detached to divorce itself from the special interests of particular sections of the class.

Moreover, capitalist societies contain working classes, and other less central classes such as professionals and the petty bourgeoisie as well as capitalists. In a modern parliamentary democracy all these can modify the nature of political institutions even if they remain in the last analysis embedded in capitalism. States and ruling classes on occasion yield to political pressure from the working class, and part of the expansion of the welfare state can be interpreted in this way as a concession. This is so even though the resulting institutions were to a considerable extent forged in ways beneficial to capitalist interests.

Not all capitalists benefit equally from state activities. Which activities expand depends, therefore, on which groups have most political sway. Firms which produce armaments want governments to raise their military budgets, while textbook publishers like to see an expansion of education, and drug companies an increase in national health services. They may not all have their way.

State interventions are not necessarily always beneficial for capitalism. They can at times become actively disadvantageous for capitalist relations. The same policies can be a help in one way, yet a hindrance in others; or they can help the survival of capitalism at one time, yet later be a threat to it. Some of these contradictions are illustrated in the final part of this chapter where we review the limits to the expansion of the state in capitalism.

All these qualifications mean that, while we have presented a logical and historical framework for looking at the various economic activities of the state, there is no all-explaining general theory of why, when and where these activities have grown. It partly depends on the particular history and the specific balance of class forces in each country.

3. CAPITALIST PLANNING

Economic planning means the allocation of resources to their uses, and the distribution of commodities to people, by some form of conscious authority, either democratic or not. On a microeconomic level, planning is a regular activity taking place in firms and state bureaucracies. Managers decide, for example, how to allocate machines and workers to tasks within the factory. But 'economic planning' refers instead to a co-ordination strategy for the whole economy.

In the fascist regimes of Germany and Italy in the 1930s the economy was closely controlled, and during the two world wars most belligerents of necessity instituted a planning mechanism of some kind. The aim was to restructure the economy as rapidly as possible towards the basic aim of military success. It meant, for example, the planned allocation of labour between civilian industries and the armed forces, the direction of investment funds and the rationing of food, furniture, clothing and other necessities. But these periods were exceptional, and though they are in themselves interesting, they do not answer the question of whether capitalism can be planned in times of peace.

At one extreme, 'imperative' planning, with powers to compel conformity by law or force, is incompatible with capitalism. It is part of the essence of the system that capitalists have the freedom to dispose of their resources in the way which will maximize their profits. If they have no control over what happens to their capital it ceases, in effect, to be their property. Some people have argued, however, that there is a halfway house – a mechanism which encourages all the separate competing businesses to conform to a coherent overall strategy for the economy, which will ensure no bottlenecks or surpluses in any industries, adequate profits and a sufficient growth of demand.

The most notable practical experiment of this kind is the system of 'indicative' planning developed in France in the 1950s. There, the legacy of wartime controls was used to institute an apparatus designed to promote growth and other varying aims over planning periods of four or five years. The various plans were apparently successful, in that the French economy grew rapidly for the two post-war decades, a fact which occasionally led to more extensive planning being proposed in other countries. Other economies, however, such as West Germany, were equally or more successful in the same period without a formal planning mechanism. So economic historians of the post-war boom period have been unable to decide whether planning is beneficial. In any case the planning mechanisms were unable to prevent the onset of the crises which beset the whole capitalist world in the 1970s. The system has now been abandoned almost everywhere.

The plans in France and elsewhere were more or less closely controlled by the capitalist class, working through its dominance over political institutions. Planning, however, is not universally regarded as an aid to the maintenance of capitalist relations, and whether plans are adopted or not has depended on the specific historical circumstances of each country and in particular on the complex relationships between big business and political institutions. The association of planning with 'socialism', and the fear that capitalist control of industry could be replaced by social control, partly explains the political opposition by big business to the Labour government's plan in Britain in the mid 1960s. In France the plans were never tainted with anything but capitalism.

4. THE GROWTH OF STATE EXPENDITURE

One way of charting expanding state activities is to examine the official figures for state expenditure (national and local) in the advanced capitalist countries. This does not fully capture what political institutions do, since some interventions can have considerable effects on the private economy without entailing much public spending – for example, the regulation of a monopoly energy supply company or the granting of tax concessions. But most state activities do involve expenditure, and we find, not surprisingly, that more state intervention is reflected in rising levels of public spending.

The best picture is gained from looking at state spending as a share of a consistently selected measure of national spending or national income (for detailed comparison of these measures see Technical Annexe 14.C). Different countries and different dates can be compared only if the same measure is used.

Reliable information on the past is for most purposes restricted to the UK and the USA, so Table 11.2 shows the long-term rise in state expenditure in these two countries, broken down to some extent by functional categories. Through several decades there were substantial rises in every category of expenditure.

Diagram 11.1 illustrates the trends in a number of major advanced capitalist countries since 1961. In all cases there was a continued rise in the proportion of public spending, apparently extending the longer-run trends identified in Table 11.2 for the USA and the UK. In some cases, the extent

Table 11.2 Public Spending as a Percentage of GNP, 1913–73

		1913	1973
(a) UK	Debt service	0.95	4.6
	Military-related	3.0	4.7
	Civil government	0.8	2.6
	Economic support to industry	4.0	7.0
	Social welfare	4.7	28.4
	TOTAL EXPENDITURE %	13.45	47.3

		1927	1977
(b) USA	Military-related	1.2	6.7
	Social welfare	0.7	11.4
	Other civilian	8.5	14.8
	TOTAL EXPENDITURE %	10.4	32.9

Sources: F. Green and P. Nore, *Economics: An Anti-Text*, London, Macmillan, 1977, p. 185. Public Sector Crisis Reader Collective, K. Fox *et al.*, *Crisis in the Public Sector*, Monthly Review Press and Union for Radical Political Economics, New York, 1981, p. 3

of the rise was remarkable and similiar trends are found on the whole for Third World countries.

Yet more detailed analysis shows that the growth in most advanced capitalist nations does not come from increased spending by governments on commodities (either labour-power or various commodities supplied by capitalists). This kind of spending remained, roughly speaking, a constant proportion of GDP (Gross Domestic Product), about 20 per cent on average for the major capitalist countries since the 1960s.

The increases have come partly from an increase in repayments of public debt but, much more importantly, from increases in transfers and subsidies: that is, flows of money, from the government to people or to firms, which are not a payment for services or goods. These consisted mainly of welfare payments of various kinds – to the unemployed, the sick and those on low incomes – as well as pensions for old people.

Explaining these rises in spending is a complex matter which would need to be answered in rather different ways depending on the country under consideration. We can, however, point to the basic ingredients of any analysis.

First, there is the development of class struggle at a political level, which in many countries obliged the ruling class to make concessions to the

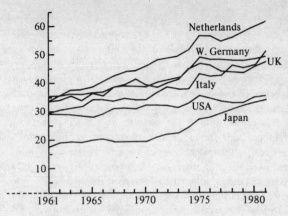

Diagram 11.1   Public Expenditure as a Percentage of GDP

principle of social welfare. In some cases this was achieved through the expansion of parliamentary democracy, in others by struggles outside parliament. In either case, once rights or expectations to public benefits are conceded, certain increases in public spending become more or less inevitable. If the numbers of old people rise, so will the amount paid out in state pensions and in health care, once the principle of social insurance is guaranteed. Apart from such demographic factors, there are also other reasons why welfare needs expand as capitalism develops. An important example is the rise of mass unemployment across the capitalist world that accompanied the end of the post-war boom. And as the structure of capitalism changes – with loss of jobs in one place followed by new jobs elsewhere often requiring new skills – the attendant social problems due to the disruption of people's lives bring with them further 'needs', for social workers, prison guards and so on, all of which have to be paid from the state.

Much of this spending serves, however inadequately, the function of helping to legitimate the system and so to maintain capitalist relationships. It can therefore usefully be categorized as necessary 'social expenses'. In the recent past nearly all the relative rise in state spending has been of this kind. An exception is the USA in the 1980s where a sharp increase resulted from an upsurge of military spending. In the longer run everywhere the rise in state spending embraces welfare entitlements, military spending (another 'social expense') and expenditures associated with social capital such as public investments in infrastructures, education and training.

5. THE LIMITS TO STATE INTERVENTION

In 1976 a senior member of the UK Labour government, which was officially committed to the principles of the welfare state, said in a speech: 'I do not think you can push public expenditure significantly above 60 per cent [of national income] and maintain the values of a plural society with adequate freedom of choice. We are here at the frontiers of social democracy.' At the time the ratio was not far from this magical 60 per cent but shortly afterwards a redefinition of the statistics brought it down to 49 per cent. Social democracy, it seemed, had been rescued by the gallant statisticians. What this really illustrates, however, is that, while all economists concur that there is *some* limit, there is much confusion and disagreement over where it comes and whether it has yet been reached.

Such arguments tend to be highly coloured by the disputant's political and ideological perspectives. The economist with right-wing political views may automatically argue that state expenditure is 'too high', forgetting to mention the positive functions it serves for capital. Conversely, left-wing people sometimes argue too naively that more state expenditure is required to meet social needs, forgetting to consider whether this is compatible with a capitalist economic basis. Here we shall list five *possible* limitations on further expanding the state's role in the economy.

(i) *The nation state*

One restriction on state action derives from the contradiction between the national basis of political institutions and the internationalization of capital. If states have come to manage the collective interests of capitalists, or more generally to be systems of political domination for capitalists, how can they continue to function when capital itself knows no national boundaries? To take a concrete example, a state's ability to maintain capitalist relations requires that it can act occasionally against individual capitalists' interests, but this becomes difficult when dealing with multinational corporations. These can play off one government against another in order to get the most favourable deal, in terms of subsidies and tax reliefs, or state controls, by threatening to withdraw their operations to other parts of the globe.

National policies of demand management may also turn out to have perverse and unexpected effects when the national economy is open to international economic forces as is increasingly the case. (Chapter 10 contains other examples of this.)

(ii) *Ideology*

There is ultimately the possibility of an ideological limit to state expansion under capitalism, though it is rather imprecise. Socially controlled enterprises, for example, if they are successful and survive without support, call into question the advantages of private ownership of the means of production. For this reason, many capitalists have opposed the nationalizations that have occurred in many European countries. Even though they are limited, and serve the interests of the bulk of capitalists, they pose in however inadequate a way the possibility of socialism. Similarly, some capitalists have opposed the expansion of social welfare – which is based on the principle of meeting needs collectively – preferring where possible to expand company welfare schemes instead. Anywhere that state institutions displace private capitalists brings the potential for questioning the profit motive.

In practice the fears of such capitalists have been exaggerated. Their premonitions of the profit system's imminent doom were never so intense as when a left-wing Labour government was elected in the UK in 1945; but they need not have worried. In the 1980s the danger (for capitalists) that more expenditure or a few nationalizations would open the door to socialism seemed rather remote, as the uninspiring experience of President Mitterrand's government in France showed; so we do not believe this to be important limit at present.

(iii) *Work incentives*

Another ultimate limit arises from the most central characteristic of capitalism: the wage relationship which economically coerces workers to sell their labour-power.

We have interpreted the rise of the post-war welfare states as in great part a project to help maintain the capitalist relationship in general. Yet if welfare were extended so far as to prevent all hardship it would diminish the fundamental capitalist coercion at work, the force of economic necessity. In a society where work is for most an alienated, boring and uncreative activity, there would be a reduced supply of labour-power, and a lesser degree of external discipline on workers since the economic threat of job loss would be lessened. Governments, therefore, may have a difficult task in balancing the need to maintain their legitimacy (which requires them to provide sufficient social welfare to avoid excessively obvious poverty), with the need to aid accumulation (which requires that social welfare should not remove economic coercion). In other words, the welfare state must not expand so far as to disrupt the reproduction of labour-power.

Although this is a limit in principle, it has not in practice proved to be a real constraint so far. It is true that in some countries very small groups of workers, usually low-paid with families, have occasionally been caught in a 'poverty trap', whereby taking a job disqualified them from some welfare benefits and raised their taxes to the point where they would be worse off. Yet for the vast majority of workers incentives have not been substantially impaired.

(iv) *Investment incentives*

It is often claimed that if public expenditure rises too high it will 'crowd out' the investment of private capitalists causing the growth of the economy to slow down and even ultimately an economic crisis. This proposition sometimes rests on a distinction between the 'productive' work which is done by private sector workers and the 'unproductive' work performed by state workers. Since the latter (except those in state enterprises) do not produce any profits, their wages must come ultimately from profits in the private sector, so that the lower limit to acceptable private profits implies an upper limit to public spending.

There is admittedly a qualitative difference between the production processes of state and private sector workers. The former are often not producing commodities for sale – normally education, welfare, health services and so on are provided free. Hence there is a difference in the discipline exercised in the absence of a market (no threat of bankruptcy), while also the quality of work can be more rewarding and self-motivating. It is clear, moreover, that many state activities have to be financed and that they have no returns.

This is sometimes how the discussion is left. It is helpful, however, to recall the two main categories of public expenditure, social capital and social expenses. Let us imagine that the state raises social expenses (welfare) spending and finances this increase by higher taxes. The immediate effect is that the taxes will have to be paid either by capitalists out of profits, or by workers out of wages (in which case they will try to negotiate a wage increase to compensate for this). In both cases rising social expenses will tend to threaten capitalist profits and so investment. But as long as there are unused resources in the economy the new spending will also tend to raise demand for goods and services and this may ultimately increase profits and investment. Only in an economy where all resources were being used would rising welfare spending unambiguously eat into profits.

Sometimes the spending is not covered by taxes but financed by borrowing. Much of the argument about crowding out has been concerned with whether government borrowing raises interest rates and corners funds which would otherwise have been used for private investment. Once again, even if this happens as an immediate effect, the indirect expansionary effect of the new spending may end up by augmenting the funds available for capitalist investment. So the way that government spending is financed is irrelevant to whether crowding out exists (though not to how it manifests itself). And even if there has been some crowding out of capitalist investment it does not follow that it has caused the rate of growth to fall.

This argument is reinforced in the case of social capital spending because this has a direct functional benefit for capitalists. It reduces the costs of the means of production and of labour-power, thus raising profits. If the spending is of the investment type (such as infrastructural spending on fixed capital, or training expenditure on skill acquisition) it will raise productivity. This means that social capital could in principle go on rising as long as it is indirectly 'productive' in the sense we have described, just as any private capital spending can go on rising while the capitalist economy survives.

Those who argue that high state expenditure caused the slowdown in economic growth in the 1970s (and hence that this fourth limit has already been reached) are apt to ignore this distinction between types of state spending.

None the less, there is some (not conclusive) evidence that crowding out has recently been a problem for capitalists. One indication is provided by the contradictory effects of militarism. As we have seen, this benefits capitalism in a number of ways, but also brings disadvantages. Chief among these is the enormous cost, which by using resources wastefully hinders the long-run competitiveness of the militaristic nation. And there is very little evidence of technological spin-offs or returns that could compensate for this by enhancing the revenues of capitalists other than the arms corporations and their subsidiaries. Statistical evidence supports the view that a relatively high level of military expenditure goes along with a low level of non-military investment. Profits are directly or indirectly reduced by taxation to pay for armaments, and the result is lower investment.

This creates a contradiction in US hegemony (dominance) over the rest of the capitalist world. Its high degree of militarism helps the USA to maintain its military and political control over world affairs; yet its economic dominance has been whittled away partly as a result of relatively low levels of investment and hence its low long-term growth in productivity.

The wider proposition that high state expenditure in general is responsible for low growth has not been convincingly demonstrated despite a great deal of sophisticated economic research. The origins of capitalist crisis and the slowdown of growth in the 1970s which we discuss in Part Five are certainly a good deal more complex. There we will see how state expenditure can modify the course which crises take (in particular, by stimulating inflation) and how a crisis can itself affect the expansion of state expenditure, reversing the cause and effect relationship implied in the notion of crowding out.

(v) *The economy as limiting factor*

A final interpretation of the view that there is a limit to the expansion of the state could, therefore, be that its expenditure is itself largely determined by the success or failure of the economy.

If profits, rent and interest fall, then tax revenue from these sources is diminished too. Total taxes could therefore only be maintained if taxes (direct or indirect) out of wages could be increased, thereby decreasing workers' net wages. If this is successfully resisted, then there must be a fall in the amount of revenue obtained. There are two possible outcomes: either expenditure would have to be limited or eventually there would be in some sense a fiscal crisis.

A fiscal crisis caused in this way would be part of a general crisis of the economy, and not a separate problem of the state (just as the state institutions should be regarded as part of the capital accumulation process, not something outside it). We shall, therefore, postpone our discussion of whether the capitalist state is in practice suffering a fiscal crisis in the 1980s until Chapter 17, where we shall be able to link the question to the wider problems of modern capitalism.

If all expenditure and production were carried out by the state then the economy would, by simple logic, no longer be a capitalist one. This means that in some sense there must be a limit to the expansion of the state sector. But it does not seem that in any specific way the rise in state spending which has occurred is approaching any kind of limit at which capitalist relations would be seriously threatened.

It is wrong, therefore, to conceive of the question in terms of advancing steadily along a road between capitalism and socialism. In practice there seem to be very strong, built-in political and economic forces in the capitalist economies which prevent state expenditure from rising to a point where the existence of the profit system would be threatened. Almost certainly the capitalists' and social democrats' spectre of state expenditure choking the private economy to death is something which could only occur in the aftermath of a major qualitative political change in which private property was expropriated on a large scale.

That, however, must not stop us from recognizing that the rise of the state during the twentieth century has effected a very major modification of the capitalist economies. Particularly in the advanced countries it has reduced somewhat, though far from eliminated, the frightening material insecurity of working-class life. It has done a great deal to rationalize the process of capitalist profit making, though it has not made it a socially coherent and accountable process. And it has immeasurably increased the repressive power under its control.

CHAPTER 12

Development and Underdevelopment

I. CAPITALISM TRANSFORMS THE THIRD WORLD

The civilizing mission of modern western society has often been extolled. In fact the arrival of capitalism in non-European countries was as often as not a hideously barbaric event.

It was the quest for profit which led to 10 million people being taken as slaves from Africa to the New World between 1500 and 1850. In Australia and the Americas the settlers from capitalist societies performed genocide on 'more primitive' (less well-armed) peoples who stood in the way of their search for land or other forms of wealth. And in many cases the accumulated wealth of non-capitalist societies was plundered with little or no payment and found its way into the capitalist circulation process.

The later history of the contact of the leading capitalist nations with non-European peoples is one of continual subjugation. By 1914 over 900 million non-European people (nearly two-thirds of the world's inhabitants) had direct or indirect colonial rule imposed on them. They were frequently coerced into becoming wage workers and pressured into being a market for capitalistically produced goods. Often, as in the more advanced countries themselves, old forms of producing goods were destroyed by new capitalist ones.

In the nineteenth century even the critics of the expansion of capitalist Europe and North America expected the African, Asian and Latin American nations to repeat the capitalist economic development of the advanced countries and even to catch them up. The spread of decolonization after the Second World War encouraged the idea that the dark ages were over and that the poorer countries would swiftly gain their prosperity.

This optimistic expectation was reinforced by the feeling that the late-comers to industrialization and development would benefit by adopting the most modern technology and so jumping from very low to very high labour productivity in a single dramatic leap; there was an associated feeling that rational economic planning would eliminate wasteful mistakes and so avoid the chaos of previous capitalist development.

Yet the actual experience of the years since decolonization has led many people to conclude that capitalism has been more a curse than a blessing to the economies of the Third World.

The disputes which rage over such expectations and judgements are bedevilled by the problems of generalization. The notion of the Third World (as opposed to the developed capitalist and developed socialist countries) has become almost universal. But it comprises well over a hundred countries in Africa, Asia and Latin America which are not homogeneous in their economic conditions. To take an extreme example, South Korea and Ethiopia have almost identical population figures but South Korea's national income per head (admittedly a far from perfect measure, as we explain in Technical Annexe 14.C) is 55 times as high as that of Ethiopia. It has been one of the most dynamic capitalist nations of the last quarter-century and has become a major industrial power, while Ethiopia has undergone a process of impoverishment and is the scene of endemic and sometimes acute famine. Today, for most relevant purposes, it would obscure rather than clarify the relationships of world capitalism to regard two such distinct countries as even extremes of a single category.

Thirty years ago, however, the similarities would have been much greater. One of the features of the post-war development of world capitalism is the kind of polarization which it has led to within the vast area of the globe which is called 'the Third World', a phrase we shall continue to use but more as a geographical than an economic category.

There are real ways in which both the astounding industrialization of South Korea and the tragic immiseration of Ethiopia are bound up with the nature of modern capitalist development and crisis.

2. IS THE THIRD WORLD PART OF CAPITALISM?

Economists have disagreed about whether the Third World countries should be described as capitalist. One way to answer this question is to look at the way in which their economic life is organized.

There are some Third World countries – the more advanced countries of Latin America like Uruguay or Argentina, the most industrialized countries of Asia like Taiwan, South Korea, Hong Kong and Singapore – where the way of life is assuredly capitalist. They are industrialized and urbanized; wage labour is widespread; and there is a significant capitalist class.

In the poorer countries of Asia and Africa the great majority live in villages and work predominantly in agriculture. Very often their work, the ownership of property and the distribution of their products are not organized on capitalist lines: often the organization has more in common with communal or feudal forms. None the less it would be hard to find a single village anywhere in the Third World where there was not at least the presence of merchant capital and in most cases wage labour as well. In the cities capitalism is more the rule. Capitalist productive enterprises are common and most workers have broken their ties with the land to become proletarians. But even in some Third World cities a disproportionate number of people do not work under capitalist relations in the strict sense: they either work for the state or in some form of petty commodity production.

In these countries the spread of capitalist production relations then tends to be much less than in the advanced countries. It could be concluded that capitalism has still not fully transformed the economic life of these areas; that they are only semi-capitalist, somewhere, perhaps, along a road between feudal and capitalist society.

Looking at some Third World countries in this way can help in understanding the important interconnections which exist between capitalist and non-capitalist realms. For instance, the fact that workers retain ties to the land in a sustaining non-capitalist community may allow employers to pay, at least to some of their workforce, wages inadequate to keep them alive and fit enough to work – to 'super-exploit' them. The existence of a non-capitalist sector which people can sometimes fall back on for security can also make it easier for the capitalist system in the Third World to function without any of the elements of welfare provision characteristic of the advanced countries.

But despite the insights which can be offered by seeing some Third World countries as characterized by a coexistence of capitalist and non-capitalist modes of production, this is at best a very incomplete view.

Capitalism is not just a mode of production which does or does not characterize a particular geographical area. It is the dominant world system of production, distribution and trade which has evolved over several centuries. Virtually all countries, if not all villages, have been touched and in some way transformed by this evolution making them, in a sense, part of the capitalist system. Even countries in which capitalist relations are less common exist economically in an enforced symbiosis with this dominant system of production.

Over the centuries what has occurred in the economically advanced countries and what has happened in the more backward ones are together aspects of the evolution of a world capitalist system. Looked at in that way development in the advanced countries is one pole and underdevelopment in Third World countries another inseparable pole of the *same* process of world-wide development of the capitalist system.

According to this view (to be found in the well-known writings of economists Paul Baran and André Gunder Frank) the development of capitalism has polarized the world into developed and underdeveloped regions.

The underdeveloped are not simply stragglers along a road to a common end result, not aboriginal states simply lacking development yet. Rather, underdevelopment is a set of characteristics which have developed as a necessary by-product of the development of the advanced area of capitalism. Underdevelopment for the many is the dark side of development for the few.

Those who have seen underdevelopment in this way have none the less differed about what is the essence of the kind of polarization which has taken place. It has been seen variously as a polarization based on the structure of production or exports – between producers of manufactures and producers of primary products; or on income levels – between growing wealth in the advanced countries and growing poverty in the under-developed ones; or on the relations of finance and capital ownership – between capital-exporting creditor countries and capital-importing debtor countries. Also many versions of the polarization hypothesis see under-development as a process involving a combination of these dichotomies. Recently, however, the whole theory has tended to be summed up in terms of another form of polarization, that between economically independent and economically dependent nations.

Dependency theory argues that the structure of power in the world capitalist economy is so unequal that efforts to repeat in the underdeveloped countries the process of industrialization and development which took place in the developed countries are more or less doomed to failure. Either they face obstacles in the world market; or the social and political systems of the underdeveloped countries, which themselves reflect the influence of the developed countries, inhibit independent development.

The theory of dependency comes, so to speak, in various strengths. The most concentrated versions argue that all capitalist development is im-possible and that economic development is only possible after a social revolution and the construction of a socialist economic system. More dilute versions tend to advocate nationalist and protectionist economic policies in the underdeveloped countries as a possible route to capitalist industrial-ization.

We would not deny that in some ways those differences in strength are very fundamental, especially at the political level. But all versions of the theory have strengths and weaknesses in common. It is genuinely illum-inating to view the economic problems of underdeveloped countries as arising from the economic development and policies of the most advanced and powerful capitalist nations. And much of the analysis of the position of underdeveloped countries within world capitalism in this chapter will benefit from this illumination.

But the light cast by the theory is often so glaring that it blots out the contrasts of the landscape. The main problem of dependency theories has resulted from their tendency to view the world as a dichotomy between two relatively homogeneous groups of nations – the rich, industrialized or imperialist and the poor, underdeveloped or dominated. It is not very well adapted to explaining the growing divergencies *within* both blocs which have characterized the last quarter-century. Later in this chapter we shall see some of the symptoms of these divergencies when we look at the Newly Industrializing Countries (NICs), the problems of famine and acute economic decline.

3. WORLD WEALTH AND POVERTY

The statistics of world poverty are very hard to assimilate especially by those who live relatively comfortable lives in western Europe or North America. The fact is, however, that some 2,000 million people in the world (two-fifths of its population) live on incomes which are less than one-tenth of the western European and North American average.

One estimate of the degree of inequality in the capitalist world's distribution of income (shown in Table 12.1) shows that, after taking account of taxes and state benefits, the richest 5 per cent of the world's people get 30 per cent of its total income; the richest 30 per cent, which would include the majority in the developed countries and a small minority from the underdeveloped countries, get over 80 per cent. The remaining 20 per cent has to be divided among over 3 billion people. And the poorest tenth get only six-tenths of 1 per cent of the total.

Table 12.1 Capitalist World Shares of Incomes after Tax and Fiscal Benefits, 1970
(10 per cent of world total for 115 capitalist countries)

Poorest 10 per cent	0.62
Next 10 per cent	0.88
Next 10 per cent	1.35
Next 10 per cent	1.81
Next 10 per cent	2.50
Next 10 per cent	4.01
Next 10 per cent	7.74
Next 10 per cent	13.41
Second 10 per cent from top	21.19
Second 5 per cent from top	16.46
Top 5 per cent	30.05

Source: Albert Berry, F. Bouguignon and C. Morrisson, 'The Level of World Inequality: How Much Can One Say?' in the *Review of Income and Wealth*, series 29, no. 3, September 1983, p. 231

To give a more specific example, the average national income of India in 1983 was $260, that of the USA $14,110 – fifty-four times as high. This ratio is about the same as that of the distance between New Delhi and Washington DC, and the distance between Washington DC and the moon.

But the relation of official national income statistics to real economic welfare is so loose, and the enormity of the difference between the USA and India so great, that it may be more helpful to think instead of the differences in the nature of life: despite widespread poverty in the USA, the average white North American has a strongly built waterproof home, heated and/or cooled as appropriate, equipped with furniture and a large number of gadgets or luxuries, a more than adequate diet and a generously stocked larder and refrigerator, a car, regular access to public entertainment and a vast variety of other costly services, one or more periods of away-from-home vacation a year and so on. An average Indian lives in overcrowded conditions in a low-quality house, has an unvaried and inadequate diet and virtually nothing else.

These differences are part of a long-established process. The US national income is much higher than a century ago. Whether the Indian figure has risen at all during that period is debatable. Even the most optimistic estimates suggest that India's average income grew no more than one-third in the whole century before 1947, its date of independence from British rule.

It is true that numerous sources of income in India today are organized in a capitalist manner (most of Indian industry and trade and a growing section of its agriculture). But history reveals other sources of income in India which were destroyed by the spread of capitalism. The British cotton textile industry got a major boost at the outset of the Industrial Revolution by replacing imported Indian textiles and ruining an early Indian industry.

There were other examples, especially in Africa, where the capitalist colonial powers left the countries as poor as or poorer than when they annexed them. In Latin America it took centuries for the descendants of the Incas and other Central and South American societies to recover from the social and economic trauma produced by Spanish and Portuguese colonialization. Even today in the Andes the living standards of many peasants are probably lower than they were in the sixteenth century.

Most Central and South American countries, however, had higher average incomes in 1950 than Asia or Africa. In countries with significant European settlement the settlers initiated some capitalist development in a much larger variety of activities than was permitted in the colonial countries elsewhere. The same was true of the white-ruled countries of southern Africa.

4. THE THIRD WORLD IN THE INTERNATIONAL DIVISION OF LABOUR

In recent times the underdeveloped countries, even after achieving formal political independence, have continued to be profoundly affected by the development of the advanced capitalist countries. Most Third World countries reaped some rewards from the post-war boom, but many suffered badly with the onset of crises in the 1970s.

But the variations were very significant (see Table 12.2). A number of Third World countries had higher than average growth rates and made some headway towards closing the gap in income levels. Among these were some of the oil-producing countries though their major gains occurred after 1973. The other major gainers during the boom were the so-called NICs (Newly Industrializing Countries) which successfully broke into the export markets for certain manufactured goods as diverse as basketball shoes and computers. By contrast the boom scarcely reached Africa. In most parts of that continent growth in average income was barely perceptible.

Table 12.2 Annual Growth in GNP per capita, 1960–84

	1960–73	1973–80	1980–84
All underdeveloped countries	3.6	3.3	0.5
India	1.3	1.9	2.5
Low-income Africa	0.9	−0.1	−2.1
Major exporters of manufactures	4.3	3.7	0.1
Middle-income oil exporters	3.5	3.1	−0.8
Industrial capitalist countries	3.9	2.1	1.4

Source: World Bank, *World Development Report, 1985*, New York, Oxford University Press for the World Bank, 1985

This gulf in economic growth was sharply accentuated by the onset of crises in the world economy. In Africa, 1973 initiated a period of first slow and then rapid decline of its already tragically low incomes. Yet NICs like South Korea, Taiwan, Singapore and Hong Kong continued to boom, even if at times their success seemed a little more precarious.

There is a remarkably close correspondence between a country's average income and the way in which its productive activity is divided up between agriculture and industry. In the low-income countries the typical situation is for three-quarters of the labour force to work in agriculture and produce a little more than one-third of the value of national production. In what the World Bank calls 'middle income economies' 44 per cent of the labour force on average produce 15 per cent of national output. By contrast in the developed countries a mere 6 per cent of the workforce remain in agriculture, producing only 3 per cent of national output.

Moreover, the industrial workforces of the Third World have only been expanding slowly, with the exception of the NICs. The typical picture is one of only very slow change from the traditional, overwhelmingly agricultural productive structure.

Generally, productivity in agriculture is much lower than it is in industry. But in the most advanced countries agricultural productivity has caught up with overall productivity. This means that the small number of farm-workers in the most developed countries are immensely more productive than the relatively numerous farmworkers in underdeveloped countries. The value of output produced by a farmworker in the USA is about a hundred times that produced by a farmworker in India.

The division of international trade to some extent reflects these differences in economic structure between underdeveloped and developed countries, but with some exceptions. As expected, the great majority (86 per cent) of world manufactured exports come from the developed industrialized countries and only 14 per cent from the underdeveloped countries (see Table 12.3).

Table 12.3 Capitalist World Exports by Commodity and Area, 1980 (in $ billion)

	Developed countries	Underdeveloped countries	Total
Primary commodities			
oil	84	348	432
others	237	118	355
TOTAL	321	466	787
Manufactures and others	885	142	1027
TOTAL	1206	608	1814

Source: Chris Edwards, *The Fragmented World: competing perspectives on trade, money and crisis*, London and New York, Methuen, 1985, p. 56

Many underdeveloped countries, especially the poorest ones, export almost exclusively raw materials (agricultural or mineral) which have been little, if at all, processed. Taken as a whole, more than three-quarters of the Third World's exports are raw materials. But this figure is misleading. It includes oil, which is a very special commodity, many of whose producers, if geographically part of the Third World, are by no means poor. It may seem surprising that, excluding oil, the other primary products exported by Third World countries are now smaller in value than their manufactured exports. But these come from a tiny handful of countries. If these NICs are also excluded, then other Third World countries, especially in Africa, do indeed display the traditional expected pattern of exports almost exclusively of primary products. For some, more than half their exports are of one commodity: Uganda, Ethiopia and Colombia (coffee), Sudan (cotton), Zambia and Chile (copper), Ghana (cocoa), Guinea (bauxite), Bolivia (tin) and Malawi (tobacco).

It may also come as a surprise that the Third World's exports of primary products, other than oil, are smaller in value than the primary product exports of the advanced countries. This fact shows that in addition to the difference between rich and poor nations in the *structure* of trade there is also a difference in the *amount* of trade. Developed countries account for about two-thirds of all world exports and about the same proportion of primary commodity exports other than oil. While their share of manufactured exports dropped a little in the twenty years from 1960 to 1980, their share of primary exports actually increased during that time.

The comparative failure of underdeveloped countries even in primary products was provoked by three factors. One was the disruption of production by the great variety of economic, political and physical problems which have beset Third World countries, including natural disasters, planning and policy errors, lack of internal and external investment, famine, wars, invasions and political upheavals. A second was the fact that many of the primary products which the Third World produces are products for which demand has not expanded very fast in the long run, or fell very sharply in the short run after the crisis of 1973. As a result of this, the average prices of the Third World's primary products have, apart from a sudden and temporary upward lurch in 1973, declined continuously since 1965, while the prices of the manufactured imports have continued to rise. Third World countries have suffered, in other words, a worsening in their terms of trade. This has exacerbated balance of payments deficits and led to indebtedness (which will be discussed later).

A third, and associated, reason why underdeveloped countries have been losing their share of primary product exports is agricultural protectionism in the advanced capitalist countries. Because of the disproportionate political weight of farming communities in North America and western Europe, they have been systematically assisted by deficiency payments schemes or by protective import-prevention and surplus-buying schemes such as the EEC's Common Agricultural Policy. The most frequently condemned feature of this policy has been the obscene coexistence of vast surplus food stocks in rich western Europe and widespread famine and hunger in Africa,

Asia and Latin America. The EEC's 'defence' of its refusal to distribute the food stocks to those who need them is that this would ruin the market and so undermine the protective effect of the policy.

A less generally appreciated consequence is that the agricultural protectionism of the advanced countries closes off potential markets for Third World agricultural producers. It has been estimated by the World Bank that in 1983 the revenues lost to the Third World as a result of trade barriers against sugar and beef and veal exporters amounted in total to about $12.5 billion, at 1980 prices, which was about 10 per cent of the Third World's total exports of primary products.

It is a frequent complaint of Third World governments and capitalists that protectionism is also a major obstacle in the way of increasing their exports of manufactured goods to the markets of the developed countries, which try artificially to extend the life of dying industries whose products could be produced more competitively in the Third World. There is a lot of justice in this complaint. The tariff structures of the advanced countries are typically graded so that goods with a higher degree of processing pay a higher rate of duty. And in recent years there has been an upsurge of non-tariff restrictions on imports to the advanced countries (known as 'the new protectionism') which have been aimed specifically against the exports of Japan and the NICs. About one-fifth of all exports from underdeveloped countries are affected by such measures.

Typical of what can happen is the case of the Bangladeshi shirts. In the early 1980s a group of capitalists in Bangladesh (a country which according to World Bank statistics is exceeded in poverty only by Ethiopia) started exporting cotton shirts to Europe. They found a loophole through which to enter the market and had an extraordinary success. Sales in the UK alone jumped from 200,000 in 1983 to over 1 million in 1984. Similar amounts were sold in France and Germany. The industry accounted for nearly a tenth of Bangladesh's export earnings though it represented only one-thousandth of Europe's garment imports. But the UK and France took steps in 1985 to impose quotas against it. In the face of such policies it is hard not to be cynical about the possibilities of any real transformation of the world division of labour in favour of the underdeveloped countries.

None the less the NICs have succeeded where others have failed. No simple explanation is possible. The NICs differ and in all cases there have been multiple reasons for their success. But one reason has clearly been that the developed countries have been prepared to allow their industrial growth by granting them special privileges. They have been given more generous import quotas than other countries, though even so they have sometimes had to exhibit some very deft footwork to dodge the effect of the advanced countries' protectionism. They have also had some special privileges with regard to finance. Undoubtedly such special consideration had political motives. The desirability of supporting countries on the borders of Asian communism (South Korea, Hong Kong, Taiwan and Singapore) or with strong anti-socialist regimes (the Brazilian military dictatorship after the 1964 coup) were no doubt important considerations.

Orthodox economists have broadcast a fable that the NICs confirm the rewards given to the traditional virtues of free competition and the market. This is hardly supported by the evidence. South Korea, to quote an example, is extremely protectionist of its home market; its government has rigidly controlled the activities of foreign capital; its own capitalist sector is dominated by a group of huge conglomerate monopolies known as *chaebols* (of which one collapsed in 1985); and the state interferes in most aspects of the economy. Political opposition and in particular the free organization of labour have been ruthlessly suppressed, as in Singapore and other NICs.

While the real experience of the NICs can give little comfort to the proponents of orthodox free market economics, they also cannot be regarded, as many dependency theorists have regarded them, as insignificant exceptions to the general rule of underdevelopment as a polar opposite of development. The NICs are authentic examples of capitalist development taking place in the modern world.

The profit system has worked in a significant group of countries to produce industrialization at a much faster rate than in any of the developed countries except for Japan. Yet it has also produced, as it did in Europe and the USA in the nineteenth century, a relatively low-paid industrial proletariat, often predominantly of women, who to avoid starvation must endure sweatshop working conditions, which irreversibly damage their health, and who are usually prevented from organizing to defend themselves. It would be hard to evaluate their lives in comparison with the rural poverty of the billions who do not live in one of the NICs.

5. FAMINE

At the other extreme from the NICs are a number of Third World countries which have not only failed to achieve structural change and income growth but which have actually experienced economic decline. Sometimes this has been apocalyptic: large sections of the population have lost even the traditional means of survival, and millions of human beings have suffered a sad and slow death through starvation.

Across the sub-Saharan region of Africa a string of countries has been ravaged by famine since the early 1970s. The most common explanation is natural disaster resulting from drought. This is certainly one of its causes but a closer examination shows it to be an insufficient explanation. Many studies have found that famines occur even when food production has not fallen very markedly. In particular, the economist A. K. Sen in his study *Poverty and Famines* has shown that people starve to death not because there is no food available to eat, but because they have lost their ability to obtain that food, either through loss of income or loss of exchangeable commodities. It has been common, in Ethiopia for instance, for food to flow out of famine-stricken areas to more profitable markets. Famine therefore is partly an example of the failure of the market.

In many African countries, however, the present famines follow long periods of declining food production. These have to some extent been the result of the lack of investment in agriculture – in irrigation, soil preservation, extension services and so on. These failures can partly be blamed on policy errors and the over-representation of urban interests, partly on the failure of more advanced countries to supply sufficient and appropriate aid to carry out the needed investments. Some portion of the blame might also be placed on the agricultural protectionism of the advanced countries which helps to hold back Third World agricultural production. None the less, some agricultural markets have remained open and this fact has itself helped to contribute to the famines. Due to their chronic indebtedness, African, like other Third World, countries are under incessant pressure to expand their export earnings. In doing this they have encouraged the development of cash crops which can be exported. Land previously used for food production – either for growing crops or grazing animals – has been converted to cash crop production. This may be profitable and may produce foreign exchange at least in the short run; but at the same time it robs peasant producers and pastoralists of their land and cuts off their normal food supplies. From an environmental point of view, cash crop monoproduction accelerates soil erosion and desertification, and so further worsens the long-term agricultural problems.

Famines, therefore, are not acts of God. They are contributed to by the profit system both because monetary incentives may lead to the destruction of food supplies and also because the capitalist world market and structure of international debt may encourage developments which bring famine as a by-product.

This has not always and everywhere been the effect of capitalism on agriculture. Many will point to the Green Revolution in India as an example of capitalist agriculture performing a role equivalent to that which it performed in Europe in the eighteenth and nineteenth centuries.

It is true that in certain areas of northern India since 1965 a technical and social revolution has taken place in agriculture. High-yielding varieties of grain have been successfully introduced by capitalist farmers, with much state assistance. As a result the level of food production in India has been very markedly improved. A nation which was once beset by frequent famines now has a large food surplus. On the other hand many people remain hungry through lack of the means to buy the food. And the introduction of the Green Revolution itself has, by benefiting the rich farmers and often driving the smaller ones to the wall, increased the poverty of some while it has enriched others. Both where it succeeds and where it fails, therefore, capitalist agriculture has created new problems for many millions of people.

6. DEBT

Famine affects only a minority of developing countries but the insidious disease of indebtedness has during the 1980s infected the majority of them.

Debt, either to governments or to banks, has always been one of the ways in which the Third World has been tied into the capitalist system as a whole. But the debt crisis which erupted in 1982 was the result of a qualitatively new situation of very recent origin, which has effected a long-term shift in the relation of Third World countries to the capitalist system as a whole.

It arose from the problems of the advanced capitalist countries themselves. Vast loans were made to many developing countries by banks confident of a sustained growth of the world economy. The world crisis of 1979 put an end to their hopes.

There are two aspects to the 'problem' of debts. There is the story of the 1970s crises, the expansion of the loans, the increased fragility of the banks and their exposure to a handful of (mainly Latin American) vast debtors, in a highly internationalized, unregulated system. We shall examine this kind of debt problem in Chapter 17. But from the point of view of the Third World, the problem is much wider. Most of the countries in debt have relatively small amounts outstanding, not big enough to trouble a bank very much, but large enough in relation to their export earnings.

International bankers have become very adept at tiding over the seemingly endless rounds of debt rescheduling to countries such as Argentina, Brazil and Mexico; by the mid 1980s, the first debt problem had not festered into something worse. But, for many other debtor countries of the Third World, debt engendered a new form of subordination to the advanced capitalist countries.

At the centre of the new relationship is the International Monetary Fund (IMF) whose status has been transformed. The IMF has become the coordinator of loan rescheduling. Banks will not reschedule debt until the government concerned has given an undertaking about its economic policies which satisfies the IMF, a system known as 'conditionality'.

The IMF's approach to the treatment of debt is rather like that of nineteenth-century doctors to the treatment of mental illness: no diagnosis of symptoms or causes, just put the patient into a straitjacket. The IMF's straitjacket is a set of universally applied policies: cut back government spending; devalue the currency to increase the competitiveness and profitability of exporting; open up the economy to imports and the inflow of foreign private capital; cut wages in order both to reduce consumption of imports and to increase the competitiveness (a euphemism for profitability) of capitalist production.

These policies conflict with domestic development objectives in the Third World and help to impose a deflationary bias on the world capitalist economy. The IMF's straitjacket, now tied around about fifty Third World countries, obliges their governments to impose material hardship on their citizens in the interests of financial institutions in New York or London operated by men of fabulous wealth. In this way the capitalist system's imperative for profits and stability are translated into an attack on the world's poorest inhabitants.

7. FOREIGN INVESTMENT IN THE THIRD WORLD

The underdeveloped countries are integrated into the world capitalist system not only through trade and debt but also through transnational investment. To the companies of the advanced countries which invest in factories, mines and other production facilities in the underdeveloped countries this is nothing special. In their search for profits, companies, especially large companies, are always on the look-out for a higher return anywhere in the world. They look everywhere for cheaper raw materials, or lower production costs, or new markets. They find them more often than not in other developed countries which are the destination of most foreign investment. Even so, the capitalists in the advanced countries own a formidable amount of property in the underdeveloped ones.

In formal colonial times most foreign investment tended to be in raw material production – in copper or tin mines and in banana, rubber or cotton plantations – and in the transportation systems needed to ship out these raw materials. The state in the producing countries became simply one arm of the capitalist producing companies. It would enforce capitalist property laws, control public order and when necessary take measures to ensure a cheap and docile labour force for the companies.

This pattern of penetration produced the small, economically illogical nations of Africa, for instance, where non-plantation agriculture was kept primitive and transport and communication systems were simply geared towards links with the colonial country.

The objective of that pattern of investment was to meet demand in the industrialized countries, not to supply the local market; profit was extracted rather than reinvested in the colonial countries themselves. Only in countries with sizeable settler populations from the industrialized countries did foreign investment take a different form – investment in manufacturing to supply the local market, usually in manufactured products.

In the period since 1950, international capital investment has often taken a different form. The legacy of colonial-style, primary-producing investment has persisted and in a number of countries remains the dominant form of investment. But by the 1960s foreign investment had come to mean pre-dominantly investment in manufacturing production facilities – mostly of consumption goods but even in some cases in investment goods also.

The reason most commonly adduced for this newer kind of investment is that it is part of an effort by capitalist manufacturing companies to search out cheaper sources of labour than exist in the advanced countries.

This has been a common motive but the evidence suggests that it is far from being the most common one. If the main inducement was the cheap labour then we would expect a considerable proportion of the products of foreign investment to be exported back to the advanced countries. On average, however, this does not happen. The great majority (over 75 per cent) of the output of foreign investors in the underdeveloped countries is sold in its country of manufacture; in Brazil the figure is 95 per cent.

This pattern results from a number of factors. Capitalists see significant markets in a number of underdeveloped countries and find it more profitable to supply them locally rather than paying transport costs from their home countries. Or they may already have a market in an undeveloped country which threatens to get cut off by tariff protection unless they 'jump' the tariff wall by installing a plant in the country in question.

Multinationals are still investing in the Third World; the evidence suggests that their rates of profit there are generally higher if more uncertain. But the inflows are not as large as they used to be, in comparison to official aid and to bank lending. Foreign investors seem to have an obsession with stability in Third World countries. They select places to invest based on what is euphemistically called their 'country risk', and they tend to support measures of political, diplomatic or military intervention designed to restore stability when it is threatened. In this sense stability tends to be equated with political authoritarianism, and the repression of trade unions and political opposition. The plot launched by International Telephone and Telegraph (ITT) to overthrow the constitutionally elected government of Salvador Allende in Chile from 1970 to 1973 is a particularly well-documented case of the extra-economic activities of foreign investors. They often require a close understanding with the government of the foreign investor's country of origin and so interconnect with official economic and military aid policies.

8. AID AND ARMS

A new feature of the post-1945 capitalist world was a nominal commitment by governments of the advanced countries to assist the economic development of the backward ones. As a result a multitude of bilateral and multilateral aid programmes has been established.

The level of aid under these programmes has been small relative both to the needs of the recipients and to the capacity of the donors. Despite the ambitious targets of the United Nations 'Development Decades' the advanced countries by the early 1980s were transferring no more than one-third of 1 per cent of their GNP in aid. At $33.6 billion this was about one-third of the net financial flow to the Third World in 1983, a little less than new loans from commercial banks. The real value of aid flows has been even lower owing to an increasing tendency for aid to be tied in various ways – for example, to purchases from the donor country. Official aid, especially in the form of export credits, has been in part a means of channelling state support to capitalists in the advanced countries. Most aid has not been invested in productive activities in the Third World. Critiques of aid programmes have pointed out how aid funds have been channelled into supporting corrupt and unproductive governments or wasted on inappropriate programmes. Model aid programmes do exist but they are few and far between.

This is partly because those countries which have taken the most radical approach towards the problem of development – especially when this involves attacking the domestic and foreign interests which stand in the way of development – have found it most difficult to obtain aid. Radical policies often lead to the cut-off of aid flows. Aid has been widely used by the advanced countries as a reward and punishment system in international relations and has been more important as an instrument of political control than as a promoter of economic development. In practice it has been less a harbinger of a new enlightenment in world affairs, more a new technique in the panoply of imperialist control, designed to benefit the donor more than the recipient.

The penny-pinching attitudes towards civil economic aid have been less evident when it comes to military spending. The US government in particular has bestowed huge volumes of military aid on selected governments in the Third World – governments which have taken the side of the USA against the USSR and have also been most supportive of 'stability', a euphemism for pro-capitalist economic policies; for them, carrots. The stick has been reserved for those governments that have tried to break clear of imperial domination. The military budget of the advanced countries, especially the USA, gives them immense power to arbitrate political affairs in the

Third World. Although the main official justification for the vast US military budget is to deter attack by the USSR, its main use in practice in the last thirty years has been to police the Third World. US armed forces have participated directly and indirectly in the overthrow of governments in Guatemala (1954), the Dominican Republic (1965), Chile (1973) and Grenada (1983). In addition the US armed forces have fought two major wars in the Third World (Korea and Vietnam) and practised more limited military interventions in countries too numerous to mention but which include Lebanon, El Salvador, Honduras and Nicaragua. The UK and French military have played similar roles, especially in African and Middle Eastern countries.

The growth of military aid has assisted the growth of Third World military expenditure, which has been associated with the very large number of civil, counter-revolutionary and international wars which Third World governments have been engaged in during the 1970s and 1980s. They are estimated to have spent $130 billion on the military in 1981 (22 per cent of the world total), to have imported $20 billion worth of arms (75 per cent of all arms imports) in order to supply nearly 16 million military personnel (nearly two-thirds of the global total). The World Bank has estimated that from 1972 to 1982 there was a significant rise in the proportion of state expenditure on arms and an equivalent fall in the proportion of spending going to education and public health. Yet a report of the Worldwatch Institute in Washington calculated that with the judicious expenditure of a mere $25 million (a little more than one-thousandth of the cost of arms imports), 7 million deaths a year could be avoided as a result of some primary health care procedure, the provision of clean drinking water and sanitation.

But primary health care and gifts of money do not necessarily help to bind societies into a world-wide capitalist system while military expenditures do. It is marines and not nurses or teachers who can be sent in to keep the peace and preserve the political pre-conditions of the profit system.

9. MODELS OF DEVELOPMENT

The Third World countries are not untouched places waiting for development to begin. In many ways they are caught up in the tentacles of the advanced capitalist world: through trade and investment, through debts and through civil and military aid. They have been transformed in some cases as profoundly as the advanced countries.

The nature of this transformation is not unambiguous impoverishment as a counterpart to the enrichment of the advanced countries. Certainly there are elements of the economic polarization produced by the development of capitalism where the dividing line is between two sets of countries – developed and underdeveloped. But the picture is in reality a more complex one than such a simple polarity would suggest. While a few NICs have been industrializing fast, a few countries have been experiencing, through famine, hyperinflation or war, a process of virtual breakdown of economic life.

Most countries lie between these extremes. Usually they have experienced some form of internal polarization – economic development for some people and areas, decline for others. Where economic advance takes place it frequently produces small islands of development rising within a sea of economic backwardness. Sometimes a racially distinct section of the population keeps the benefits of economic development largely to itself. Sometimes economic advances for some are gained directly at the expense of others (for example, the Green Revolution in India).

There is nothing in the history of the past relations between most Third World countries and the advanced capitalist world that suggests a possible future progressive transformation towards steadily greater prosperity. They have been as much held back as brought on by the meagre aid and trade that comes their way.

But this leads to a final question. Should development and industrialization be encouraged to proceed, as is normally assumed, according to the *same* model followed earlier by the already industrialized countries? A country such as South Korea is seen as 'successful' because it is approaching such an achievement. This seems to be the natural direction towards which capitalist development leads. There are two very important questions to ask about this model.

The first is whether it is physically possible. Students of the environment have begun to argue that the earth could not physically sustain the extension of US levels of consumption of resources per head to the whole planet. Somehow or other, therefore, efforts to gain this objective for the whole world will be frustrated, perhaps with catastrophic environmental consequences.

The second question is whether the objective of European- or US-style industrialization of the world is rational as a way of meeting human needs. We argue throughout this book that as a system of meeting human needs capitalism is flawed in a variety of ways. In principle, therefore, one of the lessons of capitalist development which could be learned in the future is to look for other patterns of development which are more secure, less wasteful and more endurable than capitalism. This would involve looking at what is produced, and at the ways in which it is produced, in an effort to find more economical ways of satisfying known needs, more endurable labour processes and more human and habitable environments. To ask, let alone to resolve, such questions, presupposes a system of social relations other than capitalism.

CHAPTER 13

Stages of Capitalism

I. VARIETIES OF STAGE THEORY

In its two hundred years as the dominant economic system, capitalism has transformed the world beyond recognition. In the same time capitalism itself has changed in various ways – that is what this part of the book has been about. But has it transformed itself in the process through distinct stages? Many of those who have studied it have reached the conclusion that the history of the capitalist system is not a continuous narrative but rather a series of episodes in each of which the system is qualitatively different.

There is a great deal of shared ground among those who write about the stages of development of human beings, from Shakespeare's poetic 'seven ages' of man to the drabber, but comparable, concept of childhood – adolescence – maturity – old age; but little common ground when it comes to delineating the stages of capitalism. One reason for that is that while we have a clear notion of the expected life span of a human being we do not yet know when capitalism will end, let alone the nature of economic life after its death. A striking number of the theories result from a desire to predict capitalism's demise; those with origins in Marxism or other anti-capitalist sources, especially, speak for instance of the 'highest stage of capitalism' or 'late capitalism'. Other standpoints have produced the opposite view – that capitalism is rather improving its survival prospects with each new stage. For instance old-style free-for-all capitalism is said to have been replaced by 'welfare capitalism', or economic backwardness by 'the age of high mass consumption'.

Many of the stage theories originate with Karl Marx's view of human history. Marx believed that every one of the major productive systems of the world was historically progressive in its youth in that it contributed to material advance and the growth of the productivity of labour – what he called the development of the forces of production. But sooner or later, he argued, the social relations associated with the productive system would fetter the further development of the forces of production. At that point the productive system enters a second, historically retrogressive, stage which is the harbinger of its overthrow by a new, youthful, progressive system.

Since Marx's time a number of attempts have been made to put flesh on the bones of this basic two-stage idea. The most notable of these was the theory of imperialism associated with Lenin set out in his book *Imperialism, the Highest Stage of Capitalism.*

Though this is not exactly the way he expressed it, Lenin's notion of the imperialist stage of capitalism is equivalent to Marx's second historically retrogressive phase. This did not mean that Lenin believed that no further development of the forces of production was possible after the imperialist stage began around 1900. But in a sense he believed that the counter-benefits had come to outweigh the benefits and that after 1900 capitalism would involve the certainty of bitter and destructive wars between the main capitalist countries to redivide the planet among themselves and the corporations they politically represented.

One of the major things which had led to this dire prospect was, Lenin believed, the development of monopoly. From its competitive origins as a system of relatively small firms owned by individual capitalists, capitalism had been transformed into a structure of vast corporations with world-wide interests competing to dominate and control markets. Thus Lenin argued that the briefest possible definition which could be given to imperialism was 'the monopoly stage of capitalism'.

(i) *Monopoly capital*

The idea of a competitive stage of capitalism being followed by a monopoly one is widespread. But it has been subjected to a number of different interpretations and emphases.

Noting the emergence by the turn of the century of large capitalist enterprises, employing thousands, the theories draw attention to the continued rise in the concentration of output amongst different firms. Within each industry, and over the whole economy, production is more and more concentrated among the top giant firms. Hence the degree of competitiveness in each market is said to be falling, as firms are increasingly able to parcel up market shares by agreeing not to cut prices. Furthermore, as some emphasize, while price competition has diminished, advertising has come to takes its place as a new way of competing.

We do not agree with this thesis and hence cannot accept it as the basis for a periodization of capitalism. In Chapter 2 we argued that the statistics on increasing concentration of industries yield a misleading picture. Far from falling, competition between capitalists has if anything increased over the last fifty years. Markets have widened, information about companies has become more readily available and more accurate, and firms are generally better equipped to seek high profits wherever opportunities arise.

None the less the idea of a monopoly stage has remained important in many schools of thought. Its posited effects are not merely a question of the exploitation of monopoly power over consumers and small businesses. The most theoretically sophisticated and influential of modern theories of monopoly capital is that of Paul Baran and Paul Sweezy. Their deservedly renowned and imaginative book *Monopoly Capital* deserves to be read for its wealth of ideas and stimulating analysis of western capitalism, even though its central thesis seems to us unsatisfactory.

It argues that the growth of investment leads to an increasing surplus, producible over and above necessary consumption, but that the absence of competitive, price-cutting markets means that the potential surplus can only be sold if the demand deficiency is supplied by the state or in a number of other possible ways. The surplus will tend to grow and can only be absorbed (thus leading to high levels of employment and capacity utilization) by the intervention of an agency which is, as it were, external to the capitalist system itself. The alternative is for the economy to slump back to its 'natural' state of depression.

One of the things which we find unsatisfactory about that treatment of modern capitalism is that it analyses the long period of boom and growth after 1945 (the longest and fastest capitalism has ever experienced) as in some sense an aberration, an abnormal episode supported by artificial, or exogenous, forces (of which the state is a principal one).

In addition to its misleading assumptions about competition, Baran and Sweezy's approach seems unsatisfactory for at least two reasons. One is that, if it exists, for more than half of its life up to now the monopoly capital stage has not been displaying its most 'essential' characteristics. That fact seems at least to call into question what its 'essential' features are.

A second problem is that the common theory of monopoly capital seems to take the state as being an economic institution which is in some sense external to the capitalist system. Yet the state is now so pervasive within capitalism that its activities are an integral part of that system. The state has, rather, become part of the essence of capitalism.

(ii) *State monopoly capitalism*

That idea seems to us the positive side of an extension of the two-stage competitive/monopoly theory of capitalism to a third stage usually known as 'state monopoly capitalism'.

The use of this notion, however, which became official orthodoxy in Soviet-dominated communist circles after the 1950s, has been less than illuminating. It was invented for the specific purpose of 'explaining' how it was possible for capitalism, whose obituary had been so often published by the official communist newspapers, to flourish again after the Second World War. It was thus in its origins more a response to a political embarrassment than a conclusion of scientific enquiry.

There is no doubt, however, that the growth of the economic role of the state has greatly modified the operation of capitalism (see Chapter 11). In this sense we would accept that the current period represents a new era of capitalism (a major qualitative change in its functioning compared to capitalism of the nineteenth century). We are much more dubious that this qualitative change is best captured and understood by the three-stage theory – competitive/monopoly/state monopoly capitalism – which has become so common.

(iii) *Stages in capitalist enterprise – firms, banks and multinationals*

Emphasis on the state provides a transition from stages based on the nature of the market to stages based on the dominant institutions of capitalist economies.

Within this rather different focus the dominant capitalist institution in the first stage of capitalism is the small firm, owned by an individual or a family; the owner is often also the manager.

In the next stage the typical firm is much larger, both absolutely and relative to the size of the market. It is typically owned by shareholders rather than an individual and there is separation between management and ownership. Some have seen that separation as the essence of the monopoly stage of capitalism. But, as we have argued in Chapter 2, there has in effect been no major change in capitalists' objectives of making maximum profits. The main difference is that it has introduced complications as to who are to be regarded as part of the capitalist class. The top managers are generally also owners, but when they are not they share the same objectives and depend for their livelihood on profits. It is highly dubious whether this has substantially modified the functioning of capitalism.

Others have focused on a second stage wherein banks have become the dominant large capitalist institutions, able to direct funds where they will. Summed up in the phrase 'finance capital', this has also constituted an important aspect of some monopoly capital stage theories. They see banks as facilitating the concentration of firms by supplying funds for mergers and acquisitions. Yet in our discussion of banks in Chapter 7, we found no evidence to suggest that they had achieved a unique position of prominence among capitalists. So we cannot accept that 'finance capital' constitutes a new stage.

Another version of the stage theory of capitalism based on its dominant institutions focuses on the geographical spread of companies. If the first stage of capitalism was that of the small localized firm, the second that of the national monopoly, then a third stage is based on the bursting of national boundaries and the establishment or spread of multinational corporations.

The multinational corporation is usually defined as one which either has multinational ownership or multinational operations or both. Of course, on this definition very many of today's leading capitalist corporations are multinational. But equally many of the leading corporations have always been multinational, even in the nineteenth century. The multinational corporation is certainly no new invention. Nor, as we saw in Chapter 10, are foreign trade among capitalist countries and foreign investment obviously higher in a relative sense than a century ago, though there was a period of national self-reliance, sandwiched in between the two internationalist stages. It remains true, however, that *direct* foreign investment through multinationals has been quantitatively more important in recent times. Moreover, two further features of the modern internationalism give the recent period a particular flavour: the extreme internationalization of banks, and the tendency for the production process itself to be split up and to straddle national boundaries.

(iv) *Stages of national dominance*

Another and unrelated way of looking at the stages of capitalism emphasizes the internationalization of the system, the different stages being marked off from each other on the basis of the dominant or hegemonic nation of the system.

This criterion would see an early stage of capitalism, the predominantly merchant stage, as being dominated by perhaps Holland and partly Britain, then a subsequent, early industrial stage as being definitely dominated by Britain; and then after a period of transition a further stage starting in the early part of the twentieth century dominated by the USA. This period has flowered especially in the years since the Second World War. It is characterized by the immense amount of US foreign investment, the US domination of the world financial system and its political hegemony over other capitalist nations. On this criterion there must now be some question as to whether the system is in transition from the stage of US domination to that of domination by some other nation, the main candidate presumably Japan.

This theory lends itself particularly well to linking stages with the theory of crises. So the great depression of the inter-war years has been seen by many as a crisis of transition from the hegemony of one nation, Great

Britain, to that of another nation, the USA. And a number of writers have seen the crisis of the years after 1970 as a crisis of US hegemony. This is an element of the ideas about crisis which we shall examine in Part Five.

(v) *Stages of the labour process*

A very different theory of capitalism which has recently become quite influential argues that as capitalism has developed it has been based on several stages in the organization of labour in the production process.

In Chapter 3 we discussed several systems of production: co-operation, division of labour, machine production, assembly lines and automation. It is to some extent possible to identify different stages of capitalism according to which of these was dominant. Thus we speak of the period of the Industrial Revolution, with the introduction of machines, in contrast to the earlier age of manufacture based on division of labour.

Generally, however, the various systems overlap and coexist, and so cannot correspond to definite periods. Nevertheless some recent writers have elevated their analysis of the twentieth-century production process to the status of stage theory. They point first to the era of Taylorism, the systematic application in production of the principles of 'scientific management' enunciated by F. W. Taylor. This represented an advance in capitalists' ability to extract surplus labour from workers; but ultimately it contained its own contradictions in that it tended to expand productivity without simultaneously expanding the power of consumption. It is argued that this explains, at least in part, the nature of the great economic crisis of the inter-war period.

After this crisis Taylorism was replaced, or perhaps supplemented, by a further stage of the production process and the organization of the capitalist system in general: Fordism. In Chapter 3 we defined this to mean the application of assembly-line techniques in mass production. In the stage theory we are analysing here, associated with the French writer Michel Aglietta, 'Fordism' also encompasses the simultaneous expansion of wages which provided the basis for a vastly expanding consumer market. This is seen as the basis of the great capitalist boom following the Second World War. The crisis beginning in the late 1960s is then seen as the crisis of Fordism, a system which had also, like its predecessors, outgrown its ability to secure surplus labour and hence make profits for capitalists.

This approach has the positive advantage of giving production a central place in the history of capitalism. Yet its thesis about the crisis of the 1970s is at best unproven by historical investigation, and we prefer an alternative approach to the post-war boom and its demise (discussed in Chapter 16) which stresses important factors other than work organization. Moreover, the Taylorism/Fordism dichotomy is born of a very US-centred view of the world. Other countries in Europe and, more so, Japan failed to embrace the principles in the same ways. They can hardly be said to have gone through two such definite stages.

(vi) *Stages in the composition of the output*

A further type of stage theory is based on what is being produced. The breakdown of production referred to is usually a very general one – between agricultural goods, industrial or manufactured goods (sometimes further broken down into consumers' goods and producers' goods, or light and heavy industry) and services (again sometimes further broken down into traditional and modern services). Economists who have studied the history of capitalism have developed various hypotheses about how the breakdown of production (or the division of the labour force) between these categories of output changes at different stages of capitalist development.

In the early stages of development agricultural activities remain predominant but industry is growing; the service sector remains a roughly constant proportion of the national product but this disguises a move within that sector from 'traditional' services to 'modern' services which are related more to the new industrial activities and the industrial ways of life which they promote.

The next stage is that of industrial predominance, in which the agricultural sector shrinks to a low proportion of the national product and the already mentioned changes in the services sector continue.

Finally there is then a further normal 'post-industrial' stage of development in which the agricultural sector has fallen to a minimal level, the industrial sector also begins to shrink relatively and the services sector rises to a very high proportion of total production.

There is no denying that the structure of output or of the labour force is correlated in some ways with the workings of the economy. For example, a high proportion in the agricultural sector is usually a sign of relatively high poverty and it may suggest the presence of a latent reserve army of labour to meet the needs of rapid accumulation in industry.

But we would question whether these changes are really so fundamental as to induce qualitative changes in the rules and methods of capitalism. Ultimately, while capitalism lasts, it matters little what commodities are being produced, as long as they are yielding profits for capitalists. It is a lesson increasingly learnt by the massive conglomerate firms and international banks of the modern age, that what concerns them is the 'bottom line'. They represent capital in search of profits, be it from services, industrial products or crops.

(vii) *Stages of economic growth*

A slightly different version of the developmental stage theory is that associated with Walt W. Rostow, one of the US government's main advisers during the Vietnam War. In a much-discussed and extremely influential theory he claimed to identify five stages through which all nations pass on the way to full economic development: the traditional economy, the preconditions for take-off, the take-off, the drive to maturity and the age of high mass consumption.

Like virtually all stage theories, this suffers from trying to create stages out of a process which, even if erratic, is relatively continuous. But there is an additional problem if it is applied to the capitalist system as a whole. Since it is a theory about the development of individual nations it cannot capture salient features of the entire system. In fact, if it were applied to the system as a whole, it would obscure important features. For instance, as we discussed in Chapter 12, one of the characteristics of the later stages of capitalism is the coexistence of developed and underdeveloped nations in which the former dominate the latter. This crucial inequality cannot be captured by a theory of structural change which sees all nations as at different points on a common path.

(viii) *Long waves*

A final method of periodizing capitalism is the idea that there are 'long waves' in capitalist development.

Some economists have suggested that the familiar business cycles are merely ripples on the back of a much longer and larger economic cycle – each period lasting about fifty years. These are often referred to as 'Kondratieff cycles', after the Russian economist who emphasized them and brought them to public notice in the inter-war period. They were introduced to the English-speaking world by the famous economist, Joseph Schumpeter, in his book *Business Cycles*. Kondratieff's statistical investigations have received mixed support from other economists. His contemporaries in the USSR may have been impressed, but generally they disagreed. Moreover, apart from a genuine scientific questioning of the statistics and theory, his ideas also fell foul of the dogma based on the crude interpretation of Marxism, that capitalism was tending gradually towards inevitable downfall. If, as Kondratieff argued, capitalism went in long waves of regular period and amplitude, where would the end of it be? Kondratieff himself fell victim, along with many others, to Stalin's icy purges. But the idea of long waves has not died, and some now hold that they help to explain the long historical sweep of capitalist development.

Quantitative economic historians have collected data on the growth rate of the volume of commodities produced each year, in certain countries. Table 13.1 presents this data in a way which suggests that the world capitalist economy has gone through alternating cycles of faster and slower growth.

Table 13.1   Average Annual Percentage Growth of Real Output

	USA	UK	Germany*	France	Weighted average
1848–78 (upswing)	4.2	2.2	2.5	1.3	2.8
1878–94 (downswing)	3.7	1.7	2.3	0.9	2.6
1894–1914 (upswing)	3.8	2.1	2.5	1.5	3.0
1914–38 (downswing)	2.1	1.1	2.9	1.0	2.0
1938–70 (upswing)	4.0	2.4	3.8	3.7	3.8

* Adjusted for territorial changes; excludes East Germany.
Source: David Gordon, Richard Edwards and Michael Reich, *Segmented Work, Divided Workers*, Cambridge, Cambridge University Press, 1982

The years chosen for each turning point were all trough years of the short-term business cycle, so as to avoid any spurious appearance of long waves. The table is published by three Marxist economists, David Gordon, Richard Edwards and Michael Reich, in their book *Segmented Work, Divided Workers*; they find the framework of long waves helpful in explaining the development of the US labour market. They suggest that distinct stages are reflected in differing long-term growth rates and, moreover, that other historical data (for example, in international trade) also reflect long-term fluctuations.

The evidence, however, is not extremely striking. Although the post-war boom was a period of unprecedented growth in most countries, the earlier differences in growth between, say, 1878–94 and 1894–1914 are not very great. To be confident of long waves we would have to be able to identify long-period ups and downs of fairly regular length and to explain how one phase automatically moves into another. Measured from trough to trough these swings are indeed long but they are far from regular. Moreover, different interpretations of the data can lead to different lengths for each phase.

Further to this *statistical* doubt about the existence of long waves, no one has yet adequately explained *theoretically* why a period of slow growth automatically gives way to a period of boom. In fact one might just as well say that a long phase of slow growth would automatically lead to disaffection and revolution – but this would be equally erroneous. And, finally, any long-period cyclical framework seems to ignore the political and other external shocks (such as wars) which help to shape the progress of capital accumulation.

Interest in the puzzle posed by Kondratieff has revived as economists of varying persuasions try to understand the end of the long boom and the onset of crises in the 1970s. It is possible that further research may bear fruit, in particular by throwing light on past periods of capitalism – we retain an open mind on this question. But in the absence of adequate scientific validation some of the work on long waves borders on mysticism. This is a poor substitute for concrete historical and theoretical analysis.

2. VALIDITY OF STAGE THEORIES

To sum up our conclusions about whether or not capitalism passes through distinct qualitatively different stages, there are many different arguments and criteria whereby these stages have been identified: the nature of the market, the size of firms, the dominance of finance capital, the emergence of the multinational corporation, the role of the state, the relative economic power of various nations, the nature of the labour process, the structure of production or the labour force between different sectors, and a number of others.

In some cases we have found that the changes are illusory or of no basic importance. In others we have discovered substantial transformations in the way capitalism operates. This applies to those stage theories which emphasize the rising role of the state, the changing forms of internationalization of capital and the changing relationships between capitalist nations. That is why we have devoted three chapters to these issues. Each of these changes has somehow modified the capitalist fingerprint we identified in Chapter 1, or the framework within which it operates.

Yet even though capitalism has been partially transformed, it is not necessarily valid to talk of qualitatively distinct stages as opposed to long-term processes of change. There is always the danger that the identification of distinct stages may be based on an arbitrary bench mark within a continuous process of change.

Moreover, since stage theories are usually based on only one criterion of change they suffer from a further problem: their uni-dimensionality. There is no doubt that capitalism has changed very substantially during its lifetime and will continue to do so. But changes have taken place along a number of fronts. Major shifts according to one criterion have not always coincided with major shifts according to another. It would be a gigantic and perhaps impossible task to gain a definitive idea of the interrelations of all these different kinds of change. And if the boundaries between stages tend to be rather hazy, then that haziness would thicken if we were to attempt the much greater, but possibly more important, task of identifying change based on many criteria simultaneously.

Any theory of stages seems to be based on the idea that change in the capitalist system is relatively discontinuous and relatively irreversible. In fact the history of the system shows that this is too simplified. Some changes have been sharp and discontinuous; others have been gradual and continuous but of no less importance; some permanent and irreversible, others reversed, sometimes cyclically. And since capitalist history is not yet over, it is impossible to say with absolute certainty that some changes which up to now have seemed irreversible may not be reversed at some time in the future.

It is usually convenient, when analysing capitalist history, to divide it into specified periods, bounded by obvious turning points like a world war or a major depression. Yet these successive periods normally show elements of continuity as well as of change. They do not necessarily amount to different stages.

All in all we remain rather sceptical about the stage theories of capitalism. But they can validly draw attention to long-term modifications in the operation of capitalism. It is not a system which grows steadily year in and year out, with no reason ever to change. And indeed, as the period since 1970 has demonstrated, it was prone not only to changes in its structure but to periodic dramatic interruptions in the form of various crises. It is to this overall functioning of the contemporary profit system that we now turn in Part Five.

PART FIVE

CAPITALISM IN SICKNESS AND IN HEALTH

CHAPTER 14

Capital Accumulation, Instability and the State

The answer to the question 'Does the capitalist economy work well?' would depend on whom you asked and when. People participate in it with a variety of motives and objectives: most of them simply need to survive; but a minority also want to continue as owners and controllers of the means of production. This means that they need to receive a continuous flow of profit on their existing capital and to be able to reinvest or accumulate these profits in new profitable activities. An individual who fails in these objectives experiences a crisis – the result may be a reduced standard of living; loss of wealth; in extreme cases, even death. Someone experiences such a crisis every day in the history of capitalism.

But periodically the whole system of capitalism experiences a crisis. There have been many periods when failure to find a job, loss of wealth and the other symptoms of personal crisis have simultaneously engulfed very large numbers of people. A common feature is that very many capitalists together fail to meet their objectives. They become unable to produce or sell their goods and services profitably. And they transmit their problems to the rest of society. They cut wages, sack workers, abandon expansion plans and so on.

The timing of the question is important. Take, for example, the year 1960. Very many people, at least in the developed countries, might then have replied that capitalism was working well. In that year, capitalists in business in the USA on average gained a profit rate (before tax) of about 15 per cent. In West Germany they received 23 per cent, in Japan 27 per cent and in the UK about 14 per cent. While in each country the profit rate was fluctuating somewhat from year to year, on the whole corporations, by the criterion of profitability, were flourishing.

If the other classes in society are succeeding in at least some of their aims it is likely that capitalism will work even better as a system. For example, it may be argued that workers are more likely to accept a subordinate position in society if they are guaranteed a steadily rising material standard of living. And indeed we have already seen, in Chapter 8, how the 1950s and 1960s were a time when real wages in capitalist countries were increasing, even though this left many other human needs stifled or unsatisfied. While other groups in the underdeveloped world fared less well this does not alter the fact that capitalism in this period was by many people's lights successful.

If we now look at another year, 1975, the answer would have been very different. Many individual capitalists experienced the ultimate failure, bankruptcy, or their firms were merged with or taken over by larger companies. Nearly all companies were getting lower profits than previously. Businesses in the USA had an average profit rate of just under 7 per cent, while the average West German rate had fallen to 9 per cent, the Japanese to 13 per cent and the UK to a mere 4 per cent. Had the decline gone on, the economy might have collapsed completely for capitalism cannot operate for long without profits. This, of course, did not happen; the system kept going through the crisis of 1974–5 and for the rest of the 1970s. Capitalists were even able to maintain reasonably high levels of accumulation, at least until the world crisis intensified again in 1979. But it was apparent throughout this period that something very serious had gone wrong with the system. Correspondingly, the rest of society was faring badly as well, including those groups that had benefited materially from the earlier successful period. Mass unemployment threatened the economic security of many workers, some of whom suffered severe cuts in their living standards.

The events of the 1970s were not at all exceptional or unusual in capitalist history. In the USA, in addition to some minor crises, there were major crises followed by economic recession in 1812, 1818, 1837, 1857, 1873, 1893, 1907, 1921, 1929, 1973, 1974–5 and 1979. In France they occurred in 1720, 1827, 1837, 1848, 1857, 1864, 1887, 1907, 1929, 1958, 1974–5 and 1979. A similar list could be drawn up for all the other mature capitalist countries. The historical lesson is that crises are neither isolated nor rare occasions. It is obvious that in practice periodic crises, as well as successful periods of growth, are part of the normal course of events. But why do the crises occur? And are they inescapable? We look at these pivotal questions in this chapter and the next.

2. THE DEVELOPMENT OF A CAPITALIST ECONOMY

(i) *Defining accumulation*

The capitalist system does not stand still. Even if it is running smoothly at one time, it may not – indeed does not – remain stable indefinitely. We must be looking for answers which can explain not only what the system is doing at a given time but also what it is becoming, what it is turning into. In particular, since the aim of capital is the making of maximum profit through its continuous accumulation, we need to see how that process works.

Many orthodox economic books tackle a subject closely related to this, the 'theory of growth', and try to explain why the amount of commodities produced expands. They ask: what determines the rate of increase of national income? ('National income' is a measure of the total value of goods and services produced in a country in a given period, usually a year; see Technical Annexe 14.C.) That question is important, but it is part of a larger and more pertinent one: what determines the rate of accumulation of capital? If we focus only on the quantities of goods and services produced, we fail to include in the analysis the social (as well as technical) circumstances in which they are produced – that is, by workers under the direction of capitalists.

Capital accumulation is an aspect of the continuous circuits of capital described in Parts Two and Three, through which capitalists and workers are reproduced. The continuation of the capitalist process involves the reproduction of the following elements: the means of production, the supply of labour-power and, finally, the basic relations of worker to capitalist.

The 'accumulation of capital' means this reproduction of capital on an expanded scale. It signifies that while the *qualitative* nature of the worker-to-capitalist relationship is maintained the *quantity* of money-capital laid out to buy means of production and labour-power is increased.

Also getting larger over time is the amount of commodities produced; thus 'accumulation' involves 'growth' in the normal sense. But we need to bear in mind the mechanisms and the problems of maintaining the basic capitalist relationships as growth proceeds.

The fact that growth follows from investment has given rise to the notion that it involves sacrificing something in the present to gain a reward in the future. In a limited sense this is true. If accumulation is proceeding smoothly and investment is taking place, then capitalists must be keeping their current consumption of final commodities below its possible maximum in order to free resources for investment. The result is more consumer goods at a later date; so there is a correlation between reduced current consumption and increased future consumption. It can, however, be misleading to think of growth in this way. First, the idea that future gains are balanced against current costs often conceals the historical realities of who bears the current costs and who gains the future reward. Sometimes capitalists can gain without bearing any costs – they can force workers to bear them by reducing wages. Second, even when capitalists do bear costs, they do not choose to do so in order to raise their future consumption. Their aim in buying new machinery is the making of profits and the accumulation of capital. The growth of consumption is a necessary part of this process but not, as much orthodox theory of growth claims, an end in itself. (This argument relates to our discussion of the doctrine of 'consumer sovereignty' in Chapter 4.)

(ii) *How the accumulation process works*

From the point of view of the individual capitalist the mechanism of accumulation is relatively easy to describe. Accumulation involves investment in new machinery or bigger inventories (fixed capital), and in more flows of materials and energy (circulating capital). And, unless the capitalist is scrapping much old equipment and starting with new technology which requires less labour, accumulation leads to an expanded demand for labour-power.

When we look at accumulation by all capitalists, the process is more difficult to unravel. This is because no capitalist runs his or her business in isolation – it interlocks with the rest of the economy in a variety of ways. It is therefore necessary to see how the actions of each and every capitalist are co-ordinated. Broadly speaking there are two kinds of problems to which accumulation gives rise: consistency with the supply of labour-power, and internal consistency between the plans of each capitalist.

When all or most capitalists are accumulating, an increased total supply of labour-power is required. The numbers in the 'reserve army' of un-employed and underemployed workers rise and fall according to the pace and rhythm of the expanding economy, being especially high in the period following a crisis, when some firms have gone bankrupt throwing their workers on to the labour market. When this happens no businesses should have any trouble finding an increased supply of labour-power to turn into productive capital. When, however, the numbers of unemployed are small following a sustained period of accumulation the overall supply of labour-power depends on other things – on immigration, or on changes in the family (e.g. the proportion of women who seek paid work), and ultimately on the birth rate. That, in turn, can raise problems for capital accumulation since family relations are not like capitalist relations – the reproduction of labour-power does not in principle respond to profit incentives like the production of other commodities. There may, therefore, be occasions when the increased demand for labour-power that comes with capital accumulation cannot be met, and a shortage develops.

The second kind of problem to which accumulation gives rise is co-ordinating the separate plans of many individual capitalists. Co-ordination is a necessary function in any group of independently acting units. If one set of firms producing consumer goods tries to expand, then it increases its demand for materials and orders new machinery. This presupposes that other firms are available to produce and supply the new machinery and the extra materials. By the same token those who produce machinery will be reluctant to set their production processes going if they do not expect to make a sale. In fact we can say that for accumulation to proceed smoothly (a) there must be a matching of the supplies of and demands for new machinery, (b) the supply of raw materials should equal the increased demand, (c) the demand for finance by expanding firms must equal the supply from financial capitalists, and (d) the increased supplies of finished commodities must find consumers to buy them.

What mechanism is available to ensure that such co-ordination takes place? It is the market. In an unplanned economy, as capitalism is, no central agent is available to ensure smooth accumulation. Hence the supplies of and demands for machinery, raw materials and finished products are brought into equilibrium by changes in their prices in the usual way, which we described in Chapter 7. In theory there are prices for all these commodities which would ensure that equal rates of profit are obtainable by capitalists in each industry when the supplies and demands are matched. At these prices no capitalist would have any incentive to move to another area of business. And as the supply of final goods expands, so too does the demand, since more workers are employed leading to increased consumption while also capitalists' own consumption can increase. At the same time the rate of interest would be set to ensure the supply of loan-capital matches the demand for it.

To prove this would require a rather complex set of arguments because each supply and demand depends in principle on the whole economy. Finding a set of prices to match all supplies and demands has occupied the minds of economists for many years (and is known as 'general equilibrium analysis').

We do not, however, need to consider such analysis here. The main point of this argument is that in theory a consistent set of prices exists which enables a balance to be struck between all competing capitalists who are responding to the incentives of these prices. This, or some approximation to it, is the mechanism for smoothing the process of accumulation. If the capitalist economy is working, this is, in principle, how.

(iii) *Defining 'crisis'*

While this anatomical examination is valuable it suffers from an overriding defect: it is static. All that equilibrium analysis can provide is a snapshot of accumulation in a given period where supplies and demands are matched. But snapshots tend to be of limited value. If you see a still photograph of a football match with, say, two opposing players and the ball, you can possibly infer what has just happened and what is about to happen in the next moment, but beyond that you can learn nothing.

The question we need to ask about accumulation is: as the system changes and develops over time will it remain co-ordinated? Our historical investigation has already replied with a resounding 'no'. We must now find a theoretical answer which accords with the historical record.

When the accumulation of an individual capitalist is halted for some reason – for example, a strike of workers, lack of raw material supplies or slack final demand – that firm will lose profits and might even go bust. When such interruptions are generalized to involve most or all capitalists, there is a 'crisis' in the economy. This term has come to be used fairly loosely in economics, to refer to any time when things are going badly for all or some sections of capital. Thus we witness 'banking crises', 'inflation crises', 'fiscal crises' and so on. We shall take the term to mean *either temporary or longer-lasting generalized breaks in the capitalist process*.

(iv) *Necessary and accidental theories*

More orthodox economics tends to regard crises as unnecessary or accidental events not inherent in the generation of capital. This belief derives originally from Adam Smith's idea of the 'invisible hand' of the market which acts to regulate the economy. According to his famous book, *The Wealth of Nations*, the economy was essentially harmonious despite the fact that it consisted of thousands of individuals acting independently to further their own interest. Many modern economists in the same tradition believe that the economy is always at or very close to 'equilibrium', and that any 'disequilibrium' will be quickly righted by changes in prices. It follows, if this is accepted, that crises must be caused by large external shocks to the system.

A notorious example of this approach in the nineteenth century was Stanley Jevons's 'sunspot theory'. Observing that the period over which sunspots reappeared – about ten years – was roughly the same as the length of time between business crises, he tried to explain the latter by the former. Even though Jevons's hypothesized cause of crisis lay 93 million miles away, it does not alter the methodological similarity between this kind of theory and other, superficially more plausible, theories which attribute crises to external shocks, such as war. One such notion in discussions of the 1970s blames the oil sheikhs and other members of the Organization of Petroleum Exporting Countries (OPEC) for suddenly and arbitrarily raising the oil price in 1973 and again in 1979. In criticizing such notions we do not of course say that such events have no effect on the economy. Rather, it is wrong to blame them for being the sole cause of economic breakdown.

By contrast, we, along with other economists (notably those who work in the tradition of Marx), incline to the view that occasional crises are a necessary and inevitable feature of capital accumulation. There are two kinds of argument which support this approach. First, at a purely empirical level, capitalist economies have never for long been able to avoid crises. Second, considering capitalism from the theoretical angle, the process of accumulation is basically 'anarchical' – it is unplanned. This means that the incessant drive towards accumulation is almost certain to lead to imbalances in the system. Such imbalances might involve bottlenecks (e.g. shortages of primary products and raw materials), shortages of labour-power, insufficiency of final demand, or disproportionate expansion plans of different capitalists. But whatever the actual imbalance concerns, imbalances will, almost inevitably, occur. In other words, we argue that the likelihood that the market can perform its prescribed role of co-ordinating the economy is effectively zero.

There is something special about crises in capitalism compared with crises in pre-capitalist economies. In the primarily agricultural economies of feudal Europe, and also in other social systems, crises were by no means unknown. But then the primary cause usually was an external factor, such as weather patterns – floods, droughts and so on. The result and commonest symptom of economic breakdown was *shortages*, especially of food, leading to famine and starvation. By contrast crises under capitalism are marked by massive idle resources – with factories, land and other materials lying idle, and mass unemployment. It is not a question of scarcity of resources.

No major external shock hit the US economy in the 1920s and 1930s but this did not prevent the waste of the Great Depression. In fact it took an external shock – in the shape of the Second World War – to bring the depression to an end.

(v) *The possibility or impossibility of crisis*

Why is the breakdown of smooth market regulation inevitable and necessary in capitalism? Before we can answer this question satisfactorily it is helpful first to look at a preliminary question: *why is the breakdown of the market, and hence crisis, possible?*

In the nineteenth and early twentieth century a strand of mainstream economics held that generalized crisis was impossible. The view was propounded by a French economist, Jean-Baptiste Say (1767–1832), an intellectual disciple of Adam Smith, and is summed up in the slogan 'Supply always creates its own demand', which became elevated to the status of an economic law. Those who subscribed to Say's Law conceded that overproduction of commodities was quite possible in one industry. Temporarily, at least, supply could exceed demand. However, this could not become a generalized crisis of overproduction in all industries. They argued that if supply exceeded demand in one industry, it would be less than demand in some other industry, so these 'disequilibria' could soon be eliminated by reallocating resources to the industry in excess demand and by changing the prices of the products accordingly.

Say's Law, however, has been shown to be wrong. Whether or not the market system *does* work or might be made to work is one thing. It is quite another matter to assert that it *must* work. The law is exposed as soon as we consider the possibility of 'hoarding', which was discussed in Chapter 7. Firms or consumers may from time to time withdraw from the exchange process. For example, firms unsure about the future may withhold their profits and wait a while before turning them into new machinery. Whatever the reason, the result of withholding the money would be that those businesses producing machinery suffer a loss in demand for their product.

If this happens on any scale, they will reduce their labour forces with the result that the demand for consumer products will also start to fall. Thus a deficiency of demand in one sector can spread to a deficiency in another: a shortage of demand becomes generalized. The economy behaves like a marble on a flat surface; if pushed, it continues rolling for several inches. (In the world of Say's Law, the marble rests in a gully and always returns to the same place.)

While it was Karl Marx who first saw the importance of hoarding in a monetary economy as leading to the possibility of crises, for John Maynard Keynes (1883–1946) the rejection of Say's Law was the most important starting point for understanding unemployment. Both were implicitly wrestling with the same problem: the assertion by Say that any deviation away from equilibrium in the economic system will necessarily call forth a counterbalancing force to restore its original equilibrium.

Probably no other individual economist has had more influence on the world's history than Marx or Keynes. But of the two it was Keynes whose economic thinking has dominated both theory and policy in capitalist countries ever since the 1930s. After the publication in 1936 of his most important book, *The General Theory of Employment, Interest and Money*, his policy prescriptions rapidly gained the support of economists and then, in the post-war period, of governments, too. Although many governments have now openly abandoned Keynesian policies his theoretical framework lives on through all debates on macroeconomic theory and through the methods of national income accounting adopted throughout the western world.

Keynes's analysis of the economy has been open to different interpretations. As often happens with radical new thinkers, controversy arose some years after his death over what he really meant. Fortunately we do not have to trouble ourselves with these controversies here. The analysis we shall present is based on a major part of Keynes's work, which is well enough agreed among economists. It bears out and elaborates our argument in this section: that a cumulative deviation away from market equilibrium is a real possibility.

3. KEYNES'S MODEL OF THE ECONOMY

(i) *National income and national expenditure*

It is a truism to state that wherever a commodity is being sold by one person it must be being bought by someone else. In a capitalist economy commodities are almost always exchanged for money. If an exchange takes place without cheating, the money going from buyer to seller equals the money value of the commodities passing from seller to buyer. Thus we can think of this process as two equal and opposite flows, money in one direction and commodities in the other. And since this is true for every (fair) transaction in the economy, the two-way flows picture can be applied to the whole economy, as illustrated in Diagram 14.1.

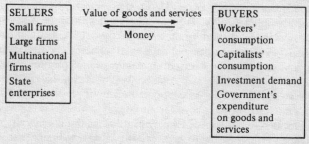

Diagram 14.1   Exchange–Money Flows and Value Flows

In our model we shall let E (for expenditure) stand for the total amount of money spent in a given period of time – say a month. This expenditure comes from several sources. The main ones, listed in the diagram, are the total consumption expenditures of workers and of capitalists, the total private investment expenditures on new means of production and the total amount that the government spends on buying goods and services. This equals the total value of commodities which firms of all types sell in the month. That, however, is not necessarily the same thing as the value of commodities produced, because in any month a firm may sell more or less than the amount produced. For example, if demand is unexpectedly low, a firm will find it has produced too much. Its unsold output will start to pile up in warehouses. Conversely, if demand is higher than output the firm will meet it by drawing down from its inventories of finished products. Of course, it will usually plan to keep some inventories – there is inevitably a short period of time between goods being produced and their being transported to consumers. But these are *planned* inventories, as opposed to *unplanned* changes in stocks when demand is unexpectedly high or low.

Let Y stand for the total value of goods produced (including any planned inventories), and Z stand for the output that remains unsold. Then our basic truism (that the total of what is bought is sold) can be expressed in the equation:

$$Y \quad - \quad Z \quad \equiv \quad E \qquad (1)$$

National income	Unsold output	National expenditure or 'aggregate demand'

The $\equiv$ sign (as opposed to a $=$ sign) signifies an important point: that the equation *must* be true. It does not, for example, depend on which economic theory you adhere to, whether firms are doing well or badly, or whether or not there is mass unemployment. The $\equiv$ sign indicates an identity, in this case an accounting identity. The two sides are defined to be equal.

Both sides of the identity represent what may be called 'national expenditure', or 'aggregate demand', the total value of goods and services bought and sold in a given period. Y is normally referred to as 'national income' (a concept explained in detail in Technical Annexe 14.C).

We have introduced the concept here because it plays a pivotal role in Keynes's model of the economy. The purpose of this model is to study what determines the overall level of employment. When Y falls sharply, so will the numbers of people employed, causing a corresponding rise in the numbers unemployed. Conversely if Y rises then unemployment will fall.

(ii) *The theory of national income*

First, it is important to remember that what matters to capitalists, who are trying to sell their commodities, is not their potential buyers' needs but their 'effective' demand (see Chapter 4). Whether they be consumers or other capitalists, buyers must be both willing and able to buy the products. They must have either the money or the credit. So an unemployed person's needs are of little interest to sellers and indeed any consumer's effective demand may be very different from his or her needs or requirements.

Suppose that a firm cannot sell all its products at a particular time – unwanted inventories are piling up in its warehouses. Very quickly, its managers will have to take some action, either to increase sales or to reduce the rate of output. It is, however, very difficult to influence demand, especially in the short run. Increasing the sales staff will not make much immediate impact. Reducing prices is not likely to be resorted to quickly since that would not substantially raise demand; moreover it would lower the normal profit margins.

The most likely *immediate* response, therefore, is to cut the production rate. Whether or not it would be advantageous to lower prices at some later date if insufficient demand persists, a quantity change will be the first reaction. To be precise, the firm will alter its output rate to meet the level of demand.

Translate this proposition to the overall economy and we have Keynes's basic hypothesis: that the *national rate of output (i.e. 'national income') will change quickly to meet the level of aggregate demand (i.e. 'national expenditure')*. In terms of our symbols,

$$Y \qquad = \qquad E \qquad (2)$$
National income   is determined by   Aggregate demand

Note that although this looks similar to the accounting identity, equation (1), it has a different meaning. In fact it represents a theory, not simply an identity. It says that national expenditure, E, *determines* (i.e. causes) national income, Y. It would be possible to conceive of it as being incorrect: for example, if it were suggested that, rather than output adjusting quickly to equal demand, prices adjusted quickly so as to bring demand into line with output.

The following hypothetical examples give the essence of the theory. Suppose that in month 1 national income equals £100 million and that there is no unplanned unsold output since total demand also equals £100 million. This is represented in the first row of Table 14.1. In month 2, we assume that aggregate demand (national expenditure) falls unexpectedly to £90 million. (This could be because capitalists have decided to hoard some money, instead of investing it, or consumers to spend less, but the reason does not matter for purposes of the present argument.) Hence if output stays the same there must be £10 million worth of unsold output, as shown in the second column.

Now we come to Keynes's theory. National income will quickly adapt to the lower level of demand. It might even begin doing this in month 2, though for the purpose of simple presentation we have assumed not. But by month 3, national income will have fallen to the lower level, £90 million. Firms reluctant to stock their warehouses any more, unable to influence

Table 14.1   The Response to the Fall in Aggregate Demand
(all figures in £ millions)

	National income Y	Unplanned unsold output, Z		Aggregate demand E
Month 1	100	0	≡	100
Month 2	100	10	≡	90
Month 3	90	0	≡	90

demand, are forced to reduce output – and begin to think about laying off workers.

The same process could work in the opposite direction. Suppose that demand has expanded to £110 million, making output 10 units less than demand. Initially the disparity could be made up by drawing on inventories; thus $Z = -£10$ million. But very quickly the capitalists would raise output to the new higher level, either by getting workers to work longer or harder or by taking on more workers.

This process of increases in demand causing increases in output is, however, inherently limited by the availability of resources. If the expansion in demand is too great then output cannot be raised and for a while some demanders may be unable to buy what they want. Capitalists may then adjust in an alternative way, by raising prices. Hence in this case changes in demand would be causing changes in prices, not in output. Hence the Keynesian hypothesis, equation (2), is meant to apply to situations where there is idle capacity. If capacity is fully used and demand is increased a different approach would need to be adopted (see Chapter 17).

(iii) *The components of national expenditure*

The theory of national income is as yet incomplete. If Y is determined by E, what determines E in the first place?

This can conveniently be answered by splitting demand into three components, consumption by the private sector (C), investment (I) and government expenditure on goods and services (G). Thus national expenditure, E, is given by:

$$E \equiv C + I + G$$

Aggregate demand | is made up of | Consumption expenditure | Investment expenditure | and government expenditure

Each of these components has been discussed previously in this book.
Keynes based his arguments around the concept of the 'marginal pro-

pensity to consume', which we reviewed in Chapter 4. He argued that consumption expenditure was composed partly of an 'autonomous' element which people would have to try to achieve regardless of their income, and partly of another element which increased according to the level of disposable (i.e. after-tax) income. For every £1 increase in disposable income, consumption would increase by a positive amount less than £1, determined by the marginal propensity to consume.

Investment, as we saw in Chapter 6, is related to profit expectations and the costs of borrowing money. It is also determined by less calculated, and often completely irrational, waves of optimism and pessimism among capitalists. In the simplest version of Keynes's model it is assumed for simplicity that the level of investment is autonomous – that is, determined independently of income.

The same simplifying assumption is made about the amount of government spending, which is assumed to be fixed by politicians.

(iv) *The working of the model*

These three simple theories about what determines aggregate demand are sufficient, together with the basic Keynesian hypothesis given in equation (2), to determine in principle the level of national income, Y. But the most interesting question actually concerns the causes of *changes* in national income. What is the effect on national income and employment in a capitalist economy of a change in the level of autonomous aggregate demand?

To illustrate its working assume that capitalists cut their level of investment by £100 million. This cut in demand leads to a cut in income – but by how much? First it falls by the initial £100 million cut in autonomous investment spending. But then it falls by more, since there will be a further induced cut in demand due to a cut in the consumption spending of those whose incomes have fallen as a result of the initial £100 million cutback. This subsequent fall itself induces yet more cuts in consumption and hence in aggregate demand and national income. The process continues cumulatively as each reduction in consumption reduces other peoples' incomes.

An autonomous drop (or rise) in investment, therefore, will lead to a drop (or rise) in national income which is some multiple of it. The process whereby this comes about is known as the 'multiplier' – the most famous concept in Keynesian economics. Suppose that eventually national income fell by £300 million, following the £100 million cut in investment: then the size of the multiplier in this hypothetical example is 3. The transition summarized by the multiplier begins to make itself felt immediately, but not for some periods is its effect fully worked out.

It is, however, a real process, and not just the product of abstract equations. Imagine a small town which is dominated by one factory, and suppose that due to a fall in demand that factory is closed down. Who can doubt that although the factory workers are the first to suffer loss of jobs, other workers in the town whose livelihood depends on selling to the factory workers will also soon suffer a loss of income and of employment? The higher is the marginal propensity to consume, the more the factory workers' consumption falls when they lose their jobs, hence, also, the greater the secondary and further effects on demand. This suggests that the multiplier is greater the higher the marginal propensity to consume – a proposition which is proved rigorously in Technical Annexe 14.A.

Although the examples we have given have assumed an initial fall in demand the arguments apply equally to a rise in demand. Suppose investment demand increases. There will be an initial expansion of national income, and firms will begin to employ their workforces for longer hours or even to take on more workers. This will increase consumption demand, which will further stimulate national income; and so on.

A further extension into more complex reality allows for the international relations of a capitalist economy. For if income is spent on imported goods the employment it creates is not domestic but in the exporting country. So the national impact of any rise or fall in autonomous demand is lessened: the higher the propensity to import, the more the multiplier process spreads itself internationally but the less its local impact.

The importance of the multiplier process is not that it leads particularly to downturns or even to upturns in the economy. It is that movements in the economy tend to be cumulative: a contractionary shock is reinforced rather than counteracted, and so also is an expansionary impetus. Even though the investment component of national expenditure may only be a relatively small one, if it is volatile it can be the source of considerable instability in national income.

(v) *'The paradox of thrift'*

Our multiplier analysis helps us to understand a well-known economic paradox. Consider the economics of peasant farmers in a non-monetary economy. The farmers choose each year how much corn harvest to consume and how much to save in the form of corn seed for next year's crop. If, one year, they decide to save a bit more and hence consume a bit less than usual, then that is their decision, but their total harvest *this* year is not affected by it. (They hope that next year their wealth will have grown a bit and they will consume more then.)

Compare this with a monetary economy, such as capitalism. If, one year, people decide (for whatever reason) to save more, the effect will be to *decrease* their income during that year. For if from every income level more is saved, then by definition less must be consumed. A rise in total savings means a fall in aggregate demand. By the Keynesian hypothesis, national income will therefore fall simply because firms cannot sell all the commodities they produce.

But will not a rise in savings call forth a rise in investment and hence leave demand unaltered? Here lies the crucial difference between this and the peasant economy. For investment depends on a number of things, not least the capitalists' confidence that they can sell the goods in the future. Those capitalists who are doing the investing may be different people from those capitalists and workers whose savings propensities have risen. To 'save' is to refrain from consumption; to 'invest' is to buy new means of production. In the case of the peasant economy consuming less corn and investing more in the ground are virtually one and the same act. In a monetary economy, saving could be merely hoarding. The Keynesian hypothesis here is that national income and output are determined by aggregate demand, which is made up of consumption and investment (omitting for now government spending which does not affect this argument). An equivalent way of stating this is to say that national income net of consumption (i.e. saving) is determined by aggregate demand net of consumption (i.e. investment). That is:

$$S \qquad = \qquad I$$

Saving   is determined   Investment
by

A rise in savings does not lead to a rise in investment. Although 'in equilibrium' savings equals investment it is investment which brings forth savings by creating income, rather than the other way round. A rise in savings out of a given income level is expressed as a fall in the propensity to consume; that means a rise in the propensity to save. If total investment causes ('determines') total savings and investment does not change, then national income will fall to match the rise in savings propensity so as to leave total savings unchanged.

The apparent paradox is that whereas workers and/or capitalists intend to save more, their intentions are collectively frustrated in the monetary economy. In the peasant economy such intentions would be fulfilled. Such is the effect of differing social and economic relations. The paradox is explained when we remember that demand is the driving force in the short-run adjustments of a monetary economy.

(vi) *What the Keynesian model shows*

The Keynesian model helps to answer some of the questions posed in the analysis of accumulation and crisis. It starts with a simple proposition about the way capitalist firms respond to a shortfall in demand for their outputs. It assumes that supply is adjusted to meet demand. When a component of demand, such as investment, falls, the suppliers of plant and machinery reduce their outputs and their labour forces. On the other hand, assuming there is some idle capacity in the industry, when demand rises suppliers' immediate response is to raise output. Prices may or may not change at a later date.

The remarkable consequence of this is the multiplier process. Its essence is that initial shocks to the economic system are magnified up, with a cumulative movement away from the initial resting place. Hence it is in contradiction to Say's Law, which had asserted that given supplies would always create their own demand. Instead falling demand would cause falling supply.

Keynes's model has been criticized for ignoring 'supply-side' factors, which are thought to be crucial. This criticism may, however, vary in meaning. Sometimes 'the supply-side critique' amounts to a blind reassertion that markets always work and that Say's Law is necessarily correct. These views are mistaken. But at another level there is some substance to the point. Keynes's analysis is most relevant to cases where there is idle capacity. If demand increases when resources are all utilized and there is full employment, then even the short-run response of firms may be different since they can only raise output to certain limits. Keynes himself recognized that in these circumstances the economics of the production process could not be ignored. And indeed, it would be surprising if we were to argue that only demand factors are relevant, given that we have devoted several chapters of this book to examining the 'supply side'.

The model also shows the way to Keynes's theoretical justification for the use of monetary and fiscal policy as means whereby the government can prevent major crises from breaking out. Since these policies have played such a major role in the management of capitalist economies for more than two decades, we describe and explain in the next section the policy principles and instruments that constitute the philosophy of 'Keynesianism', leaving discussion of its limitations and constraints till the next chapter.

4. THE KEYNESIAN PRESCRIPTION

We have already, in Chapter 11, begun to discuss the way in which the large role played by national states has become a major factor in modern capitalism. High state expenditure impinges upon the stability of the economy in two ways: automatically and via conscious policy.

(i) *Automatic stabilizers*

Consider first the following automatic way. The multiplier process, which if sparked off by fluctuating investment causes instability, rests on the assumption that consumption falls or rises as national income falls or rises. The presence of income taxes *lessens* the impact of the multiplier. As national income falls, consumers pay less income taxes: hence the fall in disposable income is not so great as the fall in national income. Similarly, if national income is stimulated then income taxes increase, so that although consumers' disposable income increases it does so by less than the increase in national income. Hence the secondary impact on consumption is lessened by income taxes. Thus income taxes play the role of an 'automatic stabilizer', acting to diminish the impact of changes in aggregate demand, rather as poor shock absorbers can lessen but not eliminate the effect on a car of bumps in the road.

Government 'transfer payments' act in a similar capacity. These are not the same as expenditure on goods and services. Rather, they are payments of money such as pensions and social security to individuals or grants to companies, who then may spend it. Many types of transfer from government to people are automatically linked with the level of income. For example, if national income decreases and workers lose their jobs, they receive unemployment pay for a while; this helps to prevent demand falling as much as it would if the unemployed workers received no income at all.

Thus without any thought-out government policy the sheer scale of government taxation and transfer payments can lessen, though not remove, the instability that derives from fluctuating aggregate demand. The main lesson, however, that Keynesians have drawn from the theory is that government can counteract shocks to the system by planning and controlling aggregate demand through conscious policy. The basic Keynesian policy principle is that aggregate demand should be managed, using fiscal or monetary policy, to stabilize national income.

(ii) *Fiscal policy*

Fiscal policy means policies either about government expenditures or about taxation. Although governments do have microeconomic fiscal policies – regarding, for example, which commodities to tax, which to subsidize and so on – we are concerned here with policies about the aggregate levels of expenditure or taxation. The role of such policies follows directly from the Keynesian model.

Thus changes in government expenditure will cause multiplied-up changes in aggregate demand and national income. Consider, for example, what happens when a government decides to spend more by building a new hospital. It makes a contract with a construction company, which takes on more workers, thus raising national income. That company, however, must purchase materials from other companies and the workers will spend their newly found income on other commodities – producing more income and jobs elsewhere in the economy. In fact, the multiplier process operates in the same way as it does for changes in capitalists' investment expenditure – except that in this case the purpose of raising the government expenditure is the conscious one of raising national income, rather than making profits.

A rather surprising corollary of this argument is that it does not actually matter what the government spends the money on. Although we quoted the example of a useful project, hospital building, the desired effect of raising national income and reducing unemployment could have been achieved even if the government had wasted the money.

An alternative fiscal means of raising aggregate demand is for the government to lower taxes. In practice, it could lower taxes of any kind, be they on income, expenditure, land, wealth or whatever. The immediate effect is that, for any given level of national income, disposable income will increase, thus boosting aggregate demand. Hence the economy will expand, unemployment will fall and national income rise.

(iii) *Monetary policy*

Another way for governments to influence aggregate demand is through policies to change the supply of money and credit, and to alter the rate of interest. Such monetary policy has been used by governments throughout the capitalist world as an alternative to or a complement to fiscal policy.

In Chapter 7 we discussed how commercial banks made their profits, and how in the process of lending to customers they created new money, on the basis of their money reserves. We also saw how the state could seek to influence the total amount of money in the economy. For example, if a central bank buys up some securities from a financial capitalist it injects more reserves into the banking system, eventually enabling commercial banks to make more loans and hence to increase the money supply. Conversely, the state could seek to contract the money supply by selling bonds.

Alternatively governments can concentrate on trying to control interest rates, either short-term or long-term or both. Since governments are continually borrowing vast amounts of funds on the open market they can influence the price at which funds are available for private capitalists. If, for example, the government raises the rate of interest it is prepared to pay on long-term bonds, private borrowers will also be forced to raise their rates. Thus companies will have to pay more for their long-term borrowings, and house-buyers more for their mortgages.

To see how interest rate and money supply policies may be used to influence demand, we can refer back to our Keynesian model. The connection in fact is quite straightforward: the interest rate is linked to investment. If the government lowers the interest rate, this decreases the cost of loan capital and raises the potential profitability for industrialists of investing in new machinery. Aggregate expenditure on investment increases and hence, via the multiplier process, national income will rise. Conversely, a rise in the rate of interest leads to a fall in national income.

Some economists argue that monetary policy affects the economy in another, more direct, way. It is proposed that both investment and consumption expenditures depend partly on the level of the money supply in relation to prices (sometimes called 'real money balances'). If the money supply is increased by the government then individual agents – both people and companies – will find they have more money than they want (though not more wealth). They therefore, it is argued, get rid of their excess money balances by spending them, trying to convert their money assets into physical assets. This mechanism is more direct than that analysed by Keynes since it does not rely on influencing the interest rate. The effect, however, is the same: aggregate demand is changed.

Like other policies, monetary policy is subject to constraints and limitations, which we shall discuss in the next chapter; here we mention two theoretical problems. First is the interrelationship between the money supply and the interest rate, which means that governments cannot for long have *separate* policies for each.

Suppose the government wished to contract the money supply (or, what comes to the same thing in a time of inflation, to slow the rate of its growth). It would have to restrict the amount of credit. Perhaps it would sell government stock on the open market. This would inevitably lower the price of bonds or in other words raise the interest rate. Conversely, a rise in the money supply raises the amount of liquidity in the banking system and, other things being equal, loans are made more cheaply. The other side of the same coin, however, is that the government can only pursue an interest rate policy, trying, for example, to keep long-term interest rates down, if it supplies enough extra money to the banking system.

A second theoretical problem derives from the international nature of capitalism. Each capitalist country's economy is woven into the fabric of the world market, and international flows of money-capital provide strong links. The interest rate in one country, therefore, is tied indirectly to rates in other countries. If in country A the rate was set substantially above that in country B then, other things being equal, financial capitalists would sell their assets held in B and buy up government bonds or other securities in A. The resultant international money flows, bringing money into A and away from B, will tend to raise interest rates in B and lower them in A – either automatically, or with the assistance of governments of A and B if they find the money flows destabilizing. This problem of international competition for money-capital will be particularly important in countries whose economies are strongly linked to a powerful economy like the USA. If rates are high in the USA, dependent countries' governments will find it hard to keep interest rates down without risking a massive outflow of money-capital.

(iv) *The practical instruments of demand management*

The principles of monetary and fiscal policy are the same in all capitalist countries, but the forms they take and the institutional arrangements and problems may vary.

In principle, tax changes or government expenditure changes may be used to control aggregate demand. Different objectives may decide which type of fiscal policy is used; moreover, institutional factors may favour one type of policy. An important technical point is the need to be able to impose changes quickly as soon as the economy is wandering off course. If tax changes require a lengthy legislative procedure before they can be imposed, expenditure changes may be preferred. On the other hand the long-term nature of many public projects often leaves little short-term room for manoeuvre in government expenditure. Hospital building cannot start until the plans are ready; and if halfway through the government were to call a halt for macroeconomic reasons, the cost would be high. For this reason, tax changes have often been preferred, where expedient, as the instrument of fiscal demand management, while expenditure plans are determined by the other aims of government.

Monetary policy instruments come in a greater variety, ranging from 'voluntary' controls whereby the central bank urges expansion or caution on commercial banks, to legal requirements such as the imposition of the minimum reserve ratio of cash to liabilities for banks. One rather useful (because quick-acting) weapon is the imposition of consumer credit controls: for example, by requiring a certain percentage deposit on durable goods purchases. But these are often not imposed for long as they discriminate against those (often powerful) capitalists who sell the kinds of commodities frequently bought on credit.

The chosen methods of monetary policy depend on the nature of a country's monetary institutions – each state should be examined separately. It is worth noting here, though, that carrying out the policy is liable to face more obstacles in some countries than in others.

First, as mentioned above, the more open the economy is to the world market, the less easy it will be to have interest rates much different from the world interest rate. A second (related) problem is that if the government tries to restrict credit, those who demand it will search for alternatives and can very often get it from different financial institutions, either inside or outside the country, that are outside the control of the monetary authorities. For example, US banks wishing to borrow from lenders above the interest-rate ceiling determined by the government could obtain dollar funds, from the 1960s onwards, from the growing Eurodollar market, not subject to US regulations. Third, the institutional links between financial and industrial capitalists vary substantially. In some countries, such as Japan and West Germany, the links are strong and intimate; by contrast, UK financial capitalists orient their business more internationally and have normally not made substantial long-term loans to industry. In such a country, it is therefore more difficult to direct a monetary policy towards expanding domestic industry. Expanding the cash base of the commercial banks may have less of an effect on domestic investment and lead to more exporting of money-capital, unless the policy is accompanied by foreign exchange controls.

(v) *Demand management and budget deficits*

It has sometimes been said that Keynesians were in favour of using fiscal policy while monetarists preferred monetary policy. But this is not really the main line of policy disagreement. Keynes advocated 'pump-priming' government expenditure expansion in times of deep recession since he felt that then it would be more effective than trying to cut already low interest rates to stimulate investment. But, in more normal times, Keynesians are happy to use both fiscal and monetary policy to 'fine-tune' the level of demand, whichever is the more practical.

In any case the two kinds of policy are in principle and practice closely related: there is no simple choice between them. This is revealed in the issues underlying a perennial argument among politicians and economic policy makers, about whether the government's budget should be balanced. Before Keynes and the events of the 1930s changed the minds of the economics profession it was assumed that budgets should always be balanced. Hence, even in a recession it was thought necessary to raise tax rates and cut expenditure if a deficit was envisaged. Many politicians concurred with this.

Keynes showed, however, that when the economy is depressed and there is much idle capacity governments can restore stability by raising expenditure or lowering taxes. It follows that budget deficits are good for the economy when it is in a recession. There are, however, two kinds of problem associated with running a persistent budget deficit: one, the possibility of creating a fiscal crisis as government debt soars too high; the other, the possibility that the deficit will unacceptably constrain the monetary policy which the government wishes to pursue.

If the government borrows large sums to finance its expenditure, its debts will rise and its interest payments to holders of government stock will increase, thereby raising the burden on future taxpayers. That does not matter if the deficit is a short-term policy measure designed to move the economy out of a recession. If full employment and growth could be achieved, tax revenues would rise and a budget surplus would be achieved: there would be no problem of rising debts. The difficulty occurs if the large deficits persist for many years. For many economists and politicians, the charge against Keynesianism was that it allowed a lax approach to public finance and stored up future problems.

There can be no dispute that large long-term deficits could destabilize governments except in special circumstances. The repayment of debt could begin to mushroom and the fiscal problem of raising enough funds become unmanageable. We discuss this eventuality in Chapter 17. For the present, we note that the call for regular budget balancing can be not only misplaced – if it ignores the occasional short-term need for deficits – but also massively deceptive in that it is based on false or inadequate statistical information and hidden political objectives.

The relevant statistical data for adequately assessing government finances have not generally been available. Arguments, therefore, have been based on the nominal monetary amount that governments borrowed each year. But in Technical Annexe 14.B we show that this is an inappropriate statistic in an era of inflation. An indication of that conclusion is suggested by the figures for national debt given in Table 14.2. In most of the years from 1970 to 1982 the advanced capitalist governments had substantial borrowing requirements: yet whether the national debt rose, in proportion to national income, varied from country to country. In the UK, for instance, despite persistent nominal budget deficits, the national debt fell substantially.

Second, the balanced budget argument becomes on certain occasions quite fraudulent, in that the real aim hidden behind the ideology of the 'balance the budget' cry is to cut government welfare expenditure. This aim derives from an altogether different approach to policy and a complete rejection of Keynesian politics. The real objective is to reduce the level of state involvement in the economy, reinforce inequality in the economic system and emphasize the primacy of the market – policies we shall discuss in Chapter 18.

Table 14.2   Government Debt in the Advanced Capitalist Countries
(percentage of GDP, 1970 and 1982)

	1970	1982
France	30	29
West Germany	19	40
USA	47	43
UK	86	54
Japan	12	62
Italy	45	74

Source: OECD Economic Studies, *The Role of the Public Sector*, OECD, Paris, Spring 1985

The second reason put forward for reducing the government deficit is in order to gain better control of the money supply. Fiscal policy is intimately related to monetary policy; in particular, running a budget deficit may constrain the options available for monetary policy. Regrettably this question can often become a technical one, tied up with the specific state and monetary institutions of a particular capitalist country. The issues, however, are general and, even if a little complex, may be presented in general terms.

Consider the following accounting identity:

What this means is that government expenditure that is not matched by income from tax revenues must be paid for somehow. First, the government could simply print more money and issue more coinage. (An equivalent technique is to allow the treasury department to write cheques against an increased account at the central bank – this expands the money supply at the stroke of a pen.) Second, the government can increase its short-term debt. Often this could lead also to an increase in the money supply, though indirectly. Those who have lent to the government deposit their short-term government debt in commercial banks, and this may allow the banks to expand their lending, since short-term liquid assets can act as reserves. Finally, the government can borrow long term, by issuing more long-term debt. This would not lead to the expansion of the money supply, since long maturity bonds are not money and cannot be used as reserves by banks. An increased demand to borrow long term, however, will lead to an increase in the rate of interest if the supply of long-term funds is unaltered. Thus the consequence of not expanding the money supply may be a rise in the rate of interest. This repeats our earlier argument: control over the money supply or over the interest rate is possible, but it is often difficult to achieve both independently.

Thus the accounting identity reveals a possible, but by no means certain, relationship between the government deficit and the expansion of the money supply. The connection could be broken in at least two important ways: the government could contract the money supply at the same time (e.g. by raising the minimum required reserve ratio). Alternatively, it could find sufficient available long-term funds from the public, without necessarily driving interest rates up too high, if private persons were ready to buy more long-term financial assets. This latter option was particularly important in the inflation years of the 1970s, when hitherto unprecedented government borrowing needs were met by willingly increased supplies of funds from the public in many capitalist countries. Technical Annexe 14.B shows why this is always likely to happen in times of inflation.

Thus the relationship between a government's financing needs and the increase of the supply of money is a complex one. That does not mean that deficits can be ignored. The logic of the accounting identity suggests that if the deficit became 'very large' it would be impossible to avoid an undesirably large expansion of the money supply, or a large rise in interest rates, or both. It is in this sense that fiscal policy ultimately constrains the options open for monetary policy. But precisely how large a deficit can be accommodated is difficult to assess in practice, because it is impossible to predict accurately the supply of long-term funds, especially in times of inflation. Moreover, with the deficit statistics and targets misleadingly presented in nominal rather than real terms, the task of relating fiscal to monetary policies is daunting. It leaves much room for cant on the part of economists, politicians and journalistic commentators.

In conclusion, government deficits are not a recipe for economic ruin and may be advantageous, especially in small doses, if aggregate demand management requires them. Those who are particularly concerned with controlling the money supply will often, because of the theoretical connection, seek to limit or remove the government deficit. The theoretical link, however, is loose, and this suggests that the real function of such pathological emphasis on budget-balancing as almost a law of nature is the often a different one – simply as a political weapon in forcing through expenditure cuts on an otherwise unwilling population.

Technical Annexe 14.A Keynesian analysis

In section 3 of this chapter we explained the principles of the Keynesian model emphasizing the multiplier process. Some readers may prefer to have the arguments presented in diagrammatic or simple algebraic terms, and this appendix is intended for this purpose. In the course of it we shall be able to prove rigorously some of the chapter's propositions about the determinants of the multiplier.

(i) *The components of aggregate demand*

We shall assume that consumption expenditure of both capitalists and workers is a function of (i.e. depends on) disposable income, Y_D. The latter concept refers to the income available to consumers to spend or to save. It is less than national income, Y, since the government imposes taxes. We therefore define Y_D by the equation

$$Y_D \equiv Y - T \tag{1}$$

where T stands for taxes. Moreover we assumed a simple relationship between consumption and disposable income, given by

$$C = 100 + 0.8Y_D \tag{2}$$

Thus the marginal propensity to consume is 0.8: if disposable income rises by \$1 then consumption increases by 80 cent. Correspondingly, the marginal propensity to save is 0.2. The figure 100 stands for autonomous consumption, being that part of consumption expenditure which does not depend on income. If we also assume that out of every dollar earned the government takes 30 cents in taxes, we can write

$$T = 0.3Y \tag{3}$$

This means, given our definition of disposable income, that

$$Y_D \equiv Y - 0.3Y = 0.7Y \tag{4}$$

Hence

$$C = 100 + 0.8 \times 0.7Y$$

or

$$C = 100 + 0.56Y \tag{5}$$

Thus, if gross income (before tax) increased by \$1 consumption would rise by 56 cents. Out of a given level of income, whatever is neither consumed nor paid in taxes must be saved. Hence

$$S \equiv Y - C - T \tag{6}$$

or

$$S \equiv -100 + 0.14Y \tag{7}$$

The numbers are to some extent arbitrary. We have chosen them to illustrate the argument to follow, but different numbers would show the same points as long as the marginal propensity to consume is between 0 and 1 (not an unreasonable proposition).

The feature of investment, I, emphasized in the chapter is that, more than consumption, it is volatile – it varies a lot from month to month, partly due to psychological swings of mood. There is no obvious direct relationship implied between I and Y, though we could not, in a more complex model, rule that possibility out. For the purposes of our model here we shall assume there is no relationship and regard I as an 'exogenous variable'. That means we shall for present purposes take I as given at a certain level and investigate the implications of that level or of any changes in it caused, say, by changes in the confidence of investors.

Finally, we take a similar approach to G, government expenditure. We regard it as given at a certain level, determined by government policy.

(ii) *Cumulative movements of national income: the multiplier process*

We can restate the Keynesian hypothesis, in terms of the components of demand, to give the relationship

$$Y = C + I + G \tag{8}$$

If we substitute our consumption equation (5), we have

$$Y = 100 + 0.56Y + I + G \tag{9}$$

We now reconsider the example introduced in the chapter to see how Keynes's argument refutes Say's Law. Suppose that capitalist firms hoard some of their money and correspondingly reduce their investment in some particular period, by 100 units. There being nothing to raise any of the other components, total demand (the right-hand side of equation (9)) would immediately fall by 100. Hence national income (the left-hand side) would quickly fall by the same amount, and there would be nothing automatic to push it back up again. Worse still, that is not the end of the story, since the equation is still not balanced. If income has dropped by 100 then consumption falls by 56, thus further reducing demand, and hence national income falls yet more. And this new fall causes yet another drop in consumption, causing yet another fall in national income, and so on. The initial shock of the fall in demand by 100 units, far from being automatically adjusted to (like the marble in the gully), is actually followed by further movements away from the starting point (like the marble on the flat surface).

How much will national income eventually fall by? This can only be answered by 'solving' our model to see how national income is determined.

(iii) *Solving the model*

Note first that equation (6) can be written in another way:

$$Y - C \equiv S + T \tag{10}$$

But equation (8), which is our statement of the Keynesian hypothesis, can also be rearranged simply, to give:

$$Y - C = I + G \tag{11}$$

Hence

$S + T$	$=$	$I + G$	
Savings	Are	Investment plus	(12)
plus	determined	Government	
Taxes	by	expenditure	

Diagram 14.A.1 shows how this equation is solved, and thus how Y is determined. Consider first the left-hand side. From (3) and (7) both savings and taxes depend on Y. In fact

$$S + T = -100 + 0.14Y + 0.3Y$$
$$\therefore S + T = -100 + 0.44Y \tag{13}$$

This relationship is shown by the upward sloping line in the diagram, with slope 0.44 and an intercept of -100.

As for the right-hand side of the equation we have assumed arbitrary values: $I = 200$ and $G = 140$. On the diagram this is shown by the horizontal line at the level of 340.

The two lines intersect at the point A where national income is 1,000. This is the solution to our model. We could equally well have found this out with some simple algebra. Substituting the assumed values for I and G into equation (12), we obtain

$$-100 + 0.44\,Y = 200 + 140$$
$$\text{Hence } 0.44\,Y = 440$$
$$Y = 1{,}000$$

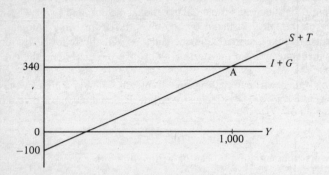

Diagram 14.A.1   Solving for National Income, Y

(iv) *The multiplier calculated geometrically*

We are now in a position to clarify the full result of the multiplier process, and in particular to investigate the effect of our supposed fall of 100 units in investment. This is illustrated in Diagram 14.A.2.

Initially Y is determined to be 1,000 at point A. The fall of 100 in I shifts the horizontal line $I + G = 340$ down to $I' + G = 240$. The new value of Y, where the $S + T$ line intersects the lower $I + G$ line at B, is 772.7. Thus Y has fallen by 227.3 units. Hence the ultimate fall in Y is 2.27 times the original fall in I: the multiplier equals 2.27.

A little consideration of the geometry of the diagram verifies that falls in investment will always lead to multiplied ultimate effects. The $S + T$ line is liable to be relatively flat, and certainly its slope is less than 45°. The slope represents the proportion of one extra dollar that is saved or taxed, which is likely to be a reasonably small fraction (in our example 0.44) and certainly less than unity. It follows that BC, the amount that Y falls, is bound to be greater than AC, the amount of the supposed initial fall in I. Moreover, the flatter the $S + T$ line the greater will be the ratio of BC to AC and hence the value of the multiplier.

Thus the multiplier tends to be high whenever the marginal propensity to save is low – or, in other words, when the marginal propensity to consume is high. In addition, the higher is the income tax rate, the lower will be the multiplier: this is illustrated in Diagram 14.A.3.

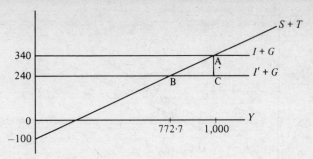

Diagram 14.A.2   The Multiplier

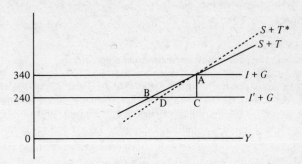

Diagram 14.A.3   The Effect of Tax Rate on the Multiplier

The dotted line through A D, marked $S + T^*$, may be compared with the solid line through A B, marked $S + T$. In the latter case, the multiplier effect of a fall in investment is given by the ratio of B C to A C, just as in Diagram 14.A.2. The line $S + T^*$ represents a case where the marginal propensity to consume is the same but the income tax rate is higher – and hence the slope is steeper. (For simplicity we have arbitrarily assumed the same initial equilibrium at A.) The multiplier is equal to D C divided by A C, which is lower than B C over A C.

Finally, Diagram 14.A.4 shows how a tax cut can be used to stimulate the economy. Suppose that the $S + T$ line going through Q A is the initial situation, so that A is the initial 'equilibrium'. If the tax rate is cut, the $S + T$ line becomes less steep. However, if there is no change in a, autonomous consumption, the starting point will still be at Q. The new line is therefore Q E, and we have labelled it $S + T$†. It is clear that the level of national income at E, where the economy moves to, is higher as a result of the tax cut.

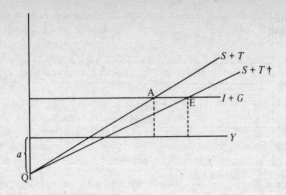

Diagram 14.A.4   The Effect of a Tax Cut

(v) *The multiplier calculated algebraically*

The diagrammatic analysis can be confirmed by solving our system of equations. At this stage, we shall generalize them by not assuming any particular values for the marginal propensities to consume and save, or for the tax schedule. Instead we shall replace equations (2) and (3) by:

$$C = a + bY_D \tag{14}$$

and

$$T = tY \tag{15}$$

Here, b stands for the marginal propensity to consume, a for autonomous consumption and t for the tax rate. Since

$$S \equiv Y - T - C$$

it follows that

$$S + T = Y - a - bY_D$$

or

$$S + T = Y - a - b(Y - tY)$$

or

$$S + T = -a + (1 - b + bt)Y \tag{16}$$

Substituting this savings equation into our Keynesian hypothesis, equation (12), we have

$$- a + (1 - b + bt)Y = I + G \qquad (17)$$

Hence

$$Y = \frac{a + I + G}{(1 - b + bt)} \qquad (18)$$

The solution for national income

(The reader may care to check this expression with the numbers from our previous example. With $a = 100$, $I = 200$, $G = 140$, $b = 0.8$ and $t = 0.3$, you find $Y = 1,000$.)

Consider, first, the effect of a fall in the tax rate, t: since it is in the denominator, national income will rise, thus confirming the conclusion of Diagram 14.A.4. Now consider what happens to Y when either I or G is changed. Since each is multiplied by $\frac{1}{1 - b - bt}$, any change in either will produce a change in Y multiplied by the same factor. For example, if I decreases by 1 unit, Y decreases by $1 \times \frac{1}{1 - b + bt}$ units. More generally, the 'multiplier' is given by

$$\frac{\Delta Y}{\Delta I} = \frac{1}{1 - b + bt} \qquad (19)$$

where we have used the symbol Δ to indicate 'change in'.

The multiplier will be larger, the larger is b, the marginal propensity to consume, and the smaller is t, the tax rate.

(vi) *An extension of the basic model: the open economy*

Our model till now has treated the overall economy as though it were a closed affair, with all commodities produced and consumed in one country. The analysis holds true in a modified form if we take international trade into account, and provides us with further insights.

It is sometimes said that 'when America sneezes, Europe catches cold, while the Third World catches pneumonia', an aphorism based on the enormous trade and capital flows between the USA and the rest of the world. US imports are Europe's exports. If its national income falls, the USA will import less – implying that Europe's exports fall. Why should this destabilize Europe's economy? For precisely the same reasons that a fall in investment leads to a multiplied fall in national income, a fall in exports also leads to a cumulative downward movement. For any country, exports to other countries constitute a component of total demand. The only special factor is that the demand is from foreign as opposed to domestic buyers. In our model we shall assume, for simplicity, that exports are independent of national income (though they may depend on other countries' national income levels, exogenous to our model).

On the other hand, if capitalists or consumers are importing commodities from abroad, this means there is less demand for the home-produced goods. Hence we must rewrite our Keynesian hypothesis, adding exports to but subtracting imports from aggregate demand.

$$Y \qquad = \qquad C + I + G + X - M \quad (20)$$

National income	is determined by	The components of aggregate demand

where X is exports, M is imports.

Alternatively, this can be stated as

$$S + T + M = I + G + X \qquad (21)$$

To solve this new expanded model we need first to know what determines the level of imports. The most straightforward and plausible assumption is that imports are some fraction, m, of national income, so that as national income increases so too do imports.

$$M = mY \qquad (22)$$

Substituting this assumption into the model (using equations (21) and (16)),

$$- a + (1 - b + bt)Y + M = I + G + X$$
$$- a + (1 - b + bt)Y + mY = I + G + X$$
$$(1 - b + bt + m)Y = a + I + G + X$$

Hence
$$Y = \frac{a + I + G + X}{1 - b + bt + m} \qquad (23)$$

Solution for national income in an open economy

Our solution shows two points of interest. First, as we suggest above, any change in X would have a multiplied effect on Y. The multiplier factor will be $(\frac{1}{1 - b + bt + m})$, and is the same in this case as for a change in I. Thus if exports fall (or rise) income falls (or rises) even more.

Second, note that the multiplier is *smaller* in this expanded model than in the previous model where we ignored the fact of international trade. This is because changes in demand are partially channelled into changes in imports, which have no effect on national income at home.

Technical Annexe 14.B
The inflation tax and measuring the government budget deficit

Money, in addition to its main function of medium of exchange, also plays the role of unit of account. When inflation occurs it both devalues the money that individuals hold and distorts its accounting function in important areas of economic life. One such is in the measurement of company profits. Another concerns the measurement of government finances. The aim of this appendix is to explain why inflation affects both the accounting and the financing of governments' budget deficits.

Inflation implies that any asset which is denominated in money – for example, some cash or a bank deposit or a bank loan – will gradually be devalued over time. If A lends $100 to B for one year and they agree a 10 per cent interest rate, A expects to receive $110 next year. However, if meanwhile prices have risen by 6 per cent the real return that A receives will only be 4 per cent. That $110 that A receives next year could only buy $104 worth of goods at this year's prices.

To cope with this effect economists distinguish between the 'nominal' rate of interest (10 per cent in our example) and the 'real' rate of interest (4 per cent). The difference between the two is the rate of inflation (6 per cent). In fact this holds true generally:

$$\text{Real interest rate} = \text{Nominal interest rate} - \text{Inflation rate}$$

Sometimes debtors (like B) and creditors (like A) will expect inflation to occur and allow for it in their bargaining. This means that inflation can often push up nominal interest rates. Suppose A and B agreed instead on a 10 per cent *real* interest rate. Expecting a 6 per cent inflation they would settle for a nominal interest rate of 16 per cent: i.e. B would pay A $116 next year.

However, whether or not inflation is fully expected by debtors and creditors, they should when it happens account for its effects. Debtors, like B, should regard it as a gain, to be offset against their interest costs: if not they will underestimate their financial positions. Meanwhile creditors like A must account for parallel inflation losses.

Since governments are always net debtors to other sectors of the economy they inevitably gain from inflation. The real value of the debt they owe to the public is continually decreasing. Hence in order to look at the true financial position of a government we need to include this gain as part of its income. Of course, it does not receive this gain overtly, like income tax and other types of tax revenues. None the less the gain is truly a tax since it increases the government's (and decreases everyone else's) command over resources.

This adjustment radically alters the apparent financial position of governments. Table 14.B.1 presents some figures for an average of the major capitalist governments, in some arbitrarily chosen years. It shows, for example, that in 1980 these governments, far from being in a dangerously large deficit, were actually in a marginal surplus, in real terms. In the case of the UK the effect of the adjustment was especially striking: it had nominal deficits throughout the 1970s but in most years a real surplus: high inflation and high amounts of outstanding debt led to a substantial inflation tax.

Table 14.B.1 General Government Budget Surplus in the Major Capitalist Countries (percentage of GDP) (deficits −, surpluses +)

	Nominal	Inflation adjusted
1971	−0.9	+0.1
1975	−4.2	−2.3
1980	−2.5	+0.1
1982	−4.1	−2.5

Source: OECD Economic Studies, *The Role of the Public Sector*, OECD, Paris, Spring 1985

These adjustments are not just the statisticians and accountants playing games with the numbers. To see this, consider the identity which we worked from in the chapter to show the possible connection between the government deficit and money supply expansion:

$$\text{Government} \equiv \text{Increase in} + \text{Government} + \text{Government}$$
deficit   money supply   short-term   long-term
                                 borrowing   borrowing

The counterpart of inflation gains by the government is the losses made by the public, in particular those people from whom the government borrows. It is reasonable to suppose that people who hold financial assets are interested in their real value. If each asset's value is eroded, they have to buy more assets to keep their total real value of financial assets equal to the amount they desire. Accordingly they buy more government bonds, *just to keep up with inflation*. This is the reflection of the accounting adjustment made in Table 14.B.1. Take, for example, 1980. There was a nominal deficit of 2.5 per cent but no real deficit. Although the nominal deficit still had to be financed, there was bound to be an increased flow of funds from the public, some of which was long-term. The above identity thus implies at best a loose link between the nominal government deficit of each country and its money supply expansion.

Technical Annexe 14.C The measurement of national income

In this chapter we have used the concept of 'national income' and on several occasions in this book we have used terms such as 'Gross National Product' (GNP) or 'Gross Domestic Product' (GDP) to refer to its official statistical measurement. In this appendix we aim to explain more precisely what these statistics refer to, how they are obtained and why they are gathered at all.

The last of these questions is easily resolved. National income accounting is a product of the Keynesian revolution in economic management techniques. As with any science, the kind of measurement that economists look for depends on the theoretical framework. Demand management could not be practised without some measurement of what was to be managed. Hence there arose a national accounting system – at first in the UK and the USA, but after the Second World War in most advanced capitalist countries – which was designed to measure the various components of aggregate demand with a view to controlling it.

(i) *Official measures*

National income accounts attempt to measure the total monetary value of all goods and services produced during a given period – for example, a year. However, when it comes to the details, sometimes several different concepts are used. It is necessary to be aware of these differences, because when other variables are compared to national income it is important to be consistent about which concept is being used. We shall briefly describe some of the most commonly used definitions here, without providing detailed explanations. (A close knowledge of national income accounting practices is not necessary here.)

The annual *Gross Domestic Product* (GDP) of a country is the value of all goods and services produced in that country in a given year. It is made up as follows:

1. Consumption expenditure   All sales of goods and services by firms to consumers, specifically excluding the sales of materials or intermediate goods from one firm to another (this avoids double counting)

2. Investment expenditure	Sales of fixed capital goods
3. Planned inventory investment	International increases of stocks
4. Unplanned inventory changes	Unplanned unsold output
5. Government expenditure	Government outputs (for example, education services) are often free or subsidized. Their value is measured by the amount spent on inputs (such as the wages of schoolteachers).
6. Exports minus Imports	Money spent by foreigners on domestically produced goods is part of national income; but money spent by domestic economic agents on foreign goods is a subtraction from it.
Gross Domestic Product	The sum total of the above

GDP differs from the concept of aggregate demand used in the chapter by the value of output produced that was unintentionally unsold – item 4 in the list.

The annual *Gross National Product* (GNP) of a country differs only slightly from its GDP. It measures the value of all goods and services produced in a given year by the nationals of that country, both at home and abroad. To get from GDP to GNP, first substract the income accruing to foreigners working and owning assets in the domestic country and then add the income obtained by domestic nationals working and owning assets abroad. Normally, GNP and GDP are not very different, and the two statistics are often used interchangeably.

The annual *Gross National Product 'at factor cost'* of a country is GNP minus indirect business taxes. If the government imposes a sales tax on a commodity, thereby raising its market price, it seems as if the value of the product has increased. Subtracting the tax is a way of trying to measure the 'real' value of what is produced.

The annual *Net National Product at factor cost* is what is most widely meant when the phrase 'national income' is used: this is, simply, GNP at factor cost minus an estimate of the depreciation of fixed capital assets. Because such estimates are usually imprecise or arbitrary, GNP and GDP are more commonly used as standards of comparison.

The most immediate way that governments actually obtain a measure of GDP is by getting direct information from firms about their sales, their investments and so on. But another major way involves measuring the incomes paid out by firms or government institutions. For the money paid to a firm does not disappear. It re-emerges either as wages, or as the profits, interest and dividend payments, or as rent payments. The government statisticians can simply add up all the incomes received by people and by firms and by government institutions to obtain another measure of GDP, assuming they have collected accurate information. Both methods – the 'expenditure approach' and the 'income approach' – should come to the same amount because they are designed to measure the same concept. In practice the information collected is never perfectly accurate, and a 'residual error' remains, the difference between the two measures.

A commonly used concept that comes out of the income approach refers to that part of GNP which accrues to individuals and which they can decide how to spend or save. The annual *Personal Disposable Income* of a country is defined as Net National Product at factor cost, minus the retained income of business, minus direct taxes on firms and on persons (income tax and so on), plus transfer incomes paid by governments to persons (social security payments and so on).

Finally, each of the above conceptual statistics is sometimes divided by the country's population to give 'per capita' figures.

(ii) *A measure of welfare?*

GNP per capita or one of the other national income concepts, is sometimes taken as a measure of a country's citizens' welfare, on the grounds that it measures the value of what is produced and hence of the resources available to the economy. Yet this conclusion is a mistake: national income accounts are in practice all but useless for any assessment of welfare.

To equate GNP with total resources assumes that everything is available through monetary exchanges only. Yet there are many non-market resources that are used to help satisfy people's needs. To be specific, GNP is a particularly sexist statistic when used as a measure of welfare, in that it ignores the productive activity of millions of women across the world – their domestic labour. If a man employs a female housekeeper, her wages enter into the measurement of GNP. If he later marries her, and she continues the same job but unpaid, her labour disappears from the official statistical view. A classic anomaly!

GNP also ignores the enjoyment of leisure and non-work activities. And even if we look only at monetary resources there are many reasons why there is no direct relation between total resources and welfare. As we saw in Chapter 8, the extent of poverty, of pollution, of military expenditure, the quality of working life and so on, all come into the picture in assessing welfare.

In Table 14.C.1 we have listed the GNP per capita figures for a selection of countries in 1983, to give an idea of the orders of magnitude involved.

But welfare conclusions are best avoided. We know that US citizens are very much better off in material terms than those of India, but one cannot meaningfully conclude from the table that they are fifty-four times better off. And when we compare two similar nations such as, say, France and the

Table 14.C.1 GNP per Capita, Selected Countries, 1983 (dollars*)

(a)	Some Advanced Capitalist Countries:	
	France	10,500
	Japan	10,120
	Sweden	12,470
	UK	9,200
	USA	14,110
(b)	Some 'Newly Industrializing Countries':	
	Hong Kong	6,000
	Mexico	2,240
	Singapore	6,620
(c)	Some Underdeveloped Capitalist Countries:	
	Bolivia	510
	Ghana	310
	Haiti	300
	India	260
(d)	Some High-Income OPEC Countries:	
	Kuwait	17,880
	Saudi Arabia	12,230

* All values have been converted to dollars at the official exchange rates averaged over three years. This gives a further powerful reason for avoiding welfare comparisons, especially in poorer countries where the bulk of goods do not enter into international trade.
Source: World Bank, *World Development Report, 1985*, New York, Oxford University Press for the World Bank, 1985

UK, one cannot deduce that French citizens are better off in the sense that social needs are better satisfied in the former than in the latter, just because its GNP per capita is higher.

CHAPTER 15

Keynesianism and Crises

I. THE CRITIQUE OF KEYNESIANISM

In Chapter 14 we pursued the question of how capitalist economies could grow but also fall occasionally into crises. Keynes's model gave the crucial insight about the cumulative effects of shocks to the economy, and we uncritically examined Keynes's policy prescriptions in order to show the principles behind them.

In this chapter we shall adopt a much more critical stance. We shall see how there arose a number of technical problems which were latched on to by monetarists, heralding not a solving of those problems but a rejection of the whole philosophy of Keynesianism. We shall also look at some more fundamental problems, as a prelude to reviewing possible causes of recurring crisis in the capitalist economies.

Keynes's model suggests that it is possible to manipulate aggregate demand so as to counteract any cumulative declines in output and employment. Just as you can tune a car engine to make it run smoothly so, it is argued, you can fine-tune the economy to prevent unemployment or inflationary pressures, sentiments well expressed by the Nobel prizewinner, economist Paul Samuelson:

Everywhere in the Western world governments and central banks have shown they can win the battle of the slump. They have the weapons of fiscal policy (expenditure and taxes) and of monetary policy (open-market operations, discount-rate policy, legal-reserve-ratio policy), to shift the various schedules that determine national income and employment. Just as we no longer meekly accept disease, we no longer need accept mass unemployment. (P. Samuelson, *Economics*, 9th ed., 1973)

Such optimism is consigned now to the history of economic thought. Few economists would argue today that things are so simple.

(i) *Technical problems with Keynesian policies*

The recipe for demand management contains three main processes: measurement, forecasting and policy making. Together these call for considerable skills and knowledge from economists and policy makers which, it is sometimes argued, they cannot possess.

Most governments now have a fairly good empirical picture of the state of economic activity seen from a Keynesian perspective (that is, focusing on aggregate components of demand). However, a problem remains in obtaining the latest measurements quickly; some figures may not appear till some time after the date to which they apply, in which case they cannot be used for economic management.

The second ingredient of demand management is forecasting economic activity. It is vital to have accurate forecasts if stabilizing policies are to be implemented. For example, if investment spending is expected to fall in the near future (leading to a fall in national income) the government can expand the economy with fiscal or monetary policy. The trouble is that it is sometimes no easier forecasting future economic activity than predicting next week's weather.

The main forecasting method is to use 'macroeconometric' models. These are essentially large-scale mathematical elaborations of the simple Keynesian model used in the last chapter, broken down into many sectors and given real empirical magnitudes on the basis of measured economic data. A model is 'estimated' over a certain period in the past, using the known values of economic variables. Then the estimated model is used to predict what will happen to income, consumption, investment and so on in the future. This principle of extrapolating from past economic relationships and assuming they will still hold in the future is not a new one. The sheer complexity of economic life, however, made such predictions either impossible or very crude until the advent of the computer. Now efficient computers produce forecasts of many economic variables in the near and medium future. While the expenditure of vast sums on developing these models has improved their accuracy, they always remain open to the possibility of economic relationships changing; and there remains much disagreement between the predictions of different models, with no one model being consistently proved the best.

For this reason, macroeconomic models are usually supplemented by consumer and business surveys of future intentions, by using business cycle indicators and also by the 'judgement' of economists who take into account the probable effect of special factors not allowed for with the other methods.

The method of using business cycle indicators has been practised in the

USA (though less commonly elsewhere) since the publication of A. F. Burns's and W. C. Mitchell's *Measuring Business Cycles* in 1946. It involves plotting the time path of various economic aggregates such as national income, industrial output, employment and many others. The historical analysis shows that all these variables go through irregular cycles. The turning points – the times at which growth turns to contraction and vice versa – usually bear systematic relationships to each other. For example, the turning points in employment occur well after those in industrial output. When output reaches its lowest point in a recession, employment will still be going down: but it is an indication that employment will turn up in the foreseeable future. We would say that industrial output is a 'leading' indicator with respect to the employment cycle. Usually, however, economists are particularly concerned to predict when output itself will reach a peak or trough, so they need leading indicators for output; one such in the USA is the index of industrial materials prices.

There are two drawbacks to indicator analysis. First, it does not predict the magnitudes of economic variables in the future – only whether they are about to reach a peak or trough. Second, the record of predictions is far from perfect. Although relatively better than macroeconomic models at predicting turning points, indicator analysis is as much a game as a serious, dispassionate and scientific technique.

After measuring and forecasting the economy comes policy implementation. We have mentioned already the argument that it is preferable to use policies that can be quickly planned, agreed and implemented. Time elapses while the policies are agreed and again before they begin to bite on the economy.

All these factors mean there is a problem of possibly long and variable time lags between the economic activity starting to go off-course and the subsequent corrective Keynesian stimulus. Drive along a straight road in a car, and whenever you hit a bump that sends the car to one side you must quickly turn the wheel to compensate. If the economic policy lags are too long the corrective measures could be useless. Worse than that, they could destabilize the economy. There is little evidence that this has in fact happened to any substantial extent. But it is a possibility. Diagrams 15.1(a) and 15.1(b) give an idealized picture of how this could happen.

In both diagrams, the continuous line represents the imagined path followed by national income over time in the absence of stabilization policy. In Diagram 15.1(a) the dotted line represents the path followed as a result of a successful fine-tuning policy. Between A and B the economy is booming and so contractionary policy is applied, thus reducing national income. Between B and C the incipient recession is avoided by expanding aggregate demand through tax-cutting and so on.

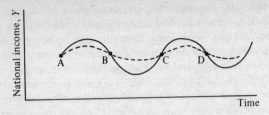

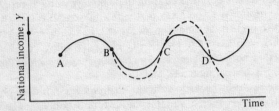

Diagram 15.1 Stabilizing and Destabilizing Policies

(a) A successful fine-tuning policy
(b) The possible consequences of lags

Diagram 15.1(b) shows the possible consequences of lags. The contractionary policy called for between A and B does not start to take effect till after point B, by which time the economy is already going into recession. The policy makes it worse. When the government realizes a recession is occurring it starts to expand the economy; but if the effect of such policy is lagged again it will not take effect till after C in which case it will exaggerate the ensuing boom. And so on.

This problem is related to, but different from, another technical hitch caused partly by lags: the 'political business cycle'. Here the main lag is the time between the good and bad effects of expanding demand. Initially, producers respond to changes in demand by changing their output plans – this is the essential Keynesian hypothesis. If, however, demand is expanded beyond the limits of existing resources prices will later start to rise as producers cannot permanently keep up a much higher output. Thus if demand remains too high, the economy becomes overheated, inflation threatens and contractionary policies have to be brought in. The theory of the political business cycle assumes that electorates vote partially on a government's economic management record and also that they have fairly short memories.

This problem of Keynesianism is essentially also one of modern parliamentary democracy. In most cases, western democratic governments *can* forecast when they need next to come up for re-election. Hence they plan to stimulate aggregate demand for the year or so prior to the election, so as to arrive on polling day with a growing economy and full employment. There is less concern that, after the election, aggregate demand will have to be contracted to avoid overheating the economy; by the next election, any bad consequences will have been forgotten. Deception is as much part of the art of politics as it is of dealing in used cars, and the destabilizing economic consequences of the political cycle involve a fair measure of it.

(ii) *Monetarism versus Keynesianism: a first glance*

The technical problems of demand management policies occupy the time and energy of many thousands of economists. They arouse various responses, but we may broadly distinguish two philosophical approaches.

The Keynesian economist aims to improve the techniques of demand management: to refine the macroeconomic models and to improve their forecasts, and to understand better the impact of monetary and fiscal policies (particularly the length of time lags involved). By contrast, the problems of the 1970s called forth a new school of macroeconomists: the monetarists. In their view, since the government was actually destabilizing the economy, it would be better not to interfere any more than absolutely necessary. In particular, since monetarists also believed that changes in the money supply had a powerful, direct, yet uncertain impact on aggregate demand, it was important to create stable monetary conditions. This could be done by having a policy rule such as: 'Expand the money supply by a constant x per cent a year.' This rule should be followed whatever the perceived state of the economy is. Even if there is a recession, there is no case for expanding the money supply faster than the rule allows.

Keynesians believe that monetary policy should be 'discretionary' – it should depend on the state of the economy. The monetarists argue that attempts to intefere, given the government's inevitable lack of information about the effect of policy, are likely to make matters worse. In their view the economy, if left to itself, would not be unstable. Although they do not necessarily hold to the discredited Say's Law, which Keynes showed to be logically false, they none the less believe that the market does work in practice, if it is allowed to.

As for the recurring crises in capitalist economies, both Keynesianism and monetarism ultimately offer explanations in the 'accidental' or 'exogenous' category referred to in the last chapter. Although Keynes pointed to the possibility of crisis, caused by a lack of effective demand, he believed the remedy was at hand given enlightened government policy. If mass unemployment remained it was the result of mistaken policy. Hence crises are not inevitable – it is merely necessary to educate the policy makers in economic theory. The monetarists by contrast discount the likelihood of effective demand crises since they believe in the market. For them, crises are caused by too much policy making by governments – the solution is to educate policy makers on how the market will co-ordinate the economy if they keep their hands off.

The foregoing discussion suggests that monetarism is more than just a particular technical response to the problems of Keynesian policies. Monetarists have never proved their technical case against Keynesianism: that the economy would do better without government demand management than with it. But many 'believe' in the ideology of monetarism. In fact, as we shall see, technical responses, like the money supply growth rule, go hand in hand with a more fundamental response to the general capitalist crisis. We shall therefore return to this discussion later, in Chapter 18.

(iii) *Fundamental problems with Keynesianism*

We argue that the technical problems are of a secondary nature. The Keynesian philosophy suffers from more basic flaws.

The first concerns the nature of governments in modern capitalism, a world of separate nation states. A capitalist government is the central institution of a capitalist state and while its policies are influenced by a great many factors, it is in the long run conditioned and constrained by the needs of capital accumulation (see Chapter 11). But to be more concrete we have sometimes to specify whether a government's policies favour all capitalists world wide, or just its domestic capitalists, or what? Capitalism may be a world system but as yet there is no world government.

We have met this contradiction before. Small countries often cannot practise Keynesian demand management without incurring or exacerbating balance of payments deficits. Suppose the economy is in recession and the government decides to expand national income using monetary and fiscal policy. As national income rises so also do imports, because imports are a part of what is consumed. But the government has no control over the demand for exports (unless the currency is devalued). Inevitably the balance of trade worsens with any recovery, especially as in the early stages imports are rising and exports are not. In the long run exports may also rise if investment bears fruit and domestic capitalists can sell to foreigners more cheaply, but in the mean time the country runs the risk of balance of payments difficulties.

Two courses are open to the government in these circumstances. It can let the currency depreciate in value on the foreign exchange market in the hope of raising exports. The problem here is that in a world recession if many countries are all devaluing their currencies in order to increase their own exports there is no real redistribution of demand but a possible collapse of confidence in world trade. The 1930s proved to be just such an era of successive competitive devaluations. The other course for a government (also followed often in the 1930s) is to isolate its economy from the world markets by widespread controls on imports and on foreign transactions, to limit the rise in imports and hence gain the freedom to stimulate aggregate demand to achieve full employment. The drawback is clear. Economic isolationism deprives capitalists of the benefits of international business; it also runs the risk of becoming generalized, like devaluation. All countries can retreat into isolated trading blocs.

Leaving aside the international question, there is a further problem with the Keynesian conception of the state as a neutral arbiter and regulator of the economy. That assumes that governments will always try to keep unemployment to a minimum. Yet governments acting in the long-term interests of capital may at times find it best deliberately to create high unemployment, in order to weaken working-class resistance in wage and production struggles. Fear of poverty and unemployment is the most potent weapon, short of physical force, for compelling work. The Keynesian view cannot explain such government behaviour – it can only call it a big mistake.

This introduces the most fundamental flaw in the Keynesian model, which is that it forgets the central purpose of the capitalist process – making profits. The basic question which Keynes attempts to resolve is: will aggregate effective demand be sufficient to create full employment? Instead, the question should be: can capitalists produce and sell sufficient commodities to make adequate profits to continue accumulation, or will accumulation come to a standstill? The concepts of aggregate consumption, investment, government expenditure and so on, while they help us to understand aggregate demand, do not require or embody a notion of class structure. But in fact the concept of class – based on the monopoly of ownership of means of production by one section of society – is essential to understanding capitalist relationships. And even if it were possible to overcome the technical problems of demand management and the limitations of nation states, there remain dynamic imbalances in the economic system which undermine profits and hence the basis of capitalism. It is to these that we now turn.

2. ACCUMULATION AND CRISIS

(i) *Production and realization of profits*

In Chapter 1 and elsewhere we have described the capitalist process as consisting of the unity of two spheres of relationships: the production and the exchange spheres. Successful profit making depends on both functioning adequately. When capital accumulation is proceeding smoothly the unity is quite apparent. The production of potential profit depends upon its being 'realized' in the selling process, and the realization of profits presupposes the potential.

Yet they are also separate processes – a fact which only becomes established in reality when a crisis occurs. The production of potential profits, examined in detail in Chapter 3, involves the unequal relationship of authority between boss and worker, where capitalists utilize the labour-power that workers have sold. The realization of profits is an exchange process and therefore it is based on typical market relationships: those between buyers and sellers of commodities.

The Keynesian model of the last section concentrates on the realization problem, rather than on the whole capitalist process. As we have seen, it identifies possible crises of insufficient aggregate demand and suggests how these can be remedied. This gives us only a partial insight into the reality of capitalism and this, like all one-sided views, is as likely to obscure as to illuminate the truth.

There is an ever-present dynamic tension which threatens to break apart the unity of the capitalist process. For there is always the danger that actions which improve the prospects for one part can make things worse for the other. For example, the state can improve the prospects for realization by expanding aggregate demand. But in the long run that leads to higher taxes. If they fall on capitalists, profits are reduced directly. If they fall on workers, wage demands are raised to try to protect living standards, again making it more difficult to make profits.

On the other hand, if at another time capitalists manage to force cuts in wages generally this can increase their profit margins – but if this happens nationally, or even globally, workers' effective demand for consumer goods will fall and the danger is that a realization crisis can ensue.

This dilemma or contradiction is always there. And it can prevent successful capital accumulation at any time.

This does not mean, however, that capitalist crises are always just round the corner. Some radical economists have argued not simply that capitalism is prone to crises, but that it is always about to break down completely. They argue that because of capitalism's internal contradictions it is a system always in crisis – hence that it could never work successfully. This is as dogmatic as the opposite extreme view taken by pure orthodox economists who, relying on the market, argue that the capitalist economy always works, provided it is not subject to external shocks. Neither of these extremes can be substantiated either theoretically or by reference to historical facts. Rather, a successful theoretical approach should aim to account organically for both the success and the failure of the system, and to say how it can go from one to the other.

The contradiction between production and realization can certainly be overcome for a while through capital accumulation. As the expansion of production of commodities proceeds so also can the demand for them as wages rise slowly and as more workers are brought into employment. The realization problem can be resolved. That is exactly what happened in the 'golden years' of post-war capitalism.

(ii) *Crisis of overproduction*

Successful periods of capital accumulation, however, have all sooner or later come to an end. It is impossible for capitalism to stand still. It is driven forward by inner forces: in particular the forces of capitalist competition and of class antagonism with workers. The individual capitalist who does not invest risks being excluded from the capitalist class, since others are continually investing, changing production processes and trying to reduce costs. Moreover, expansion means wage rises, which helps to maintain a docile, subordinate working class. One way of understanding the seeming inevitability of crises is to suggest, as many writers have done, that these inner forces driving capitalism to expand lead inevitably to the 'over-accumulation' of capital and to the 'over-production' of commodities. By 'over-production' we do not mean that too much is being produced relative to human needs (seeing the poverty of so many millions of people all over the world, this would be absurd) but rather that accumulation has proceeded so fast and so far that capitalist relationships are coming under increasing strain: capital is no longer able to reproduce itself in the way we described in Chapter 14. In other words, imbalances are liable to arise, sooner or later, either between different capitalists' expansion paths or between capitalists and workers. As the nineteenth-century French economist Clement Juglar put it, 'The only cause of depression is prosperity.'

Concretely, prosperity might turn into depression in one of a number of ways. Some sectors of capital may not expand as fast as others, thus creating bottlenecks and shortages of intermediate products. Market forces may not be able to cope sufficiently quickly by raising accumulation in the shortage sectors. This can be especially significant in the case of raw materials where production may depend partly on the co-operation of forces and people outside the capitalist world.

For some writers, a more fundamental bottleneck is that the available labour force becomes used up. As capitalism expands it can draw on any unemployed workers, and then on the latent reserve army of potential workers in agriculture and in the home. The reproduction of workers, however, is not a capitalist process and does not respond to the market as a capitalist firm would. Inevitably the shortage of workers puts upward pressure on wages, both by raising competitive pressures and by strengthening the bargaining powers of organized workers. The rise in wages leads to a fall in profits.

An alternative scenario, even if the reserve army of labour remains available and wages do not rise, is that the production of commodities can expand faster than the effective demand for them, thus triggering off a realization crisis. Writers who emphasize this are sometimes referred to as 'under-consumptionists'.

(iii) *The organic function of crisis*

When there has been a break in capital accumulation, all sorts of readjustments and restructuring become possible. As profits fall, so does investment. The Keynesian multiplier effect ensures a fall in demand and a rise in unemployment. If this gets high enough, it can begin to redress the imbalances that have grown up during the period of expansion: workers' strength may be reduced and wages cut. At the same time other imbalances may be removed as some capitalists become bankrupt and only the strongest survive. In this way the conditions for successful accumulation can be re-established. The unity of production and exchange can be forcefully reimposed, at the expense of working-class people and the weaker capitalists.

Because of this, crisis may partly be seen as cleansing and restoring a system that has gone wrong. This function, however, is far from automatic or inevitable. The course of the crisis and its aftermath depends to some extent on the strength of the working class and its ability to resist cuts in living standards. Moreover, there is no automatic way to resolve the realization problem. If the depression following a crisis is deep, the economy can get stuck in it, just as the world's economies did following the 1929 crisis. No amount of restructuring production and of wage cutting can necessarily create the required demand. To extricate the economy and set it back on the path of successful accumulation might need the stimulus of some external event such as war or, as Keynes argued forcefully in the 1930s, massive pump-priming expenditure by governments.

Finally, again depending on the specific condition of class struggle at the time, crises can lead instead to fundamental questioning of the capitalist system itself. They can raise the consciousness of workers and their willingness to resist and to seek for change. In sum, it is safer for ideological reasons to keep most workers employed and to prevent large wage cuts; but occasionally a crisis and the restructuring which follows are inevitable. Rather like a surgical operation, economic crises are necessary to ensure survival but carry some risk of fatality.

(iv) *Crises in the abstract, and in history*

In this chapter and the previous one we have established the most basic feature of the 'laws of motion' of capitalism. It consists of bursts of accumulation interrupted by periods of crisis, restructuring and perhaps questioning of the system. In doing this we have given abstract answers to our abstract questions about the success or failure of the profit system.

Fundamental as these questions are, we have as yet only touched on specific historical developments. Moreover, in discussing crises we have even kept to a rather abstract definition of them, as interruptions in accumulation. We now set about putting flesh on to these bones, beginning in Chapter 16 with a historical account of the post-war successes of capitalism and its return to crisis in the 1970s. And in Chapter 17 we examine some of the many different ways that the crisis tendency has manifested itself in modern capitalist economies.

CHAPTER 16

From Boom to Stagnation

I. THE TWO PHASES OF POST-WAR CAPITALISM

Starting about 1950 the capitalist economies of the world embarked upon a quite unprecedented era of success, bringing fortunes probably undreamt of by those who had lived through the doldrums of the 1930s. Many people nowadays have long since forgotten this time of success, many others are too young to remember it, but there are real connections between these former successes and the current, much deteriorated, state of health of capitalist economies.

Capitalism during this period became increasingly integrated, which makes it easier to talk of the experiences of the advanced capitalist countries as a group without too many substantial exceptions. From the 1950s onwards their progress can be roughly divided into two episodes. The first, variously termed the 'post-war boom' or the 'golden years', lasted till the early 1970s. It is convenient to mark 1973 as the last year, since it was followed by the crash of 1974 which ushered in the era of relative stagnation. The precise date however, is somewhat arbitrary for, as we shall see, the profit system had begun to turn sour well beforehand.

Placing 1973 as the start of a new period can perhaps exaggerate the difference between the two episodes, in that we start the second with a recession which might have reflected only a short-term cyclical downturn rather than the beginning of a new long-term phase. None the less, even with this qualification, the difference between the economic performance of the two periods, shown in Table 16.1, is striking. The earlier period had high profits, an exceptionally high rate of accumulation of capital stock and an extraordinary growth rate of output, compared to the stagnation period when profits, investment and growth rates were lower. Meanwhile, the 'problems' of inflation, unemployment and recessions that have plagued the current era were relatively absent in the earlier 'golden' years.

In addition to the differences in such economic aggregates, the two eras may be contrasted through their institutional and political environments. The early period had a stable international monetary system and a

Table 16.1 From Boom to Stagnation

	Boom	Stagnation
World manufacturing profit rate 1.	26.0% (1955)	12.0% (1975)
Average annual output growth 2.	4.9% (1950–73)	2.3% (1973–81)
'Recessions' 3.	14 in 23 years (1950–73)	25 in 8 years (1973–81)
Average unemployment rate, OECD countries 4.	3.2% (1960–73)	6.2% (1974–83)
Average annual inflation rate 5.	4.0% (1950–73)	10.9% (1973–9)
Average annual rate of change of capital stock 6.	5.2% (1950–73)	3.6% (1973–9)

Sources and Definitions: 1. OECD weighted average; Philip Armstrong, Andrew Glyn and John Harrison, *Capitalism since World War II*, London, Fontana, 1984. 2. Arithmetical average of sixteen advanced capitalist countries; see Angus Maddison, *Phases of Capitalist Development*, Oxford and New York, Oxford University Press, 1982, p. 68. 3. Incidences of annual reductions in GDP in any of sixteen countries; see Maddison, *op. cit.*, p. 89. 4. OECD Economic Outlook, *Historical Statistics, 1960–1983*, OECD, Paris, 1985. 5. Arithmetical average of the six largest countries. 6. Arithmetical average of US, UK, West Germany and Canada; see Maddison, *op. cit.*, pp. 227–32

supremely powerful 'world policeman', the USA. In many nations predominantly social democratic governments geared themselves to the steady expansion of social welfare and the pursuance of Keynesian demand management policies and provided a favourable environment for the expansion of unions. The stagnation period has been accompanied by the 'non-system' of floating exchange rates and a changing balance of international relations as capitalists in other countries, notably Japan, challenged Europe and the USA for economic supremacy. The principles of social welfare have been widely called into question, and in many countries there was an ideological switch from the Keynesian promise of full employment to the monetarist argument for total reliance on markets, together with a widespread attack on trade unions.

2. THE VIRTUOUS CIRCLE

In the 'golden years' the course of capitalism became for a while caught in a high-growth groove, a 'virtuous circle', in which high and rising rates of accumulation of capital chased high profits, which in turn led to high investment. The various mechanisms of this self-sustaining boom have been discussed individually at other points in this book, but in order to get a picture of how they can work in relation to one another we shall briefly review them here.

The structure of the circle is shown schematically in Diagram 16.1. Starting arbitrarily at the point where there are high profits we may trace the mechanism around as follows. High profits generate high investment in two ways: through raising profit expectations and through providing the liquidity to finance investments when borrowing is constrained (see Chapter 6).

The direct effects of high investment are twofold. First, it leads to high productivity increases as machines are substituted for workers. Second, growing investment orders provide a major direct source of increased market demand, which is necessary for profits to be realized. With the exception of 1958, investment across the capitalist world expanded throughout the golden years.

But high investment also has indirect effects through its effect on wages.

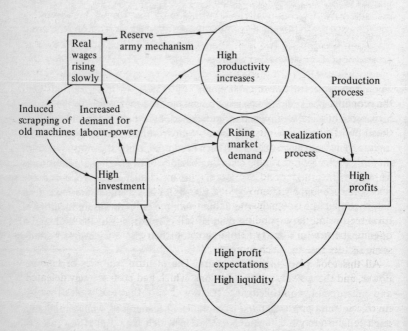

Diagram 16.1   The Virtuous Circle of the Self-Sustaining Boom

As we saw in Chapter 5, a number of factors can affect wages and no absolute law can be laid down about their rising or falling. The two main effects of high investment work in opposite directions. As investment is high and output rises so also must the demand for labour-power expand, as workers are required to operate the new machines. Yet at the same time these machines are replacing workers in all sectors of the economy, particularly the backward agricultural sectors, thereby releasing redundant workers on to the labour market (the reserve army mechanism). A further factor is the increased supply of labour-power from other sources (e.g. population growth and more married women seeking paid labour). Although real wages can theoretically move up or down, in practice the high accumulation rates bring gradual rises which have beneficial effects for the virtuous circle. It reinforces the high investment, because those capitalists operating in backward and labour-intensive sectors are induced to mechanize their production processes; and it provides an additional market demand for consumer goods, allowing that market to rise substantially faster than the base population increase.

Together, the regular high increases in productivity and the expansion of market demand for consumer goods and services and for machinery were the ingredients for continually high profitability. The former enhanced the conditions for production of profits, the latter their realization: the contradiction between the two had, at least for a while, been held at bay. An extreme and ideal practical example of the virtuous circle mechanism is the frankly astonishing performance of the Japanese economy in the years after 1955. The circle was drawn most boldly in the next six years. In that time the economy was boosted up on to a new and hitherto unknown plane of high accumulation and high profits that was to sustain it for a long time thereafter. In 1955, the rate of accumulation of fixed capital was 4 per cent a year. By 1961 this figure had risen to 12 per cent. The effect was a vast rise in productivity (86 per cent in manufacturing industries) which, apart from raising profits, augmented the reserve army of labour as workers were released more quickly from working on old machines. This, together with ample supplies of new industrial labour-power from the declining agricultural sector and the expanding population, provided sufficient workers to operate the new machinery. Total employment rose by 10 per cent, and some sectors rose by much more.

All this took place in just six years. The plentiful supplies of labour-power, and the weakness of trade unions, which had been severely defeated and subsequently controlled since the war, meant that real wages rose by much less than productivity. The workers' consumption demand did not rise enough to buy the increased outputs, but this did not matter since the expanding investment orders, together with increased exports, provided the extra market demand. Profits kept rolling in: the average pre-tax profit rate outside agriculture rose from the already high level of 19 per cent in 1955 to about 27 per cent in 1961.

Nowhere else in the major capitalist countries has the circle been as virtuous as in Japan at this time. Investment rates were always much lower elsewhere. None the less, the idea of a self-sustaining boom provides the abstract model for post-war growth which characterizes the success of the advanced capitalist countries in the golden years. It was the bandwagon which all countries were trying to climb on to, and most succeeded to a greater or lesser extent.

3. THE MATERIAL AND INSTITUTIONAL FRAMEWORK

The virtuous circle harboured contradictions. But four factors allowed capitalism several years before any of them came to the surface. These factors were the plentiful supplies of new labour-power, the existence of a large technological backlog to draw on, the availability of cheap raw materials and the maintenance of stable national and international economic relations. None of these are in themselves 'causes' of the boom. History is too complex for such an easy conclusion. Rather they are better thought of as 'enabling factors', or collectively as a framework within which to understand the recent past of capitalism, hence also the present.

(i) *Reserves of labour-power*

The first, and some would contend the most crucial, potential contradiction of rapid bursts of accumulation, is that the demand for labour-power can increase so fast that the reserve army of labour becomes exhausted, even though it is being replenished by productivity increases; and workers are able to obtain high wage rises which counteract their exploitation and reduce profits.

Some rise in real wages is possible, given that productivity is also rising. In fact, it is normally beneficial, if the boom is to be sustained, since otherwise market demand may not rise fast enough unless supplemented by exceptional rises in exports or government expenditure. Thus real wages tread best an intermediate path of slow growth in order to meet both production and realization conditions.

Such a path was indeed followed in the golden years in most countries. Despite the unprecedented rates of accumulation, wages were prevented from rising too fast by the addition of new and elastic supplies of labour-power. The proletariat in the largest capitalist countries (the USA, the UK, Japan, West Germany, France and Italy) grew on average by about

2.25 per cent per year from the early 1950s to the early 1970s – much faster than the 1.1 per cent annual rate of increase of the working-age population. Moreover, these extra workers could be drawn in yet more rapidly over short periods of time – which is why, for example, the Japanese burst from 1955 to 1961 could be sustained without encountering a substantial shortage of labour-power. The sources were mainly the emptying fields and deserted kitchens (Chapter 5).

(ii) *The availability of technology*

A related material condition for continued high accumulation is that the technology should be available to allow sufficient productivity rises and high profit expectations from new investments. If more advanced technology does not already exist, capitalists must rely on their Research and Development (R & D) expenditures to generate it, which is generally a slow and uncertain process. Without new production methods, investment and profit expectations would fall.

But in the boom this danger was absent for a wide range of businesses, especially outside the USA. Many countries had old and relatively small stocks of fixed capital, partly as a result of the destructions of the Second World War. The level of US technology was much more advanced, because for the previous half-century capitalists' investment had been generally higher than in Europe or Japan, and because it had avoided the setbacks of two world wars fought on home territory. So, long after 1950, firms elsewhere were able to draw on US technology to make their productivity improvements, while US firms could only expand productivity at a much slower rate as new methods were invented. Japanese corporations in particular proved to be especially adept at appropriating US methods; by 1961 over half of their manufacturing industry was using imported techniques.

(iii) *Raw materials*

A third potential contradiction is that rapid accumulation could lead to shortages of raw materials. More generally, it is necessary that no great disproportionalities should develop between the growth of different sectors of the economy. Some unevenness can be coped with, for the price mechanism can work to induce capitalists in search of greater profits to switch production to commodities which are in short supply and experiencing price rises. If a major sector develops a hitch, however, it may prove impossible to switch resources to that sector quickly enough to cope with a fast-developing disequilibrium. As a result, the price of the commodity in short supply may continue to rise, thereby lowering the profits of all other capitalists who use it. Exactly this perspective is often thought to apply to primary products. Many of these are produced in underdeveloped countries, with politically less stable regimes, where growth may not keep pace with that of capitalists elsewhere.

Yet no major raw material constraint ever appeared in the golden years of capitalism, nor were there yet any major ecological constraints on the political agenda. In fact, the 'terms of trade' for the Third World's primary products with the developed countries' manufactured products steadily decreased by about 12 per cent overall between 1952 and 1970.

Despite the fast accumulation rates no sectoral or geographical disproportionality arose to interfere with the virtuous circle. The reason was partly that multinational companies were able to invest and reap profits in primary product industries. But this in itself is due to the conscious role of imperialist nations, especially the USA, in providing the conditions for secure access to primary commodities produced abroad (see Chapter 6).

(iv) *The regulation of capitalism and the hegemony of the USA*

Secure raw material supplies were related to the fourth general factor which was needed to allow the self-sustaining boom to proceed: the maintenance of a stable political and economic environment for profit making. The institutions for regulating capitalism were functioning well during the golden years, in a number of ways.

First, successful accumulation depended on an industrial relations system that guaranteed that workers would comply with capitalist control. Trade unions in many places were expanding and often resisting; but the legitimation of trade unionism, and the unions' right to fight for better wages, were traded for their acceptance of capitalist relations. In Japan, many workers' unions were defeated altogether and replaced by company unions, which although formally constituted to look after workers' interests were in effect incorporated into the company hierarchies. In many other countries unions typically accepted management's prerogatives to impose 'Taylorist' control over the production process, in return for gradually rising wages.

At the national level the task of providing an orderly economic environment fell mainly to individual nation states. They provided increasing social welfare, tried to stabilize demand through Keynesian techniques and intervened where necessary to help boost the profits of industry (see Chapter 11).

National state institutions played some part in providing the required environment for growth to proceed, but it is impossible to assess just how important each one was. We cannot, for example, say that the French planning agencies contributed x per cent to the growth rate of the French economy or to the profits of French capitalists. Nor, as we saw in the last chapter, is the record of Keynesian demand management an unmitigated success.

It is on the international front, however, that much of the interest centres, for as we saw in Chapter 10, there has emerged no supranational world capitalist state capable of performing the regulatory functions that a national state undertakes in its own domestic economy. Yet this was a period in which capitalist relations became increasingly international. The void was filled instead by one particular government, that of the USA.

From the Second World War onwards successive US governments set out to mould a stable international economic environment that would be congenial to US capitalists wishing to do business in and with foreign countries. At the start of the boom, output in the USA was some 60 per cent of all the advanced capitalist world's produce. US workers were several times more productive than those elsewhere, so that despite their higher wages their products could undercut most European producers. The economy was thus so strong that the US government was usually able to compel other governments to accept its plans for the world. If persuasion failed it could simply threaten to cut off aid and loans.

The US hegemony provided stability to international capitalist relations in a number of ways. On a political level it was able to exert pressure on underdeveloped nations to remain part of the capitalist world – as opposed to turning to the Soviet bloc or trying to remain neutral. The carrot was US aid and loans to friendly governments. The stick was the covert or open subversion of unfriendly (anti-capitalist) governments, and even occasionally military invasion. The policy was first clearly enunciated in 1947, becoming known as the Truman Doctrine, which declared that the US would intervene on the side of 'freedom' (i.e. anti-communism) wherever necessary. It still remains the basis for US foreign policy at the time of writing (1986) despite major setbacks in Vietnam and in Cuba.

The purpose of such political and military intervention was to maintain stable (capitalist) economic relationships with the rest of the world. This meant, first, that US-based multinational firms could freely operate in other countries, second, that their markets would remain open to receive US exports, and third, that supplies of primary products from abroad could be assured. And while US corporations perhaps benefited most, others could also take advantage of the stability.

Parallel to its operations in the Third World, the US ruling class also set about managing its economic relationships with the other, more advanced countries in western Europe and with Japan. The main objective could be summed up as attempting to 'open up' the world's capitalist economies. This view was not universally held within political circles. After 1945 those with an internationalist perspective had to defeat those who wished America to withdraw into a national capitalism. This battle won, the USA proceeded to try to stabilize the economic affairs of Europe.

It pumped in aid under the 'Marshall Plan' to European governments that were prepared to conform to US policy notions (particularly, deflation) and from 1950 onwards there was a massive rearmament programme, helped along by the Korean War. This provided the European governments with military aid against possible internal and external subversion, while it also injected vast amounts of dollars to bolster the European economies and their demands for US exports. At the same time US political pressure gradually moved world opinion towards a multilateral lowering of trade tariffs and barriers and an easing of restrictions on foreign exchange deals so that currencies could become mutually convertible. Thus were the economies of the world opened up.

The changes took a long time – for example, full convertibility of currencies did not arrive until 1958 and there were many setbacks along the road. The development of international institutions followed the path of competitive struggles between the USA and other powers as well as internal political struggles within the US. None the less it may be reasonably stated as a broad generalization that US governments succeeded in imposing and policing a set of international economic relationships that proved sufficiently durable and stable to permit the virtuous circle to function.

Dominating these relationships was a particular institution located in Washington DC, the International Monetary Fund (IMF). It is through this that the international monetary system, which was set up at a famous conference in Bretton Woods, New Hampshire, in 1944, was organized. Capitalist world integration has not gone so far as to impose one currency on all countries, any more than one language or one culture has displaced all others. But the dollar did for a long time become the international language of commerce; and it was inevitable that it should have been the basis of the Bretton Woods system.

4. THE BRETTON WOODS SYSTEM DURING THE GOLDEN YEARS

(i) *The nature of foreign exchange markets*

The foreign exchange market is not a geographical location but an economic arena, wherein dealers (normally bank employees) buy and sell the world's currencies on behalf of business clients. For example, importers of goods from West Germany must buy marks, whereas exporters to West Germany will have marks to sell. US tourists in Europe will be selling dollars and buying pounds, francs and so on. Investors who wish to buy shares on the Australian stock market need first to buy Australian dollars.

As in any other market, the demands and supplies are sensitive to price (that is, the exchange rate) and the exchange rates vary in response to imbalances (though especially quickly in this case). Another feature is the presence of speculators, who aim to make quick profits from currency devaluations or appreciations.

But since exchange rate fluctuations affect all capitalists who directly or indirectly are involved with trade, a strong presumption in favour of fixing the rates emerges if the aim is to provide stability. In order to do so, governments have to intervene in the free market each day and buy up any excess supplies or meet any excess demands for their national currencies, to prevent the exchange rate fluctuating very much. And that implies, above all, one vital requirement: a sufficient stock of foreign exchange reserves for each government. For if, due to a balance of payments deficit, there is an excess supply of, say, French francs, then the French central bank (or one of its allies) must use some of its stock of gold or foreign currency and be able to sustain its intervention long enough for the balance of payments to swing into a surplus, when there will be an excess demand instead. So a government's reserves in a fixed rate system must be plentiful. It is in the light of this that we can see the crucial stabilizing role of the US dollar during the boom years.

(ii) *The Bretton Woods agreement*

In the nineteenth century British governments had regulated the system through their dominance over international trade and the imposition of a 'gold standard' – a fixed exchange rate system whereby all currencies were pegged directly to gold, or to the pound, which was itself convertible into gold at a constant price. In the inter-war period no overall system had prevailed. The decline of British hegemony had led to the demise of the old gold standard and there were frequent devaluations as each country tried to cheapen its currency. In the 1930s trade became concentrated amongst specific blocs, based on the traditional imperial spheres of influence. Monetary instability mirrored and reinforced the economic stagnation of the Great Depression years. After the Second World War, the US government aimed to break into the vicious circle of stagnation and uncertainty by devising a stable monetary system which would survive and would itself permit the long-term growth of the economy.

Harry Dexter White, an influential economist in the US Treasury Department, proposed the setting up of a world central bank, with massive lending resources to provide the financial capital required for reconstruction, which would intervene to stabilize exchange and stock markets all over the world. It was the financial embryo of the possible supranational state. But the US Congress would never have agreed both to provide sufficient resources and at the same time to cede control to an international body. The grand plan was dropped. In the final agreement, sealed in 1944 at Bretton Woods, the World Bank was reduced to a small lending agency that would mainly concentrate on raising finance to lend to underdeveloped countries. Much more important in the longer term was the founding of the International Monetary Fund (IMF).

The IMF was to allocate quotas to member countries' central banks, which would be allowed to borrow from the fund to augment their reserves when it was necessary in order to maintain their exchange rates. The precise terms reflected the influence of Keynes, who had negotiated on behalf of the UK government, aiming to maintain some independence for smaller nation states from the USA. Its role was later transformed following the death of Keynes (1946) and the fall from grace of White in the course of the post-war communist witch-hunt. The terms of access were made more restrictive under US influence and essentially the IMF became an instrument through which the USA could influence the macroeconomic policies of member countries. Governments wishing to receive loans typically had to agree to follow deflationary policies and to maintain open access to international capital (mainly US corporations) – though the details of the terms differed from time to time and place to place.

The system which evolved was essentially a product of the competition between different groups of capitalists and their political representatives: between those with a national and those with an international perspective in the USA and between the US internationalists and capitalists elsewhere. The Americans had the clout and usually got their way. So it was not just a technical solution to the technical 'problem' of regulating the foreign exchanges. The protagonists were aiming together to expand or defend the arena for profit making; but separately each was competing for as big a share as possible.

The Bretton Woods rules were to survive for a quarter of a century and to provide that degree of certainty in international trade which was an essential background to the rapid bursts of accumulation achieved during the golden years. Central banks were charged with maintaining exchange rates essentially fixed (though they could vary within a very small range) by buying and selling their currencies on the markets, using their reserves of gold, dollars and, in a few cases, pounds. If reserves were being depleted over a long period it was open to countries to devalue by adjusting the exchange parity downwards in a discrete jump – but this possibility was to be used rarely. The stability was to be facilitated by access to IMF quota loans. The system survived the post-war economic disorders not because of the IMF but because the many restrictions on trade and capital movements were only gradually removed. Later it lived on into the period of open economies and rapid growth because, as we shall now see, countries were able gradually to increase their reserves and hence better to withstand the fluctuations in supply of and demand for their currencies.

(iii) *The US balance of payments deficit*

The success hinged on there being an adequate source of additional reserves to match the increased volumes of output and of international trade. Although gold output was expanding, so also was its use for industrial purposes, and in practice the increase in gold stocks provided only 17 per cent of the rise in international reserves in the 1950s and hardly any of the rise in the 1960s. The gap was filled by the one currency that was 'good as gold', namely US dollars. Central banks accumulated dollar assets which provided small interest returns but much more importantly certainty of value, for the price was fixed at $35 to the ounce of gold, and they were acceptable means of payment everywhere.

For eighteen years during the boom period, a massive cumulative deficit of some $32 billion was chalked up by the USA (see Table 16.2). This flowed into the rest of the world's coffers mainly in the form of dollars. Some of those dollars were converted into gold, which had to come out of the USA's own reserves; so these were substantially reduced.

The deficit was not just a fortuitous accident: it was related in a complex but definite way to the USA's hegemonic position in the world hierarchy of nations.

Looking at the details, it is clear how the bottom-line deficit occurred despite the fact that the current account was in surplus. To begin with there was a surplus of $68.9 billion on trade over the eighteen years: the US superiority in production always enabled exports to exceed imports. But the long-term capital balance was hugely in deficit. A specially large outflow was due to direct investment abroad – for example, as US multinationals spent their dollars to build factories in Europe. This was actually more than matched by an inflow of profits from past investments which appears in the current account balance as 'Net interest and dividends received'. A further large deficit item totalling altogether nearly $94 billion arose from the government's own transactions – both through making foreign loans (recorded in the capital account) and through its grants and military

Table 16.2   The US Balance of Payments, 1950s and 1960s ($ billion)

	1950–9	1960–7
Merchandise trade	29.3	39.6
Net military transactions	−23.1	−20.5
Services and remittances	−5.3	−8.5
Net interest and dividends received	25.5	36.5
US government grants (ex-military)	−20.5	−14.8
Current account balance	6.0	32.3
Direct investment (net)	−17.2	−27.9
Investment in shares and bonds (net)	−3.7	−6.4
Government loans	−4.1	−10.6
Long-term capital balance	−25.0	−44.9
Basic balance on current and long-term capital	−19.0	−12.6
Dollars held abroad by private sector	1.5	−2.8
Financed by:		
Dollars held abroad in reserves	13.0	8.1
Reduction in US reserves	4.5	6.7
(of which gold)	(5.1)	(7.4)

Source: Philip Armstrong, Andrew Glyn and John Harrison, *Capitalism since World War II*, London, Fontana, 1984

expenditures (see under the current account): the price of its imperialism.

To sum up, the inflow of dollars from the trade surplus and the re-patriation of profits was insufficient to match the dollar outflow from further foreign investments, government loans and grants and military spending. The difference was largely provided by printing new dollars and accepting a massive loss of gold reserves.

Corresponding to this flow of dollars was an opposite flow of goods, services and machines that effectively constituted international seignorage: the transfer of resources from the rest of the world to the USA (see Chapter 7). Foreign producers accepted dollars willingly because they represented certainty of value and could be traded everywhere. So in that sense they were not really being cheated. In effect, international seignorage was the fee exacted by the USA for providing stability to the other capitalist economies during the golden years.

Moreover, it is difficult to see how the situation could have been different if the boom was to be enabled to continue. The US deficit was a con-tradictory yet necessary aspect of its objectives in reshaping and regulating the world's capitalist economies: contradictory because it was eventually to prove the downfall of the Bretton Woods system (even during the years of success US commodities were higher priced, and so less competitive, than if the dollar had been devalued in response to the deficit; the long-run dangers of a persistent deficit were perceived by some at the time); necessary because very little could have been done that would not have radically worsened the path of the advanced capitalist economies. Despite occasional attempts to 'cure' it, and despite the very large flows of money each way across the exchanges, every year (except 1957) produced a deficit. If the government had seriously tried to eliminate it through devaluation it would have met with united opposition from European and Japanese capitalists for making their commodities less competitive with US commodities. To impose capital controls (restricting international movements) was to go against the philosophy of the open economy which the USA was hoping other nations would embrace. When things got bad in 1964 some controls were imposed, but the problem still would not go away. To deflate the economy in order to reduce imports would have meant raising unemployment, contrary to domestic requirements. To reduce military spending would also have meant raising unemployment and in addition implied abandoning the role of capitalism's military policeman. And, above all, to eliminate the outflow of dollars by any of the above means would have risked bringing the boom to a halt, as then many other countries would have been forced through loss of reserves into balance of payments problems.

5. THE ONSET OF CRISES

The four conditions underlying the post-war boom and enabling long and sometimes rapid periods of accumulation to take place, by their very nature could not last indefinitely.

The fundamental contradiction of the international monetary system was the increasingly shaky foundation on which it was built: the dollar. The political and economic stabilization of the capitalist world had decreed the US balance of payments deficit – but this very deficit eventually meant such a build-up of foreign-owned dollars that its price could not be sustained.

The most visible feature of this contradiction was the Vietnam War which, from 1966 onwards, began to pull dollars abroad as fast as the army could draft soldiers over to spend them. A second factor was that the trade surplus was being steadily whittled away as corporations in other countries grew much faster and were able to compete more effectively with US products. This in itself was partly due to the fact that high military spending had diverted resources away from civilian investment. By 1968 the trade account went into deficit for the first time since the Second World War.

Meanwhile the evident structural problems of the dollar led foreign central banks to convert more and more dollars into gold. This began to provoke periodic runs on the dollar, whereby speculators sold them in the expectation that the price would fall and that they could later buy them back at a lower rate. After a similar panic the British pound sterling had been devalued in 1967, and with it went a psychological buffer between the dollar and the rest of the world's currencies. In 1968 the US government ceased convertibility into gold and permitted the private gold price to float upwards. It still maintained the notion that it was prepared to buy back dollars from other central banks at the old price of $35 an ounce, but in practice it discouraged them – especially the West German Bundesbank – from attempting to sell.

What followed in the next four years resembled a Hollywood B movie in which the hero – or villain – staggers on, mortally wounded, through the absurdly protracted final death scene. The Bretton Woods system, which had been slowly poisoned by the US deficit, was now stabbed in the back. There were further speculative runs on the dollar in 1971 and on 15 August the US government formally renounced any further obligation to sell gold to defend it. After negotiations at the Smithsonian Institute in Washington the crippled fixed exchange rate system staggered on with a devalued dollar. But it could not survive the now more convulsive international economy and after fresh waves of speculation, in which simply unprecedented sums of 'hot' money flowed out of the USA, the dollar was allowed to float downwards and the Bretton Woods system was finally laid to rest on 19 March 1973.

The regime thereafter was a system of 'dirty floating'. Central banks recognize they have not got the reserves to impose fixed rates and withstand speculative runs of hot money across national boundaries, especially in view of the enormous size of the Eurodollar markets and the impossibility of supervising them. Hence instead they 'manage' the rates, intervening in order to prevent excessively sudden swings in them.

As a result, governments still need to keep up reserves. In 1970 the IMF began to issue Special Drawing Rights (SDRs) – sometimes called 'paper gold' – which increased the reserves of member countries. The SDRs were convertible into gold and other currencies. Yet far too few were issued to meet the demands for reserves and once again governments across the world have built up their stocks of dollar assets, even if they also now include other strong currencies, such as marks and yen, in their reserves. Thus the USA continued to extract international seignorage from the rest of the world. But the strict rules of fixed exchange rates that had prevailed in the boom were notably absent – as from 1973 onwards rates for most countries floated substantially both up and down. Some countries reduced uncertainty by maintaining nearly constant rates of exchange between themselves. The European 'snake' system and the European Monetary System, to which most EEC countries belong, are examples, based on the principle that even though their currencies remain fixed against each other, they can float jointly up and down against the dollar and other currencies.

The death of Bretton Woods did not mean the end also for the dollar, but it signalled an end to the certainties – the safe assumptions of the 'golden years'. Through the 1970s and 1980s the dollar showed such volatility as to confound experts' predictions time and again. In a real sense the decline of dollar stability reflected the decline of US hegemony over the world. But as we write (1986), the dollar still remains the foremost international reserve currency and US imperialism remains as pugnacious as ever.

If the collapse of the stable monetary system and the unsteadying of the visible hand of US hegemony were not on their own enough to break the virtuous circle of high profits and high accumulation, the gradual exhaustion of reserves of extra labour-power was perhaps a contradiction of even greater importance.

As the 1960s wore on and accumulation across the capitalist world proceeded at feverish pace with few interruptions, millions of potential extra workers were drawn into wage work. Meanwhile the latent reserve army of agricultural workers was also diminishing. By 1970 the proportion of agricultural workers in the advanced capitalist countries had dropped below 12 per cent and subsequently fell more slowly. The clearest indications of labour shortages were the official unemployment figures, which were reaching an all-time low in many countries while vacancies (unfilled jobs) were attaining new highs. The system had reached full employment, an achievement rarely if ever managed except in wartime; but the subsequent collapse only proved the fundamentally contradictory nature of the feat.

The lack of a substantial under-employed sector would not in itself necessarily have been disastrous, for the usual reserve army mechanism could still have worked. The problem was, however, that even though investment remained high in the late 1960s and early 1970s, productivity failed to increase any faster and indeed in the early 1970s its growth actually slowed a little. (After 1973 it was to drop substantially.) This may have been partly the result of full employment, which reduced discipline on the shop-floor, leading to lower intensity of work, and partly because the new machines did not embody such great leaps in technology (see below). Whatever the cause, the effect was that the reserve army mechanism was being impaired.

So labour markets grew yet tighter and real wage growth accelerated in many countries in the late 1960s and early 1970s. This had been exacerbated, to the surprise of capitalist employers and many working-class leaders, by a rise in militant worker resistance that spread across several countries in

Europe. Most notably a brief alliance was struck between students and rank-and-file workers in the 'May events' in France in 1968. A general strike took place and it was some weeks before the ruling classes re-established their control of events. And in Italy's 'Hot Autumn' of 1969 an unprecedented wave of strikes swept across industry leading to massive wage rises well in excess of productivity growth.

Just as the uneven development of capitalist economies across the world gradually undermined US domination of international economic relations, the relatively slow development of the USA also meant that the technological basis for self-perpetuating boom was being steadily undermined. As European and Japanese production methods were catching up with US methods the time was approaching when further advances would have to rely on R & D expenditures and scientific progress to push forward the frontiers of production knowledge. The latter process is much slower than adopting and improving existing technology, which Japanese capitalists had so ably succeeded in doing.

It is difficult to assess precisely how important was this process of 'catching up' and the possible closing of the technology gap in bringing the boom to an end. By looking at some detailed comparative case studies of the techniques used by capitalists before and after the boom, we can attempt to build up a picture. In the 1950s US factories were in all known cases far more advanced than their counterparts elsewhere; by 1970, they remained more advanced in many cases, but in a few industries the Europeans or Japanese were employing the newest techniques.

Another way of measuring the process is to recall that the quality of the technology used is an important factor in determining productivity. So we can use the productivity gap between the USA and elsewhere as a rough proxy for the technology gap. This gives a similar picture to that of the detailed case studies. The average productivity (GDP per man-hour) of France, West Germany, Italy, Japan and the UK combined was about 36 per cent of that of the USA in 1950, 65 per cent in 1973 and 72 per cent in 1979. These figures suggest, even if very crudely, that other countries were indeed catching up with best-practice US technology, but that a considerable difference still remained at the end of the boom period.

Finally, a further contributory problem arising from rapid accumulation in the golden years was that there gradually developed an imbalance between the growth of the primary product sectors and the expansion of the rest of the economy. The terms of trade, after 1970, began to turn massively in favour of the underdeveloped countries. Two particular factors underlaid the rise in price of raw materials in the early 1970s: the collapse of the 1972 grain harvest, and the dramatic rise of OPEC oil power which we shall review in the next chapter.

6. EXPLANATIONS OF THE END OF THE BOOM

Capital accumulation is always prone to possible imbalances and disruptions. During the golden years the possibilities were largely buried. The high growth/high investment virtuous circle proceeded, against the background of the enabling material and institutional conditions. But these were themselves undermined by the very success of the boom over two decades. Capital accumulation was thereby confronted by barriers of its own making. It meant a return to an era of periodically crisis-torn economies. All this may be summed up in the statement that there was an 'over-accumulation' of capital.

(i) *The rate of profit*

Since profit making is the fundamental aim of capital accumulation, estimates of the rate of profit give a basic indication of the health of capitalism: they act as its thermometer.

The rate of profit broadly measures the ratio of profits gained to the value of capital laid out. Table 16.3 shows some figures for the average

Table 16.3   The Decline in Profitability

| | Manufacturing net profit rate | | | Business net profit rate | | |
	USA	Europe	Japan	USA	Europe	Japan
Peak year*	34.9†	19.9‡	46.5§	22.3†	16.3‡	32.0§
1973	22.5	12.1	33.5	14.8	11.3	19.6
1975	16.7	7.9	10.4	12.3	7.3	13.5
1981	10.3	5.2	13.3	11.8	7.6	14.2

* Year before the sustained decline in profit rate
† 1966
‡ 1960
§ 1970
Source: Philip Armstrong, Andrew Glyn and John Harrison, *Capitalism since World War II*, London, Fontana, 1984

profit rate in the main capitalist blocs over the years. But some cautionary words are necessary because there are many technical issues involved in correctly measuring both the amount of profits and the value of capital. For example, it is difficult to assess a firm's real profits in times of inflation, because the money values of its assets and debts are changing every year. These changes should be included in the measurement of profits, but there remain differences of opinion amongst accountants as to how this is best done. A further problem is that, in order to measure the value of the stock of a firm's fixed capital (existing machinery and so on), one has to make tentative assumptions about how much the machines bought in the past are worth at present, how fast they deteriorate in usefulness, and so on. Finally, lumping together and averaging across all capitalists in each bloc conceals large differences between the performance of individuals.

But the main message of the table would not be substantially altered even if the underlying statistical assumptions were changed in generally acceptable ways. Some time in the decade from 1960 to 1970 the profit rate began to fall, so that even though in 1973 most economies were at the crest of a wave the profits by then were on average already considerably down. In 1975 the devastating effects of the crash of 1974 are shown; and although some recovery was obtained in the late 1970s, the renewed crash of 1979 left capitalists still reeling in 1981. The fact that these are averages indicate that the falls were widespread, but in some places they were even more dramatic: in the UK, for example, the profit rate fell to 3.9 per cent in 1975, and then even to 1.7 per cent in 1981 as a result of the Thatcherite recession.

(ii) *Over-accumulation with respect to labour-power*

One major fundamental explanation of the long-term falling profit rate is based on the second contradiction which we discussed in the previous section: the depletion, by the end of the boom, of the reserve army of labour. Among those who have developed this approach are the British Marxists, Philip Armstrong, Andrew Glyn and John Harrison.

This explanation gives emphasis primarily to the profit share (the ratio of profits to the value of output); but there is a straightforward connection between this and the profit rate. It may be summed up in a simple equation:

$$\text{`Profit rate'} = \frac{\text{Amount of profits}}{\text{Value of capital stock}}$$

$$= \frac{\text{Amount of profits}}{\text{Value of output}} \times \frac{\text{Value of output}}{\text{Value of capital stock}}$$

That is:

$$\text{`Profit rate'} = \text{`Profits share'} \times \text{`Output-to-Capital ratio'}$$

A close examination of the figures has shown that both these 'components' of the profit rate have tended to fall. The 'full-employment profits-squeeze' explanation, which concentrates on the 'profits share' component, derives from the connection between the profits share and labour productivity: the higher that productivity is, in relation to the average wage rate, the higher is the profit share. This may be encapsulated in an equation:

$$\text{'Profit share'} = 1 - \frac{\text{'Wage rate'}}{\text{'Productivity'}}$$

(This relationship is further explained in Technical Annexe 16.A.)

The theory suggests that the depletion of reserves of available labour-power was manifested in a profits squeeze: the profit share, and hence the profit rate, fell. In short, capital accumulation was no longer able to liberate enough new workers through productivity increases, through scrapping old machines and mechanizing previously labour-intensive processes. Meanwhile other sources of extra labour-power were drying up. The full employment which the boom had created became, like Frankenstein's monster, its undoing.

There was over-accumulation, in that the forces of competition had driven the system to expand so fast that it came up against a classic contradiction. Ultimately labour-power is a commodity not itself produced by capitalists and although massive social transformations can in some circumstances bring greater proportions of the population into the pool of potential wage workers, the rate of expansion cannot ultimately and always match the voracious demands for more labour-power that a successful period of capitalism brings. Thus at some stage the wage rate begins to accelerate upwards and productivity increases cannot match it. So the share of profits falls.

Such an interpretation does not by any means ignore other factors. For example, the destabilization of the international monetary system must have contributed to a lack of investors' confidence, to the failure of effective demand to rise fast enough in the 1970s and hence to some under-utilization of capacity. If machinery lies idle for a time, the output-to-capital ratio falls. Additionally, it may fall because workers, strengthened by full employment, have gained a shorter working week, so that machines are being used less intensively. These and other factors will eventually have to be accounted for in a full assessment of all the proximate reasons behind the falling profit rate. In the 'full-employment profits-squeeze' framework, however, they are treated as of secondary importance behind the prime contradiction, which is the over-accumulation of capital with respect to the supply of labour-power, as manifested in a falling profit share.

(iii) *Other explanations*

One possible alternative approach is to put no primary importance on any one 'cause' of the boom's ending, but to argue that each of the four contradictions played a contributing role in creating barriers to accumulation.

Thus, the collapse of total US hegemony and the deteriorating regulation of international economic relations, the closing of the technology gap, and the shortages of raw materials as well as the depletion of the reserve army of labour, are assigned equal importance. They may be manifested either as a falling profit share or as a rising output-to-capital ratio or both – but in effect the relevant result is a falling profit rate. Such an eclectic approach may yet survive when economic historians have further examined the recent era.

We have mentioned, in Chapter 13, another influential account of the golden years in terms of the theory of 'monopoly capital'. There are yet other explanations of the end of the boom which we do not find helpful. For example, the approach of most orthodox economists is to treat the fall in the rate of profit as due to specific and accidental ('exogenous') forces that rocked the capitalist boat, placing it in a temporary disequilibrium. All crises are attributed in this view to shocks, as we discussed in the last chapter. Our whole approach in this chapter has taken the opposite view: we have emphasized how the very success of the boom helped to undermine the material and institutional conditions on which it was based. The disequilibriating forces were aboard the boat and not confined to the waves.

The reasons for the ending of the boom years remain a controversial subject. Other approaches to crisis have asserted in different abstract ways the necessity of crises occurring as a result of falling profit rates. But they have not yet elaborated the connections with real historical events. The mere fact of the profit rate falling is common to a number of accounts of capitalist crises, just as a high reading on a thermometer indicates a fever but not which type of disease. It cannot, therefore, be used to 'prove' that one or other theory is correct. Moreover, even though one explanation is accepted as the best available for the recent period, it does not follow that it applies also to previous periods of capitalism. For example, the origins of the 1930s Great Depression are not easily described in the same framework of depletion of labour-power, tight labour markets and so on that we have put forward to account for the end of the post-war boom.

Whatever the cause, however, it is certain that by the middle of the 1970s the profit system had developed a malaise, the most visible symptoms of which were the varying forms of persistent and recurring crises which altered the lives of both workers and capitalists. A massive but slow restructuring of the world's capitalist economies began as new technologies were introduced, labour processes intensified, factories closed down and relocated, and welfare state ideologies brought into question. The two uppermost features of the crisis and the restructuring were the rise of inflation and of mass unemployment, but the disease broke out in other ways too, including fiscal and financial crises; all are symptoms of a seemingly almost universal malaise, which we shall discuss in the next chapter.

Technical Annexe 16.A   Wages, Productivity and the Profit Rate

The relationship between productivity slowdown, wages rates and the profit share, used in the 'full-employment profits-squeeze' theory discussed in the text, may be demonstrated in simple algebra as follows.

Let π be total profits, W total wages, w the wage rate, Y total income and L total employment, Productivity is therefore represented by $\dfrac{Y}{L}$ If we assume (for simplicity) that all output is shared between wages and profits, profits must be given by

$$\pi = Y - W$$

So the profit share is

$$\frac{\pi}{Y} = 1 - \frac{W}{Y}$$

Next we may write that

$$W = w \cdot L$$

The wage bill is the wage rate times total employment

From these it follows, simply, that

$$\frac{\pi}{Y} = 1 - \frac{w \cdot L}{Y}$$

$$= 1 - \frac{w}{\dfrac{Y}{L}}$$

or that

$$\text{The profits share} = 1 - \frac{\text{The wage rate}}{\text{Productivity}}$$

CHAPTER 17

Symptoms of Malaise

The story told in the last chapter was one, for the capitalist system, of Paradise Lost. Its tale of lower profits and slower growth of production and productivity demonstrated that after the early 1970s the basic accumulation processes were functioning more precariously than before and were being frequently interrupted. For this reason it seems reasonable to say that this period of capitalism was one of economic crisis conditions, though there have been many other ways of describing it (from 'slowth' to 'stagflation').

The scourge of crisis in capitalism has not, as many euphorically believed in the 1960s, been eradicated by the Keynesian vaccine. A new strain of it has returned. Whether or not it will prove more virulent than earlier ones has yet to be shown. This chapter does not attempt any systematic narrative of the course of this new infection but rather examines four of its most-discussed symptoms: inflation, unemployment, the role of oil and the fiscal crisis of the state.

I. INFLATION

(i) The present inflation

The generalized rise in prices, or in other words the fall in the purchasing power of money, has been a recurrent phenomenon of monetary economies. There have been slow inflations and fast ones; long ones and short ones; and neglected ones – but none quite like the inflation which broke out in the early 1970s.

The new inflation was much less spectacular than the hyperinflations which followed both the First and Second World Wars: in 1922–3 prices in Germany rose by 10 billion times in little more than a year; and in 1945–6 in Hungary they rose by 4,000 trillion, trillion times. Such inflations can only be cured by root and branch replacement of the existing monetary system. Nor is the new inflation yet as long-lasting as the one which began in Europe in about 1530, with the inflow of silver and gold from the New

World, and which lasted 110 years, during which it raised prices fivefold. Much remarked upon at the time and much discussed by economic historians, in today's capitalist world it would seem like no inflation at all. At the rates which existed in the advanced capitalist countries in the mid 1970s, prices increased fivefold in a mere seventeen years.

Table 17.1   Inflation in the Main Capitalist Countries, 1960–83

	Annual average percentage increase in consumer prices			
	1960–8	1968–73	1973–9	1979–83
USA	2.0	5.0	8.5	8.2
Japan	5.7	7.0	10.0	4.3
West Germany	2.7	4.6	4.7	5.1
France	3.6	6.1	10.7	12.1
UK	3.6	7.5	15.6	10.7
Italy	4.0	5.8	16.1	17.5
Canada	2.4	4.6	9.2	9.8
All OECD countries	2.9	5.6	10.0	9.1

Source: OECD Economic Outlook, *Historical Statistics, 1960–1983*, OECD, Paris, 1985

Aside from the always relatively short-lived hyperinflations, the post-1973 inflation has been the fastest substantial period of international inflation in the history of capitalism. The figures in Table 17.1 and Diagram 17.1, which give price rises for a number of major capitalist countries and for the OECD countries as a whole, show a relatively slow inflation during the boom, which doubled in the years of transition from boom to crisis, and then doubled again during the early years of the crisis before falling back considerably by the mid 1980s.

(ii) *Common theories of inflation*

Any sustained inflation must be accompanied by an expansion in the quantity of money. Exchanges in a monetary economy naturally involve the circulation of money, so any rise in the total money value of exchanges must involve an increase in the amount of money circulating. The latter may be expressed as the total stock or supply of money, M, multiplied by the velocity at which it circulates, V. The logic is then expressed by the famous equation:

$$MV = PT$$

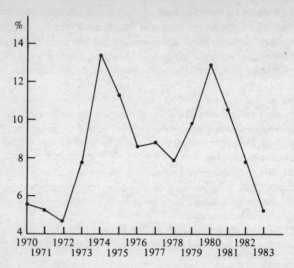

Diagram 17.1   Inflation (rate of increases in consumer prices): Average for All OECD Countries, 1970–83

Source: OECD, *Economic Outlook, Historical Statistics, 1960–1983*, OECD, Paris, 1985.

where *T* stands for the total quantity of commodities exchanged (transacted) while *P* is the price level.

As it stands, the equation is no more than an identity – something that is necessarily true if commodities are exchanged with money. It means no more than 'total sales must be equal to total purchases'.

Yet, with the help of additional assumptions, this obvious-seeming idea can become an analysis of inflation. The assumptions are that the velocity of money (*V*) and total transactions (*T*) vary very little or not at all. That means that only *P* and *M* are variable so that a rise in *P* must be accompanied by an equivalent rise in *M*. Hence any sustained inflation is certain to be associated with sustained rises in the money supply.

In practice these assumptions are seldom exactly fulfilled. But from this quantity theory can be derived an important if limited lesson: that inflation is (by definition) a monetary phenomenon and it cannot be investigated without some reference to the money supply. In the long run inflation and monetary expansion inevitably accompany each other. This proves neither that a rise in the money supply *causes* inflation nor that inflation *causes* a rise in the supply of money, simply that they are closely related. That relationship may not be a simple causal one at all: they may be connected by a long chain of causes which includes many other phenomena.

Many economists, however, have unfortunately become mesmerized by the connection between the two variables and assert that a rise in money supply causes inflation. For them it follows, as the night the day, that to stifle inflation governments have only to control, fix or reduce the money supply. Inflation therefore is simply the result of mistakes in monetary policy.

According to these mechanical monetarists the mechanism of the relationship is that an increase in the money supply causes an increase in demand for goods and services and it is this which raises prices. They fall, therefore, into a category of frequently proffered explanations of inflation which have been grouped under the heading of *demand-pull theories*. Most of the theories in this category attach less weight to the money supply as a causal factor. Following Keynes, they point to all the many influences on the level of aggregate demand – fiscal policy, the determinants of consumption and investment spending and so on – which can cause increases in demand. The Keynesian versions of demand-pull theories all associate inflation with an excess of aggregate demand in a situation of full employment of resources.

A rival camp of inflation explanations has been called *cost-push theories*. They attribute inflation to the presence of monopolistic practices either by firms or by workers in trade unions. Particular favourite sources of inflation for this school are the militant behaviour of greedy workers and the 'exogenous' oil price increases of 1974. According to them, some outside factor (such as the politics of OPEC) starts off the inflation. Firms put up their prices to recoup their costs, and workers claim more wages to compensate for their lost real earnings. The result is a wage-price spiral. This school usually claims that the money supply is irrelevant as a *cause* of inflation: it will always rise passively accordingly as more money is demanded. Thus even this school expects a connection between the expansion rate of the money supply and inflation: the latter causes the former.

These widely held theories of inflation have some deficiencies in common. They all tend to trivialize the question of inflation by seeing it as a problematic phenomenon in its own right, which can be sufficiently isolated from all the other phenomena of capitalism to be allotted its own unambiguous cause or causes. They ignore the possibility that it is, at least in part, a manifestation of other, more fundamental problems. They do not probe deeply enough.

The theories also oversimplify by looking for causes in one direction only whereas in reality economic phenomena can at the same time mutually relate as cause and effect. And they tend to insist that there is only one cause, or at the most a very few, rather than allowing that the causes could be multiple.

Finally, they tend to asume that inflation is an unambiguous evil which everyone in society wants to avoid. This results from a general failure to analyse capitalist societies in terms of different classes with sometimes divergent interests. They fail in general to appreciate that there may be circumstances in which certain groups in the society – in particular, capitalists and the state – might find inflation beneficial to their interests and as a result deliberately try to bring it about.

We cannot say that all common theories of inflation possess these deficiencies equally. Nor do we deny that some of them can provide useful partial insights – for example, the observed relationship between money supply and the price level, and the wage-price spiral. But none of them have been able to provide a convincing theory to account for the special peculiarities of the crisis-related inflation of the years following the early 1970s. All of them are led into supporting, implicitly at least, the category of accidental or external theories of crisis, which was outlined in Chapter 15. Excess demand explanations lead to accusations of mistaken government policies; cost-push views tend to blame greedy workers or oil sheikhs.

To get deeper than that we need a theory of inflation which takes into account the primacy of the profit motive, the conflict of interest between capitalist and worker, and the role of the state as ultimate guardian of the interests of capitalism.

(iii) *The modern dynamic of inflation and unemployment*

The historically unusual combination of prolonged high inflation and mass unemployment can be jointly understood as a consequence of two major features of modern capitalism: the ending of the high profit rates of the long boom and the vastly increased economic role played by capitalist states.

When threatened with declining profits capitalists will spontaneously seek to protect themselves by raising their prices. But this will not work if they are constrained by the level of demand. They can only raise prices and still sell the products if the state collaborates by raising effective demand, mainly by increasing the money supply. During the boom years this was precisely the policy of most western governments. It was part of the Keynesian programme to keep unemployment low – it helped to legitimate capitalist relations and the state itself. At the same time it ensured the best possible conditions for the realization of potential profits.

So if, at one time, unemployment was relatively high and profits were sluggish, governments could expand aggregate demand. Even if that had little effect on the amount of goods produced, capitalists could still defend or increase their profits through raising prices. The inflation eroded the real wage gains of workers, keeping up the capitalists' share of national output at the expense of the other main class, the workers.

So the key to the success of the policy of permitting slow inflation was that workers should not be able fully to protect themselves against it. This effectively meant that they should not be able to anticipate it in their wage bargaining.

In the successful years it was possible for inflation to fluctuate by a few per cent a year, going high in years when unemployment was low, and vice versa. When unemployment was high, both workers and capitalists would be less aggressive in their claims and so inflation would be low: workers would have to settle for lower wage claims, capitalists would be unable to raise prices much, due to insufficient demand. Governments could turn the inflation tap on and off as thought necessary. But for several reasons it was a policy that could not last indefinitely.

As the boom continued into the 1960s high employment levels seemed increasingly secure and trade unions grew. With the depletion of the reserve army of labour, and the increasing militancy of many groups of workers, more aggressive wage claims threatened the terms of the trade-off between inflation and unemployment: for any given level of unemployment, the greater militancy led to higher wage claims and higher inflation.

A second factor was the rising share of national income being taken by the state. Whether taxes were taken from corporations or from workers, capitalists had to be more aggressive in their conflicts in order to maintain their after-tax incomes.

A third factor relevant in some countries was the rising share taken by foreign capitalists, via an increasing import bill – for example, if imported raw material prices rise, out of any fixed total output, the amount left to be shared out among workers and capitalists is diminished: thus also intensifying their conflict.

These factors simply intensified the capital-labour conflict, but another factor fundamentally wrecked the whole mechanism: as inflation was pushed too high, workers began to *anticipate* higher inflation levels in their bargaining. In some countries workers even gained systems of automatic compensation (sliding-scale escalators). As the working class improved its protection against existing levels of inflation, the profit protection mechanism required even higher rates of price increase. One way of viewing this startling difference between boom and crisis is via the fate of a well-known statistical relationship, known as 'the Phillips curve'. The economist A. W. Phillips had observed that there was a long-term, relatively stable statistical relationship between the level of unemployment and the rate of inflation. It was concluded from this widely accepted analysis that governments faced a trade-off, a choice, between these two evils. The Phillips curve predicted (as

Keynes had) that low unemployment would coincide with high inflation and high unemployment with low inflation. This, however, is exactly the opposite of what was observed in the period after 1970. The increasing ability of workers to anticipate inflation had rendered the Phillips curve 'unstable' – that is, its predictions were wrong.

A more technical version of our explanation of the present inflation, couched in terms of the reasons for the breakdown of the Phillips curve, is presented in Technical Annexe 17.A. A real empirical picture of the breakdown is given in Diagram 17.2. It shows how the earlier trade-off between the two 'evils' of inflation and unemployment was replaced by a spiral of one chasing the other in apparent chaos.

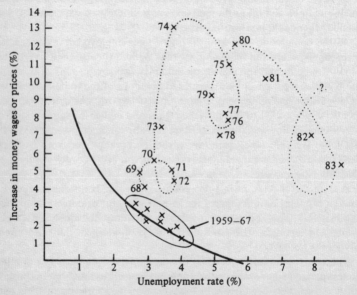

Diagram 17.2   The Breakdown of the Phillips Curve and Spiralling Inflation

The continuous line shows the stable trade-off between wage inflation and unemployment (the Phillips curve); it is based on British data from 1861 to 1957. The points show the change in consumer prices and rates of unemployment for the seven major capitalist countries from 1959 to 1983.

Source: Chris Edwards, *The Fragmented World: competing perspectives on trade, money and crises*, London and New York, Methuen, 1985, p. 146.

The factor underlying the chaos was the ability of all parties to anticipate inflation and fight to protect themselves against declining incomes. But the precise course of the inflation narrative in the 1970s varied from country to country, and the first, second and third factors may have been more important in some places than in others.

What is certain is that most countries were launched into the unstable wage-price spiral during the first half of the 1970s, helped partly by the oil price shock; and that when most states tried to jump off the spiral, at the end of the decade, by rejecting their Keynesian aims, the numbers of unemployed people escalated at an extraordinary rate.

Whatever mechanisms were most important, the 1970s inflationary spiral is just one reflection of the end of the boom and the increase of state intervention is one form taken by the return to crisis conditions. Testimony to this is the fact that inflation became a general feature of modern capitalism (with hardly any exceptions), reflecting its transformation into an internationally integrated system. The end of the long boom affected all countries; and the increased interventionist role of governments can also be seen everywhere. It is unsurprising therefore that the disease of unstable inflation soon became an epidemic.

There was, however, more to the international inflation. As we saw in the last chapter, the dominance of the USA over the world economy meant that it has been able to have a chronic balance of payments deficit, thus spreading dollars throughout the world's economies. This accumulation of dollar reserves was the basis on which other governments increased the money supply and supported inflation in their countries. The US deficits were 'oiling the wheels' of the world's economies.

(iv) *Ideology about inflation*

Inflation has come to be perceived as almost the most important problem facing the capitalist world, sometimes rivalling mass unemployment. Yet it becomes a problem only when it fails, as it eventually did, to sustain profitability. The real crisis is the underlying lack of profits rather than the inflation itself. Increasingly uncontrollable inflation can make matters worse by disrupting trade – for traders become less sure of the value of their financial assets. But such an effect would be secondary to the fundamental problem.

However, unlike unemployment, inflation also has a direct impact on everybody in the economy – it is indeed the device through which real wages and living standards are often reduced. That is why many people come to see inflation as the 'cause' of the drop in or stagnation of their living standards – since they understandably mistake the immediate factor for the fundamental cause. The fact that most people perceive it as the 'number one' problem paves the way for governments' proclaimed anti-inflation policies. The real object of many government policies in the late 1970s was to create unemployment in order to weaken the working classes: but their purpose was usually stated in the more neutral guise of policies to reduce inflation. Anti-inflation policies, therefore, are really anti-working-class policies. There is no clearer instance of money veiling the ugly face of economic reality.

2. UNEMPLOYMENT

(i) *Whose problem?*

During the years since 1973 workers across the capitalist world have lost their jobs at the rate of one every few minutes. That is their bitter experience of crisis and stagnation.

The dire effects of unemployment on personal health and social life have been mentioned in Chapter 8. Here we are concerned with its role in the capitalist system. From the point of view of workers, even those in developed countries, the immediate tangible impact of unemployment is a cut in income and hence in their standard of living.

It is also likely that a worker who finds another job after a spell of unemployment will have to accept lower pay than before. As unemployed people are concentrated among those groups in society who in any case receive relatively low pay – women, minorities and unskilled manual workers – it is not surprising that most unemployed people suffer, at least for a while, from real poverty.

Unemployment, therefore, is an overwhelming and unambiguous problem for those who have to live through and adjust to it. But that does not mean that it is necessarily also a problem for the profit system, whose objective is not the meeting of human needs.

There are, however, two main ways, one political, the other economic, in which unemployment can contribute to instability. Politically, mass unemployment can contribute to general disaffection and undermine capitalism's legitimacy. It is hard for the rulers of a system which extols enterprise and diligence to explain enforced idleness. This is why capitalist politicans so often feel obliged to blame the unemployed for their own plight. Whether the resistance to unemployment will lead to major political upheaval depends on the specific balance of class forces at a particular time in each country. It is more often advantageous to the capitalist class because it can lessen the solidarity of working people by dividing them into two groups: the employed and the unemployed.

Economically, unemployment can help to generate instability in so far as it puts pressure on government finances. Each unemployed person costs the government a certain amount in foregone tax revenues as well as in the benefits it pays out. Mass unemployment can today be very expensive for governments: in 1980 in western Europe this cost was already as much as one-tenth of government current expenditures in the countries with the highest unemployment rates. That figure rose during the 1980s.

Unemployment reduces aggregate demand and so makes the realization of profit harder for some capitalists. But unemployment is not *in itself* an economic problem for capitalists as a whole. In fact the replenishment of the reserve army of labour has an important role to play in enforcing the discipline and control of labour-power.

The complete absence of unemployment is a greater problem because it dulls the economic incentive for work and discipline and enhances labour's bargaining power. Full employment is thus a contradictory objective for capitalist nation states. The real problem for corporations in the crisis is the reduction of opportunities for profitable investment. Rising unemployment is a reflection of this, not the problem itself. At times pro-capitalist governments have even deliberately created unemployment.

(ii) *Unemployment statistics*

International data

The extent of the rise in unemployment is shown in Table 17.2. The first column shows the unemployment rates typical of the long boom period. There was some variation across countries, with North America being on

Table 17.2 Unemployment Rates in the Main Capitalist Countries, 1960–83

	Annual averages (percentage of labour force)			
	1960–7	1968–73	1974–9	1980–3
USA	5.0	4.6	6.7	8.4
Japan	1.3	1.2	1.9	2.3
West Germany	0.8	0.8	3.5	5.7
France	1.3	–	4.6	7.6
UK	1.5	2.4	4.2	9.0
Italy	4.9	5.7	6.5	8.6
Canada	4.8	5.4	7.2	9.4
All OECD countries	3.1	5.4	5.2	7.6

The data have been adjusted to ensure comparability (see p. 317).

Source: OECD Economic Outlook, *Historical Statistics, 1960–1983*, OECD, Paris, 1985

the high side. The remaining columns show that unemployment rose in *all* the main capitalist countries over the decade of the 1970s and beyond. There were no exceptions.

During the long boom, unemployment in each country moved up and down cyclically, from month to month and year to year. After the boom ended these cyclical movements were combined with a strongly rising trend. Diagram 17.3 shows the unemployment rate for all OECD countries combined: on the whole the unemployment rate did not recover from the 1974–5 crisis before it began to swing upwards again with the renewed slump in 1979.

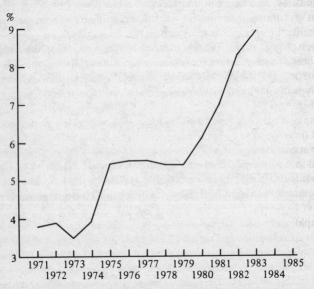

Diagram 17.3   Unemployment Rate: Average for All OECD Countries, 1971–83

Source: OECD, *Economic Outlook, Historical Statistics, 1960–1983*, OECD, Paris, 1985

Measurement difficulties

The unemployment rate is defined as the number of unemployed workers divided by the size of the labour force, but exactly what is meant by the 'labour force'? The numbers of unemployed people depend crucially on the definition of what is meant by being *in* the labour force yet *out* of employment. As a result, the data on unemployment rates mean much less than they seem to at first sight; and they are easily subject to manipulation for political purposes.

At different times the numbers of unemployed have been counted as the numbers of trade union members without jobs, or the numbers of workers applying for jobs at employment exchanges, or the numbers found to be unemployed from censuses, or from sample surveys of the population. Of these four the last is the most comprehensive way of counting and has been used in the USA for many years. The data in Table 17.2 from other countries which used different methods have been adjusted to make them comparable with the USA.

According to the survey method, a person of working age is in the labour force and unemployed if he or she is actively looking for a job and is unable to find one. Such a definition includes many who would not otherwise count as unemployed under, say, the UK method where only those registered for unemployment benefit are officially 'unemployed'.

Even the survey method is not necessarily accurate. It may overstate the numbers of those who are involuntarily unemployed; in any economy some people may choose not to work and live off unemployment benefit or family support, though most evidence shows these are relatively few in number. Conversely, it may considerably understate the real level of unemployment. To begin with, many workers working part time or on short time due to recession would prefer to work full time if they could. Yet these are counted as employed. In addition many millions throughout the world are discouraged from seeking paid work simply through the knowledge that they have no hope of getting it. This is normally more important for women workers, but it applies to all groups, particularly at a time of recession. Thus when official unemployment rises, real but hidden unemployment rises further since many people withdraw from the official labour force and do not therefore count as officially unemployed. This is sometimes referred to by economists as the 'discouraged worker effect'. Another means of 'reduction' is the encouragement, by firms or by governments, of early retirement of workers who would otherwise be quite happy to continue working. As statistics of the labour force they no longer exist. Redundant 'guest workers' also disappear from the unemployment statistics if they are obliged to leave the country (though they may reappear in the data for other countries), like the *gastarbeiter* from poorer Mediterranean areas (such as southern Italy, Turkey, Algeria), who came in their millions to fill jobs in western Europe in the long boom period. Finally, in the mid 1980s younger workers were increasingly being placed in education or training schemes if they could not get work. Though the training they received was often fictional, they were none the less removed from the count of officially unemployed.

These various forms of statistical vaporization of workers are not always easy to quantify. One estimate by the British Trades Union Congress found that in 1982 true unemployment was about 5.5 percentage points above the official rate. Whether or not this figure is accepted there can be no doubt that the extent of undercounting is considerable. Unsurprisingly, little effort is devoted by governments to calculating precise estimates of true unemployment since their publication would be a political embarrassment.

These statistical deficiencies mean that the precise number of people counted as officially unemployed in any country is not a particularly significant statistic. Those who are not employed for money are not necessarily idle; they include those doing housework and other productive activity in the home, those at college, those following a hobby, and so on. For some, these activities may be in the wider sense just as valuable as doing paid work. We should not put too much store, therefore, on the welfare implications of the precise numbers who are officially unemployed.

The statistics are more use, however, as an indicator of the macroeconomic stability of the economy. Provided they are gathered from year to year on a consistent basis, they will reflect the fortunes of capital accumulation. Even then, the importance of the discouraged worker effect will change over the years and this must be borne in mind.

(iii) *The mechanisms that create unemployment*

In any one month there will be many workers who leave their jobs, either voluntarily or involuntarily, to join the reserve army of labour, the unemployed. Others, like many school-leavers, may find themselves automatically recruited into the reserve army as they enter the labour force. At the same time, others are leaving the reserve army, either to take up jobs or to exit from the labour force.

Of those that return to jobs, some will have been unemployed for only a short time, a few weeks at most, while they have been looking for employment. There will always be a certain number of 'frictionally unemployed people between jobs' even in a full employment economy. They are a necessary adjunct of normal labour mobility. When unemployment is low these form a substantial part of the total. But when mass unemployment arrives, frictional unemployment becomes fairly insignificant. At the same time the really long-term unemployed become an increasing proportion of the total. Such a process is illustrated in Table 17.3, for five major western countries hit by the 1979 recession.

The overall level of unemployment increases when the numbers entering the reserve army exceed those leaving it. Apart from frictional unemployment there were two main sources of the mass unemployment of the 1970s and 1980s.

Table 17.3 Long-Term Unemployment* as a Percentage of Total Unemployment

	1979	1983
USA	4.7	15.8
West Germany	16.6	29.6
France	31.7	42.7
UK	27.0	39.5
Canada	4.4	11.0

* 12 months or more

Source: OECD, *Economic Outlook*, June 1985

The most important is called the 'deficiency of aggregate demand'. In most countries the populations of working age have been growing; and the labour forces (however defined) have grown even faster. To maintain full employment, aggregate demand for goods and services has to grow at least as fast as the labour force, and faster when labour productivity is also rising. A simple rule of thumb about this has been dubbed 'Okun's Law' after the Keynesian economist, Arthur Okun. Referring to the USA, it says that the unemployment rate will remain unchanged if aggregate demand grows by about 3 per cent in a year. If demand grows slower/faster than this, the unemployment rate will rise/fall a certain amount each year. Similar rules of thumb can apply to other capitalist countries although the numbers tend to be different. Taking the advanced capitalist world as a whole, between 1971 and 1983 demand grew at an average annual rate of 2.8 per cent. This was not enough to prevent an upward trend in the unemployment rate of just under 0.5 per cent a year on average.

The slow demand growth reflects the general slowdown in capital accumulation at the end of the long boom. The level of investment expenditures did not grow as fast as previously, and in some cases it fell. The leaps in unemployment in 1975 and from 1980 onwards reflect the precipitate drops in investment demand throughout the world in the recessions of 1974 and 1979. As we shall see (p. 327–9), the rises in the price of oil had a partial role in cutting demand.

In addition to this, the policies of governments were turned, from the mid 1970s onwards, in the direction of fighting inflation – or, what is the same thing, deliberately fostering unemployment by limiting the growth of aggregate demand. As we saw in the previous section, the main reason for this was that the earlier inflationary policy was no longer working to maintain profits. To some extent the different pace at which unemployment rose in each country reflected the differing policy stances of various governments. Those countries with a particularly strong unemployment-creation policy produced relatively greater rises – an example is the Conservative government in Britain after 1979.

The second main source of unemployment is usually referred to as 'structural'. As capital accumulates, and especially at times when it is restructuring in the wake of a crisis, required skills change as new methods of production are introduced. Often, the new methods require fewer skills from most of the workforce and highly specialized skills from a small minority (see Chapter 3). Workers with unwanted skills can find themselves unemployed even though there are vacancies for workers with new or different skills; there is thus a mismatch of jobs and workers. A second part of structural unemployment consists of a geographical mismatch: jobs are available but not in the area where the unemployed people live. Often for workers to move to the jobs can be prohibitively expensive.

Some orthodox economists have developed a concept known as 'the natural rate of unemployment' which is roughly, though not exactly, equivalent to what we have called 'frictional' and 'structural' unemployment. They argue that for governments to try to reduce unemployment below this natural rate would be to cause accelerated inflation. By arguing that the 'natural' rate has been rising, they sometimes use the concept to make higher levels of unemployment seem more politically acceptable. The choice of vocabulary is an interesting example of the way that economics often disguises the fact that capitalist economies are based on human social relations by describing them as if they were relations of nature. It must be small comfort to, say, unemployed steel workers to discover that their unemployment is 'natural'.

There is in fact very little good evidence about how much unemployment can be accounted for by these structural factors. They may have become more important over the years, especially with the decline of old industrial areas, and so probably account for some of the long-term rise in the unemployment statistics. They would however, be slow long-term changes and cannot explain the huge leaps into mass unemployment of 1975 and 1980. These are the result of the events and policies which reduced aggregate demand.

It is widely believed that a large proportion of joblessness is 'technological unemployment'. The new technology, based on the microchip, which is revolutionizing the production techniques of the service industries, as well as manufacturing, is usually held responsible. Again, the evidence is inconclusive. From 1973 onwards the measured rate of increase of productivity (output by labour input) has been noticeably lower than in the previous two decades in most countries; this makes it unlikely, therefore, that new technology has yet had a major and decisive impact on jobs by displacing skilled or unskilled workers in the economy as a whole, though it has done so in particular instances. That is no guarantee that it will not be a much more important source of job loss in the future. If productivity starts to rise rapidly again as a result of the new technology, then any given rise in aggregate demand and in output will cause a much smaller rise in the demand for labour-power.

(iv) *The distribution of unemployment*

In an unequal economy it would perhaps be surprising if the costs of its malfunctioning were not also unequally distributed. If a 10 per cent unemployment rate were to be shared equally among workers, each person could expect to be out of work one month in ten, or perhaps one year in ten. But a considerable proportion of workers hardly ever experience unemployment throughout their lives. That leaves a minority, often large, who have to endure frequent and maybe prolonged spells without work. Not only is unemployment an aid to disciplining the workforce, it can diffuse opposition to capitalist oppression by dividing the working class.

The essential principle is that it is always the marginalized workers who experience the brunt of unemployment. Many workers are at least partially protected from the insecurity of a job loss by the rules of internal labour markets. Only if their firm goes bankrupt or if their factory is closed down are they likely to be thrown on to the job market. Workers in secondary labour markets (as we showed in Chapter 5) tend to be less unionized and less skilled and are usually hired on more casual or temporary terms.

Consequently, the unemployment rate among manual workers, particularly the unskilled, is in all countries much greater than for professional and other non-manual occupations. Female workers tend to be disproportionately concentrated in secondary markets, as do racial minorities in the USA and other countries, and these facts are also reflected in relative unemployment rates. Table 17.4 shows how in almost all countries the rates for men are less than for women. The differences are probably understated, since the 'discouraged worker effect' tends to be greater for women. Table 17.5 illustrates the large variations that can occur between the average unemployment rates of different ethnic groups.

A particular feature of unemployment since 1973 has been its disproportionate effect on young workers. Firms (and often unions as well) are able to impose much of the burden of job cuts on new entrants to the labour force since they have not had time to establish themselves in internal labour markets. Table 17.6 illustrates this disproportion in a number of countries. In all of them, youth unemployment is much greater than the

Table 17.4 Unemployment Rates for Men and Women

| | 1970 | | 1980 | |
	Males	Females	Males	Females
Austria	1.2	2.8	1.4	2.0
Belgium	1.8	2.3	7.5	12.9
Denmark	1.4	0.5	6.4	7.8
Finland	2.6	1.0	4.8	4.9
France	1.4	4.2	4.1	9.7
West Germany	0.5	0.6	2.6	4.6
Italy	3.7	9.4	5.1	13.9
Netherlands	1.4	0.9	4.3	5.3
Sweden	1.4	1.8	2.0	2.2
UK	2.9	0.9	7.0	5.1
Canada	5.6	5.8	6.9	8.4
USA	4.1	5.9	6.7	7.4

Source: United Nations, *Economic Survey of Europe in 1981*, New York, UN, 1982

Table 17.5 Unemployment Rates of Blacks and of All Workers in the USA

	White	Black	Hispanic origin
1965	4.3	8.5	n.a.
1975	8.5	14.7	12.8
1984	9.7	21.0	16.3

Source: US Department of Commerce, Bureau of the Census, *Statistical Abstract of the United States*, Washington DC, 1985

average. This poses special problems for government social policies and for the problems of legitimation of the profit system. A substantial proportion of a new generation of potential workers is being offered no prospect of a means of livelihood other than, in some cases, meagre welfare benefits. Neither diligence and discipline, nor mass consumption, are likely to arise out of that experience. This particular concentration of unemployment among young people has not appeared before in major crises. Its social consequences are, therefore, hard to predict.

Another source of unequal burden is the uneven geographical distribution. Industries tend to bunch together, so when a particular industry declines, the whole area in which its component firms are mainly located declines too. In such areas unemployment can reach enormous proportions, much higher than the national average. It can create despair in communities and eventually destroy them.

Table 17.6 Youth Unemployment Rates in Selected Countries, 1984 (per cent)

	Youths (aged up to 24)	All workers
USA	13.3	7.4
Japan	4.9	2.7
West Germany	10.1	8.6
France	26.1	9.7
UK	21.8	13.2
Canada	17.9	11.2
Italy	34.1	10.2

Source: OECD, *Economic Outlook*, June 1985

3. OIL CRISIS

In the Himalayan mountains and valleys of Nepal, hazardous landslides happen regularly because the land is gradually being denuded of its trees and, with nothing to hold the soil together, the earth is washed away by the monsoon rains. The trees are being used to give energy for daily living, for people unable to afford the new high costs of modern energy sources such as oil or electricity. Shortage of traditional fuel is indeed a growing problem for over 2 billion people in Asia, Africa and Latin America. It not only impoverishes those people, already poor, who have to draw on other resources to buy sufficient fuel. It also contributes to ecological deterioration in the form of widespread soil erosion, silting up of rivers and canals, and the generation of excess carbon dioxide in the world's atmosphere. This, in other words, is a real energy crisis – a shortage of fuel in relation to human needs.

The 'energy crisis' of the 1970s was different: it had very little to do with physical resources and needs, but a great deal to do with exchange, profits and international competition, centring on the exceptional role in the world capitalist economy of petroleum. So much importance is attached to this single commodity that the problems of the 1970s are sometimes referred to as 'oil crises' almost as if there were no other source of instability in modern capitalism.

In this way the responsibility for generalized capitalist crisis was identified as external to the capitalist system and traced to the behaviour of the rulers of some rather backward societies, the kings, sheikhs and shahs of the Arabian Gulf who had raised the price of oil. More generally 'the Arabs' became scapegoats for the troubles of the capitalist system. This fanciful notion was, especially in the western media, implicitly and sometimes explicitly supplemented by racist sneers and jokes at the expense of a group of non-white nations who, for a change, were able to put one over on the white leaders of western imperialism. But if the capitalist crisis was not in essence an 'oil crisis', oil did none the less have a starring role in it.

(i) *Oil as a special commodity*

There is nothing fundamentally new in the emergence of oil as a major politico-economic issue. Capitalism has always depended on its supplies of raw materials and this has often been a source of problems. Oil, however, *is* rather a special commodity and there is a particularly powerful set of mutual influences between the structure of the oil industry and the general course of capital accumulation and the re-emergence of crises.

Three basic features of the oil industry determine its special role:

(a) Oil plays an inordinate role in the provision of energy. Throughout the long boom period, energy supplies were rapidly expanded to meet the growing demands of industry and people. About 80 per cent of this increase was met by oil and gas, as they widely replaced coal, previously the basic staple fuel. By 1973, 53 per cent of energy in the advanced capitalist countries was supplied by oil while another 20 per cent came from natural gas. Since energy is an indispensable input in just about all production processes, the importance of reliable supplies of oil for the stability of all parts of an economy is clear.

(b) The oil industry is dominated by a small number of giant firms. Sometimes they compete with each other but often they have limited the competition between them – for example, by unofficially dividing up the world market between themselves into spheres of influence. In essence they often operated as a cartel. Together they have been able to make vast profits by keeping prices much higher than extraction costs. And as their enormous profits were reinvested they grew into the largest corporations on earth. Twelve out of the top twenty US industrial corporations are suppliers primarily of oil but also of other forms of energy. And oil companies are among the largest in the rest of the world.

(c) The advanced capitalist countries are for the most part highly dependent on importing their oil supplies from elsewhere. In the 1970s the twenty-four countries of the OECD imported two-thirds of their oil supplies, much of this from the Middle East. Through most of the twentieth century, the power of western imperialism was so great that the international oil companies could rely on a steady and increasing supply of crude oil. They harvested enormous profits from countries such as Iran, Iraq, Saudi Arabia and Venezuela, and ploughed back little to promote development. Royalties were paid to the ruling group who controlled the state, frequently a small and authoritarian elite, usually with the backing of the imperialist powers.

Beginning perhaps with the assumption of control of the Suez Canal by the Egyptian President Gamal Abdul Nasser in 1956, the domination over the exporting countries began to weaken. OPEC – the Organization of

Petroleum Exporting Countries – was formed in 1960, and though for many years it was impotent, it survived into the 1970s when its strength and expertise enabled it to play a decisive role in wrenching control of production from the western oil companies and claiming a share of the surplus profits. The oil companies, and the economies of the advanced capitalist world, could no longer rely so closely on a compliant ruling elite in the oil-exporting countries.

By the 1970s the demand for oil had grown so much that even the USA ceased to be self-sufficient, despite being at the time the capitalist world's greatest producer. By then oil had already become a strategic commodity – one whose supplies it was necessary to guarantee in case of war. If foreign countries could turn off the oil tap they could now disrupt the US economy in time of peace, as well as the other capitalist countries. Thus, even before the oil price explosion of 1974, oil had appeared on the agenda of major political problems for capitalism.

(ii) *Implications*

Among the implications of these features of the oil industry, there are three which stand out as strikingly important for the way in which capitalism developed after the end of the long boom.

The price of oil

The oil market is far from the traditional economist's model of perfect competition. The major companies have exercised enough monopoly control in the past to choose a price for the oil they sell without too much fear of undercutting. Their ability to vary the price depends mostly on how sensitive is the demand for it. Since energy is such a fundamental input into modern production processes, the demand for it (and oil in particular) has been very insensitive to increases in price.

Thus, to use the economists' technical term (p. 71), the elasticity of demand for oil is low. In 1980, the OECD reported its rough estimate of the elasticity of demand for energy: it was 0.15 after one year. In other words cutting back by 15 per cent the quantity of energy supplied would permit producers to raise their prices by 100 per cent (the immediate possible rise in price would if anything be greater, as it takes a while for people to economize even a little on energy).

In practical terms this means that the price of oil is especially subject to political forces which can cause sharp and substantial fluctuations. Just as the demand for final energy by consumers is relatively inelastic, so is the oil companies' demand for the crude oil. If the producer countries gain control over the *quantities* of oil extracted from the wells each month the effect on the price can be both sudden and dramatic. This is exactly what happened in 1974 when in a matter of only a few months the price jumped astonishingly by a factor of 4. The same extreme volatility, only in the reverse direction, was seen in early 1986.

The immediate stimulus for the 1974 price shock was the Yom Kippur War in October 1973 between Israel and the Arab states, which brought in its aftermath an embargo on oil exports to the USA and the Netherlands. It is doubtful, however, whether this caused any substantial shortage of oil, since the oil companies could easily divert supplies covertly from other countries. Part of the reason why the price rose so sharply was the panic buying and speculation that took place.

The main political reason why prices rose was that three major actors wanted it. Obviously it was in the interests of the OPEC states to raise their share of the the surplus profit, both by pushing up the crude oil price and by raising their demands. The international oil companies acceded to the increases, because they saw an opportunity to raise the price of their marketed products. Their profits were actually enlarged, even though the share they were forced to concede to the producer countries increased. Finally, there is evidence that the US government was to some extent in favour of raising the price (though perhaps not by so much) as a means of warding off the increased competition from its rivals in Europe and more particularly Japan, which were more highly dependent on oil imports. Here is another effect of the decline of US hegemony.

Table 17.7 Oil Price

(US $ per barrel)	
1972	2
1975	11
1978	13
1981	35
1984	29
1986 (May)	12

Source: OECD, *Economic Outlook*, July 1983 and June 1985; *Financial Times*, 2 May 1986

Trends in the price of oil are shown in Table 17.7. After the first shock increase it remained roughly steady for five years until 1979. Then the low elasticity of demand for oil was again demonstrated in the wake of the revolution in Iran and a well-organized move by OPEC to cut production.

This time the price more than doubled. It should be noted that these changes are in nominal terms; the *real* oil price (i.e. relative to the price of other goods) was gradually falling between the two shocks due to the rapid inflation. Throughout the period 1972 to 1979 the nominal oil price rose by a factor of close to 8; the real price by less than three times.

After the peak reached by oil prices in 1981, the situation changed considerably. Continued stagnation in a number of countries and some economizing on energy use reduced the pressure of demand. And the development of oil production in non-OPEC countries meant that by 1985 OPEC controlled well under half of the world's exports. It has also suffered an increase in internal disputes so that its ability to act as a cartel and control the world price was very much diminished. There was a precipitate decline in oil prices in 1986, following Saudi Arabia's decision to raise production.

The effects of the oil price shocks

The oil price rises of the 1970s were definitely not the causes of the end of the long boom or of the re-emergence of crises. As we saw in the previous chapter, the end was signalled by the decline in profit rates some years beforehand. Moreover, the general downturn in the capitalist economies that happened in 1973 is known to have begun some months before the oil price shocks.

The dramatic ups and downs of the oil price are part of the unstable world's political and economic relations. Moreover, their effects do not simply cancel out. The volatility both reflects and intensifies the fragility.

The changes *did* considerably affect the course of events. They helped to shape the pace and direction of capital accumulation in several ways. First they exacerbated recessions that were happening anyway. The immediate effect of the 1974 price rise was a redistribution of income away from the western oil-importing nations towards the OPEC countries. Household consumers had to pay more for their fuels, and corporations' input costs were raised. The effect of that was to cut profits at a time when profits were already generally decreasing. As a result there was a sharp cutback in private investment through much of the western world. The cumulative multiplier process was set to work and output and employment began to fall.

The 1975 recession occurred despite two counteracting forces. One came from the major capitalist governments which tried to offset the cut in investment by shoring up profits. They did this partly by reducing taxes on final energy products (particularly gasoline) so that their prices rose much less than that of crude oil. They also accommodated price rises by expansions of the money supply, accelerating the wage-price instability discussed earlier in this chapter.

The second counteracting force came from OPEC. While investment spending fell in the oil-importing world, the spending of the newly rich oil producers was increased. Table 17.8 gives an idea of what happened in the course of the first oil shock. OPEC spending got under way gradually, lagging behind their increased export revenues. Their imports came largely from the advanced capitalist countries, as they sought to develop their economies. A particular beneficiary was the arms industry of the west. The Shah of Iran spent billions of oil money in purchasing the latest military hardware from the USA, whose government saw him as their sheriff of the Middle East. Later on, after his deposition, OPEC was to be substantially weakened as two of its members, Iran and Iraq, expended countless billions on a tragically futile war with each other.

Table 17.8 OPEC Revenues and Spending ($billion)

	1973	1974	1975	1976	1977
Exports	42	116	107	132	145
Imports of goods and services *	35	56	80	96	116
Surplus	7	60	27	36	29

* includes transfers abroad

Source: OECD Economic Outlook, OECD, Paris, July 1980

What the OPEC countries could not spend in the mid 1970s was recycled back into the western banking systems, at first mainly to London and later elsewhere. These funds became known as 'petrodollars' and they enabled the countries which borrowed them to withstand their balance of payments deficits for a while without substantial expenditure cutting or devaluation: hence, again the recession was lessened by mitigating the cut in aggregate demand.

Yet OPEC spending and the recycling of petrodollars took some time, and in the intervening period the slackening of aggregate demand across the capitalist world was aggravated by the redistribution away from the advanced capitalist countries.

Another way in which the oil price rises affected capital accumulation is that more resources in the west came to be devoted to lessening the dependence on OPEC. The spectre of the main imperialist nations being held to ransom for lack of oil was a real one. Attempts were made to reduce the growth of energy demand, to step up exploration for more oil in politically 'safe' yet high cost areas such as the North Sea and to make more use of nuclear power.

The oil shocks had a major impact also on further impoverishing many of those underdeveloped countries which do not have their own oil. Like the advanced countries, they were faced with a substantial real income loss as a result of the 1974 price jump. They found it less easy to substitute other energy sources, so the effect persisted. As a result the collective balance of trade deficit of all these countries rose from $11.5 billion in 1973 to $46 billion in 1975, and remained averaging around $33 billion for the next few years before leaping up once more to $70 billion in 1980 after the second shock.

Many of these economies did not substantially contract as a result because vast amounts of the petrodollars were recycled in their direction by the banks. But thereby this acute source of disturbance was to lead to another. The oil shocks watered the seeds of a debt problem that came both to threaten the living standards of workers and peasants in Third World nations and to undermine the financial position of the western banks which lent to them, raising the ominous prospect of a major financial crash. Ironically, though, some of the heaviest debtors were poor countries in possession of oil, thereby raising the danger that a substantial cut in its price can be as destabilizing as large rises.

4. PROBLEMS OF GOVERNMENTS AND BANKS

(i) *State budgets: is there a fiscal crisis?*

As we saw in Chapter 11, the changing social requirements of capital accumulation have led to a huge expansion in the economic activities and spending of the state in the twentieth century. It is, therefore, not surprising that a new period of crisis has displayed some of its symptoms in the area of state finances.

During the boom years governments were able to raise increasing tax revenues to match their rising expenditure. Taxes were raised from wages and workers acceded as long as their pre-tax wages were rising fast enough – which, in an era of expanding productivity, they were. Taxes could also be raised from profits, as long as the rate of profit remained sufficiently high. With the ending of boom conditions and the fall in the profit rate, raising taxes out of incomes, whether profit or wages, became more problematical.

This situation has led to some economists arguing that there is a fiscal crisis of the state which is general to advanced capitalist countries. Some support has been lent to this idea by the almost obsessive concern of their governments in the 1980s with reducing programmes of public spending; and by the generally unfavourable, and sometimes doom-laden, publicity attached to the size of government budget deficits in the 1980s especially in countries such as Italy, where the deficit was around 12 per cent of GNP, and the USA, where, although relatively much smaller, its absolute size – over $200 billion in 1985 – was mind-boggling.

In one sense the situation of state finances unambiguously creates a crisis. Where governments have cut spending on welfare services when requirements for them are rising, this creates a real crisis of human need. That, however, is regrettably not the primary concern of the capitalist class and of the authorities of the state.

A fiscal crisis of the state would imply that as a result of its economic position, the state's financial or political viability as an institution was threatened, or at least that its financial situation represented an acute threat to the stability of the rest of the capitalist economy.

In its most extreme sense, a fiscal crisis could mean that the state was obliged to default on its financial obligations – not pay wages, bills and debts that were due – quite literally to go bankrupt.

A local state institution, or a state which owes money in foreign currencies, can certainly encounter fiscal crisis in this sense. And both situations have been seen during the 1970s and 1980s: the debt crisis experienced by a number of underdeveloped countries after 1982 (discussed in the next subsection); and the fiscal crisis of a number of large city administrations in the advanced countries, especially in the USA. Both these types of fiscal crisis have been more than purely financial; they have been heavily laced with politics.

Many city governments were particularly badly hit by the economic problems of the 1970s: their local tax revenues were limited as the rich moved out and firms also left or closed down. Moreover, much welfare spending became concentrated at the city level as a result of rising unemployment and urban poverty. In the 1970s New York and several other cities found themselves unable to meet their expenditures and were forced into various crisis measures in the absence of federal help. In essence the local fiscal crises were the mechanism through which the federal government was able to force through a policy of cuts in welfare expenditures. The role played by political, as much as economic, forces can be seen in the case of Cleveland, Ohio, forced to default on $14 million of short-term debt. The banks had been prepared to lend much more than that to the previous administration. But Mayor Dennis Kucinich was at odds with them for trying to pursue the reformist programme on which he was elected and for his refusal to follow the policies the bankers insisted on, such as selling off some of the city's assets.

Central governments in advanced countries are very unlikely to experience a fiscal crisis in this extreme sense because most of their obligations are denominated in their own currency which, unlike Cleveland, Ohio, they can in the last resort print. There may, however, still be a fiscal crisis in a less extreme sense, namely a tendency for the growth of government resources systematically and seriously to fall behind their expenditures.

In the short term, the gap between expenditure and revenue – the budget deficit – has to be met either by long-term borrowing (issuing government bonds) or by other methods which essentially mean an increase in the money supply (analysed in detail in Chapter 14). Hence a budget deficit of crisis proportions would result either in a serious destabilizing rise in interest rates or in a massive rise in the money supply causing a substantial inflation. Thus a high and accelerating rate of inflation and/or rocketing real interest rates would be a symptom of a fiscal crisis – though, as we have seen earlier in this chapter, accelerating inflation can be a symptom of a general crisis and is not therefore necessarily a proof of a specifically fiscal crisis.

It is difficult to predict whether a fiscal crisis tendency exists in contemporary advanced capitalist countries, though it has certainly been a recent feature of some underdeveloped ones such as Argentina and Bolivia. Some economists and politicians have tried to argue that the current nominal budget deficits of the 1980s were evidence of a trajectory towards fiscal crisis, But, as we explained in Technical Annexe 14.B, nominal deficits are almost meaningless in times of inflation. To assess the long-term financial viability of governments we would need regular balance-sheet accounts of their assets and liabilities, which are not provided by official statisticians. We are forced to reserve judgement about whether there truly exists a fiscal crisis in advanced capitalist countries in the 1980s, or whether one existed in the 1970s when most governments began their policies of expenditure cuts. And in Chapter 18 we suggest an alternative explanation of why these cuts have been implemented.

(ii) *The debt crisis*

That there exists a fiscal crisis in some underdeveloped countries is, however, beyond doubt. The long fuse which ultimately resulted in the explosion of the debt crisis in August 1982, when first Mexico, and then a number of other countries, in all but name defaulted on their huge international debts, was set in the late 1960s. The sluggish economy's demands for funds were falling behind the supply, and banks began to channel some loans to the Third World instead.

The subsequent oil-price rises of 1974 served to make the later event more dramatic and potentially catastrophic. Their impact was, first, to add a large sum to the balance of payments deficits of the underdeveloped non-oil-producing countries, which were already high. It was extremely difficult for most countries to take measures to reduce these deficits. A cutback in imports would threaten either urgent development programmes or existing consumption standards and provoke social unrest. An increase in exports was ruled out by the world recession which followed the oil price increase. This itself worsened the original deficit problem.

Many countries, therefore, were forced to look for a way of filling the increased deficit by greater financial flows from the developed countries. The recession in the advanced countries themselves led to reductions in their willingness to give economic aid. The suddenly enriched OPEC nations took some guilt-stricken but woefully inadequate measures to lend more money to the underdeveloped countries. But most of their new, as yet unspent, funds they placed in banks in the USA or western Europe, which thus suddenly found themselves awash with funds which few in the recession-torn advanced countries wanted to borrow.

So the banks went looking for new borrowers and they found them in the underdeveloped countries. This marriage of the need for funds to their availability was consummated with enthusiasm – many argue with reckless abandon. It led to an increase in the debts of underdeveloped countries from about \$60 billion in 1973 to about \$900 billion in 1984. Most of these increased debts were owed to banks, who are less able than governments to renegotiate or even wipe out debts since their survival as institutions depends upon the earning of profit and on perceived financial stability.

As world economic instability continued in the late 1970s and early 1980s, the debt contracts which had been so blithely entered into became increasingly burdensome to the debtors. By 1982 some countries needed *more* than their total export earnings to pay their obligations in capital repayments and interest. This was impossible.

Two alternatives, therefore, presented themselves: default or the rescheduling, or roll-over, of the debts. Major defaults would threaten the stability of major world banks and perhaps the whole capitalist financial system. So the banks were obliged to reschedule or roll-over the loans. The indebtedness of different Third World countries varied enormously. The vast majority of the debt was incurred by a handful of countries of which Mexico, Brazil and Argentina have been the most prominent. But virtually all countries incurred some new debts in this period. And over forty debtors experienced a repayment crisis and were forced to reschedule – some on the most favourable terms because of 'the debtor's power' implicit in the possibility of a default. But the smaller debtors, unable to secure multi-year rescheduling deals, had to renegotiate their position every year and accept more rigorous conditions.

The debt crisis, therefore, implies a crisis of human need on a vast scale. It is not that, however, which made it fill the financial pages of the capitalist world's press for several years but rather the continued threat which it posed to the financial stability of the banks. By the mid 1980s the vast debt of Third World countries to the banks had become an ineradicable feature of the world capitalist landscape, a huge, occasionally grumbling volcano.

(iii) *The problem of the banks: is there a financial crisis?*

Revolutions and national liberation movements in the Third World have posed occasional political threats to capitalism, through removal of markets and of areas for capitalist exploitation and profit making. The 1980s is the first period in which the Third World has posed a major financial threat.

The question is being posed time and again; will inability successfully to negotiate rescheduling lead one day to default, the failure of a crucial bank and hence to more general banking collapse in the capitalist world? The banking system is built on confidence: the guarantee that you can get your deposited money back if and when you want it. If you feel the bank is unsound, you immediately take your money out. If *everybody* feels that at the same time, then almost *nobody* will be satisfied and the bank collapses. If this happens it will only be repeating, though possibly on a more catastrophic scale, what has happened many times before in history. Major breaks in capital accumulation have always been accompanied by financial crises and bank failures. As capitalists borrow at increasingly short-term rates of interest in search of expected profits which fail to materialize, the point comes when suddenly many firms and banks are unable to repay their debts and are declared bankrupt. Thus financial crises sharpen the breaks in accumulation and to call them crises is no exaggeration.

Bank failure is a highly contagious disease. Since the nature of the banking system is countless endless circles of debt, then one failure spreads very rapidly to others. The contagion can only be avoided by rapid and decisive action by central banks and governments acting as 'lender of last resort' and rescuing banks on the brink by flooding them with the funds they require.

Even without a major Third World debt default, the financial instability and uncertainty of the mid 1980s saw a growing number of bank failures. So far (1986), in every case state intervention has been in time to arrest the contagion. In the early 1970s a near panic was avoided in Germany after the Herstadt Bank failed, and the UK banking system was saved after the collapse of several smaller 'secondary' banks by the timely action of the Bank of England. Meanwhile twenty-seven banks failed in the USA in the aftermath of the 1974–5 recession.

In 1982, the collapse of a relatively insignificant financial institution in New York, Drysdale Government Securities, imposed serious losses on two major commercial banks, Chase Manhattan and Manufacturers Hanover.

In 1984, the US government had to intervene to save the Continental Illinois Bank, the country's twelfth largest bank, at a cost of $4.5 billion. In 1985 the Governor of Ohio ordered a three-day closure of the state's savings banks in the face of a run on some of them, reminding the world of March 1933 when President Roosevelt closed all the US banks for a week; and there was also an increase in savings bank and other bank failures in other parts of the USA.

This list of failures and problems looks ominous. Yet it would be unbalanced not to add that the banks and the various state agencies responsible for overseeing them have during the 1970s and 1980s shown themselves to be extraordinarily flexible and inventive in stopping the holes in what to many looked like a sinking ship.

Optimists in the banking world rely on the existence of a lender of last resort to prevent any major banking collapse from occurring. This, however, does not necessarily solve the problem. Knowing that the lender of last resort will always rescue it leads a bank into loose banking practices: it encourages bankers to make excessively risky loans in their search for profits. Charles Kindleberger, the American economic historian, has argued the curious yet beguiling position that bankers should be made to believe they would not be rescued in a liquidity crisis – but that in fact they should be rescued when the time came. But his diagnosis of the financial and economic crises of the 1930s was that there was, in any case, no *international* lender of last resort: the UK government was unable to perform this role and the US unwilling to. This may be a disputed interpretation of that period, but it does raise issues for the present: who is going to be the lender of last resort in the event of a major international banking collapse in the 1980s? Will the capitalist world's indisputably fragile banking system avert collapse? These are the economic equivalent of the breathless questions posed at the end of old radio soap operas. We will not be so foolish as to try to give the answers.

We cannot predict the future of capitalism in any detail. But it is certain that, whether they become more acute or whether they subside somewhat, many of the problems discussed in this chapter will persist for some time. No one is optimistic enough to believe that low profitability, mass unemployment, Third World indebtedness and financial fragility will disappear in a short time. This is partly because of what has been the main overall theme of this chapter, that these problems are not separate diseases treatable on their own. They are the observable symptoms of some much more fundamental malaise which may well manifest itself in further forms we cannot yet foresee. This malaise has transformed not only the economic functioning of the profit system compared with the golden years of the boom, but also its politics, the subject which we turn to next.

Technical Annexe 17.A A model of unstable inflation

In the text it was argued that the Phillips curve became unstable because it was no longer possible, with the intensification of conflict over income, to contain the claims of workers and capitalists without inflation coming to be anticipated in wage bargaining. A precise analytical model which suggests how this process can happen has been developed by the British economist, Bob Rowthorn, in his book *Capitalism, Conflict and Inflation*.

Assume that in a national economy there are four groups which make a claim for a share of national income: the capitalist class, the working class, foreigners and the state. The state's share is obtained by levying taxes, while the foreigners' share comes from the nation's import bill. Assume further that the foreigners' and the state's shares are, for the moment, fixed. That leaves a given share to be divided between capitalists' profits and workers' wages, a situation of conflict in which both classes aim to maximize their share of income at the expense of the other.

The arguments in this chapter suggest that the workers' and the capitalists' claims on the national income are both inversely related to the rate of unemployment. The consequences of these assumptions are illustrated in Diagram 17.A.1 which is a hypothetical Phillips curve. At a low level of unemployment, U_1, aggregate demand is relatively high. Workers are able to bargain for reasonably good wage increases as productivity rises. Capitalists are able to increase their profits by raising prices by a small amount. In this way, the conflicting claims for a share of national income are reconciled. At a higher level of unemployment, U_0, workers are inhibited from claiming wage rises while capitalists are unable to raise prices; hence inflation is zero.

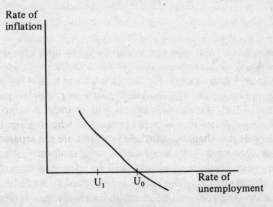

Diagram 17.A.1 A Hypothetical Phillips Curve

Suppose that at one time the economy is at U_0, with low profits. The government could influence the economy through its management of aggregate demand. By increasing demand and allowing the money supply to expand it can cause *some* level of unanticipated inflation. Thereby it can both ensure a low level of unemployment, so as to assist in maintaining social cohesion, and help to support the profitability of capital.

But the relationships implied in Diagram 17.A.1 cease to hold when people start to anticipate inflation in their bargaining. Let us suppose that if inflation is below a given threshold it is too small for workers to take much notice of it (especially if their real wages are rising), but as soon as it rises above that level they always push for wage rises to compensate for future inflation. The effect is shown in Diagram 17.A.2.

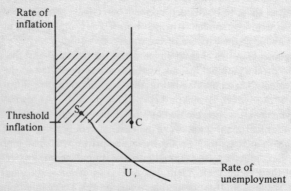

Diagram 17.A.2   The Breakdown of the Phillips Curve

If the government pushes its inflation policy too far the economy goes initially to a point such as S, where it is hoped it will mean only a small increase in inflation. But now the workers start to anticipate inflation in their wage bargaining, and the conflict for a share of national income hots up. Wages rise by increasing amounts each year, but capitalists can push inflation higher still. The economy cannot stay at S. Evidently, there is no point at which the economy could settle down to a steady inflation rate while the government continues to ensure enough aggregate demand. In fact, anywhere in the shaded area is an unstable region for the economy: it is the area of the classic wage-price spiral. Capitalists and workers are both powerful enough to push up prices and wages in pursuit of their conflicting claims. The only way the conflict can be reconciled is if aggregate demand is decreased and high unemployment is created, thus reducing the bargaining power of workers and the price-raising ability of capitalists. In the diagram we have shown this as a vertical line drawn through C.

At any point on the line the economy would settle down to a steady rate of inflation and constant high unemployment – high enough, that is, to stifle capitalists' and workers' claims so that inflation does not exceed what is anticipated. (Note that this does not mean prices do not go up – only that they go up at a steady and anticipated rate.)

Thus, if the government pushes the economy into the shaded region, its inflation policy will eventually break down as the economy becomes unstable: it will sooner or later be forced to create or facilitate crisis by cutting back demand and creating unemployment. If it resolves to intensify the crisis it can even bring inflation down by creating mass unemployment, to the right of the vertical line through C.

The process we have traced is the breakdown of the Phillips curve. We have sharply distinguished the two regions, that below threshold inflation where the Phillips curve is valid, and that above the threshold where it breaks down. In reality the borderline between the two is not so precise, but our model does capture the essence of the distinction.

Up till now, we have assumed that the shares of the state and of foreigners were constant, but there is good reason to consider what happens when their shares increase. The share remaining to be apportioned between workers and capitalists is reduced. To a certain extent workers and capitalists might accept this reduction in their share, and if they together accepted it fully their wage and price behaviour would not change, nor would the position of the Phillips curve, and there would be no additional conflict.

But this is unlikely. If workers demand higher wage increases to compensate for having to pay more for imported goods and to pay higher taxes, and capitalists try to push up their prices to compensate for the extra costs implied by higher taxes or import costs, the result is illustrated in Diagram 17.A.3, which depicts the shift in the Phillips curve.

Consider an initial situation which is stable, at the point of Q. The effect of an increased share of either the state or the foreign sector is to shift the Phillips curve from AB to A'B'. Since conflict is intensified a higher level of unemployment is necessary to ensure zero inflation at A'. The shifting curve could cause two possible results. If the government did not allow an expanded demand for domestic goods there would be a rise in unemployment as the economy adjusted to the point R. There, the workers and the capitalists would be forced to accept the extra burden placed upon them. If on the other hand profits are already low, and if in addition the government does not wish to risk higher unemployment, it can expand the money supply and pursue an inflation policy up to the point S. But there we are again in the unstable wage-price spiral region, where workers correctly

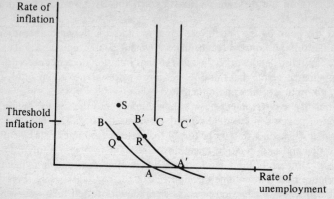

Diagram 17.A.3   The Shift and Breakdown of the Phillips Curve (as a result of rises in the state's or foreigners' shares)

anticipate future inflation. Sooner or later the economy explodes, the Phillips curve breaks down and the government finds itself creating unemployment, at least as far as the line above C′.

CHAPTER 18

The Politics of Crisis

I. THE FALL OF KEYNESIANISM AND THE RISE OF AUSTERITY

In 1970 a now infamous political leader of the capitalist world, President Richard Nixon, made a revealing and ironic declaration: 'We are all Keynesians now.' It revealed that the most powerful right-wing politician of the time had been converted to the notions which had become associated (though not quite accurately) with Keynes – namely that governments, through a judicious combination of their spending, taxation and monetary policies, could keep capitalist economies prosperous and stable. The converted president now believed that government intervention should, if appropriate, involve spending more than is raised through taxes; and also that the aims of government economic policy included fast growth and full employment as well as the absence of inflation and a stable balance of payments. To an American right which had traditionally tended to associate Keynesianism with communism and immorality, Nixon's statement remained unacceptable. But it shows the broad consensus on economic questions which had developed in the advanced capitalist countries in the course of the long boom. By 1970 anyone who was not in some such sense a Keynesian was on the fringes of politics.

Twenty-seven years earlier, in the closing stages of the Second World War, the economist Friedrich Hayek wrote a treatise in defence of classic liberalism, the political and economic ideas which predominated in the nineteenth century. *The Road to Serfdom* was unusual for a book on political economy in that it became a bestseller. It argued against the over-expansion of social security and of state intervention in the economy. Any partial moves towards a system of planning for needs would become unstoppable and would end up inevitably with a totalitarian society. Only the principle of the free market, of social control through impersonal competition, could prevent this. This book was soon read by millions, but for many years it made no impact on the development of the Keynesian consensus, which came to dominate the economic policy of the major political parties in the advanced capitalist world.

The irony is that, just as Hayek's treatise had arrived at the start of the long Keynesian era, so Nixon's conversion occurred on the point of its collapse. By the 1980s nobody was in the old sense a Keynesian any more. Virtually all governments in the advanced countries, whatever their political hue, espoused stability and repudiated prosperity and full employment except as distant goals. Hayek's pleas had been heard at last.

The new policies and the new politics arrived not because they were the best ones for capitalism at any time, for Keynesianism in many ways suited the needs of profit making during the boom period. Rather they were an integral part of the most recent era of capitalism and reflected its characteristic frequent crises. For many years the 'new' ideas were rehearsed in certain academic surroundings without much wider recognition. Monetarism's guru, Milton Friedman, was for a long time the intellectual head of a minority school of macroeconomists. The ideas came into their own only in the 1970s when it became necessary to re-create the conditions under which profits could be made and capital accumulated.

The policies appear under a number of guises, which we shall shortly examine, but we believe their most important essential objective is to increase profits through an attack on the position of the working class. In other words, they signal a return to more open class confrontations, to struggles which had been hidden in the Keynesian era. They threaten the collective consumption needs of most workers by cutting the welfare state; they aim to reduce workers' power of resistance by creating mass unemployment; they restore incentives for capitalists to make profits by reducing taxes, denationalizing state enterprises and removing controls on private ones; all inevitably creating greater inequality with more rewards for the rich and less for the poor.

All these policies can be summed up in one word: austerity. In the mid 1980s the policies of austerity have become the new orthodoxy, a new belief that has spread more rapidly than any mass religion, throughout the capitalist world. In the underdeveloped world it has been imposed on dozens of countries by the IMF and by their creditors as a response to indebtedness which has grown out of control. In the more advanced countries it has been adopted by domestic right-wing political parties with less pressing outside constraints.

And if the origins of the new orthodoxy in economic policy are to be found in right-wing and conservative parties, there are now many centre and centre-left parties whose words in praise of austerity are hardly any less reverent. In the US presidential election of 1984 Ronald Reagan was attacked by the Democrats for being too spendthrift: so much had the tables been turned.

The most widely advocated alternative to the orthodoxy retains a strong flavour of Keynesianism. It generally involves expanding government expenditure and a concomitant nationalist and protectionist element. But the modern Keynesians have lost the confidence they had in the 1950s and 1960s. They have become much more modest in what they regard as possible in modern capitalist society. Talk of full employment and rapid economic growth has been replaced by the more limited objectives of reducing the current high levels of unemployment and the arrest of deindustrialization. In many respects the ideas of the new orthodoxy have penetrated almost throughout the political spectrum in the advanced countries. In the years of the long boom the success and popularity of the welfare state dragged the traditional conservative parties to the left. In the 1980s in many countries a defensive left has been dragged to the right.

2. THE NEW ORTHODOXY IN THEORY

These new consensus economic policies could be traced back a long way in the history of capitalism, even before the time of Adam Smith. They rest fundamentally on a belief in the market mechanism both as a reference point for describing the capitalist world and as a normative principle. Hayek, for example, states that the price system, backed up by an appropriate legal framework, should be used to make 'the best possible use of the forces of competition as a means of co-ordinating human efforts'. Not only does the market mechanism work successfully, if promoted and not interferred with, it does so better than other systems of control. Hayek embellishes this argument by suggesting that there is eventually only one other viable system of control: totalitarian central planning. Given the choice the market, therefore, is an offer we can hardly refuse. Not many people would agree that these are the only alternatives. Yet there remains among the intellectuals of the ruling class an almost religious faith in the market as a social mechanism.

It is this deep belief that underlies and motivates the specific arguments and policies of this period of austerity. The centrepiece of the strategy is the objective of reducing state intervention in the economy, through expenditure-cutting, denationalizations and deregulation.

An intellectual case for cuts in expenditure has generally rested on the theory of 'crowding out', whereby higher (lower) public spending would be met by a fall (rise) in private investment. But as we discussed in Chapter 11, despite great efforts no one has found any decisive evidence to suggest that the crowding-out process has been important. Rather the intellectual and technical arguments have sometimes hidden the real basis of the policies, which was the pro-market ideology. Implicitly this entails causing a recession, re-creating the reserve army of unemployed workers and thereby weakening the bargaining power of the working class. And, as we saw in Chapter 17, the same objective underlies the major stated macroeconomic aspect of austerity policies, the attempt to reduce inflation.

As adjuncts to the more general strategy, various more detailed and more technical policies are tried. One of these is monetarism, the policy of controlling the growth of the money supply, letting it grow at a fixed and steady rate and shunning discretionary fiscal policy (see Chapter 15). In the mid 1980s the term has become, less technically, virtually synonymous with the austerity policies as we have defined them.

The problem with technical monetarism is that it is extremely difficult in practice for governments to control the money supply. They can only do so through their arms-length controls over the banking system. Yet banks are subject to the fluctuating demands for their loans and in any case are often able to avoid national controls through their international operations. As a result, governments practising technical monetarism typically have had to set a wide range of target rates of growth for their money supplies and they have often missed even these targets despite frequently changing the precise definition of money supply which they use. With some partial justification, monetarists are able to respond to criticisms of technical monetarist strategies by arguing that they have not been consistently tried out in practice. The doubt is whether they ever could be, to the purist's satisfaction.

Whatever the technical failures or successes, the doctrine of monetarism is none the less also useful as part of the justification for expenditure cuts. For if money growth is thought to cause inflation (a view we criticized in the last chapter), and if government deficits cause excessive money growth, it appears that public services must be cut in order to protect the value of money.

This point is related to another technical policy, introduced in some countries, to control the level of government borrowing as part of the strategy of 'fighting inflation'. Here the policies normally degenerate into an irrational morass, for the methods of accounting for governments' present and expected future finances are primitive. In Technical Annexe 14.B we showed how, in a time of substantial inflation, the nominal budget deficit is almost meaningless as a measure of fiscal rectitude or recklessness. Despite this obstacle to making a target of nominal borrowing, some governments have made a fetish of this policy.

Another strongly held fallacy has been used to support a policy of raising profits through tax cuts: the set of ideas which arose in the USA, known as 'supply side economics'. According to this, tax cuts would result in an upsurge of entrepreneurial activity and growth of national product, owing to greater private incentives, so gigantic that the problem of government revenues would solve itself: total revenue would stay the same or even increase at lower tax rates because taxable income would have grown so much. There are those who argue that this theory has been vindicated by the rapid growth of the US economy between 1982 and 1984. In fact, however, it was almost certainly the massive fiscal stimulus of a traditional Keynesian kind which was more responsible for this short-term growth. And the size of the US budget deficit grew larger, not smaller, during this time.

In Europe, the term 'supply side economics' has been interpreted more widely, to refer to policies to change the industrial relations climate, to improve management techniques, to introduce 'labour flexibility' and so on. In this respect the stated policies are more honest: they more closely reflect the reality of the underlying strategy which is to reorganize the economy, largely at the expense of workers, to enable profit rates to be restored. In the US 'supply siders' of the early 1980s and in the ill-informed targeting of nominal government borrowing, we see two examples of what is perhaps a general tendency: a proliferation of economic policy fantasies at a time when a generally repressive strategy needs all the 'scientific' legitimation it can gather.

Belief in the market mechanism and in the maximum amount of competition seems to be a neutral ideology, and is often so regarded by its disciples. It can mean that some sectors of capital are deliberately threatened by the new policies, in that their traditional monopolist privileges are removed. But we have argued throughout this book that the whole approach of seeing capitalist society just as a system of market exchanges between equals is one-sided: it masks the unequal and hierarchical organization of capitalist production and the capitalist class monopoly of the means of production. So the philosophy of *laissez-faire* amounts in effect to a policy of letting the inequality prevail, removing protections from working people and exposing them to the full glare of competition with capital.

3. THE NEW ORTHODOXY IN PRACTICE

The shortcomings of the exclusively market view of capitalism help to explain why the market-oriented policies encounter obstacles. Before examining whether the policies can succeed in restoring profits we must look first at the contradictions they give rise to.

Foremost among these are the political problems of reducing state expenditure, which have meant that the most radical aims have not been implemented. In the USA, for instance, it turned out to be relatively easy politically to introduce the part of the policy which called for tax cuts (especially for the better-off) but much more difficult to implement the policy of spending cuts. This was true everywhere; but in the USA it was complicated by President Reagan's decision simultaneously to raise military spending. This has meant that in practice, ironically, with a government in power pledged to the ruthless pursuit of fiscal rectitude, US state expenditure actually rose from 35.0 to 38.1 per cent of GDP in the three years from 1980.

It is interesting to examine why the policy of reducing government expenditure proved so difficult to implement in practice. The answer is hinted at by a statement made by the US Director of the Office of the Budget between 1980 and 1985, David Stockman, whose task it was to identify possible cuts on behalf of the Reagan administration:

[The budget] isn't something you reconstruct each year. The budget is a sort of rolling history of decisions. All kinds of decisions made five, ten, fifteen years ago, are coming back to bite us unexpectedly. (*Atlantic Monthly*, December 1981)

This perceptive remark illustrates the fact that high state expenditure is not simply a question of government policy. It has become entrenched in the structure of modern capitalism. To reduce it very substantially involves not just a decision to spend less this year but a decision to change that structure; and that means changing major laws, which in turn means transforming basic political relationships. Any thorough-going attempt to implement austerity policies – for example, to abolish unemployment benefit – would lead to confrontations with the organized labour movement and many other political forces in capitalist society. When the austerity policies themselves create mass unemployment it leads to an automatic rise in public expenditure which parliamentary governments cannot do anything about.

A second contradiction of austerity policies arises from the competition between nation states in an increasingly integrated capitalist world. If austerity is practised by one national government it is no longer unambiguous that *its* capitalists will be the ones to benefit: it could be the multinational corporations with owners in other countries. Moreover, if all countries' governments practise austerity to the full, there arises the problem of insufficient export demand; so that even if workers are forced to accept wage cuts by a successful policy of mass unemployment and austerity, the potential profits are not obtained because not all commodities can be sold. This is a third contradiction: that the conditions that are suitable for high potential profits (especially, lower wages) may not match those necessary for 'realizing' those profits (namely, higher public expenditure and growing wages leading to higher effective demand).

Increasing pressures for protectionism alongside IMF austerity policies exemplify these contradictions on a world scale. The principle of the free market implies that inevitably some capitalists must lose out in the process of competition. One group that lost badly in the 1980s was the American textile industry. They duly formed a strong pressure group (Fibre, Fabric and Apparel Coalition for Trade – or FACT, for short) with much financial backing to press the US government for further protection. This is but one example of a growing political movement to reverse the openness of the US economy that had prevailed for four decades. Between 1980 and 1983 the proportion of US imports subject to some form of non-tariff trade barrier doubled.

If protectionism expands, as competition between nation states intensifies, so as qualitatively to change the nature of the world economy, not only does it go against free market principles, it further undermines the austerity policies being imposed on Third World governments.

The problem is vividly shown in the interrelations between countries' balance of payments. A surplus in one country must show up (errors apart) in a deficit somewhere else in the world. Between 1981 and 1984 the USA and the Middle Eastern oil exporters jointly raised their deficits by some $170 billion. This was largely matched by surpluses in the Third World and the other advanced capitalist countries, chiefly Japan. The world balance of payments accounts therefore pose the following problem: if the Third World countries must stay in surplus (in order to meet their debts through carrying out IMF-imposed austerity policies), and if the USA tries to reduce its deficit (by bowing to protectionist tendencies or through self-imposed austerity), then increased deficits or reduced surpluses *must* appear elsewhere. The imposition of austerity policies in Europe can only work to increase surpluses there. The only other major bloc is Japan – by far the most successful capitalist economy, with a long tradition of state intervention in industry and protectionism which has served it well. There may be a tendency, therefore, towards policies which are mutually inconsistent and thus in aggregate unattainable.

The outcome of the various contradictions is that, just as the technical policies such as strict monetary control have proved difficult to enact, so the more general strategies have been implemented everywhere in an irregular fashion. And occasionally the rhetoric of austerity can diverge widely from the reality. While the US high priests of austerity urged retrenchment on many other countries, President Reagan's massive military expansions violated the strategy within his own domain.

None the less, even President Reagan carried on the offensive to reduce state welfare benefits and to inflict defeats on the working class. Environmental, banking and other restrictive controls on capitalists were reduced. And across the capitalist world many less militaristic governments succeeded in at least limiting the growth of, if not reducing, public expenditure. There arises therefore the question: are the policies effective in meeting their objectives?

In one respect the answer normally given is yes: the rate of inflation in advanced capitalist countries was reduced substantially from the double-digit levels of the 1970s to an average of 4.7 per cent by 1985. This 'success' is not surprising, since the policies also succeeded in generating a massive recession, with many countries experiencing unemployment levels unknown since the 1930s.

But the more basic aspect of capitalist life is profits. In the short term, the effect of a recession is to send actual profits plummeting, as demand falls and the potential profits cannot be realized. In the UK, for example, the average manufacturing profit rate reached an all-time low of 1.7 per cent in 1981 before beginning to recover somewhat. So in order to assess whether profitability has been re-established on a stable long-term basis we would have to disentangle long-term trends from cyclical movements.

The contradictions implicit in the austerity programmes make it extremely unlikely that the world could regain the conditions that fostered the golden years of the 1950s and 1960s. But it is virtually impossible to evaluate, in the midst of the programmes, whether they can be at least partially successful or whether they will prove to be as disastrous for the ruling capitalist class as they assuredly have been for the world's working classes and peasantry.

4. OLD AND NEW POLARIZATIONS

Austerity policies have frequently been accepted by some of the leaders of the left; but unlike Keynesianism, which had earlier gained a wide consensus in all sections of society, they have generally been opposed by millions of people throughout the capitalist world. As we have argued, the gap between the theory and practice of the new orthodoxy remains wide partly because of the political power of the forces which oppose it or may suffer from it.

The end of the post-war boom coincided with the emergence of new centrifugal forces in many capitalist countries. Political parties began to diverge more in their policies, and widespread worker militancy led to a tidal wave of strikes; and the time since then has seen the birth of new social movements.

Workplace struggles intensified as trade unions engaged in defensive action against the crises of the 1970s. The austerity policies of the 1980s were in part designed to weight the scales in favour of the capitalist classes in these struggles. Governments initiated legal and constitutional attacks against the rights of labour to organize. In addition capitalist states increased their expenditure on anti-riot and similar police forces, which have been increasingly used to control public protest in industrial and other disputes. Business corporations themselves became increasingly efficient at and dedicated to breaking the strength of trade unions. In particular in the USA, but also elsewhere, many of the major corporations, especially in the newer and growing industries, with the assistance of consultancy firms which specialized in union-busting tactics succeeded in outlawing unions and becoming non-union companies. Such factors combined with the effects of mass unemployment to reduce both the size and the strength of unions in the 1980s in the main capitalist countries.

None the less union strength remained well in excess of what it was during the 1930s. And the conditions of militant resistance by no means disappeared even after more than a decade of crisis conditions and several years of austerity policies. This was demonstrated vividly by the British miners' strike of 1984–5, one of the most tenacious struggles in the history of the British labour movement. More widely, the early 1980s saw no very substantial decrease in strikes and other industrial conflict in most other countries, and a small increase in some.

The years of crisis in the capitalist world saw not only a political polarization around the traditional issues of class struggle – wages and jobs – carried out by the traditional means – strikes and occupations – but also the emergence of many new radical forces, all of them challenging in some way the existing values and practices of advanced capitalist society.

One of these forces, by no means a single homogenous one with common and consistent objectives, was the women's movement. The years of boom had seen a great growth of women's employment in most advanced capitalist countries, yet women continued to suffer discrimination. Some of the issues they raised related to their inferior position within capitalist work relations; they engaged in trade union struggles about low wages, or union recognition. But because of their continued role within the family they also found themselves in the vanguard of struggles relating to the welfare state – education, health and social services. Other sections of the women's movement challenged broader aspects of women's position in modern society, especially their enforced subordinacy to men within the structure of the typical family. In political terms the influence of the womens' movement has sometimes reinforced the more traditional class struggle, sometimes complemented it, and sometimes also cut across it.

The second major conflict within capitalism outside the traditional class struggle has been the fight against racial discrimination. In many ways US politics was dominated in the latter part of the 1960s by the civil rights movement and reactions to it. But resistance to race discrimination has also been a significant feature of politics in France, West Germany and the UK. Black people and other national minorities tend to have significantly lower wage rates and higher levels of unemployment than members of the dominant culture. Again, their struggles have sometimes but not always been in harmony with those of the labour movement. Capitalists have often realized the value of racism in enabling them to divide the working class, and black people have been forced to struggle against a combination of classes of the dominant culture when they demand their rights.

A third area has been the struggle of oppressed nationalities, either within the advanced capitalist countries themselves (the Irish Republicans in the UK, the Basques and other nationalities in Spain, the Corsicans in France) or the fight of Third World nations against imperialism which is often reflected in solidarity movements in the advanced countries. On occasions in the post-war period such issues have dominated the politics of some major capitalist countries and have created the same combination of co-incidence and contradiction with class struggles shown by the other arenas of struggle.

The lesbian and gay men's movement, starting in the United States in 1969, then spreading throughout the advanced capitalist world, has raised many personal, political and moral issues which are almost completely new to the political life of capitalist countries.

Then during the late 1970s and the 1980s more movements came to occupy an important part on the political stage especially in Europe: the peace and disarmament movements, the anti-nuclear movement, the environmentalist ('green') movements.

In the wake of the crises of the 1970s, modern capitalist politics in the advanced countries now consists of both the traditional alignments of political parties and organizations, and the struggles and mobilizations raised by these various newer political forces and organizations. On the whole, the major conservative parties which most closely represent the interests of the capitalist class (the Republicans in the USA, the Christian Democrats in Italy and West Germany, the Gaullists in France, the Conservatives in the UK) held to a remarkably consistent set of political positions on all the issues which we have mentioned. They support capital in the class struggle, they oppose the demands of nationalists, feminists, lesbian and gay liberationists, the peace movement, the environmentalist movement and so on. Governments which have espoused the new orthodoxy in economic policy have characteristically adopted exceptionally reactionary positions on the other questions as well. The Reagan government in particular has taken a very strong stand in favour of massive arms expenditure, against many established rights of women such as the right to abortion and against demands of all the modern radical movements.

The other extreme of politics contains a very tiny and scarcely significant number of revolutionary socialists who argue in support of radical anti-authoritarian and anti-capitalist positions on all the questions we have mentioned but who have been practically devoid of political influence and remain effectively marginalized despite brief waves of hope stimulated by dramatic events like the 1968 general strike in France. Between the two extremes lies a host of different political forces, parties and movements, partly allied, partly conflicting. For instance, if women or black people receive better treatment in the labour force, white male workers may suffer; and the disarmament movement would mean many workers in armaments-related industries would lose their jobs. It is idealistic to argue that anti-capitalist politics could be an uncomplicated alliance of these various interests and movements.

Modern capitalist society is a complex of different forms of oppression and exploitation in human relations which are in very important ways interlinked. But it is impossible to reduce all such issues to consequences of capitalist economic exploitation only. There are real contradictions between the various interests involved in the political struggles we have mentioned.

Nevertheless, the diversity of the social and political currents which find themselves in opposition to the established authorities of modern capitalism expresses and confirms something of the diversity of ways in which capitalism exploits and maintains its power – in the factory, the office, the council chamber, the home, the bed and the human mind. Capitalist society now finds itself challenged, if not with greater strength than at times in the past, then over a wider and more varied front. If there is a trend, it seems to be towards the increasing inclusion on the political agenda of aspects of the way capitalism legitimates itself, in addition to the way it economically exploits and politically rules. But as long as they can exploit the contradictions which exist among the opposing forces, then the rulers of capitalism will not be shaken.

A successful challenge to the existing system, therefore, seems to depend on whether the sometimes divergent, but absolutely very numerous, forces which oppose it can find some basis on which existing divisions can be overcome and a social and political unity constructed. It depends, to put it in other words, if they can collectively evolve a viable socialist alternative.

PART SIX

ALTERNATIVES TO CAPITALISM

CHAPTER 19

Actually Existing Alternatives

I. ACTUALLY EXISTING SOCIALISM

One-third of the world's population now lives in what are variously known as communist, socialist, centrally planned or non-market economies. For various reasons our book would not be complete without discussing these other economies which officially claim to have replaced capitalism.

First, we have presented a critical picture of capitalism as a productive system based on exploitation and the pursuit of profit, which does not very effectively meet human needs. We are bound therefore to look, albeit briefly, at the existing alternative to see whether it supersedes the faults and problems of capitalism.

Secondly, some observers of the so-called socialist states, noting their exploitative character, have contended that they contain many elements that are found in capitalism, or even that there is no essential difference between them and capitalism. This is a feature of the theories which characterize societies like the USSR as 'state capitalist'. And it is also in another way a feature of the theories which see both capitalism and communism as having been transformed and as having converged into some form of state bureaucratic society. This idea of converging systems is reinforced by the existence of widespread movements for economic reform in communist countries. The common themes of these, such as more reliance on the market mechanism, and giving more attention to cost and profit calculations, might suggest the possibility that these economies are partially retracing their steps towards capitalism.

Third, whatever is their true nature, the communist states are by no means completely isolated blocs. They are related economically to the capitalist world through trade, technology, debt, military competition and so on. They therefore in some sense constitute a part of the world capitalist economy and their presence and behaviour make a difference to the way in which capitalism functions.

Most of the names which are conventionally given to these economies involve, at least implicitly, some conclusions about their nature. We prefer to use the term popularized by the writer Rudolf Bahro (formerly of East Germany, now of West), 'actually existing socialism', which suggests the difference of such societies from capitalism without implying that they have attained any theoretical ideal.

From the start, however, there is a danger that in lumping all these economies under one phrase we miss the heterogeneity of the various different countries. It may, for example, be useful for some purposes to distinguish the relatively developed countries such as the USSR, East Germany and others in eastern Europe from less developed countries such as China and Cuba, and, poorer still, the fledgeling communist-oriented countries of Africa. For other purposes we could distinguish a country like Czechoslovakia, still firmly under Soviet hegemony, from one like Yugoslavia, which has broken from the USSR and is more closely linked to the west.

Hence it may be misleading to posit a single model of 'actually existing socialism' for such a wide group of countries, and too optimistic to expect to settle on objective truth when the range of views about the nature of the countries concerned is so extreme. Nevertheless we shall, somewhat heroically, initially consider all the countries together. We want to find their identifying common features, their fingerprint, in order to compare them with capitalism.

We identified the essential features of the capitalist system as the predominantly private ownership and control by a minority capitalist class of the means of production, and the profit motive which arises from this. Here there are obvious differences from actually existing socialism.

Despite the existence of pockets of small-scale private ownership and the trend towards private ownership in some recent reform programmes, the means of production in actually existing socialism are overwhelmingly owned by the state or by some other collective body. The form of property is not the same as the nationalized industries in the capitalist countries since these exist in some sort of symbiotic relationship with a dominant private sector. In the USSR and similar economies virtually all the means of production are part of a state economic system. No substantial class receives income as a result of the private ownership of the major means of production. That does not mean that there are no capitalists; commerce (especially illegal or semi-legal markets) and even some small-scale production can be based on pure capitalist forms of ownership and profit motivation. But in no actually existing socialist country do capitalists own the major means of production. In that sense, therefore, such countries are very different from capitalism.

But that answer is not sufficient. The essence of capitalism relates not only to ownership but also to control. Here the similarity between the two systems is much more marked. The nature of the production process, and within it the degree and kind of authority exercised by the management, does not seem to be qualitatively different between the two systems. Many would argue that, if there is a difference, then actually existing socialism generally exhibits more hierarchical and authoritarian forms of control over workers, partly because of the absence of any trade unions which are *de facto* independent of the management. The influence of Taylorism on the production process has not been confined to capitalist countries; it was, for example, explicitly embraced by Lenin in the 1920s.

It is also true in both systems that working people have no control over the economy as a whole. In fact, economic control in actually existing socialist countries is very much a 'top–down' affair. A typical pattern is that a central planning authority, such as Gosplan in the USSR, determines priorities and strategies both for each year and over each five-year plan. The authority's policies are themselves determined by the leadership of the Communist Party. Managers of enterprises are then charged with the task of fulfilling the production targets they have been given, or for which they have negotiated.

Many of the administrative and other functions of Soviet managers are hardly distinguishable from those performed by capitalist managers. Both devise and implement the production processes in their enterprises and both seek to maintain labour discipline. Yet there are are also essential differences. Managers in actually existing socialist countries are inevitably linked closely with the state through the central planning apparatus; whereas capitalist managers are more independent of their national governments and subject instead to the coercive forces of the market. They also differ in respect of their motives: to implement a state economic plan or to make profits on behalf of private owners.

2. MEETING HUMAN NEEDS

Differences in motivation can be expected to result in differences in the way in which the systems meet human needs. We have already discussed in detail the various reasons why the pursuit of profit does not lead very satisfactorily to the meeting of human needs by capitalist production systems. We tend towards the conclusion that actually existing socialism is in an overall sense neither better nor worse at meeting human needs than capitalism; but its successes and failures are different.

Part of the problem of comparison springs from the fact that we are not comparing like with like. The USA and the USSR are very different, both physically and socially, and, more specifically, they are at different levels of economic development.

It is sometimes argued that this fact itself should be part of the comparison

– that socialist countries tend to be relatively underdeveloped because socialism is not conducive to development. The evidence shows this to be untrue. During the twentieth century a number of actually existing socialist countries have sustained over quite long periods remarkable rates of growth of industrial and economic development, faster than the average for capitalist countries, though slower than the most successful capitalist nations such as Japan and a number of South-East Asian countries. Again the simple comparison is not a reasonable one since socialist countries have often had to contend with an unusual number of economic obstacles to development being placed in their way by the major capitalist countries. And it should be remembered that the USSR suffered incomparably greater physical and human destruction in the Second World War than its capitalist allies.

The estimates of long-term growth of national income in the USSR are extremely variable and unreliable. But its progress in industry is well illustrated by figures for the growth of particular sectors. For instance, between 1928 and 1970 electricity production rose from 5 billion kilowatt hours to 740 billion, steel production from 4.3 million tons to 166 million; coal from 35.5 million tons to 624 million.

Growth rates, however, are far from an adequate measure of the changing extent to which people's needs are satisfied. For one thing, one cannot ignore the costs of economic growth. If a higher standard of living is achieved today, at whose expense in the past has this occurred? The untold miseries of the British working class during nineteenth-century industrialization might be set against those millions who suffered and died during Stalin's farm collectivization drive after 1929. There is no objective calculus to compare such costs with the benefits of later growth.

If we are forced to generalize about how the systems of actually existing socialism have met human needs, we would argue that among the poorer countries, at least, socialist revolutions have had almost unambiguously remarkable benefits, especially in the first few years. This is true even when accompanied by wild adventurism such as China's Cultural Revolution and the 'Great Leap Forward', because typically the provision of minimal subsistence, literacy, basic sanitation and public health and the elimination of backward pre-capitalist customs were accomplished quickly. These became permanent gains which in other similar countries without socialist revolutions tend to be accomplished only slowly after decades or centuries of growth.

The case of Cuba is well known. After the revolution of 1959, despite the imposition of a total economic embargo by the USA, the majority of the Cuban people, especially the poorest and most oppressed sections, found their way of life positively transformed in a very brief space of time. Welfare, wage and employment-creating policies virtually wiped out poverty and unemployment, which had been considerable. A legendary literacy campaign and a crash programme of education-spending opened new cultural possibilities to many; and the prioritization of public health has provided accessible and high-quality medical facilities. The contrast with pre-revolutionary Cuba, or with capitalist Latin American countries at similar levels of economic development, is immense.

These notable gains had been achieved by the mid 1960s. But other economic problems have been much more difficult to overcome. This is partly because of the objective difficulties of socialist economic development in an isolated small island only ninety miles from the world's most powerful capitalist nation. But it has also been because of the growing influence of the bureaucratic political and economic planning structure which Cuba has taken over with modifications from other actually existing socialist countries.

In those countries where such a structure has existed over a long and stable period, we can observe several systematic differences from capitalist economies in the way certain human needs are met.

First, involuntary unemployment, so widespread in the west, is virtually absent from the actually existing socialist countries (excepting Yugoslavia and China). Partly this is associated with the fact that economic activity and growth have been less subject to cyclical fluctuations than in capitalism. Those fluctuations which have occurred have been traceable more to abrupt shifts in state policy and the political climate than to the apparently less controllable factors which create them in capitalist economies. The achievement of full employment is basic to the communist regime's legitimation. The USSR, which claims full employment since 1931, has formally guaranteed it since the 1936 Constitution.

Second, a greater proportion of national economic resources tends to be devoted to health and welfare provision in actually existing socialist countries than in capitalist ones at the equivalent stage in their economic development. It should, however, be noted that the absolute level of provision may not be as good as that in the richer capitalist countries. Strict comparisons are not easy, partly because statistics from autocratic 'socialist' nation states are more often open to greater manipulation than those in countries where they are more easily questioned. Moreover, with even less democratic control of social provision than in capitalist countries, it is possible for the quality and type of provision to deviate more from people's needs.

Third, the actually existing socialist countries do not suffer so badly from the wastes associated with competition. There are no vast expenditures on advertising in order falsely to differentiate identical products from each other. Nor is it common for factories and enterprises to be set up and then their assets abandoned as they lose out in the competitive struggle. Such factors should in principle have led to resources being used in a less wasteful way and hence human needs being met more effectively.

We might thus expect actually existing socialist countries to have a systematically much better record at using their economic resources to meet human needs than their capitalist rivals in the profit system. But, in the longer-established ones, at least, we do not think this conclusion is valid, even when allowances are made either for their low initial level of development or for the effects of capitalist hostility.

It is a telling fact that despite increasing standards of living, and despite the relatively low levels of inequality compared to many capitalist countries, there remain substantial numbers of poor people in the USSR; it has been estimated from government statistics that between 35 and 40 per cent of the population were below the official poverty line as late as 1970. The Soviet citizen may not be subjected to exploitative TV advertising of detergents; none the less it is a commonplace to find no detergent at all available and the TV broken down. This particular example may appear trivial but it illustrates some seemingly inherent failings of the highly centralized system of running the economy which has been the norm (with substantial variations) in eastern Europe, China, Cuba and elsewhere.

3. PROBLEMS OF AUTHORITARIAN PLANNING

It is hard to escape the conclusion that authoritarian planning has many problems. Speeches by major leaders such as Mikhail Gorbachev, Fidel Castro or Deng Xiaoping and many treatises on the subject have identified the same list of problems.

(a) Excessive centralization makes planning uninformed, inflexible and unresponsive to needs and possibilities. On the other hand, the attempt to restrict bureaucracy by limiting the numbers of instructions to enterprise managers can lead to inappropriate criteria for the fulfilment of plans. To illustrate with a simple example: if nails are being produced then the size, weight and quality are all important to the users. Yet if only, say, the weight is specified in the plan, the manager of the nail-producing enterprise will be tempted to produce only large heavy nails, to meet the weight target most easily. Such problems form the basis of a whole genre of eastern European humour.

(b) A chronic state of excess demand in the absence of price movements leads to arbitrary and bureaucratic modes of distribution of scarce resources, even if it helps to abolish unemployment.

(c) Widespread corruption diverts resources from planned purposes for private gain (though such corruption seems quite low compared to that in capitalist countries at equivalent stages of development).

(d) Extreme conservatism at the enterprise level limits the introduction of new techniques and technical improvements.

(e) Material privileges accrue in the hands of privileged sections of the population, in particular members of the ruling communist parties.

If we add to this list the well-known problems of an autocratic political system, which not only limits the quality of social provision but also tends to stifle through censorship the cultural and spiritual needs of people, as much if not more than in some parliamentary democratic countries, it is absolutely clear that 'actually existing socialism' may not be equated or even approximated to any ideal form of socialism.

This list is not one of occasional problems but of basic and chronic deficiencies which result in a gigantic waste of productive resources and a systematic failure to meet human needs as effectively as is consistent with the level of economic development. The problem is so vast that it has led to almost continuous campaigns to reform economic policy in some way. All actually existing socialist countries have been characterized by occasional sudden and extreme shifts of policy when some new idea is dogmatically introduced as a cure of existing ills: more centralization, less centralization; more moral and political incentives to work, more material incentives to work; more use of prices and the market, less use of prices and the market; more emphasis on agriculture, less emphasis on agriculture; collectivization and nationalization, private property; more foreign technology, less foreign technology. Often associated with swings in the political fortunes of factions of the ruling party, the shifts themselves have been at times extremely disruptive; and they have not seemed to resolve basic problems, though they often lead to a small spurt in growth or a sudden improvement in known problems before new ones develop.

4. CONVERGENCE WITH CAPITALISM?

In the years since the mid 1960s the reforms in many actually existing socialist countries have in general (with exceptions) been directed more consistently towards a greater role for prices and the market and for the profitability of the enterprise (and so of cost reduction), both as a measure of efficiency and as a basis for incentive and bonuses, greater decentralization of enterprises and greater material incentives for work. This sometimes involves the expansion of private ownership and enterprise, or the decollectivization of agriculture, sometimes the admission of foreign investment from the capitalist countries, or the greater opening of the economies to trade, finance and technology transfers with the capitalist countries. In some countries, such as Hungary and China, these measures have gone quite far. In others, such as the USSR, reforms have met entrenched political opposition and have not yet been so radical.

No country, however, has abolished collective ownership of the main productive industries or some form of centrally planned economy. This seems to us the crucial counter to the proposition occasionally argued that just as the capitalist economies had been transformed into a 'mixed economy' by the growth of the state, so the actually existing socialist economies are moving towards this 'mixed economy' middle ground from the opposite side. We have already criticized the idea of the 'mixed economy' as a description of the advanced capitalist countries. And we think that it is too early to speculate on how far economic reforms might go in the USSR or elsewhere.

The prior question is whether, as some have argued, the actually existing socialist countries are intrinsically the same as the capitalist ones, since both are exploitative systems. The actually existing socialist societies are exploitative in that the direct producers are forced to surrender a part of their product to a category of people who due to their privileged positions within the party and state apparatus have a materially privileged standard of living. In capitalist countries exploitation through private ownership and the market is primary while exploitation through state taxes and state-sanctioned salary structures is secondary and dependent. In actually existing socialism this has been reversed: political power, that is, power over a part of the state, is the primary source of privilege and of control over the means of production and the economic aspects follow from that.

This exploitation is manifested in part by the degree of systematic material inequality between citizens. But it is very difficult to give a quantitative measure of it, for the rewards of the ruling classes are kept very secret. There are many wage differentials between ordinary workers, as well as between them and the enterprise managers. For example, in 1970 in the USSR industrial workers could expect an average of about 130 roubles a month, while directors' rewards ranged from 150 to 500 roubles a month. These figures suggest some degree of inequality. But in general it is less, on the face of it, than in most capitalist countries. You do not see the same stark contrasts between 'good' and 'bad' neighbourhoods in Moscow as in Manhattan.

The salaries received by Soviet ministers, party officials, deputy ministers and senior bureaucrats are not known, but rumoured to be very high. Moreover, those with privileges obtain relatively much more than any salary figures would suggest. No monetary value is put on the disproportionate access to education, medical facilities, good housing, private cars and other transport, the ability to travel abroad, holidays, second homes, tickets to the opera and so on. Since many of these things are in no way allocated through money and the market they are obtained by those with 'pull'. There is now a substantial number of people in the USSR and eastern Europe with numerous domestic luxuries, an impressive public life-style, two homes, one or more cars, perhaps chauffeur-driven – that is to say, people who would be relatively rich even by the grotesque standards of the USA, the UK or Switzerland.

So, even if the mode of exploitation is substantially different between capitalism and actually existing socialism, the fact of exploitation in both systems is clear.

5. RELATIONS WITH CAPITALISM

The very existence of the actually existing socialist countries has economic as well as political implications for the capitalist system. We shall look here at three economic ways in which the systems are related: trade, foreign investment and debt.

(i) *Trade*

Through trade with capitalist corporations and western governments, actually existing socialist countries have become a part of the world market. But it remains only a very small part, around 3 per cent of the total trade of the advanced capitalist countries. At various times in the 1970s and 1980s, partly in response to the problems of capitalist crisis, leading luminaries waxed rhapsodic about the vast untapped markets in eastern Europe and Asia. And periodically groups of them fly off in search of sales. But in fact the market has expanded relatively slowly (no faster than trade generally) and has not really constituted a significant way out of crisis.

Nor is there much sign that any of the actually existing socialist countries are going to open up so much of their internal markets to capitalist exporters as to become fully integrated into the capitalist world. This is an unlikely prospect since they have limited possibilities of developing hard currency exports and so a large proportion of their recent growth of imports has been financed by capitalist loans, often at particularly generous rates of interest.

There is one way in which it helps advanced capitalist countries to have available a relatively isolated trading bloc such as the Comecon countries. The failure of agriculture, particularly in the USSR but also in some other eastern European countries, requires them to import large quantities of food to maintain existing living standards. By contrast, in the west the policies of agricultural price and production supports adopted have in recent decades led to vast food surpluses. These are both expensive to store, or even destroy, and embarrassing to keep when 800 million people on earth are believed to be undernourished. But they continue to accumulate because they are a sop to the disproportionately strong farmers' vote. It has become extremely convenient, both for the US government and the EEC, to sell them off relatively cheaply to the USSR and other eastern European states.

(ii) *Foreign investment*

A casual look at the streets or homes of most capitalist countries would not reveal much that was made in an actually existing socialist country. One exception might be a Lada motor car, at a distance indistinguishable from an Italian Fiat; made in Togliattigrad in a vast factory established by the Italian Fiat company, it is an example of foreign investment by capitalists in socialist countries. If it was thought, however, that Ladas would be a prelude to a whole new field of opportunity opening up for capitalists, such hopes remained unfulfilled. And such projects as do exist are hemmed in by state limitations. In Togliattigrad Fiat established the factory, the technology and the work methods, and permitted their cars to be produced under licence, but they do not own the means of production; they continue to provide management and technical services for which they receive a continuous stream of fees from the Soviet government; and the extent to which the Soviet producers can compete in third markets with the home Fiat company is restricted. From the point of view of Fiat, and other firms in a similar position like Levi Strauss jeans in Hungary, these deals are very different from investment in capitalist countries. But they may be more advantageous because they are negotiated with a state and in an economy with generally less fluctuations of demand.

This is perhaps one of the reasons why such deals have been popular with capitalist corporations in the last fifteen years when stable profits have been more difficult to come by in the capitalist countries themselves. It is certainly possible that some actually existing socialist states may start to open up their economies more in the future. This is supported by China's agreement to let Hong Kong remain a capitalist enclave even when China takes over in 1999, and even to establish some kind of free enterprise zones on the mainland itself. If this trend is intensified it will be a strong force pulling them into the capitalist fold. As yet, however, this movement is not widespread.

(iii) *Debt*

Finally, a word must be said about debt which, in the case of some countries, particularly Poland and Yugoslavia, has become the strongest tentacle drawing the actually existing socialist world towards world capitalism. In the 1970s such countries borrowed extensively from commercial banks and from official capitalist sources. Essentially the Polish debt was accumulated because the government was politically unable to impose enough restrictions on private consumption and because it embarked on a highly optimistic investment programme which did not have the desired results.

The outcome is that Poland had a debt of $26 billion in 1985 which it was unable to repay within the foreseeable future and which it had been forced to renegotiate several times. In addition to the state there emerged two strong influences on the economic situation and economic policy in Poland: the illegally organized Polish working class and the committee of capitalist bankers to which the government was answerable for its debt. This committee, despite capitalist politicians' hypocritical and opportunist support for the independent Polish trade union movement, tried to impose the same disciplines of austerity as on capitalist debtors. Many of the economic policy statements of General Jaruzelski proved almost indistinguishable from those of Prime Minister Thatcher, President Reagan or President Mitterrand. The Polish government supplied far more information about its economy to banks in New York than to any 'socialist' institution inside Poland.

Not so drastic was the case of Yugoslavia. But with debts of $9 billion in 1983 it was also embroiled in the debt crisis and had to make repeated resettlements with its capitalist creditors. At the economic level Yugoslavia was even more integrated into the international capitalist system in that it was a member of the IMF, which supervised its debt rescheduling programme.

There seems no doubt that the debt link has become a significant one. The debts are yet one more layer of the dark cloud hanging over the world's banking systems which we discussed in Chapter 17. Yet indebtedness and other economic links are still nowhere near to converting actually existing socialist economies into integral components of the world capitalist system. Nor, in reverse, has their own internal system yet been altered by the contacts in any fundamental way. For the present we see them as being neither imminent recruits to the capitalist club, nor authentically socialist or communist societies.

Such, however, is the strength of the idea that capitalism is to be followed by socialism in the historical evolution of societies that most people have been unwilling to accept that any contemporary society may be neither capitalist nor socialist. In the next chapter, therefore, we have chosen to take a brief and inevitably speculative, even utopian, look at the concept of authentic socialist society, in particular at what would be the characteristics of a form of economic organization devoid of the exploitation, injustice and wasteful destructiveness of capitalism and of the only actually existing alternatives to it at present.

CHAPTER 20

Socialism

I. THE ESSENCE OF SOCIALISM

A critique of the profit system of capitalism and of the existing alternatives to it involves an implicit statement that there is some feasible alternative to both. In this chapter we aim to make that assumption a little more explicit but not to lay down a blueprint. The fundamental bases of a socialist economy and society would be the freedom of those who live in it to decide on its nature, and the equality that would entitle them to their own conception of what it should be like. Its actual nature would be the outcome of debates and struggles between rival conceptions.

But it *is* possible to discuss what is meant by such essential socialist principles as peace, freedom and equality. For instance, although one can hardly imagine any human society without conflict and contradiction, it is equally impossible to imagine true socialist society developing without peace, in the sense of the absence of military conflict. The conditions of war are the implacable enemies of freedom and equality.

In a negative sense the socialist endeavour conceives of freedom and equality not as perfect ideal states but as the reverse of the conditions which have prevailed in class society. It emphasizes freedom from hunger and want; freedom from the need to labour incessantly merely to survive; freedom from oppression and tyranny whether it be exercised by monarchs, slave-owners, capitalists, generals, bureaucrats, whites or men.

Equality does not mean identity. It means the removal of the pervasive material inequalities which characterize capitalism; and the removal of barriers or discriminations based on race, age, sex, sexuality, disability and so on. In these negative senses freedom and equality are very similar to each other.

But socialism is also a more positive vision. It also embraces the freedom *to*: the freedom to create, to decide, to participate fully in the running of one's own society. These freedoms cannot be exercised except by human beings who are in some way equal to each other. But in another sense to exercise them fully creates the opportunity to be *different*, to be individual, to be oneself. Authentic socialism would be not the prevalence of the collective, let alone the state, over the individual – which is how it is so often conceived; it would be the liberation of individuality through the social co-operation of equals.

2. THE ECONOMIC BASIS AND PROBLEMS OF SOCIALIST SOCIETY

Although no detailed blueprint is possible, a set of broad economic principles can be set out on which there would be a wider measure of agreement.

(i) *Abundance*

Freedom and creativity will be impossible if every waking moment is absorbed in necessary toil. They require a sufficient material basis for every-one to live comfortably and securely free from the most pressing material wants – in other words, a development of the productivity of labour to provide a considerable surplus over basic needs. That means a tech-nologically sophisticated, advanced, developed economy – but not on the model of today's advanced capitalist countries. There would be no pro-duction of goods devoted to destructive ends rather than meeting needs, such as armaments and many of the 'services' rendered by police and military personnel; no deliberate waste; no productive resources lying idle; no non-informative advertising; no destruction of produced goods to keep prices up; no private property in ideas and knowledge: instead technological and scientific knowledge could be more widely available and research could be reoriented, away from solving the problems which are obstacles to capital-ist profitability or military domination, and towards resolving problems associated with human needs, like the elimination of diseases, or the de-velopment of more appropriate technologies for poorer countries.

A socialist economy would be better able to husband resources. While the globalization of present-day US levels of resource utilization could bring environmental catastrophe, a developed socialist economy based on a relationship between humanity and nature, and not on the profit motive, would make it easier to replace renewable resources and leave non-renewable ones unplundered until adequate substitutes are available.

Abundance does not mean luxury or opulence, or the ability to supply costlessly every conceivable want, but generalized sufficiency and security in the supply of necessities and the existence of a considerable surplus above this. We live today, perhaps for the first time in human history, in an epoch of potential abundance. That potential could be realized by using existing resources more rationally and fairly. It is hard to imagine the widespread existence of abundance without also some international redistribution of income, some development in the underdeveloped areas of the world and some rationalization, including some deindustrialization, in the more advanced sections of the world.

(ii) *Ownership of the means of production*

The private ownership of the means of production contradicts the principles of freedom and equality and is the basis of exploitation in the capitalist system: its abolition is necessary for socialism.

What are the possible alternative forms of non-private or social ownership? To date the most significant has been the state-owned nationalized corporations; they could be operated in ways which would make them much more answerable to their workers and consumers than they are now, although there will always remain a problem in making such vast centralized organisms completely democratic. Municipal-, district- and community-owned services constitute another form of socially owned enterprise, which in principle it will be easier to democratize. The workers' co-operative, which may be especially suitable to small enterprises, and independent self-employment by craftspeople, artists and those who provide a vast variety of personal services, should be maintained and even extended. As for the many medium-sized plants, a socialist economy would require a radical extension of workers' management of enterprises, with management being chosen by and answerable to the workforce.

(iii) *The nature of work*

In order to break free from the alienating routines which are forced upon most workers in capitalism, workers in a socialist economy will have to become the *subjects* of the work process, not objects to be used for the ends of others, not, as Marx put it, 'mere appendages to machines'. But the control of work involves society as a whole and a solution would need to embrace the whole of the social division of labour.

If work is to become a source of satisfaction and pleasure, and if workers are to be able to exercise some control over it, they need to have some knowledge of the production process as a whole. The acts of conception and execution must as far as possible be reunited. Only thus can work become a liberating human activity rather than mindless drudgery.

The abolition of the capitalist division of labour is sometimes mis-interpreted as meaning that socialism would do away with all divisions of labour. A saying of Marx is often quoted in support of this:

In communist society, where nobody has one exclusive sphere of activity but each can become accomplished in any branch he wishes, society regulates the general production and thus makes it possible for me to do one thing today and another tomorrow, to hunt in the morning, fish in the afternoon, rear cattle in the evening, criticize after dinner, just as I have a mind, without ever becoming a hunter, fisherman, shepherd or critic. (*The German Ideology*, p. 45)

This is alleged to mean that everybody could (and would) do any task in a socialist economy, with frequent switching between jobs virtually according to whim.

But the socialist principle we are here asserting has a more plausible and practical interpretation. Instead of specific tasks within a production process being broken down in a narrow way, even manual work would regain some variety. There would be no detailed lifetime specialization in certain jobs, though people might typically choose and follow careers or 'fields of activity'. The opportunity to do this would be open to all, though it is hard to see how this could be totally unconstrained by social needs. Technological research could be reoriented to give priority to workers' needs and to find ways of eliminating (through mechanization and other means) dirty, dangerous and tedious jobs. As long as such jobs remained they could be shared on a rotation basis, or those who performed them could be permitted shorter working hours or some other reward.

A wide-ranging education system would shun elitism and discrimination. Citizens would be free to follow several fields in the course of their lifetimes so education and training would have to be a continuous resource, available at any age, rather than one which is arbitrarily restricted to the young. Marx's proposition is much more realistic if we take it to mean that people do not become fixed indefinitely in one single job – be it fisherman, critic or bus mechanic.

The vertical division of labour between manager and managed would also be transformed. Clearly some 'direction' is necessary in almost any production process but the plan should not be external to the workforce, nor should the managers be a class apart. Managerial skills could be acquired by anyone who wished. The managers would be accountable to and interchangeable with other workers. And their authority would have a rational and democratic foundation.

The quality of active life could also be improved through technical progress by giving priority to cutting working time in the most unpopular kinds of necessary labour. Where possible, with non-alienating and potentially satisfying activities, the distinction between work and leisure characteristic of capitalism could become blurred.

Finally, the first and most enduring division of labour, that between men and women, must be abolished by an attack on all the constituents of systemized women's oppression. Behind its economic aspects lie such profoundly ingrained forces – social, religious, psychological – that the task of creating women's equality is destined to be as difficult as any which a socialist society would face.

(iv) *Democracy in production*

Democracy in production can be most real if enterprises are small and decentralized. The catchphrase 'small is beautiful', popularized by the economist E. F. Schumacher, is essentially a call for a humanizing technology, a reaction against the dehumanizing constructions of twentieth-century capitalism. Small scale enables people to relate more closely to their work and to participate in management more easily. Happily, in an increasing number of industries technical change is making small units as efficient as large ones or even more so.

Decentralization maximizes the range of decisions which workers can take collectively without reference to some other level. It may allow the needs of consumers to be more effectively conveyed to producers through the process of competition and facilitate innovation of new products or production processes.

There are, however, very real problems with decentralization and small scale. Numerous aspects of an abundant and rationally organized economic system (regional and national transport, basic energy and much industry) are still inconceivable without large-scale operation and some centralization. Centralization may be needed as a result of the nature of the technology, or because of the need to co-ordinate the inputs and outputs of interrelated sectors of the economy, or because economic actions have external effects proponents cannot see, no matter how socially minded they may be.

The tensions, conflicts and trade-offs between the advantages of large scale and small scale and between centralization and decentralization seem destined to be a permanent problem for a socialist society, unresolvable if resolution means striking a perfect and stable balance between the two.

Centralization carries with it the threat of bureaucratization and the separation of rulers and ruled. Those who see the need to defend the potentiality for freedom and equality which a socialist society contains, will have to give priority to the construction of forms of democracy at the central, perhaps national, level. Unless the problem of centralized decisions is resolved (however imperfectly), the economic preconditions of a society of freedom and equality will not survive.

Recent developments in information technology may help national democracy by permitting frequent consultations of public opinion via

computer terminals in homes, communities or workplaces. This is an imaginative notion – but one which seems to offer a technical solution (which
may also be needed) to a political problem. New technology also offers
tyrants more sophisticated ways to manipulate, deceive and brainwash. The
means of consultation may be magnificent but will they be controlled or
used democratically?

(v) *Co-ordinating the economy*

The new information technology does open a route towards solving another
problem – the alleged impossibility of solving simultaneously all the equations necessary to produce a consistent economic plan.

An economy can be represented by an input-output model (a technique
first developed in the 1920s by the US economist Wassily Leontief) which is
made up of a set of equations showing all the inputs needed to produce a
unit of every output. A vast amount of technical information is necessary
but once it has been collected and the planned outputs decided upon, the
solving of the model to produce a balanced and consistent plan would,
with today's computers, be feasible, although still liable to become highly
technical and remote from popular understanding.

Some socialists argue that centralized planning in a socialist country
would have to rely to a considerable extent on the mechanism of prices and
the market; others recoil in horror at such suggestions which they see as
tantamount to the restoration of capitalism. We would argue that prices
and the market as such are neutral – neither essentially capitalist nor essentially socialist. There is a difference between a price system which is designed
merely to give signals to producers about relative demand and supply, and
one which is used to create material incentives and so economic differentiation between people, though one admittedly grows easily into the
other. Both of them are different in turn from a price system which operates
in the context of the private ownership of the means of production and
through which the fruits of exploitation are realized.

Without private ownership a price system may be the most efficient and
even the most democratic means of effecting some production and distribution decisions, especially when its possible ill-effects (the creation of
inequalities) are constantly monitored. Socialists have habitually contrasted
the blind, inhuman price system with conscious rational planning. But if the
conscious planners are ignorant of people's needs and politically remote,
then a price system may constitute a lesser evil. This difficulty reflects an
inbuilt problem of a socialist economy to which there is probably no utterly
perfect solution.

(vi) *Democracy in distribution*

The fruits of production would be distributed in a socialist society as they are currently, partly through social provision of services, such as education, and partly through private purchases, but the mechanisms would be modified.

Freedom from poverty could be ensured by a guaranteed income for all. This would not reduce production substantially, since other changes would mean that there were many more incentivies to work than simply to earn income. A tax system and maximum wage regulations could prevent the receipt of unnecessarily high individual incomes. A degree of income dispersion would be inevitable, for some production units would be more successful than others and workers would be free to elect to have some differences within their own units. The extent could be limited by placing a floor and a ceiling to incomes, the distance between them being determined by the principle that persons at the floor would not be excluded through lack of resources from freely participating in the same social activities as those at the ceiling. There should be no stratification of society on the basis of income levels (or any other criteria).

Income differences could in any case be offset by distributing increasing numbers of goods and services socially, without payment, on the basis of need: health care, education, social services, housing, public transport and basic foodstuffs. The distribution system would require close monitoring by consumers. Technology could facilitate the information flow between supplier and consumer and substantially reduce the costs of democracy.

Other social changes can be expected to alter the units of consumption as well. People would find it easier to adopt patterns of living other than the conventional family unit, if they wished. Communal and individual households might well increase. And some of the distinction between consumption and production would become blurred, with people living and working in the same communities.

(vii) *Internationalism*

Socialism will have to confront the problem of relating to a non-socialist world, the quicksand in which many socialisms in the past have perished.

Poor and militarily weak countries lack all or most of the material preconditions for socialism. They are apt to be subjected to economic and military pressures from the advanced capitalist countries, which either destroy their socialist experiments altogether or compromise them by forcing them into the protection of more powerful, bureaucratically ruled, socialist countries. Their only visible, if difficult, third course would be to survive through the building of a broad and powerful solidarity movement, especially inside the most threatening capitalist countries.

An authentic socialist experiment in one of the now advanced capitalist countries or in a coalition of some of them would possess more of the needed preconditions and might therefore have more room for manoeuvre. If it managed to survive or neutralize the inevitable attempts at military or economic sabotage (such as trade boycott, currency flight and currency speculation), it would then have to find a way to regulate its trade and other economic relations with other, still capitalist, countries.

If there is no free internal market, international trade will also have to be planned and controlled. By contrast, if there is a free market in the unplanned sector of the economy it makes sense to permit some free international trade as well. Consistent internationalism demands that trade controls are not imposed as a protective measure to favour domestic production over imports but only to ration the available foreign exchange.

But a problem arises when some socialist production units, because of their attention to social needs, prove to be less effective at cost cutting than producers elsewhere. Lack of competitiveness can lead to rising imports, or to a diminished ability to sell abroad and hence to buy foreign products, and may result in a tendency towards autarky, exacerbation of the contradictions of socialism, and loss of some material welfare.

These problems add up to another of the fundamental difficulties which any socialism in practice could encounter but to which no pure and perfect solution exists.

International economic questions would provide one of the basic tests of the commitment of socialism in an advanced country to the principle of equality – its posture towards the Third World. The degree of inequality on a world scale is incomparably greater than it is in any single country. A serious socialist experiment in an advanced country could very easily eliminate poverty at home but to make a significant contribution to eliminating global poverty would require a vast augmentation of material and technical aid to Third World countries for productive investment and poverty relief, especially in those countries which were themselves attempting to build a fairer society. It would need a willingness to allow some transformation in the world division of labour by removing the domestic protection of industries which could be feasibly established in Third World countries and a readiness to permit immigration from the poorer countries. No one would reasonably expect that a single socialist country could accomplish the earth in this regard. Some form of international co-operation may be required. The precondition for such a radical shift would be a fight against the nationalist, xenophobic and racist prejudices which the profit system has helped to nurture in the advanced countries and which often lie as deep as sexism in human consciousness.

(viii) *A socialist fingerprint*

We have been careful not to outline a fully developed, ideal communist society such as has been conceived by many socialist thinkers: one which will have completely resolved material problems, where all work is done according to ability, all distribution made exclusively according to need, where money has been abolished and where the state has withered away. Such a vision is valuable but we have preferred here to remain more pragmatic in order to visualize a society which seems less distant and more imaginable. But the principles of socialist economy which we have outlined contain in a diluted form most of the attributes of the more perfect model.

A society which implemented these principles would, we believe, be qualitatively distinct from others which have called themselves socialist, from the USSR where workers' power is virtually non-existent to Prime Minister Wilson's UK or President Mitterrand's France, which have remained securely capitalist. Its fingerprint would be distinctive and unique. Work would be a social act shared as fairly as possible among members of the society; increasingly the main motivation for work would be not money but personal satisfaction and social commitment; drudgery would be reduced by the maximum extent compatible with necessary production; work would be organized under democratic control so that the authority and direction were not external to the worker; the institutions of production would be socially owned and the motivation of the producers would be to meet people's needs; there would be a narrow limit on permitted differences of income; wherever possible, goods and services would be distributed through direct provision according to need.

If we compare this socialist fingerprint with that of capitalism which we described in the opening chapter we see that there can be no possibility of mistaken identity. In all significant respects they are totally different from each other.

3. OBJECTIONS TO SOCIALISM

'Cloud-cuckoo land', 'pie in the sky', 'castles in the air', 'never-never land' . . . there is no shortage of dismissive, incredulous put-downs of any serious socialist project in capitalist society. We have tried not to deny the inevitable difficulties of socialist experimentation or the potential contradictions of socialist society. So we do not wish to take the objections lightly.

But virtually every item in our list of principles of socialist economy has, in existing capitalist societies or sometimes in non-capitalist ones, either been partially implemented or existed in embryo, even though the form may have been distorted by the environment. So nationalized industries, workers' co-operatives, workers' control, aspects of the welfare state, adult education opportunities, progressive income tax, technical progress which removes drudgery, economic assistance to underdeveloped countries, positive discrimination or affirmative action in favour of women or blacks, are all partial or distorted but actually existing elements of a socialist economy within capitalism. We are dealing with real experiences. Why could they not be expanded and altered to the point where they qualitatively change the whole of society?

The answer which is most often given by even sympathetic sceptics is: 'Socialism goes against human nature.' They quote Adam Smith in support of the idea that a free market capitalist economy harnesses the essentially anti-social nature of human beings in order to create social cohesion:

It is not from the benevolence of the butcher, the brewer, or the baker that we expect our dinner, but from their regard to their own interest. We address ourselves, not to their humanity but to their self-love, and never talk to them of our own necessities but of their advantages. (*The Wealth of Nations*, p. 119)

Human nature is not infinitely malleable; self-love will not be abolished by socialism. But we would contend that capitalism is an economic system which systematically rewards this aspect of human nature and penalizes others which are equally essential. Too little self-love under capitalism and you find yourself out of a job and penniless.

Most people have experienced situations in which self-love and humanity towards others are not in contradiction with each other: friendships, clubs, interest groups, community and co-operative ventures, even families and, for a lucky few, work all exhibit such characteristics. Socialism need not be a society of saints; but it would be organized so that the characteristics most rewarded were not greed, avarice, cheating, competitiveness and aggression.

A second common objection is that the world cannot afford socialism. We have argued that potential abundance, in the relevant and not fanciful sense, already exists and that the principal obstacles to its realization are not technical but social and political. They lie in the nature of the world capitalist system.

A third objection, frequently raised by economists, is that planning an economy is an impossibly complicated task. We have argued that a socialist economy should incorporate as much decentralization as possible and that there is more to socialism than just planning. Moreover, the information-processing capabilities of computers are now such that though problems remain, they can hardly be said to be so basic that planning is effectively precluded.

It is often objected that, since no country or society yet exists that conforms to our characterization of socialism, there must be some intrinsic reason why it cannot work. This argument reaches deep into people's beliefs and ideas. There would, after all, be no better proof of the viability of socialism than to point to an actual society that works according to socialist principles. Yet even places that have proclaimed socialism have failed to conform to its principles.

Our response, which we cannot prove, is that socialism's failure to appear so far is due to a number of contingent historical reasons but not to the intrinsic impossibility of a socialist economy. Those countries that have embarked on a journey to socialism, from the USSR onwards, all have begun from a very low material base. Many have also been too small to survive on their own as viable economic entities. Generally, during the period of growth countries have lost their socialist aim in practice, even if it continues to be declared in name.

In the case of the richer countries of Europe, America and the Far East, the experiment has never been tried. Endorsed by the successful capitalist boom in the 1950s and 1960s, the political power of their capitalist classes has remained strong while socialist movements have been weak and divided. The most powerful and aggressively anti-socialist country, the USA, has had one of the weakest socialist movements even though anti-racist, anti-sexist and anti-war movements have been particularly powerful there.

The non-appearance of authentic socialism is related to another question which we have up to this point begged – the process of transition between capitalist and socialist society. We have considered the ends, or partial ends, without considering the means by which they may be reached. But the way in which any social revolution is achieved is bound to affect its outcome. This problem is crucial but it is too vast for us to tackle here, even if we felt qualified to do so. Our purpose in outlining the principles of a hypothetical socialist economy has been mainly to demonstrate that a coherent alternative to capitalism really does exist in principle.

But we will make one observation on the question of transition. A change which is not to result in a twisted caricature of socialist society will require not only a sense of the injustice of existing society but a very widespread vision of how a socialist alternative would be different and better: an element of utopianism.

4. VISIONS OF THE FUTURE

Traditional utopian socialists have been reviled by much of the socialist movement because they advocated the building of islands of socialism within a society which did not have the material preconditions for the generalization of socialist social relations. But ours is a world which has the potential for abundance. The main function of utopianism today is to create and spread a believable or inspiring vision of an alternative society, counteracting that which arises from the observation of actual existing socialism.

Socialist utopianism can be practical or imaginative. There have been centuries of attempts at practical utopianism (e.g. the Diggers during the English Revolution, or Robert Owen's factory communities in the nineteenth century) and the contemporary capitalist world abounds with practical experiments as alternatives to capitalism: co-operative movements in housing, in retailing and in working, people who, unrelated by family ties, have evolved ways of combining communal living with the need for privacy, self-contained communities that merge co-operative working and communal living. The workers of some capitalist companies have developed detailed plans for products which meet social needs (e.g. workers at the U K Lucas factory proposed to devote their skills to non-military production, such as making kidney machines for the National Health Service). Many other models of worker participation and degrees of self-management can be found.

All these experiments are limited at present, hemmed in by capitalist relationships. Workers' plans for social need tend to undermine profits, and so will normally encounter opposition. Co-operatives have to live and often die with the market. Yet they constitute seeds, some or all of which would grow and flourish in a socialist world. They help to highlight the possibilities for new forms of organization and provide a realizable vision. They are images of a future, distorted by the mirror of the present time.

A few socialist writers, however, have attempted to open a window on a future world. Among those influential utopian visions which are still instructive and even inspiring to read today are Nikolai Chernyshevskii's *What is to be done?* and William Morris's *News from Nowhere*.

Chernyshevskii's novel, which was read approvingly by Marx, above all looked forward to the day when the 'moral power' of women would not be destroyed by the oppression of male-dominated society. It also tried to show how co-operative non-hierarchical ways of producing things could succeed. William Morris's vision was part radical and part conservative, the latter most particularly in relation to women, sex and sexuality, respects in which he remained eminently Victorian, like Marx and many other socialists. The modern rise of the women's and of the lesbian and gay liberation movements have raised items for the agenda of utopia which might have made Morris and other Victorian utopians blench.

But he had faith in the ability of human beings to build a genuinely creative society. 'How do you get people to work if there is no reward of labour?' The question is put by a nineteenth-century time-traveller to an inhabitant of the twenty-first century utopia.

'No reward of labour?' said Hammond gravely. 'The reward of labour is *life*. Is that not enough?' 'But no reward for especially good work', quoth I. 'Plenty of reward,' said he – 'the reward of creation. The wages which God gets, as people might have said time agone.'

Morris, as a utopian, perhaps trespasses too far into the incredible in his belief that all work could be pleasurable and equivalent to art, and the near-complete absence of conflict and the permanent joy of his characters are both cloying and unconvincing.

Part of the incredibility of many utopias has been their naive and magical interpretation of abundance as a state where unlimited quantities of material goods can be obtained as if by rubbing a magic lamp. There is a shortage of utopian visions based on a more plausible definition of abundance where scarcity and material choice remain. But a more contemporary, sober, and indeed sobering, utopia is that of Ursula Le Guin in her novel *The Dispossessed*. Hers is not a utopia of wealth, leisure and joy but of a society of people who have chosen to pursue equality in a universe still dominated by capitalism. They endure physical hardship but at the same time express their humanity and above all gain dignity. It is perhaps a less inviting vision than many, but one which is an antidote to the danger that utopianism instead of being a mobilizing vision becomes a source of false promise and demagogy.

We have written this book in the belief that some form of authentically socialist society is not a false promise; that it is physically attainable given today's level of human knowledge and that it could reverse the inequality, alienation, oppression and periodic crisis which characterize the devil we know – the profit system.

Sources of Data used in the Text

Chapter 2

Fortune, 30 April 1984.

Herman, Edward S., *Corporate Control, Corporate Power*, Cambridge, Cambridge University Press, 1981.

Nyman, S. and Silbertson, A., 'The Ownership and Control of Industry', *Oxford Economic Papers*, new series, vol. 30, March 1978, pp. 74–101.

OECD Economic Studies, *The Role of the Public Sector*, Paris, OECD, Spring 1985.

Chapter 3

Gartman, D., 'Origins of the Assembly Line and Capitalist Control of Work at Fords', in A. S. Zimbalist (ed.), *Case Studies on the Labor Process*, New York, Monthly Review Press, 1979.

Chapter 4

Harbury, C. D. and McMahon, P. C., 'Inheritance and the Characteristics of Top Wealth-Leavers in Britain', *Economic Journal*, vol. 83, September 1973, pp. 810–33.

Chapter 5

Employment Gazette, vol. 93, no. 1, January 1985.

International Labour Office, *Yearbook of Labour Statistics*, Geneva, ILO, 1968 and other years.

Maddison, Angus, *Phases of Capitalist Development*, Oxford and New York, Oxford University Press, 1982.

Rist, Ray C., *Guestworkers in Germany*, New York, Praeger Special Studies, 1978.

US Department of Commerce, Bureau of the Census, *Statistical Abstract of the United States*, Washington DC, various years.

Vining, Daniel R., Jr, 'The Growth of Core Regions in the Third World', *Scientific American*, vol. 252, no. 4, April 1985, pp. 24–31.

Chapter 6

Maddison, Angus, *Phases of Capitalist Development*, Oxford and New York, Oxford University Press, 1982.
OECD, *Economic Outlook, Historical Statistics 1960–1983*, Paris, OECD, 1985.

Chapter 7

Armstrong, Philip, Glyn, Andrew and Harrison, John, *Capitalism since World War II*, London, Fontana, 1984.
Central Statistical Office, *National Income and Expenditure*, London, HMSO, 1984.
Fortune, 30 April 1984 and 11 June 1984.
US Department of Commerce, *The National Income and Product Accounts of the United States, 1929–76*, Washington DC, 1981.

Chapter 8

Central Statistical Office, *Social Trends*, London, HMSO, 1982.
Council on Environmental Quality and the Department of State (USA), *The Global 2000 Report to the President of the US*, Harmondsworth, Penguin, 1982.
International Labour Office, *Yearbook of Labour Statistics*, Geneva, ILO, 1968 and other years.
OECD, *Economic Outlook, Historical Statistics 1960–1983*, Paris, OECD, 1985.
US Department of Commerce, Bureau of the Census, *Statistical Abstract of the United States*, Washington DC, 1984.
World Bank, *World Development Report, 1985*, New York, Oxford University Press for the World Bank, 1985.

Chapter 10

Feinstein, C. H., *National Income, Expenditure and Output of the United Kingdom, 1855–1965*, Cambridge, Cambridge University Press, 1972.
International Monetary Fund, *International Financial Statistics*, Washington DC, IMF, various issues.
Kenwood, A. G. and Lougheed, A. L., *The Growth of the International Economy, 1820–1980*, London, Allen & Unwin, 1983.
OECD Economic Outlook, *Historical Statistics, 1960–1983*, Paris, OECD, 1985.
US Department of Commerce, Bureau of the Census, *Statistical Abstract of the United States*, Washington DC, various years.
Versluysen, E. L., *The Political Economy of International Finance*, Farnborough, Gower Press, 1981.
World Bank, *World Development Report, 1985*, New York, Oxford University Press for the World Bank, 1985.

Chapter 11

Smith, Dan and Smith, Ron, *The Economics of Militarism*, London, Pluto Press, 1983.

Chapter 12

Crow, Ben and Thomas, Alan, with Jenkins, Robin and Kimble, Judy, *The Third World Atlas*, Milton Keynes, Open University Press, 1983.

Edwards, Chris, *The Fragmented World: competing perspectives on trade, money and crisis*, London and New York, Methuen, 1985.

Hayter, Teresa and Watson, Catharine, *Aid: rhetoric and reality*, London, Pluto Press, 1985.

Kaplinsky, Raphael (ed.), *Third World Industrialization in the 1980s; open economies in a closing world*, London, Frank Cass, 1984.

Sen, Amartya, *Poverty and Famines: an essay on entitlement and deprivation*, Oxford, Oxford University Press, 1982.

Sivard, Ruth Leger, *World Military and Social Expenditures, 1983*, Washington DC, World Priorities, 1983.

World Bank, *World Development Report, 1985*, New York, Oxford University Press for the World Bank, 1985; and previous years.

Chapter 14

Armstrong, Philip, Glyn, Andrew and Harrison, John, *Capitalism since World War II*, London, Fontana, 1984.

Kindleberger, Charles, *Manias, Panics and Crashes*, London, Macmillan, 1978.

Chapter 16

Armstrong, Philip, Glyn, Andrew and Harrison, John, *Capitalism since World War II*, London, Fontana, 1984.

Edwards, Chris, *The Fragmented World: competing perspectives on trade, money and crisis*, London and New York, Methuen, 1985.

International Labour Office, *Yearbook of Labour Statistics*, Geneva, ILO, various years.

Maddison, Angus, *Phases of Capitalist Development*, Oxford and New York, Oxford University Press, 1982.

OECD Economic Outlook, *Historical Statistics, 1960–1983*, Paris, OECD, 1985.

Chapter 17

Cagan, Phillip, 'The Monetary Dynamics of Hyperinflation', in Milton Friedman (ed.), *Studies in the Quantity Theory of Money*, Chicago, University of Chicago Press, 1956.

OECD Economic Outlook, *The Impact of Oil on the World Economy*, Paris, OECD, July 1980.

World Bank, *World Development Report, 1985*, New York, Oxford University Press for the World Bank, 1985.

Chapter 18

Employment Gazette, vol. 93, no. 4, April 1985.

Chapter 19

McAuley, Alastair, *Economic Welfare in the Soviet Union: poverty, living standards and inequality*, Hemel Hempstead, Allen & Unwin, 1979.

Nove, Alec, *An Economic History of the USSR*, London, Allen Lane, 1969 and Harmondsworth, Penguin, 1972.

OECD Economic Outlook, *Historical Statistics, 1960–1983*, Paris, OECD, 1985.

Bibliography of Works mentioned in the Text

Aglietta, Michel, *A Theory of Capitalist Regulation*, London, New Left Books, 1980.

Armstrong, Philip, Glyn, Andrew and Harrison, John, *Capitalism since World War II*, London, Fontana, 1984.

Auerbach, Paul, *A Critique of Industrial Analysis*, mimeo, Kingston upon Thames, Kingston Polytechnic, 1985.

Baran, Paul A. and Sweezy, Paul M., *Monopoly Capital*, Harmondsworth, Penguin, 1966.

Braverman, Harry, *Labor and Monopoly Capital*, New York, Monthly Review Press, 1974.

Burns, A. F. and Mitchell, W. C., *Measuring Business Cycles*, New York, National Bureau of Economic Research, 1946.

Chernyshevskii, Nikolai Gavrilovich, *What Is To Be Done? a romance*, 4th edition, translated by B. R. Tudor, New York, Manhattan Book Co., 1909; republished in an abridged edition, New York, Vintage Books, 1961.

Council on Environmental Quality and the Department of State (USA), *The Global 2000 Report to the President of the US*, Harmondsworth, Penguin, 1982.

Davies, Margery, *Woman's Place Is at the Typewriter*, Philadelphia, Temple University Press, 1982.

Friedman, Milton, *Capitalism and Freedom*, Chicago, University of Chicago Press, 1962.

Fromm, Erich, *The Sane Society*, London, Routledge & Kegan Paul, 1963.

Galbraith, J. K., *The Affluent Society*, New York, Houghton Mifflin, 1958.

Giedion, Sigfried, *Mechanization Takes Command*, New York, W. W. Norton, 1969.

Gordon, David, Edwards, Richard and Reich, Michael, *Segmented Work, Divided Workers*, Cambridge, Cambridge University Press, 1982.

Hayek, F. A., *The Road to Serfdom*, London, Routledge & Kegan Paul, 1962.

Hilferding, Rudolf, *Financial Capital*, London, Routledge & Kegan Paul, 1981.

Keynes, John Maynard, *The General Theory of Employment, Interest and Money*, London, Macmillan, 1967.

Le Guin, Ursula, *The Dispossessed*, London, Gollancz, 1974.

Lenin, Vladimir Ilich, *Imperialism, the Highest Stage of Capitalism*, New York, International Publishers, 1940.

Leontief, Wassily, *Input-Output Economics*, New York, Oxford University Press, 1966.

Marx, Karl, *Capital*, vol. I, translated by Ben Fowkes, Harmondsworth, Penguin, 1976.

Marx, Karl and Engels, Friedrich, *The German Ideology*, Moscow, 1968.

Morishima, Michio, *Why Has Japan 'Succeeded'?*, Cambridge, Cambridge University Press, 1982.

Morris, William, *News from Nowhere, and Selected Writings and Designs*, Harmondsworth, Penguin, 1984.

Rostow, Walt W., *The Stages of Economic Growth*, Cambridge, Cambridge University Press, 1960.

Rowthorn, Bob, *Capitalism, Conflict and Inflation*, London, Lawrence & Wishart, 1980.

Samuelson, Paul, *Economics*, 9th edition, New York, McGraw Hill, 1973.

Schumacher, Fritz, *Small is Beautiful*, London, Sphere, 1974.

Schumpeter, Joseph A., *Business Cycles*, New York, McGraw Hill, 1939.

Sen, Amartya, *Poverty and Famines: an essay on entitlement and deprivation*, Oxford, Oxford University Press, 1981.

Smith, Adam, *The Wealth of Nations*, Book I, Harmondsworth, Penguin, 1970; complete edition, New York, Random House, 1937.

Thompson, E. P., *The Making of the English Working Class*, Harmondsworth, Penguin, 1968.

Townsend, Peter, *Poverty in the United Kingdom*, Harmondsworth, Penguin, 1979.

Veblen, Thorstein, *The Theory of the Leisure Class: an economic study of institutions*, New York, Augustus M. Kelly, 1965.

Weber, Max, *The Protestant Ethic and the Spirit of Capitalism*, London, Allen & Unwin, 1976.

Index

FOR THE BEST IN PAPERBACKS, LOOK FOR THE

In every corner of the world, on every subject under the sun, Penguins represent quality and variety – the very best in publishing today.

For complete information about books available from Penguin and how to order them, write to us at the appropriate address below. Please note that for copyright reasons the selection of books varies from country to country.

In the United Kingdom: For a complete list of books available from Penguin in the U.K., please write to *Dept EP, Penguin Books Ltd, Harmondsworth, Middlesex, UB7 0DA*

In the United States: For a complete list of books available from Penguin in the U.S., please write to *Dept BA, Viking Penguin, 299 Murray Hill Parkway, East Rutherford, New Jersey 07073*

In Canada: For a complete list of books available from Penguin in Canada, please write to *Penguin Books Canada Limited, 2801 John Street, Markham, Ontario L3R 1B4*

In Australia: For a complete list of books available from Penguin in Australia, please write to the *Marketing Department, Penguin Books Australia Ltd, P.O. Box 257, Ringwood, Victoria 3134*

In New Zealand: For a complete list of books available from Penguin in New Zealand, please write to the *Marketing Department, Penguin Books (N.Z.) Ltd, Private Bag, Takapuna, Auckland 9*

In India: For a complete list of books available from Penguin in India, please write to *Penguin Overseas Ltd, 706 Eros Apartments, 56 Nehru Place, New Delhi 110019*

FOR THE BEST IN PAPERBACKS, LOOK FOR THE

A CHOICE OF PENGUINS AND PELICANS

The Second World War (6 volumes)   Winston S. Churchill

The definitive history of the cataclysm which swept the world for the second time in thirty years.

1917: The Russian Revolutions and the Origins of Present-Day Communism
Leonard Schapiro

A superb narrative history of one of the greatest episodes in modern history by one of our greatest historians.

Imperial Spain 1496–1716   J. H. Elliot

A brilliant modern study of the sudden rise of a barren and isolated country to be the greatest power on earth, and of its equally sudden decline. 'Outstandingly good' – *Daily Telegraph*

Joan of Arc: The Image of Female Heroism   Marina Warner

'A profound book, about human history in general and the place of women in it' – Christopher Hill

Man and the Natural World: Changing Attitudes in England 1500–1800
Keith Thomas

'A delight to read and a pleasure to own' – Auberon Waugh in the *Sunday Telegraph*

The Making of the English Working Class   E. P. Thompson

Probably the most imaginative – and the most famous – post-war work of English social history.

A CHOICE OF PENGUINS AND PELICANS

The French Revolution Christopher Hibbert

'One of the best accounts of the Revolution that I know . . . Mr Hibbert is outstanding' – J. H. Plumb in the *Sunday Telegraph*

The Germans Gordon A. Craig

An intimate study of a complex and fascinating nation by 'one of the ablest and most distinguished American historians of modern Germany' – Hugh Trevor-Roper

Ireland: A Positive Proposal Kevin Boyle and Tom Hadden

A timely and realistic book on Northern Ireland which explains the historical context – and offers a practical and coherent set of proposals which could actually work.

A History of Venice John Julius Norwich

'Lord Norwich has loved and understood Venice as well as any other Englishman has ever done' – Peter Levi in the *Sunday Times*

Montaillou: Cathars and Catholics in a French Village 1294–1324
Emmanuel Le Roy Ladurie

'A classic adventure in eavesdropping across time' – Michael Ratcliffe in *The Times*

Star Wars E. P. Thompson and others

Is Star Wars a serious defence strategy or just a science fiction fantasy? This major book sets out all the arguments and makes an unanswerable case *against* Star Wars.

FOR THE BEST IN PAPERBACKS, LOOK FOR THE

A CHOICE OF PENGUINS AND PELICANS

Adieux   Simone de Beauvoir

This 'farewell to Sartre' by his life-long companion is a 'true labour of love' (the *Listener*) and 'an extraordinary achievement' (*New Statesman*).

British Society 1914–45   John Stevenson

A major contribution to the Pelican Social History of Britain, which 'will undoubtedly be the standard work for students of modern Britain for many years to come' – *The Times Educational Supplement*

The Pelican History of Greek Literature   Peter Levi

A remarkable survey covering all the major writers from Homer to Plutarch, with brilliant translations by the author, one of the leading poets of today.

Art and Literature   Sigmund Freud

Volume 14 of the Pelican Freud Library contains Freud's major essays on Leonardo, Michelangelo and Dostoevsky, plus shorter pieces on Shakespeare, the nature of creativity and much more.

A History of the Crusades   Sir Steven Runciman

This three-volume history of the events which transferred world power to Western Europe – and founded Modern History – has been universally acclaimed as a masterpiece.

A Night to Remember   Walter Lord

The classic account of the sinking of the *Titanic*. 'A stunning book, incomparably the best on its subject and one of the most exciting books of this or any year' – *The New York Times*

FOR THE BEST IN PAPERBACKS, LOOK FOR THE 🐧

A CHOICE OF PENGUINS AND PELICANS

The Informed Heart Bruno Bettelheim

Bettelheim draws on his experience in concentration camps to illuminate the dangers inherent in all mass societies in this profound and moving masterpiece.

God and the New Physics Paul Davies

Can science, now come of age, offer a surer path to God than religion? This 'very interesting' (*New Scientist*) book suggests it can.

Modernism Malcolm Bradbury and James McFarlane (eds.)

A brilliant collection of essays dealing with all aspects of literature and culture for the period 1890–1930 – from Apollinaire and Brecht to Yeats and Zola.

Rise to Globalism Stephen E. Ambrose

A clear, up-to-date and well-researched history of American foreign policy since 1938, Volume 8 of the Pelican History of the United States.

The Waning of the Middle Ages Johan Huizinga

A magnificent study of life, thought and art in 14th and 15th century France and the Netherlands, long established as a classic.

The Penguin Dictionary of Psychology Arthur S. Reber

Over 17,000 terms from psychology, psychiatry and related fields are given clear, concise and modern definitions.

Metamagical Themas Douglas R. Hofstadter

A new mind-bending bestseller by the author of *Gödel, Escher, Bach*.

The Body Anthony Smith

A completely updated edition of the well-known book by the author of *The Mind*. The clear and comprehensive text deals with everything from sex to the skeleton, sleep to the senses.

Why Big Fierce Animals are Rare Paul Colinvaux

'A vivid picture of how the natural world works' – *Nature*

How to Lie with Statistics Darrell Huff

A classic introduction to the ways statistics can be used to prove *anything*, the book is both informative and 'wildly funny' – *Evening News*

The Penguin Dictionary of Computers Anthony Chandor and others

An invaluable glossary of over 300 words, from 'aberration' to 'zoom' by way of 'crippled lead-frog tests' and 'output bus drivers'.

The Cosmic Code Heinz R. Pagels

Tracing the historical development of quantum physics, the author describes the baffling and seemingly lawless world of leptons, hadrons, gluons and quarks and provides a lucid and exciting guide for the layman to the world of infinitesimal particles.

Asimov's New Guide to Science   Isaac Asimov

A fully updated edition of a classic work – far and away the best one-volume survey of all the physical and biological sciences.

Relativity for the Layman   James A. Coleman

Of this book Albert Einstein said: 'Gives a really clear idea of the problem, especially the development of our knowledge concerning the propagation of light and the difficulties which arose from the apparently inevitable introduction of the ether.

The Double Helix   James D. Watson

Watson's vivid and outspoken account of how he and Crick discovered the structure of DNA (and won themselves a Nobel Prize) – one of the greatest scientific achievements of the century.

Ever Since Darwin   Stephen Jay Gould

'Stephen Gould's writing is elegant, erudite, witty, coherent and forceful' – Richard Dawkins, *Nature*

Mathematical Magic Show   Martin Gardner

A further mind-bending collection of puzzles, games and diversions by the undisputed master of recreational mathematics.

Silent Spring   Rachel Carson

The brilliant book which provided the impetus for the ecological move- ment – and has retained its supreme power to this day.

FOR THE BEST IN PAPERBACKS, LOOK FOR THE 🐧

A CHOICE OF PENGUINS AND PELICANS

Setting Genes to Work Stephanie Yanchinski

Combining informativeness and accuracy with readability, Stephanie Yanchinski explores the hopes, fears and, more importantly, the realities of biotechnology – the science of using micro-organisms to manufacture chemicals, drugs, fuel and food.

Brighter than a Thousand Suns Robert Jungk

'By far the most interesting historical work on the atomic bomb I know of' – C. P. Snow

Turing's Man J. David Bolter

We live today in a computer age, which has meant some startling changes in the ways we understand freedom, creativity and language. This major book looks at the implications.

Einstein's Universe Nigel Calder

'A valuable contribution to the de-mystification of relativity' – *Nature*

The Creative Computer Donald R. Michie and Rory Johnston

Computers *can* create the new knowledge we need to solve some of our most pressing human problems; this path-breaking book shows how.

Only One Earth Barbara Ward and Rene Dubos

An extraordinary document which explains with eloquence and passion how we should go about 'the care and maintenance of a small planet'.

FOR THE BEST IN PAPERBACKS, LOOK FOR THE

A CHOICE OF PENGUINS AND PELICANS

A Question of Economics Peter Donaldson

Twenty key issues – the City, trade unions, 'free market forces' and many others – are presented clearly and fully in this major book based on a television series.

The Economist Economics Rupert Pennant-Rea and Clive Crook

Based on a series of 'briefs' published in the *Economist* in 1984, this important new book makes the key issues of contemporary economic thinking accessible to the general reader.

The Tyranny of the Status Quo Milton and Rose Friedman

Despite the rhetoric, big government has actually *grown* under Reagan and Thatcher. The Friedmans consider why this is – and what we can do now to change it.

Business Wargames Barrie G. James

Successful companies use military strategy to win. Barrie James shows how – and draws some vital lessons for today's manager.

Atlas of Management Thinking Edward de Bono

This fascinating book provides a vital repertoire of non-verbal images – to help activate the right side of any manager's brain.

The Winning Streak Walter Goldsmith and David Clutterbuck

A brilliant analysis of what Britain's best-run and successful companies have in common – a must for all managers.

A CHOICE OF PENGUINS AND PELICANS

Lateral Thinking for Management   Edward de Bono

Creativity and lateral thinking can work together for managers in developing new products or ideas; Edward de Bono shows how.

Understanding Organizations   Charles B. Handy

Of practical as well as theoretical interest, this book shows how general concepts can help solve specific organizational problems.

The Art of Japanese Management   Richard Tanner Pascale and Anthony G. Athos   With an Introduction by Sir Peter Parker

Japanese industrial success owes much to Japanese management techniques, which we in the West neglect at our peril. The lessons are set out in this important book.

My Years with General Motors   Alfred P. Sloan   With an Introduction by John Egan

A business classic by the man who took General Motors to the top – and kept them there for decades.

Introducing Management   Ken Elliott and Peter Lawrence (eds.)

An important and comprehensive collection of texts on modern management which draw some provocative conclusions.

English Culture and the Decline of the Industrial Spirit   Martin J. Wiener

A major analysis of why the 'world's first industrial nation has never been comfortable with industrialism'. 'Very persuasive' – Anthony Sampson in the *Observer*

A CHOICE OF PENGUINS AND PELICANS

Dinosaur and Co   Tom Lloyd

A lively and optimistic survey of a new breed of businessmen who are breaking away from huge companies to form dynamic enterprises in microelectronics, biotechnology and other developing areas.

The Money Machine: How the City Works   Philip Coggan

How are the big deals made? Which are the institutions that *really* matter? What causes the pound to rise or interest rates to fall? This book provides clear and concise answers to these and many other money-related questions.

Parkinson's Law   C. Northcote Parkinson

'Work expands so as to fill the time available for its completion': that law underlies this 'extraordinarily funny and witty book' (Stephen Potter in the *Sunday Times*) which also makes some painfully serious points for those in business or the Civil Service.

Debt and Danger   Harold Lever and Christopher Huhne

The international debt crisis was brought about by Western bankers in search of quick profit and is now one of our most pressing problems. This book looks at the background and shows what we must do to avoid disaster.

Lloyd's Bank Tax Guide 1986/7

Cut through the complexities! Work the system in *your* favour! Don't pay a penny more than you have to! Written for anyone who has to deal with personal tax, this up-to-date and concise new handbook includes all the important changes in this year's budget.

The Spirit of Enterprise   George Gilder

A lucidly written and excitingly argued defence of capitalism and the role of the entrepreneur within it.